D1480483

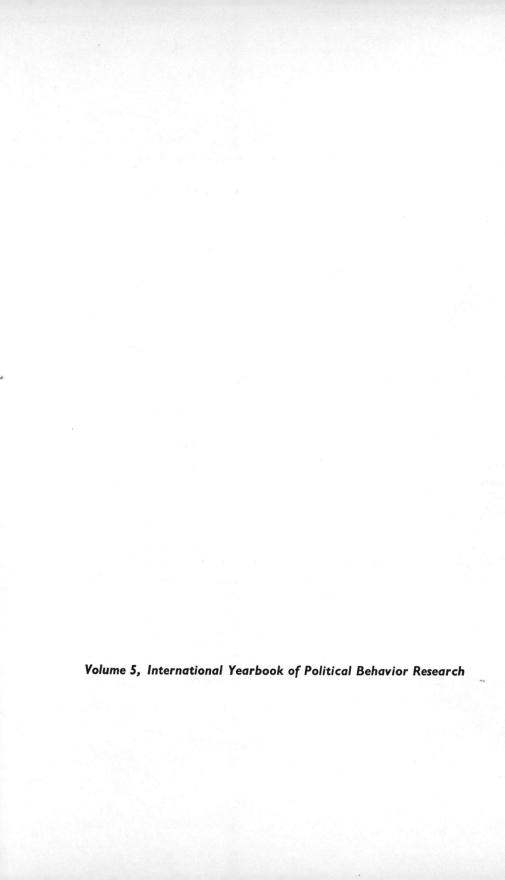

Volume 5, International Yearbook of Political Behavior Research

INTERNATIONAL YEARBOOK
OF POLITICAL BEHAVIOR RESEARCH

General Editor: HEINZ EULAU, STANFORD UNIVERSITY

Ideology and Discontent

This book was prepared for publication under the sponsorship of the Institute of International Studies. The Institute is devoted to research in the comparative and international fields at the University of California, Berkeley. Information about the activities of the Institute may be obtained by writing to

The Secretary
2250 Piedmont Avenue
Berkeley 4, California

Ideology
and
Discontent

EDITED BY *DAVID E. APTER* UNIVERSITY OF CALIFORNIA

THE FREE PRESS
A Division of Macmillan Publishing Co., Inc.
NEW YORK

Collier Macmillan Publishers
LONDON

The Free Press
A Division of Macmillan Publishing Co., Inc.
866 Third Avenue, New York, N.Y. 10022

Collier-Macmillan Canada Ltd., Toronto, Ontario

Library of Congress Catalog Card Number: 64–20305

Printed in the United States of America

printing number
4   5   6   7   8   9   10

Preface

AN EARLY manifesto of the behavioral persuasion in political science specified as a requisite of analysis that political theory and research be placed in a frame of reference common to social psychology, sociology, and cultural anthropology. Implicit in this call for an interdisciplinary focus was the realization that politics is not a behavioral phenomenon *sui generis*, unrelated to other aspects of human conduct, and that, if political scientists are to study what they are studying in any meaningful way, they will have to do so with the help of the conceptual and technical tools of the other social sciences.

It is quite clear that the study of politics is no longer the exclusive domain of the political scientists, if it ever was. Sociologists, social psychologists, and anthropologists have increasingly come to deal with things political, and they often do so in ways that are more convincing and incisive than the ways of political science, at least of conventional political science as it was cultivated before the behavioral impact on the discipline made itself felt.

This fifth volume of the *International Yearbook of Political Behavior Research* is eminently representative of the interdisciplinary orientation in the study of politics. The volume, edited by a political scientist of the new generation of comparative analysts, contains contributions by political scientists as well as by an anthropologist, a social psychologist, and a sociologist. Perhaps more significantly, we know from the work and the institutional affiliations of some of these scholars that their formal disciplinary labels are quite supererogatory. The volume, then, suggests that all social scientists can make significant contributions to political inquiry, just as it suggests that at least some political scientists have caught up in their interdisciplinary education and can make contributions of interest to the other behavioral sciences.

Does that mean that political science has lost its autonomous status in the family of the social sciences, as it was feared it might some years ago? I do not think so. Regardless of whether one defines politics in terms of a set of institutions truistically labeled "political," in terms of particular relationships among human actors (as in the case of "power"), or in terms of generic processes of action whatever the institutional context or the relationships among actors (as in the case of decision-making), it seems to me that there is enough scope in the division of labor among the various disciplines for political science to make its own contributions.

But what can or will these contributions be? I think that this question can be answered only if one surrenders whatever presuppositions he may enter-

tain about a hierarchically ordered disciplinary universe with "higher" or
"lower" forms of analysis and therefore more prestigious and less prestigious
academic pursuits. Time was, not so long ago, when political scientists con-
gratulated themselves on their discipline's place as "the queen of sciences,"
the master science. But time passed political science by. If political scientists, a sensitive member of the profession wrote only a dozen years ago,
"were to eavesdrop on the whisperings of their fellow social scientists, they
would find that they are almost generally stigmatized as the least advanced."
Not that these whisperings among other behavioral scientists did them much
honor. As even they have come to realize, the graveyard of obsolescence
claims its corpses without prejudice to disciplinary labels. And, I believe,
there is more modesty now being shown by most social scientists in making
their claims to knowledge than was the case even a decade ago.

In the division of labor, then, the various behavioral sciences do not occupy
positions of subordination or superordination, nor is one ancillary to another.
Each depends on the others for theoretical, methodological, and substantive
developments. Because political science is, perhaps more immediately than
the others, a "policy science" in its concern with the fates of societies and
civilizations, it does not follow that it is for this reason of a superior order,
as even today some political theorists, preoccupied with such classical problems of human intercourse as justice, security, freedom, or "the good life,"
would have it. If anything, political science finds itself in an interstitial
position among the social sciences and between the latter and the physical
sciences, in that it must of necessity be more alert to the intricate and un-
solved problems that arise out of the styles of discourse and the aims that
characterize behavioral and physical science, on the one hand, and social
philosophy and ethics, on the other.

Whatever else political scientists may be doing, and they are doing many
things, they are bound to raise questions about the inevitable gaps between
what we know about things political and what we may prefer to be the consequences of disinterested scientific inquiry for public policy—and about
the ways and means by which political knowledge can be brought to bear
on the issues of the public forum. But asking these questions does not mean
that they can be readily answered. For to answer them, political science will
have to rely on inquiries and new knowledge in many fields, from neuro-
biology to analytic philosophy, from history to moral philosophy. Its own
role inevitably depends on its being in step with the other social sciences—in
a concert without a conductor. It is toward this end that the interdisciplinary
orientation of behavioral research in political science finds its reason for
being.

STANFORD, CALIFORNIA   *Heinz Eulau*
November, 1964   General Editor

Acknowledgments

I am grateful to Walker Percy and to the directors of the *Journal of Philosophy* for permission to quote from Mr. Percy's "Symbol, Consciousness and Intersubjectivity"; to Dr. Th. Piegeaud and the Koninklijk Instituut voor Taal-, Land-, en Volkenkunde, The Hague, for permission to quote from Dr. Piegeaud's *Java in the Fourteenth Century*; to HRAF Press of New Haven, Connecticut, for permission to quote from Herbert Feith's article, "Government and Politics," which appeared in *Indonesia,* edited by R. McVey; to Editions du Seuil, Paris, for permission to reprint excerpts from *Ethiopiques* and *Nocturnes* by Léopold Senghor; and to Random House, Inc., for permission to quote from *Capital* by Karl Marx.

In addition, I wish to express my gratitude to my wife, who patiently handled the proofreading of the entire book.

David E. Apter

CONTRIBUTORS

Charles F. Andrain, SAN DIEGO STATE COLLEGE

David E. Apter, UNIVERSITY OF CALIFORNIA

Reinhard Bendix, UNIVERSITY OF CALIFORNIA

Leonard Binder, UNIVERSITY OF CHICAGO

Philip E. Converse, THE UNIVERSITY OF MICHIGAN

Joseph W. Elder, UNIVERSITY OF WISCONSIN

Clifford Geertz, UNIVERSITY OF CHICAGO

Kenneth Prewitt, WASHINGTON UNIVERSITY

Sheilah Rosenhack, STANFORD UNIVERSITY

Robert A. Scalapino, UNIVERSITY OF CALIFORNIA

Barbara Kaye Wolfinger, CALIFORNIA DEPARTMENT OF PUBLIC HEALTH

Raymond E. Wolfinger, STANFORD UNIVERSITY

Contents

Ideology and Discontent

Ideology and Discontent

BY *DAVID E. APTER*

I.

IN THIS introductory essay, I intend to pursue several themes that are to be found elsewhere in the book, but in an almost muttering kind of way; picking up an idea, putting it down again, returning to it as the mood strikes me. I have done so deliberately, in order to establish an attitude of mind, as it were, about so trying a subject. For ideology has no specific referent, although, despite its elusiveness, it remains powerful, meshing as it does at so many different points in our organized lives and intimate selves. While there are therefore main themes here—the role of ideology in society, in personality, in new nations, as well as in old ones—there is also a random quality to these remarks, which are designed to explore the outermost limits of the significance of the subject.

Perhaps the main reason for studying ideology is its mirror-like quality, reflecting the moral and material aspects of our understanding. These aspects become intensely interesting, especially in an age of science when they can no longer be rooted in faith. For all their sturdy tenure together, reason and morality have remained uneasy partners. In his book, *The Logic of Liberty*, Michael Polanyi has commented that science is in a paradoxical condition that reflects the modern mind. "A new destructive scepticism is linked here to a new passionate social conscience; an utter disbelief in the spirit of man is coupled with extravagant moral demands. We see at work here the form of action which has already dealt so many shattering blows to the modern world: the chisel of scepticism driven by the hammer of social passion."[1]

This paradox is to be found in all modern societies; those in the first stages of their development (where the freshness of self-discovery gives way to the discipline of organized power), as well as those that have gone through earlier upheavals in the effort to transform themselves. At a time when the Russians have conquered space, their new writers and poets, Voznesensky, Yevtushenko, Tertz, and others revolt against, rather than exult in, the achievements of science. Their counterparts can be found in the West.

We have refined our moral sensibilities along with our skepticism. At no time in history has the world been so sensitive to moral subtleties and more likely to take its transgressions seriously. This sensitivity is expressed in many ways: among the developing nations in a search for new political forms, among the older ones in a public desire for reform. In both, there is a new willingness to apply scientific research to human problems. Yet experience tells us that the more we desire to ameliorate our ills, the more they crowd in upon us. Each fresh solution uncovers more problems. The truth is that men at work on these matters are troubled men.

This "Polanyi paradox" is reflected in our attitudes to modern ideologies. None seems able to capture the public imagination either programmatically or morally. This observation is true of the developing areas as well as of our own. In the former, it is the heroic individual or leader, more than the content of his ideas, around which the many rally in order to organize themselves. In their eyes, leadership and progress go together. It is more complex than that in the highly developed countries, where offended morality leads to outrage. We still do not know where outrage will lead.

One clue is offered by the study of ideologies. Ideology and outrage have affinities, which reflect something of what men claim to strive for even when their thinking is contrived and dull. The vaguest of ideologies can be made to shine in the reflected glow of moral indignation.

Why is that? Because ideology is not quite like other subjects. It reflects the presuppositions of its observers. The study of ideologies soon draws one into the analysis of social science itself, into meta-analysis, with all its peculiarities and its uniqueness. Weber and Mannheim after him pointed out this fact because they were struck by the capacity of social scientists to understand the meaning of events from the inside, as it were. One cannot comprehend the motives of stars because they do not have motives. The inner life is the unique quality of living man. Furthermore, each place has its own mood and its own special problems which are expressed in ideologies. That is why the subject remains important. Our assumption here is that, if we examine ideology contextually and comparatively, we shall learn something about the coherence and intellectual cultures of modern nations and their degrees of integration.

This book is concerned with various ideological formulae some of which have arisen in response to the problems of development. Development is not an ideology, but it embodies hope and a positive notion of the future (even though it may reveal, at any moment, consequences so negative that they are blinding). The ideologies employed in development seek to transcend negativism and to define hope in programmatic terms. Of the many ideologies we could discuss, three are of interest because of their general acceptance. The first is the ideology of socialism. The second is the ideology of nationalism. The third, which is presently evolving in modern development systems, results from the adaptation of the scientific spirit to social science. We can properly refer to it as a social-science ideology and discuss its conditions and consequences.

Ideology Defined

Before going on to these matters, however, some definition of ideology is essential. "Ideology" refers to more than doctrine. It links particular actions and mundane practices with a wider set of meanings and, by doing so, lends a more honorable and dignified complexion to social conduct. This view is, of course, a generous one. From another vantage point, ideology may be viewed as a cloak for shabby motives and appearances. The more generous version lays emphasis on the behavior of individuals in a setting of action-in-relation-to-principle.

"Ideology" is a generic term applied to general ideas potent in specific situations of conduct: for example, not *any* ideals, only political ones; not *any* values, only those specifying a given set of preferences; not *any* beliefs, only those governing particular modes of thought. Because it is the link between action and fundamental belief, ideology helps to make more explicit the moral basis of action. It is not a vulgar description of something more noble and sacred than itself, like a cartoon of a stained glass window.

Furthermore, ideology is not philosophy. It is in the curious position of an abstraction that is less abstract than the abstractions contained within it. Powerful ideologies and creative ideologists (like religious ideas and innovative clerics) do much to enlarge the role of the individual. That is why the role of ideology is central to the thinking of revolutionaries. Working out an ideology is for them a way of stipulating the moral superiority of new ideas.

Political ideology is an application of particular moral prescriptions to collectivities. Any ideology can become political. Hegelianism became the "ideological" justification for the Prussian state. Marxism-Leninism is the "ideology" of Communist societies. Both claims to superiority lie in a presumed relationship between higher human consciousness and more evolved forms of material relationship. The ideologist is the one who makes the intellectual and moral leap forward; by virtue of his superior knowledge, his view ought to prevail.[2]

In the Western world, ideology has changed considerably from the more dogmatic statements that periodically in the eighteenth and nineteenth centuries heralded total solutions to world problems. Today our ideologies are disguised. Their language has changed. The utopian element has disappeared. One might say that our own society holds some vague belief in democratic progress through the application of science to human affairs and that in recent times this belief has come to include social science. The special application of science in social affairs represents our commitment to the rational improvement of our society. Not only does this application fall within our definition of ideology, but, as applied to collectivities, it is increasingly political. This way of putting things is no doubt somewhat troublesome because it extends our ordinary notions of ideology into new areas. But if these notions have any merit, then the subject of ideology is more important to study than ever before.

Why? Perhaps not much more need be said in answer than it is hard to understand the meaning of human conduct without some knowledge of it. As Inkeles remarked in his book on the Soviet Union, "Certainly a knowledge of their fundamental beliefs is hardly sufficient for the explanation of men's actions in the real world. But insofar as these actions reflect a mutual adjustment between ideology and social realities, an understanding of ideology becomes a necessary condition for an understanding of the action."[3] As I have already suggested furthermore, the study of ideology reveals the "scientific" status of social science more clearly than does any other subject. To study *about* ideology (as distinct from examining specific ideologies) raises issues about the scientific quality of social science methods. These issues are: the role of the observer—aloof social scientist or passionate but reflective participant; the degree to which we can assume the motivations and attitudes of others by "empathizing" with their roles or playing similar ones; the degree to which we can separate observer roles from previous ideological commitment, or put more generally, the problem of bias in research; and the nature of prediction.

Such matters have become more pressing as the social sciences have become more interested in precision. A science is, in the long run, evaluated on the basis of the useful predictions it can make, and these predictions depend in turn on the power of the independent variables used in analysis. Ready or not, social scientists are being asked to do research leading to policy formation. What happened first in the natural and physical sciences is now beginning in the social sciences—that is the modification of change through the application of planning and control. Some years ago, Bertrand Russell made a comment about the role of science that is increasingly applicable to social science as well. "Science used to be valued as a means of getting to *know* the world; now, owing to the triumphs of technique, it is conceived as showing how to *change* the world." [4]

These themes then serve as the underlying rationale for this book. Methodologically, the contributions range from the broadly structural to the more precise and behavioral. The units of analysis are nations because the roles and contents of their ideologies seem particularly interesting. We have included older development communities of the West and some newer ones in other areas. We have excluded the Soviet system largely because the changes going on there are so great and wrapped in so much conjecture that they require a volume by themselves.

II. A Functional Approach

I am inclined to the view that ideology helps to perform two main functions: one directly social, binding the community together, and the other individual, organizing the role personalities of the maturing individual.

These functions combine to legitimize authority. It is the relation to authority that gives ideology its political significance. In "early-stage" development communities, authority becomes legitimized on the basis of those ideologies that lay claim to superior planning and rationality and that provide moral bases for social manipulation for development purposes. Such authority is supported by large bodies of technicians, economists, administrative specialists, and fiscal experts. In short, ideology helps to support an elite and to justify the exercise of power. This observation is no less true for highly developed societies, even though in them the position of ideology is shakier, with corresponding weaknesses in social solidarity and individual identity. It is the curious mood of our time that the rise of unlimited opportunities in the development sphere, through the applications of social science to modern problems, is accompanied by much ideological restlessness.

The Solidarity Aspect

The solidarity aspect of ideology was first made explicit by Marx. His views can be briefly summarized as follows. Change in the material conditions of life is expressed in two forms: the intensification of class struggle resulting in the emergence of different kinds of systems and the evolution of a higher form of consciousness that coincides with the evolutionary pattern of system growth.[5]

Less clear is the degree of determinism Marx attributed to productive relations. This vagueness in the Marxian theory has, of course, been the basis for a great deal of debate. If productive relations determined all, then it ought to be unnecessary to study ideology. Yet ideology is very much a concern of the Marxians.

Lenin, the ideologue of Marxism, reinforced his polemics with claims to superior wisdom. From analysis of "material conditions," the ideologue can lay down a "correct" political line for the public to follow. Superior wisdom is equated with ideological authority by means of which the public is converted to the political line.[6] Indeed, ideological purity becomes the rock against which waves of deviationism must be dashed unless they submerge the promontories of revolution.[7]

Lenin made ideology into a form of philosophical propaganda. He was both ideologue and ideologist. In his hand, communism became a revolutionary dogma. Not a philosophy, it contained one; not an epistemology, it prescribed one; not a system of values, it was a program for achieving one. But he did not transform ideology into much more than propaganda. It is Sorel, rather than Lenin, who spins out the implications of solidarity to the fullest and "completes" Marx "instead of making commentaries on his text as his unfortunate disciples have done for so long."[8]

The feature of Sorel's work that makes explicit the solidarity function of ideology is the role of myth—more particularly the myth of the general strike. Myth is the social equivalent of metaphor, or, to put it another way, myth is to solidarity what metaphor is to identity. It is a way of binding the individual and the social together. For such myths to be useful, Sorel argues, they must be in tune with the worthier moral tendencies. It is on a moral basis that ideologies must be evaluated rather than on vague belief in dialectical progress. He taxes Marxians for failing to recognize that old myths can be revived in order to modify the historical processes, thus leading to reactionary revolutions. "Marx does not seem to have asked himself what would happen if the economic system were on the downgrade; he never dreamt of the possibility of a revolution which would take a return to the past, or even social conservation as its ideal. . . .

"These are dreams which Marx looked upon as reactionary, and consequently negligible, because it seemed to him that capitalism was embarked on an irresistible progress; but nowadays we see considerable forces grouped together in the endeavour to reform the capitalist economic system by bringing it, with the aid of laws, nearer to the medieval ideal. Parliamentary Socialism would like to combine with the moralists, the Church, and the democracy, with the common aim of impeding the capitalist movement; and, in view of middle-class cowardice, that would not perhaps be impossible."[9]

The myths and the utopias provide each great event with its moral dimension. Sorel asks, "what remains of the Revolution when we have taken away the epic of the wars against the coalition, and of that of the victories of the populace? What remains is not very savoury: police operations, proscriptions, and sittings of servile courts of law."[10]

For Sorel it is the myth of the proletarian general strike that activates the class struggle and carries it forward. In this sense, we can say that he carries Marx to an ideological conclusion, for without the ideology of the general strike, regardless of the full weight of material development or the evolutionary emphasis in dialectical materialism, the revolution may fail or become reactionary. Ideology is a necessary ingredient of progress.[11]

What makes Sorel interesting to us, however, is not his doctrine of the proletarian general strike or his justification of violence. It is, rather the claim he makes for ideology. Its role is to build solidarity, and solidarity is the moral basis of society. Solidarity is for Sorel a moral system based on class and held together by myths. It is the foundation of change. Solidarity-producing myths are "good" when they lead to a higher morality. His plea for solidarity is thus also a plea for a more moral social personality and a superior human community.

This connection between solidarity and morality is the essence of authority, a fact well recognized by leaders of new nations. Solidarity and myth as expressed in ideology are commonly manipulated in order to supply a moral dimension to political forms. In this sense, the creation of myth, the moral solidarity of the community, and its authority are intimately linked.

The Identity Aspect

Sorel helped to clarify the function of ideology for society in building its bonds of affect, social commitment, and historical perspective. The natural outcome of his analysis centers attention less on the particular polemics of his own ideology than on the diverse but concrete manifestations of solidarity in ideological form. These manifestations include the use of historical myths, the rewriting of history, the search for a golden age—all ingredients that serve to promote the ends of a political community. So far, ideology in society has been our point of reference. But ideology, like language and dreams, is related to morphologies of behavior by universal psychobiological variables. Balance, mastery, and control are the desired results of ideological behavior. Ideas help men to control and change their environment. Such ideas arise out of action rather than out of pure speculation. Such was Freud's view. He wrote "It must not be assumed that mankind came to create its first world system through a purely speculative thirst for knowledge. The practical need of mastering the world must have contributed to this effort."[12] These views of Freud's would apply to all forms of belief, including animism, magic, taboos, and presumably political beliefs.[13]

For Freud, ideology is a form of personal *rationalization*. (In this view, he might have agreed with Marx.) Both he and Marx saw ideas as a cloak behind which "reality" hides, although, of course, each had a different idea of reality. For Freud ideologies are elaborate mental fictions, which the observer must penetrate in order to understand personality. Ideology in his view is uniquely personal. The scholar who seeks to understand ideology is the psychotherapist who unravels the mental rationalizations of his patients. It is hard to say whether or not this attitude defined ideology as a pathological condition for Freud. Certainly he would consider political extremists emotionally suspect. He did not have much taste for the bizarre, despite the novelty of his views.

Yet Erikson, who recently became concerned with such matters, does not do too great violence to the ideas of Freud when, in his study of Luther, he emphasizes the forbidding emotional complex that led to greatness. His concern with the conditions leading to the formation of creative personalities leads him to both the study of ideology and its role in personality. In psychohistory more than in any other form of social analysis, the observer relies on unorthodox sensitivities as he sniffs for evidence, clues and data, much of which has barely been touched by previous analysts. He is more on his own in social analysis than either the ordinary historian or the social scientist. Erikson's point is that, since he observes ideology in the context of personality, the psychotherapist *cum* social-science observer can contribute a great deal to the understanding of why individuals are so receptive to ideology. Erikson establishes a theory of personality formation based on that aspect of maturation he calls the search for identity. Because identity search coincides with role search, youth (as well as others who have never quite "found" themselves, as the vernacular goes) is particularly vulnerable to ideologies. This point adds another aspect of the study of ideology to the one offered by the Marxians, motivation. None of the Marxians can explain why class interest ought to *be*, and they are confused enough to deny the universality of the proposition by showing how it is possible for some individuals to emancipate themselves from that class interest. This contradiction is an important weakness in Marxian theory, for, much as Marx would have liked to deny the independent validity of ideas for action, he had to leave some loopholes for the gratuitous entry of nonworking-class Marxian ideas. The link between material conditions and class behavior cannot therefore be axiomatic. The result is an incomplete and inconclusive treatment of ideology. Erikson defines ideology as "an unconscious tendency underlying religious and scientific as well as political thought: the tendency at a given time to make facts amenable to ideas, and ideas to facts, in order to create a world image convincing enough to support the collective and the individual sense of identity. Far from being arbitrary or consciously manageable (although it is as exploitable as all of man's unconscious strivings), the total perspective created by ideological simplification reveals its strength by the dominance it exerts on the seeming logic of historical events, and by its influence on the identity formation of individuals (and thus on their 'ego-strength')."[14]

This formulation helps us understand why individuals are receptive to ideology, by showing how ideology satisfies the identity function. It also helps us to realize how it is that the creative ideologist is formed. By relating identity to maturation—by defining it as a critical problem for youth—Erikson suggests why it is that ideology has a particular attractiveness to youth. The first point provides some insight into the conditions of personal conflict that lead to the acceptance or rejection of ideologies. The second helps to explain prophets, charismatic leaders, and manipulators of ideology. The third is of particular relevance to new-development communities, where the emphasis on youth raises it to a particularly high level of prominence in society at the precise time when the search for identity is at its most critical stage.[15]

III. Ideology in the Developing Areas

So far we have been exploring the significance of solidarity and identity as laid down by social theorists who have had something appropriate to say about them.[16]

In this section, we shall discuss these matters with respect to both new and old nations. Rightly or wrongly, I visualize developing communities as if they were strung on a continuum. The new developing communities are trying to sort out certain problems that the older ones have more or less resolved, although not in all cases. These problems involve the more "primordial" sentiments based on race, language, tribe, or other factors, which, although not relevant to the development process, may be relevant to the maintenance of solidarity or identity. What I call "nationalism" is the ideology that embodies these primordial sentiments. It is well to bear this special meaning in mind as we discuss the relationship between nationalism and socialism. In the highly developed communities, such primordial sentiments are less a problem than are confusion, irresponsibility, withdrawal, and cynicism. Here we can find conditions pointing to what Durkheim called *anomie*. More common is something like Scheler's *ressentiment*. Generally there is a feeling of fear and disappointment in the consequences of development. Boundless confidence in the benefits it will bring (common in new nations) is not very widespread in the older nations.

Countries that are neither new nor old in this process include Japan and the U.S.S.R. We shall briefly mention the former because in Japan nationalism has played a crucial part in relating solidarity, identity, and development to one another. The Soviet system we shall not discuss—partly because there is insufficient data. We do not know the role of ideology there at the moment; nor is it clear what ideologies are prevalent. If we can consider the ideology of the Soviet Union conservative, embodying as it does principles that are to be realized through the Soviet state, it is also true that we cannot evaluate its role without comparing it to an ideology of rebellion. The only hints we have are in the poems, plays, and novels of the angry young Soviet men. As the U.S.S.R. moves toward the highly developed end of the continuum, we may expect that a new language and a new ideology will emerge. But such a time is in the rather distant future!

What we are suggesting then is that the role of ideology in the new developing communities is to promote authority. In the middle of the continuum it maintains authority. In the older societies, ideologies compete, weakening solidarity and identity with the resulting danger of alienation. Paradoxically, however, consensus varies in the opposite direction. In the new developing areas consensus is low, primordial loyalties high. Ideology blends them. In the old developing areas, consensus is high and primordial loyalties low. Ideology makes minor differences important. Correspondingly, the identity problem in the new development communities is to achieve a political consensus—the problem of political socialization and indoctrination —while in the older ones it is private, associated with a lengthy period of role search. Let us explore these propositions a bit further.

Almost all communities at the beginning stages of their development are seriously handicapped by various antipathetic cultural strains. Ideology, often consciously manipulated for the purpose of building authority, helps to minimize the consequences of such strain. That is how ideology performs its solidarity function. Similarly, in the case of identity, competing socialization processes, new and traditional, make the identity problem a complex one; ideology is employed to introduce greater coherence.

Two contrasting cases come to mind from Africa: Mali and Nigeria. In Mali, cultural discontinuities are being made to give way before new political arrangements in society represented in a Malian version of Marxism. In Nigeria, no single ideology defines political orthodoxy, and instead there is a host of competing traditions and ideas.[17] The young are enthusiastic supporters of the regime in Mali. In Nigeria, youth is estranged from the leadership, and no ideology has caught on. In Mali, solidarity is brought about by the conscious manipulation of ideology.

Socialism as an Ideology

Most of the political leaders in the developing areas profess to be socialists. This ideology enables them to repudiate prevailing hierarchies of power and prestige associated with traditionalism or colonialism. Furthermore, socialism helps to define as "temporary" (as a phase in economic growth) the commercial "market place" or "bazaar" economy.[18] Socialism, while it accepts the secularism of the market place, rejects the form; that is, roles associated with the market place are minimized.

In this sense, socialism has a very special meaning. It becomes the ethic for a system of political discipline leading to an emphasis on "science"— science for its own sake as a symbol of progress and as a form of political wisdom. In keeping with this aim, it offers a set of unified developmental goals that stress roles functional to the achievement of a workmanlike, rational society in which people extend helping hands to one another because they value highly the process of industrialization through community effort.

Such forms of socialism have very little to say about property or religion. Indeed they are largely silent on the subject of class antagonism. They are vague about the role of property, a factor central in Western ideas of socialism. The African variety, for example, prefers at present to delineate core values appropriate to modernization rather than to limit itself prematurely to particular economic forms.

In this sense, African socialism, like its counterparts in other developing areas, tends to look backward and forward at the same time. Although they may speak in the name of "revolution," in most cases political leaders are forced to make changes slowly by opening up the system to modernized roles. The result is that quite often what is called "socialism" is merely another name for "nationalism."[19]

What the various forms of socialism have in common, irrespective of their other ingredients, is an emphasis on development goals, for which individuals must sacrifice. Government is seen as a main source of development. Unity, represented in national citizenship, is the critical form of allegiance, with no other loyalties taking precedence over the state itself. Behind unity is the concept of society as a natural and organic body in which all the parts have their appointed functions, especially those linked to the development process.

Socialism is viewed as more rational than capitalism because of its emphasis on planning—more scientific, more secular, and more in keeping with the need to fit together and develop functionally modern roles. Socialism then has two aspects. In the content of its ideology, it defines modernity. In the application of its ideology, it defines social discipline manifested in solidarity groupings whose *raison d'être* is functionally for development. This functionality in turn lays down the terms of individual identity and establishes a new system of motivation that emphasizes achievement.[20]

Nationalism and Ideology—The Japanese Illustration

Quite often socialism, no matter how vaguely defined, breaks down into a number of competing dogmas that have the effects of weakening solidarity and confusing identity. When this danger arises, political leaders may opt for nationalism as the dominant ideology in new development communities. Nationalism incorporates primordial loyalties in a readily understandable synthesis, taking up the "slack" in identity and solidarity where socialism fails. Diffuse enough to encompass all specific forms of loyalty and tradition, it elevates them to a national inheritance. The value of nationalism lies in its functional flexibility.[21]

As Herskovits has pointed out, "African leaders faced with the challenge of economic growth and the need to establish higher living standards began to re-examine traditional communal patterns with the objective of shaping them to fit the requirements of a new economic order. This re-examination occurred both where patterns of individual effort had become established and where socialistically oriented plans sought to use traditional communalism as an instrument to make the new system function." In this process, certain older values had to give way—the emphasis on age, hereditary status, kinship, and chieftancy, for example. Once these values have given way, the remaining aspects of traditional life can be translated into more modern circumstances.[22]

Then nationalism takes on a more explicitly ideological complexion. Perhaps the best example, and certainly the best studied, is Japan. What made the Japanese case so interesting was the ability of the country to develop rapidly within the shell of traditional culture. Existing social beliefs, mainly of an instrumental nature, allowed a bending and shaping of well-understood institutions, which, despite their alteration, provided a public sense of continuity. Some of these beliefs were represented in an emphasis on education for instrumental ends. Bellah points out that, in Japan, learning for its own sake "tends to be despised. The merely erudite man is not worthy of respect. Rather, learning should eventuate in practice. A truly learned man will be a truly loyal and filial man."[23]

The same considerations held for Japanese religion. "It was seen almost as a system of training which aided in the self-abnegating performance of actions expressing loyalty to one's lord."[24]

Religion and education, community and family, found their natural and practical expression in the state, which could therefore contemplate change while continuing to hold the loyalties of its members. (We have in mind the massive alterations occurring when Tokugawa evolved into Meiji Japan.) The primacy of political values and the emphasis on the polity allowed modification in social institutions, particularly economic ones, without dramatically rupturing the values and social beliefs of the Japanese.

It is not our concern, nor are we qualified, to discuss the many factors relevant to this process. Even in the Japanese case, however, the accumulated changes could not all be absorbed by the nationalist ideology and political framework. The result can be seen in the growth of Japanese militarism from 1900 onward. If the Meiji government represented a "logical fulfillment of a conception of the polity which already existed in the Tokugawa Period," as Bellah indicates, militarism was a natural outgrowth of both, to the extent that it combined instrumentalism in the economic sphere with nationalism in the political.[25] Militarism was the imperial answer to the rise of trade unions, liberal and left-wing political thought, and advocacy of genuine parliamentary government.

As a result, education, religion, and the polity were brought together in an explicit orthodoxy, perhaps most clearly stated in the Japanese document, *Kokutai No Hongi* or *Cardinal Principles of the National Entity of Japan.* This document illustrates the uses of ideology in building and maintaining solidarity and identity in Japan. (It also illustrates how ideology as an instrument of solidarity can be applied through education.) As the editor points out in his introduction to *Kokutai No Hongi,* it is "primarily an educational book written for educators."[26] Hardly a pamphlet or tract in the ordinary sense, it is rather a religious document, which links together mythical history ("The great august Will of the Emperor in the administration of the nation is constantly clearly reflected in our history"), the role of the emperor in religious ceremony ("The Emperor, venerating in person the divine spirits of the Imperial Ancestors, increasingly becomes one in essence with Imperial Ancestry"), loyalty ("Loyalty means to reverence the Emperor as our pivot and to follow him implicitly"), and familial and national harmony ("In order to bring national harmony to fruition there is no way but for every person in the nation to do his allotted duty and to exalt it"). The nation then is like the family, the emperor like the father, and in the cultivation of both, people venerate themselves and realize higher purposes.

What makes this document so interesting is its explicit rejection of occidental individualism and liberalism. War is regarded as an expression of development, leading to great harmony. The martial spirit is sacred.[27] Life and death are basically one. "The monistic truth is found where life and death are transcended. Through this is life, and through this is death. However, to treat life and death as two opposites and to hate death and to seek life is to be taken up with one's own interests, and is a thing of which warriors are ashamed. To fulfill the Way of loyalty, counting life and death as one, is Bushido."[28]

Here we have a striking emphasis on loyalty and filial bonds that extends the notion of sacrifice and service further than in any Western ideology. At the same time, the primacy of national solidarity is linked to specific institutions, which trace their lineage to antiquity. The most immediate effects of modernization and industrialization are thereby deflected without hindering the modernization process in its economic sphere. Rather, education, industrial employment, and the enlargement of urban life help to reinforce rather than destroy the organic conception of society. Individual identity is found in service to the state and the emperor. Solidarity is expressed through the network of familial obligations, which includes the royal house. What are thus normally, in other systems, sources of tension, dislocation, and cultural strain are in the Japanese case twisted the other way around. Theirs is an explicitly traditionalist ideology, embodying instrumental ends, that was deliberately employed to make the identity and solidarity problems simpler. (Witness, for example, the unbelievable expansion of the educational system in the nineteenth century.) Nationalism in Japan was able to do what socialism in the developing areas could not do: to serve its functional purposes while transmitting a scientific temper.

Some Relationships between Nationalism and Socialism

"The process of shaping new principles or changing old ones is not without its tensions. One could almost say that there is a kind of 'dialectical' relationship between an ideologically oriented party and reality. The ideological party attempts to change reality and, in this way, is a revolutionary force; the new changed reality for a while corresponds to the ideology even while gradually changing itself; in time the ideology may become a conservative force; a new adjustment is eventually forced, and the ideology may then again become a revolutionary force."[29] In the new development communities, this "dialectic" takes place between nationalism and socialism. Each of these ideological forces emphasizes different attachments, meanings, and evaluations of solidarity, identity, and motivation.[30] Socialism is more universalistic and secular in tendency. Nationalism incorporates specific elements of tradition and employs them to bring meaning to the establishment of a solidly rooted sense of identity and solidarity.

In countries moving from dependent to independent status, the periods of nationalism build up slowly. At first there is emphasis on common citizenship, leading to more effective participation in agencies of rule and to greater educational opportunities. Nationalism also allows primordial loyalties to serve as the basis of the society's uniqueness. This attitude promotes pride in identity. In the period of nationalism, therefore, the main structure of society is accepted as it stands while greater opportunities are sought. It is "radical" in only one political context, colonialism.

Quite often a nationalist movement takes a leftward turn during the last phase of a people's struggle for independence. The "radicalization of nationalism" results from a changed political emphasis. Independence is no longer the issue. The act of transferring authority from outside to inside turns out to be less simple than it had appeared. The radicalization of nationalism therefore employs socialism as a developmental ideology. A secular system of loyalties replaces more traditional forms. One effect of this radicalization is to add a sense of community to the earlier nationalist emphasis on common membership in the national state. Egalitarianism and a sense of shared purpose in the scientific evolution of the society are aspects of this sense of community.

A second effect of this radicalization is more individual. For those who have been involved in nationalism, identity is bound up with roles of daring innovation, often involving personal risk—"Robin Hood roles."[31] Many nationalist leaders have had no regular occupations other than political life, and they thrive on uncertainty. Once the nationalist period has achieved its main objectives, the socialist period takes over—different from the earlier ones because it involves leaders in a coldly calculated priorities system. For a few, possibilities open up for pioneering in new political and economic forms, rejection of approved and well tried formulae of political practice, and the search for new forms related to the special conditions of the country. Whatever the political form adopted, however, society now becomes bureaucratized. In a bureaucratic state, legitimacy is based on a system of roles functional to the development of the society.[32] Under such circumstances, the Robin Hood role is replaced by a bureaucratic one. But the continuation of these two role tendencies is a chronic problem.

Perhaps a diagram will summarize more adequately this relationship between socialism and nationalism.

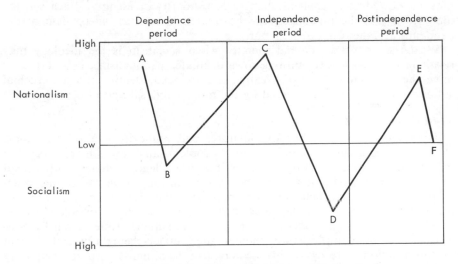

Figure 1.   Relationship between Socialism and Nationalism

At point A, we have the drawing together of a variety of social groups, which become increasingly "politicized" in a national sense, seeking a sharper definition of national society in political terms. At point B, a socialist "revolutionary" theme usually coincides with the appearance of a new group of political entrepreneurs, who take power away from the older and perhaps more "establishment"-minded members of the community. At this point, there is an emphasis on corporate community and functionally significant roles. Just after independence, nationalism goes through its apotheosis, and parochial and personal interests pale before the accomplishment of independence. Here solidarity and identity are linked with achievement. Old institutions become honorable and new ones exciting. At point D, the contradictions in culture, in social groups, and in solidarity and identity have resulted in a sweeping re-evaluation of society in the name of progress. It is the high point of socialism. Point D is the major ideological crisis point in the political life of a country, because it is at this point that the country becomes either a militant socialist state, or choosing moderately socialist ideas, turns accommodationist. In the case of Africa, this turning point pinpoints the dialogue between proponents of the more revolutionary view of socialism and of the more moderate African socialism—a dialogue affecting not only competition among leaders but policy toward education and indoctrination, or what is more broadly known as political socialization. When point F is reached, neither nationalism nor socialism is particularly relevant. At that point, what we have called the ideology of social science takes over. To achieve that point, however, involves not only a long period of time but a very complex process as well.

Changes among the four main variables we have been discussing form one basis for evaluating the tendency described. For example, the conditions of solidarity and identity change when nationalism is weakened and socialism strengthened. From a different angle, the need for nationalism or socialism may be viewed as a result of changes in solidarity or identity. Each set, the ideological and the functional, can be treated in turn as independent or dependent variables for research purposes.

Weakness in solidarity and identity when socialism is the ideology may result in political leaders turning toward greater nationalism. This turn may have the unwanted effect of creating a provincial identity and a parochial solidarity that must be countered by the more universal appeal of socialism.[33]

Youth and Identity

These problems of solidarity, identity, and authority can be seen most sharply among a nation's youth. Identity problems among youth are very often exaggerated in modernizing societies because identity choices often lead to culturally discontinuous sequences resulting in inconsistent and often mutually misleading behavior. Furthermore, the search for identity coincides with a period of relative social freedom—the period of role search—when role testing and observation are at the maximum. Role search leads to anxiety over premature identity choices, such anxiety being a crucial element in the searching process. This anxiety can lead in its turn to temporary alienation from society. There have always been angry young men. In new nations, which rely heavily on youth as the backbone of society, identity problems can seriously undermine solidarity. This situation leads to serious political difficulties.

Resentful of the anxieties that result from role search, youth in new nations characteristically seeks its identity through revolt against the system. Socialism (among the young) may result in an attack on nationalism and an urge toward universality, while "socialists" who have come to power through *nationalism* respond by becoming more nationalist than socialist. The long-term trend is the nationalization of socialism. For example, Sékou Touré, once the exponent of the militant left in Africa, is widely regarded as a right-wing "deviationist" by members of the Federation of African Students in France.[34]

Furthermore, this anti-authority reflex can be demarcated generationally. A political generation in a developing society is quite often short (perhaps only four or five years), during which time a new group makes its claim to political power. This group consists of the angry young men of the post-revolutionary period who have no other direction than the political in which to direct their energies. The generational variable thus links up with the larger problem of role search, alienation, and irresponsibility, which is centered largely on the identity problem. And where development depends heavily on the training and commitment of youth (both politically and technically), a group of alienated counterelites commonly emerges. They develop their own ideologies and identities through solidarity in a subgroup based on deviance from society. Indeed, if one treats solidarity and identity as independent variables, it is quite often the youth group with a high-deviance solidarity potential that triggers the ideological shift from socialism to nationalism, in order to achieve wider solidarity in the development community. Political parties take social pains to prevent this occurrence. As Eisenstadt has put it, "Almost all such modern movements have developed a special 'youth ideology.' The essence of these ideologies (from the point of view of our analysis) is that the changes which they advocate and struggle for are more or less synonymous with rebellion against the 'old' order and generation—a rebellion of youth, a manifestation of the rejuvenation of national social spirit."[35]

In the developing areas, youth cultures continue to be at variance with the regimes except during the short honeymoon periods after the success of national-liberation or revolutionary movements. Nor can the problems be solved simply by putting the young into uniforms and transforming them into obedient wards of the state. In many of the developing areas, each youth group brought under such "control" becomes a new center of local resistance within the existing party or other control group.

When is it likely that a transition will take place from both nationalism and socialism to a "higher" ideology of science associated with roles functional to the development community itself? It is hard to say. When nationalism can secure some honorific and traditional ideological inheritance and make it useful for maintaining solidarity and identity purposes and when socialism becomes a name for the values of science—then both will have lost their significance.

We have stressed the backward and forward movement between socialism and nationalism for two reasons. The first is that, in themselves, each represents the classic use of ideology in binding loyalties around major themes of political life and providing more than purely rational satisfactions from political activity. Second, an emphasis on functional skills in both socialism and nationalism places the technician and the scientist in an important political position, though clearly subordinate to the topmost level of leadership. This latter level is reserved for those who embody more than science and who do all the nonempirical things required of leadership, including supplying those meanings and identities that are central to the cultural hunger of a world in extreme transition. Such are the usual uses of ideology that have reached their greatest significance today in the developing areas of the world. Indeed, at times they take on the proportions of a political religion.[36]

In the developed areas (where it is commonly thought that ideology has disappeared), however, we find that it is only this "vulgar" aspect of ideology that is disappearing. Gone are the rather simple-minded explanatory notions of ideology (wrapped up in simplistic dogmas) that attribute behavior to explicit motives like desire for wealth or power. But if the new ideology is more sophisticated than the old, it is no less significant. Indeed it buttresses the authority of politicians with a universal appeal to scientific reason. Where the scientist or technician is frequently used as a basis for the legitimacy of political acts, whether the issue is development or civil rights, the Common Market or nuclear disarmament, legitimate action depends for its legitimacy on the advice of professionals. The battle of the politicians is in some measure enlarged to include charge and refutation by opposing experts employed by novices. In the West, the war had a great deal to do with stimulating this new ideology. It also fits into our traditions that the appeal to reason requires the competitive play of ideas in order to maximize information, which leads to the correct course of action. In the new societies, the professional becomes the symbol of progress. He is the "establishment" employed by the politicians. The social-science ideology, then, embodies a new form of solidarity and identity based on professional status. The appeal to science is an appeal to authority. The scientific establishment is itself based on a natural hierarchy of talent in which equal opportunities become the means to unequal political significance. We can conclude our discussion of modern ideology with examination of two conditions common in highly developed societies.

IV. Science and Ideology in Highly Developed Communities

We have said that developing countries are engaged in the process of rationalizing all aspects of social life. There is another aspect to this process; the corresponding erosion of durable beliefs and traditions. Increasing complexity leads to less sure guides to social and political practice than those to which people have been habituated.

In highly advanced development communities, ideology takes its most elaborate and complex form when the following conditions are present: There is general acceptance of common membership in the society, so that nationalism has become internalized and implicit; sufficient development has already occurred so that social dislocations require fine adjustments rather than gross "solutions"; consensus prevails about which roles are functional to the continuous process of development. Advanced development communities are no longer in the process of changing from traditional to modern forms of social life. As a consequence, they look beyond programmatic ideologies with their simplified remedial suggestions. One of the outstanding characteristics of such communities is broad agreement on fundamentals and corresponding magnification of minor issues. In highly developed areas, these problems come to a head in what is called status competition. As a result of increasing differentiation in the economic sphere, neither class nor caste is so significant as status, with its gradations extending indefinitely up and down the hierarchy scale. Some individuals strive for status differentiation, while others work consistently to undermine status distinctions. The result is an elusive power and prestige system which provides only temporary advantages for those who achieve high status. Only the professional role, based on skill, is durable. This distinction reflects itself more and more in a division between a scientific elite and the rest of the community.

Bifurcation in the Community

This phenomenon helps to explain a peculiar lack of personal constraint in performance among many occupants of high-status positions. Knowing their status tenure is temporary, they do not have the same sense of obligation or duty to the community that a more permanent high-status group might develop. When status competition is a motivational system, the result is grave weakness in solidarity and an agonizing search for identity.[37] The reasons for this weakness are not hard to find. Functional hierarchies allow equality of access to unequally distributed sets of roles. One result is that the lower the position he occupies on the scale, the more fundamentally incapacitated, incapable, and unrewarded a person feels. Functional hierarchy (based on achievement) intensifies the hostility and personal anguish of those on the bottom of the hierachy. No one can draw satisfaction from lower-status roles. The prospect now facing the highly developed communities is a large proportion of functionally superfluous people, particularly in unskilled occupations, and by that I mean those who are largely unemployable.[38]

How does a democratic society come to rationalize this bifurcation of the community into members of the "establishment" and the functionally superfluous, the responsible and the nonresponsible, the scientifically literate and the scientifically illiterate? Any major political issue serves to illustrate how. Any political conflict quickly becomes a problem of evaluating evidence. Each interested body employs its own experts to bring in findings in conformity with its own views. Laymen must decide which expert advice to accept. But the expert has been involved in the decision-making process. What happens to the nonexpert? Too often he cannot follow the debate. He withdraws, and the resulting bifurcation is more complete than one might ordinarily imagine. Modern society then is composed of a small but powerful group of intellectually participant citizens, trained, educated, and sophisticated, while all others are reduced in stature if they are scientifically illiterate.

In practice, of course, there is no single professional group. It is possible to be scientifically intelligent about some subjects and a complete fool in others. The dividing line between the "establishment" and the "disestablished" is therefore not sharp. There is a full-time and a part-time "establishment," and people with very little training may belong to the latter. But their participation in political problems and their interest in the community is largely limited to their fields of expertise. The result is, for them, a decline in their civic responsibilities and obligations.

One consequence of this decline in democratic societies is that government is almost always ahead of the public on most issues, in the sense that it is more progressive. Oil men interested in concessions, tide lands, and real estate are concerned with atomic disarmament only as it affects power resources and prices. We could cite other examples. Each particular interest group forces government to pay some attention to it, and to yield some special concessions. Each group is then partially satisfied in its functional interest, while bored with, alienated by, or positively opposed to government actions directed toward satisfying other functional interest groups.

Of course, this process can also work the other way around. A good illustration is the slow but increasingly steady intervention of government on the side of Negroes in the matter of race relations. The majority of the white population remains opposed to major change in the *status quo*. (Most whites would prefer to hide such opposition in vague sentiments of liberalism and moderate good works.) How do we attempt to quiet white objections? By bringing in the experts. Science is equated with democracy. The primacy of equalitarian values is asserted in the name of science, which asserts that there can be no genuine equality between races until all sorts of special programs are put into practice: training schools for Negroes, special fellowships, the breaking up of neighborhood patterns, and so forth. Research on this problem, the results of which are widely distributed through the public press and the mass media, points the way to a "political" solution. Making the problem "scientific" makes it somewhat more manageable.

The case of race relations in the United States is a particularly interesting one, bringing into play as it does a number of competing social norms affecting solidarity and identity in the face of ingrained prejudice. I would argue, however, that this problem is much smaller (and will be more easily solved) than the one that lies ahead: the problem of inequality on the basis of differences in ability. Science can help to resolve all problems other than that one, for it is science itself that sets the conditions of that kind of unequal society.

Alienation and the Ideology of Science

Democracy is a system of government that requires a high level of self-restraint. Where this self-restraint does not prevail, democracy rapidly degenerates into a system of plunder, restricted only by the mutual check of hostile and antagonistic groups in the society. Social reforms become bargaining points—by-products of political life. Under such circumstances, democratic reform "does not have any unifying appeal, nor does it give a younger generation the outlet for 'self-expression' and 'self-definition' that it wants."[39]

Perhaps such alienation is a permanent feature of democratic society.[40] Even the "establishment" feels it, particularly if its members have well-developed sensitivities. Not easily corrupted by power, the new "establishment" can easily feel compromised by it. The scientific personality is, on the whole, a modest one, especially at the top. (Technicians are less so.) It can become alienated by its own successes. It does not like to be a pawn in the politician's game. One illustration of the "establishment's" ambiguous attitude can be found in its distaste for politics at the same time that it participates in politics—evident among scientists all over the world. There is, furthermore, a universality in the scientific ideology and role. Soviet scientists too are likely to push political matters aside in order to maintain a certain scientific chastity unviolated by political dogma. Despite noticeable lapses, especially in the biological field, they wear their professional status like a caste mark.

The ideology of science has very peculiar and diverse effects. On the one hand, it serves to identify a group of people who are themselves important and significant because they can manipulate the scientific culture. On the other, it casts out of the charmed circle those who are hopelessly incapable of understanding it.

But it is not science itself that causes alienation. This phenomenon arises when boundless hope becomes tempered with realization of the limits of one's abilities. This realization causes considerable bitterness against the system, if only because the alternative to alienation is self-hatred. Modern societies harbor large proportions of people with extraordinary degrees of self-hatred and self-doubt.

Some Consequences of Bifurcation

Our society is subject to a dangerous bifurcation, the "establishment" versus the "disestablished." The latter, in turn, is divided into the functionally useful (but with lower status) and the superfluous. The "establishment" derives its power from the expertise embodied in advisory and appointive posts; the middle from electional strength; and the bottom from threat of local violence. Opportunities to move from the bottom to the top exist, but they are rare, as with Negro members of the "establishment" (the extreme case, showing the great obstacles to be overcome). The middle group tries to restrict mobility from the bottom into the middle and to restrict the growing "establishment" (growing both in proportion and significance). Squeezed by the new "establishment" and the functionally superfluous, the disestablished middle fights back either by attacking the social-science and scientific ideologies or by attempting to ensure entry into the "establishment" for its children.

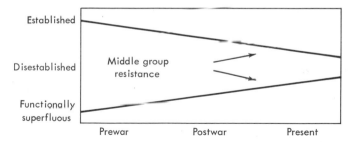

Figure 2. Division in the Community

The search for talent begins at an early age—witness the eleven-plus examination in England, aptitude tests and intelligence tests in American elementary schools. Parents who want their children to be members of the new "establishment" try to instill in them the proper desire for study and work. Solidarity, centered around the "establishment," makes nonestablishment people increasingly superfluous. Functional roles are those relevant to planning, policy, and research. The new "ideology" is increasingly rooted in a professional cadre of highly trained men. Solidarity within—alienation without; identity within—lack of identity without. What Weiss and Riesman have suggested holds true for the working class is increasingly true of all nonprofessionals in Western society. They point out that one of the things wrong with the working-class job is simply that it is a working-class job. "In a culture where the worth of a man is measured by how far he has gotten, the unskilled laborer or service worker, despite the pieties that may be uttered periodically about the dignity of labor, knows that he has not gotten very far."[41]

Technological superfluousness leads to social superfluousness. Nor is this matter simply a technological one. The alleviation of distress and the requirements for planning and calculation involved in modern politics, whether in urban planning or overseas aid, have helped to create a revolution in social science. The businessman, once the heroic figure of Western society, is increasingly an administrator. The old-fashioned ideal of capitalism, particularly in its more rural forms, becomes the ideological defense of the business and older professional groups against their own social displacement. It is no wonder that social science is so often identified with socialism and regarded as the enemy.[42]

In each of the three groups, solidarity and identity are different. Solidarity in the "establishment" centers around high-status *esprit* and a desire for more effective communications between disciplines and specialists. The recent discussion of C. P. Snow's Rede Lectures can be seen as an exhortation to solidarity between literary intellectuals and scientists. His concern over possible differences in their points of view presumes, on his part, a more fundamental identity of outlook.[43] Solidarity involves greater intellectual breadth and a shared appreciation of the values of the modern scientific community. Identity derives from the significance of the work engaged in by the individual, whose own personal satisfactions are in some measure a reflection of the recognition he receives within the "establishment."

For the disestablished, the situation is different. Their solidarity and identity have in the past been associated with the business community and territorially localized in villages, towns, and cities throughout the country. The "establishment" is a national elite. The disestablished have been a localized elite, their solidarity centered around churches, voluntary associations, and similar bodies.[44] These bodies have become increasingly parochialized and no longer provide solidarity satisfactions. The result among some of the disestablished is an increase in the significance of patriotic organizations associated with the radical right. Such solidarity groupings try to link the local with the national and to embody a new unity by means of which the disestablished would become powerful. On the other hand, the disestablished are losing the identities provided by middle-class business values and, in suffering this loss, are left bewildered and insecure.

The functionally superfluous have virtually no solidarity and are extremely difficult to organize, for their lives are preoccupied not only with basic poverty and all its consequences but in some measure also, in an affluent society, with escape. For them there are very few permanent identity symbols but only shifting popular ones, with resultant behavior divided between apathy and hysteria. For these people, the present situation is critical and utterly devastating.

V. Science and Democracy

Rather deliberately the concept of ideology has been thrust to the center of the stage, making it a point of entry for the discussion of many problems, both methodological and substantive. So far, I have tried to show the significance of ideology for society, for personality, and for authority, first in the context of the problems of developing areas and now those of developed ones. In the process, both the virtues and the deficiencies of ideology as a theoretical interest are easily demonstrated. Touching on problems of a very diverse sort, it also exaggerates them and casts them bolder than life itself. So, it might be argued, the use of ideology as a category of analysis is itself a distortion of reality. Does it not do violence to the actual role of the scientist or social scientist and give him too prominent a place in modern society? Even worse, to consider ideas about science in the context of ideology does not make ideology scientific—but science ideological.

I think the answer is yes. As a category of analysis it does exaggerate, but it does so usefully. If the problems of solidarity and identity, for example, are real ones, then the answers to them will have a special ethno- and ego-centeredness about them. That is why they become matters of dogma and passion, relevant to ideology. Furthermore, the argument I have made about the bifurcation of culture in modern society between the educated and the uneducated is surely exaggerated. But if it has any merit, we should be able to find the instruments of bifurcation empirically. And we do. The schools reflect the differentiation of the public into the dis- established and the established. Fifteen or twenty major universities provide professional education and postgraduate training. A number of small and high-quality colleges derive their status as feeder institutions, providing a high proportion of those students who go on to the postgraduate programs. A somewhat wider group of universities is anxious to move into this "academic establishment." Then suddenly the dividing line sharpens. Below the line is the main bulk of our universities and colleges, representing education by the disestablished for the disestablished.

These institutions incorporate all the exaggerated socializing functions of college life, with few of its compensating intellectual advantages. And, as with the disestablished generally, the faculty members of these institutions— and the students too—are embarrassed and harassed by the identities created. Critical of one another, and divided, they work at cross purposes.

I cite the case of educational institutions because they, more than any other institutions in our culture, frankly adopt the natural hierarchy of ability and talent as an adjustment to inequality. Each institution recruits in its own image of ability, with minor variations. The norm of quality is accepted by all, but the functions of each set are different. With society too, the norm of quality is accepted by all, but the functional definition of it is different. So too with science, and increasingly with social science as well. Indeed, the norms of science are rooted in our ideas of education, and they are the standards on which a scientific ideology is based.[45] Furthermore, the hierarchy of educational establishments intensifies bifurcation. The schools, colleges, and universities are becoming a major screening device. Theirs is a monitor role, instilling the values of democracy in the elect, while to the nonelect de- mocracy becomes an overpowering burden. This observation is true of Europe as well as of the United States.

In politics, social science assumes a new force. Its ideology differs in out- ward appearance from other forms. It is not polemical. On the contrary,

its practitioners embody the norm of "scientific" modesty. Social scientists
are the first to warn of the inadequacies of their disciplines when applied
to social problems.[46]

Underneath the modesty, however, is a lively belief in the norms and
values associated with science and the useful potentialities of social science
in political life. Special studies on every subject imaginable, from race
relations to nuclear disarmament, represent the application of social-
science techniques to problems of everyday life. Training, specialization,
and research are the basis of knowledge, which is why, as we suggested
earlier, the public is increasingly divided into the expert in social-science
matters and the layman. The layman, as a citizen, does not have the facts.
Nor does he have the ability to make important decisions. He may be
irritated in the face of such expertise, but it is difficult for him to contradict
it. Indeed, one token of the rising significance of the social scientist as a
member of the political "establishment" is the attacks against him, particularly
from members of the "old establishments," namely law and medicine. Law-
yers are, by definition, manipulators of custom, that is, of laws. A developing
community is less constrained by law than are more stable systems. It
cannot wait for law to catch up with its own needs for development. In the
field of medicine, emphasis is increasingly on the medical theorist or scientist
rather than on the practitioner. The latter is being reduced to the status
occupied by the pharmacist of two or three generations ago.

Another characteristic of the modern development community is the
primacy of the political. Social welfare, development, reform, and revolution all place new responsibilities on governments. In order to live up to
these responsibilities, governments seek advice. Authority is enlarged as responsibilities become more complex. The exercise of power is justified by
the prospect of endless political reform through technical expertise.

This whole process has the effect of polarizing identities and undermining
solidarities. Lacking a heroic dimension and requiring a wide range of intellectual discrimination, it imposes the burden of natural inequality upon
the members of a single community. Superfluousness is not an article of
faith in the social-science ideology, but an unfortunate consequence of
science in an industrial age, punctuated by a growing gulf between those with
status and those without. But those who represent the social-science ideology
in the community come to represent, for the disestablished, a threat to the
solidarity of the society and a deforming identity. Those inside the "establishment" are profoundly convinced, not only that it is highly desirable and
a force for good, but also that their role within it is the critical one. Those
outside the "establishment" become the ideologues of the extreme left or
the extreme right, sniping at the "establishment" and increasingly frustrated by its imperviousness.

We have suggested so far that ideology helps to establish solidarity for
society and identity for individuals within it. We have indicated that, in the
development of new societies, socialist ideology is relevant in bringing about
integration in the system and programmatic guides to functional roles, while
nationalist ideology helps to promote solidarity and identity. We have also
suggested that the political leaders in developing areas find sanction for
authority in the claims of socialism to be scientific—but that these socialist

ideologies do not belong in the same intellectual class with nineteenth century socialism or, for that matter, Marxism. Claiming the heritage of "socialism" enables political leaders in developing areas to make some wider connection with the philosophical heritage of Marxism without necessarily applying it.[47]

The West has gone beyond this stage. "Socialism has become an unthought-out assumption, a collection of economic recipes, and a nagging critique, from a distance, of existing institutions. The fresh self-confidence, the wonderful feeling of relevant discovery, the convincing air of ethical righteousness, and the vibrant expectation of a total—and significant—transformation of the entire life of society have nearly disappeared from the socialist movement and from socialist thought since the mid-twenties. The belief that socialist aims enabled one to see reality more realistically and fruitfully, the belief that socialism was a 'way of life' and not just a scheme for operating factories and wholesale enterprises has in the main evaporated."[48]

The New American Dilemma

The United States has clearly opted for science, and precisely because it has done so it must take the consequences. One of these consequences is that power and prestige will be based on functional roles germane to modern industrial society, in which science and efficiency go hand in hand. Equality of opportunity means that social life is a continuous screening process that begins with education. Parental status is no guarantee of future success. Ours is a system of downward, as well as of upward, mobility—but a special kind of downward mobility. The "downwardness" is a measure of inability, while "upwardness" is a measure of ability and proficiency. The criteria are based on natural talent.

This phenomenon is as yet only dimly understood and only beginning to emerge in our society. Luck, fortune, special advantages—these excuses could always be used to explain personal failure or success. Increasingly they cannot and an individual of the future will have to confront himself with some agonizing questions. Can the less gifted accept the fact? We have developed an elaborate rhetoric to disguise low status and to give it false dignity through titles, euphemistic job descriptions, and other accommodations that the "establishment" uses to salve its conscience. This rhetoric does not help to prepare us for the bifurcation that is occurring in our country—in which society divides into two mutually antagonistic and, in many ways, lonely groups. One is composed of ideologues who devoutly defend unreason because they are afraid that, in the face of reason, their orientation to the world around them will fall apart and that in the process their world will disappear. Ideology becomes a protection for people alienated from their society—a protection against the final alienation. They therefore stubbornly hang on to their ideologies in the hope that, by sheer persistence, they will prevail against other ideologies or even against reason itself. They represent the "disestablishment."

The second group is also alienated. Theirs is an alienation brought about by "superior wisdom," that is, by the ability to penetrate the ideologies of others and thereby to emancipate themselves. In this group is the social scientist, who is the objective observer. He penetrates all the disguises created by the untrained mind or the ideological mind and attaches himself to the image of the wise. He represents the "establishment."

The social scientist and the ideologue represent two increasingly antagonistic roles in modern society. The antagonism is all the sharper because, in an age of science, the nonrationality of the ideologue only makes him more defensive about his beliefs. More and more the social scientist is at the center of the society, and his probing and inevitably remorseless search for deeper levels of reality confuse the ideologue. The latter, more alienated, is therefore likely to engage in bold behavior calculated to inhibit the scientist and cause him to refrain from probing too deeply. To the disestablished, the language of social science is obscure and dangerous. The levels of reality probed by the social scientist are only dimly understood, if at all. Meanwhile, the universities controlled by the established set higher and higher standards of "quality." The insurance salesman, the bank clerk, the businessman, the retired army officer, and the other nonprofessional representatives of the middle class most often in possession of university degrees become the most concerned. They cannot find their places in the functionally unequal society.

The pattern of mutual alienation between these two groups is only intensified by the spread of quality education. With the increased dependence of the population on educational qualifications for positions that a generation ago did not require the same knowledge, the social scientist controls many of the main routes to power and prestige. The only recourse of the ideologue is intimidation of the social scientist by arousing the public against unorthodox or heretical views. And, episodically, he does so. So well entrenched are the universities, however, and so widely accepted is the norm of academic freedom that the ideologues as a group are rarely very successful, although individual ideologues may successfully enhance their personal careers by becoming professional witch-hunters.

Today's American ideologue is a middle-class man who objects to his dependence on science even when he accepts its norms. He is resentful of the superiority of the educated and antagonistic to knowledge. His ideology is characteristically not of the left but of the right. It is, in extreme cases, of the radical right, looking back to a more bucolic age of individuality and localism, in which parochial qualities of mind were precisely those most esteemed—to a simple democracy, in fact. Robbed of its individuality, the middle-class "disestablishment" forms loose associations with others who are escaping from the fate of superfluousness. Social hatred is directed against the Negro, the black enemy who can destroy the disestablished, and against the Negro's protector, the establishment man whose belief in rationality and equal opportunity has altered the system of power and prestige so that it is based on universalistic selection and talent. *Today, the radical right fights against the bifurcation of society on the basis of talent.* It is the resistance ideology of all those who hitherto were the *Stand* figures of our society in an earlier day; the models of once sober, industrious, and responsible citizens.

For the truly superfluous men, there is no ideology, only generalized hatred. Speed, violence, a frenetic round of petulant actions, or perhaps more simply despair, characterize these groups, which have been largely ignored by a prosperous society. Black or white, they are an embarrassment to the "establishment," which would like to take drastic remedial action—action that they find consistently blocked by the disestablished majority, which on the contrary, tries to preserve its superiority over those beneath it. And in the process, the disestablished look more and more alike. Violence, militancy, activism, in the name of a conservatism for which, especially in the United States, we have no traditional rhetoric—the result is seen in comical but dangerous extremist groups, which by their activities give to a nebulous conservatism greater appeal and mystique.

VI. Conclusion

Mannheim argues that the discovery that much thought is ideological challenges the validity of thought itself. "Man's thought had from time immemorial appeared to him as a segment of his spiritual existence and not simply as a discrete objective fact. Reorientation had in the past frequently meant a change in man himself. In these earlier periods it was mostly a case of slow shifts in values and norms, of a gradual transformation of the frame of reference from which men's actions derived their ultimate orientation. But in modern times it is a much more profoundly disorganizing affair. The resort to the unconscious tended to dig up the soil out of which the varying points of view emerged. The roots from which human thought had hitherto derived its nourishment were exposed. Gradually it becomes clear to all of us that we cannot go on living in the same way once we know about our unconscious motives as we did when we were ignorant of them. What we now experience is more than a new idea, and the questions we raise constitute more than a new problem. What we are concerned with here is the elemental perplexity of our time, which can be epitomized in the symptomatic question, 'How is it possible for man to continue to think and live in a time when the problems of ideology and utopia are being radically raised and thought through in all their implications?' "[49]

To expose the ideological aspects of human thinking does not, however, make ideological thought impossible. It divides it into new forms. One is that of dogma, which easily leads to violence and dissension. Those who see the world in stereotypes seek to protect their beliefs from those who would undermine them.

The more hopeful alternative is the spread of social science. It is in this sense that we can say that social science has become the ultimate ideology and science the ultimate talisman against cynicism. It defines its own purposes through the logic of enquiry. Some years ago, Michael Polanyi pointed out this process very clearly. What he said then of scientists in general applies more and more to the *social* scientist today: "Professional scientists form a very small minority in the community, perhaps one in ten thousand. The ideas and opinions of so small a group can be of importance only by virtue of the response which they evoke from the general public. This response is indispensable to science, which depends on it for the money to pay the costs of research and for recruits to replenish the ranks of the profession. Why do people decide to accept science as valid? Can they not see the limitations of scientific demonstrations—in the pre-selected evidence, the pre-

conceived theories, the always basically deficient documentation? They may
see these shortcomings, or at least they may be made to see them. The
fact remains that they must make up their minds about their material surroundings in one way or another. Men must form ideas about the material
universe and must embrace definite convictions on the subject. No part of
the human race has ever been known to exist without a system of such
convictions, and it is clear that their absence would mean intellectual annihilation. The public must choose, therefore, either to believe in science or else
in Aristotle, the Bible, Astrology or Magic. Of all such alternatives, the
public of our times has, in its majority, chosen science."[50] But the "Polanyi
choice" (like the "Polanyi paradox" with which we began this essay) embodies some very troubling and universal problems. His statement shows
a certain comfortableness about the majority choice. But what happens if,
having chosen, the majority does not follow through on its choice and indeed rejects many aspects of it? What is the effect, too, upon the minority
that has not made this choice—and by effect I mean particularly political
consequences? Perhaps one illustration of what occurs is to be found in the
United States at the present time.

What is happening in the United States may well be typical of other highly
developed societies. In a functional and rationalistic universe, the scientists
and social scientists are accorded an increasing monitor role in political life
—though not because they possess a kind of Platonic predisposition that
prepares them for the role of leaders. Quite the contrary, they share all the
ambiguity about their roles that their fellow citizens have. By gaining
a superior insight into the conduct of their fellows, however, they create a
new role and an ideology that follows from it, a hierarchy of power and
prestige based on intellectual ability, which, in its extreme form, is what
Michael Young called the "meritocracy." Once the social scientist discovered that there is a discrepancy between behavior observed and behavior
felt, between the act and the rationalization, between the conscious and the
subconscious, and between virtue and conduct, he fashioned a new role for
himself—the theoretically omniscient observer. Human mysteries have become technical problems. In the modern development communities, he is
asked to apply his knowledge. He displaces the physician as a new symbol
of aloofness. (The professional intellect is antiseptic.) He regards the
layman as irresponsible or, at best, uninformed. It is therefore not surprising that the recourse of the disestablished is intimidation of the social
scientist by arousing the public against unorthodox or heretical views.

The major propositions that emerge from this brief examination can now
be indicated: (1) Science is a well defined ideology possessing norms
of empiricism, predictability, and rationality as guides to conduct. (2) Social
science is becoming accepted as scientific, and scientific norms are increasingly accepted as guides to social conduct. (3) There is a universal trend
toward planning, calculation, and rationalistic goals concerned with the
future in both the developing and developed areas. (4) In the developing
areas, vulgar ideologies express the urge to science in some form of socialism
associated with national independence movements (African socialism, Egyptian socialism, Indonesian socialism). (5) In the developed areas, the new
ideology expresses itself in the "meritocracy." Recruitment of talent is on

the basis of competitive school and university examinations, with increasingly close links between the educational "establishment" and the bureaucratic "establishment."

Durkheim remarked about the pioneering role of economics that "for two centuries economic life has taken on an expansion it never knew before. From being a secondary function, despised and left to inferior classes, it passed on to one of the first rank. We see the military, governmental and religious functions falling back more and more in the face of it. The scientific functions alone are in a position to dispute its ground . . ."[51]

What was true for economics is increasingly true for the other social sciences. Both science and technology are, in application, intertwined with the social sciences. In modern scientific communities, governments are the greatest single consumers of social science. They not only stimulate policy research but consume the product as well.[52]

It is in the political sphere that the battle between social scientists and ideologues will be the most intense. More and more political leaders rely on the social scientists, as we have suggested. This reliance is growing both in the early- and later-stage development communities. As long as social science cannot perform functions of identity and solidarity, recourse will be had to ideology in its more dogmatic forms. Certainly there will be antiscientific ideologies. Political leaders will need to learn how to tread lightly between the alienated ideologues and the desire to apply science to human affairs.

We have suggested earlier that the dialogue in the developing areas is between nationalism and socialism. In the more developed countries, it will be between social science and nonrational vulgar ideologies. The ideologue will manipulate the slogans. The social scientist will ignore him. Political leaders will learn to rely on the latter without unduly arousing the former. Perhaps the long-run trend in both types of development community is a drawing of the lines between idiocy and intellectual merit more sharply until the ideologues fall of their own weight. But this end is too much to hope for.

What is the antidote? We need to understand problems of solidarity and identity more clearly. A kind of settling-down process is in order. With respect to ideology, social science differs from all others in one respect. The only antidote for it is more of it, addressed to solidarity and identity problems. Both new and highly developed communities need to accept the openness of spirit, the attitudes of questioning that probe the innermost secrets of social and political life (without feeling threatened). Such a spirit, essential to democracy, will perhaps have a destructive effect on all other ideologies.

We need, too, to pay more attention to the total educational system. I do not mean simply to refer to education in a pious way and to argue that modifying it will solve all our problems when obviously it cannot. But more social science education, the early development of a questioning attitude toward human affairs, and attention to discovery as a means of identifying the self, will help to break down the growing dichotomy between layman and specialist. That this process will take place has always been part of our liberal faith. It will not occur, however, through the trickling-down of jargon and a few manipulative ideas (as advertising executives, for example, pick up psychological jargon). What is needed, in addition to the modesty and propriety inherent in the scientific enterprise, is an understanding of relevant criteria for the evaluation of conduct, our own as well as others'.

We have suggested that the main uses of ideology in the developing areas are to promote solidarity and identity. The one represents the linking up of institutions, some of which are old, some new, and most of which emerge at the interstices between them. The other is the assertion of self (identity) through the marking out of new roles and the fulfillment of personality through such roles. The survival of "vulgar" ideologies, which are programmatic and explanatory, depends on the effectiveness with which they perform these two functions.

The scientific ideology can do little to promote solidarity and identity. The obligations implied in either are not very relevant, and a scientific ideology tends to downgrade the beliefs and intimacies that the vulgar ideologies promote. On the other hand, the scientific ideology handles these matters through professionality. The key to the "establishment" is its professional status. Its authority derives from superior knowledge. It has a code of ethics that enshrines integrity. The integrity of the research worker is only slightly less entrenched than the code from which it derives, academic freedom. This code, in turn, is linked with the concept of free enquiry. And, in an area where free enquiry produces a superior range of technological social alternatives for decision-makers, its concrete advantages become manifest.

Professionalization creates a sense of obligation among individuals, which by becoming moral is therefore much more significant than a simple contract and more reliable. A feeling of custodianship derives from this professional form of obligation, for it is the profession, the body of theory, the set of ideas that contain universals and represent the human intellectual inheritance that need to be enlarged by the incumbents of professional roles. Older professional roles that cannot make this kind of contribution become more mechanical rather than professional; become trades rather than professions. A move into the "establishment" begins when a particular group adopts a code of ethics and tries to establish some theory for its work, some transmittable body of ideas that can be called "scientific." The public relations experts who run polls, do sample studies for private firms on a contract basis, and function between the universities proper and corporate business are an example. The Bureau of Applied Social Research at Columbia University, the National Opinion Research Center at the University of Chicago, and the Stanford Research Associates are other examples of bodies that, although clearly professional, are doing contract work. The next step is for the large-scale private firms to claim the same professional status, followed by the more skilled advertising technicians. By this means, relating the needed skills to transmittable theory and the theory to some opinion—professionalization occurs.

Professionalization then gives identity to the role and solidarity to the organization. Such organizational identity and solidarity link the professional to the "establishment." Once in the "establishment," the individual has "arrived."

In this respect, the long-term aspects of ideology in the developing areas are the same as for the developed countries. Subordinate but senior roles on the basis of technical ability are already associated with civil-service positions, planning positions, and fiscal and other technical roles associated with development in the new nations. The occupants of such roles are like their counterparts from abroad. They have been trained in more or less the same institutions, and similar professional standards obtain. To this degree, the vulgar ideologies decline, and the scientific ideology takes over. Perhaps the long-run basis of association between new nations and old ones will take place largely between members of the professional establishments; for the sense of shared solidarity and identity, like the canons of science themselves, are more or less universal for professionals.

What we have been saying has, of course, been said before—and better. I know of no more adequate summary of these remarks than Werner Jaeger's introductory paragraph in *Paideia*. "Every nation which has reached a certain stage of development is instinctively impelled to practice education. Education is the process by which a community preserves and transmits its phsyical and intellectual character. For the individual passes away, but the main type remains. The natural process of transmission from one generation to another ensures the perpetuation of the physical characteristics of animals and men; but men can transmit their social and intellectual nature only by exercising the qualities through which they created it—reason and conscious will. Through the exercise of these qualities man commands a freedom of development which is impossible to other living creatures . . ."[53]

It is in this spirit that we examine ideology and discontent.

NOTES

1. Michael Polanyi, *The Logic of Liberty* (Chicago, 1958), p. 4.
2. George Lichtheim, *Marxism: An Historical and Critical Study* (London, 1961), Parts 1 and II.
3. Alex Inkeles, *Public Opinion in Soviet Russia: A Study in Mass Persuasion* (Cambridge, Mass., 1950), p. 21.
4. Bertrand Russell, *The Impact of Science on Society* (New York, 1951), p. 45.
5. Lichtheim points out that there is a conflict here, which Marxists in their "objectivism" do not like to admit. Although it is "in accordance with Marx's own manner to take a historical view of his work, such an approach presupposes a vantage-point made available by developments beyond the stage reflected in the Marxian system. In other words, it assumes that the Marxian categories are no longer quite applicable to current history. For obvious reasons, this is an admission which orthodox Marxists find it hard to make, while others may wonder why this particular scruple should arise in the first place. Its emergence is due to the fact that Hegel and following him, Marx, took a view of history which is not the familiar positivist one. They saw history as a process whose meaning reveals itself by stages, the succession of the latter reflecting man's growing awareness of his role in creating the historical world. To comprehend its past, mankind must raise itself to a higher level; hence, our ability to understand our predecessors suggests that we have reached a new altitude." Lichtheim, *op. cit.*, p. xv.
It was this problem that concerned Mannheim. Although Marxism supported the objectivist school of thought, the consequences of his theories were to produce the neo-Marxian subjectivist school of the sociology of knowledge. Mannheim and his followers, however, cannot avoid the same criticism to which Marx was subject.
6. This view is nicely brought out in the conflict between the "Economists" and Lenin. Consider, for example, the criticisms leveled against *Iskra*, Lenin's newspaper, and Lenin's reply. The criticism: "*Iskra's* excessive predilection for controversy is due primarily to its exaggerated idea of the role of 'ideology' (programs, theories . . .) in the movement, and is partly an echo of the internecine squabbles that have flared up among Russian emigrants in Western Europe, of which they have hastened to in-

form the world in a number of polemical pamphlets and articles. In our opinion, these disagreements exercise almost no influence upon the actual progress of the Russian Social-Democratic movement except perhaps to damage it by introducing an undesirable schism among the comrades working in Russia. For that reason we cannot but express our disapproval of *Iskra's* polemical zeal, particularly when it exceeds the bounds of decency." Lenin's reply was characteristic. He flayed the "Economists" for not staying ahead of the revolutionary consciousness of the people. He charged that the authors of the attack "fail to understand that an 'ideologist' is worthy of that name only when he marches ahead of the 'spontaneous movement,' points out the road, and when he is able, ahead of all others, to solve all the theoretical, political, tactical and organizational questions which the 'material elements' of the movement spontaneously encounter. In order to give 'consideration to the material elements of the movement' it is necessary to be critical of it, to point out its dangers and defects, and aspire to elevate spontaneity to consciousness. To say, however, that ideologists (i.e., conscious leaders) cannot divert the movement created by the interaction of environment and elements from its path is to ignore the elementary truth that consciousness participates in this interaction and creation."

Lenin equates ideology with more than the simple manipulation of ideas. Rather, it is created by those who share a higher consciousness and a more informed intelligence about social matters. He calls ideological "elements" those "conscious elements [who] operate according to plan." Nicolai Lenin, "A Conversation with Defenders of Economism," in Alexander Trachtenberg, ed., *Collected Works of Lenin*, IV (New York, 1929), Book II: "The Iskra Period," 66-7.

7. This aspect of ideology, building solidarity within confusion and vulnerability without, is one of the reasons why Marxism as an ideology is attractive to many youthful leaders of new states. Marx considers ideology to be those ideas that represent a particular mode of social organization. "To consider ideology as a set of ruling ideas which have been separated from the ruling individuals and given an independent force, an element of creativity in social affairs," he considers nonsense. The real basis of ideology, he points out, is in the material conditions of life, particularly in social relationships, division of labor, and productive power. Ideology is thus a screen for reality, a cloak. Karl Marx, *The German Ideology* (New York, 1939) pp. 41, 42, 43; see also Karl Mannheim, *Ideology and Utopia* (New York, 1946), p. 110.

8. Georges Sorel, *Reflections on Violence* (New York, 1950), p. 59.

9. *Ibid.*, p. 107.

10. *Ibid.*, p. 119.

11. Sorel, although an admirer of Marx, is by no means dazzled by his doctrine. He quotes with relish a "learned exponent of Socialism" who said that "the art of reconciling opposites by means of nonsense is the most obvious result which he had got from the study of the works of Marx." *Ibid.*, p. 138. See also Ernst Cassirer, *The Myth of the State* (New Haven, 1946), Part 1.

12. A. A. Brill, ed., *The Basic Writings of Sigmund Freud* (New York, 1938), p. 867.

13. Perhaps Freud's most direct concern with ideology is his analysis of the "chosen people" myth. Freud's transposition of the Moses legend is remarkable for its imaginative skill. More to the point, Freud argues that "the human intellect has not shown itself elsewhere to be endowed with a very good scent for truth, nor has the human mind displayed any readiness to accept truth. On the contrary, it is the general experience that the human intellect errs very easily without our suspecting it at all, and that nothing is more readily believed that what—regardless of the truth—meets our wishes and illusions half-way." Sigmund Freud, *Moses and Monotheism* (New York, 1939), p. 204.

14. Erik H. Erikson, *Young Man Luther: A study in Psychoanalysis and History* (London, 1958), p. 20. He goes on to describe his book as a study of "identity and ideology."

15. "Youth stands between the past and the future, both in individual life and in society. It also stands between alternate ways of life. . . . Ideologies offer to the members of this age-group overly simplified and yet determined answers to exactly those vague inner states and those urgent questions which arise in consequence of identity conflict. Ideologies serve to channel youth's forceful earnestness and sincere asceticism as well as its search for excitement and its eager indignation toward that social frontier where the struggle between conservatism and radicalism is most alive. On that frontier, fanatic ideologists do their busy work and psychopathic leaders their dirty work; but there, also, true leaders create significant solidarities." *Ibid.*, pp. 38-9.

16. "Solidarity" is a highly abstract term for the bonds that hold individuals together through shared emotions about the same highly valued ideas and objects. Ideology cannot therefore be other than significant in solidarity. Identity is the self-definition of individuals with reference to their roles and the roles of others. Ideology

cannot help but suggest guidelines to the self-definition process. It is also the case, however, that ideology responds differently to different demands made upon it in both the solidarity and identity spheres. In addition, the relationship between solidarity and identity deeply affects the appropriateness of particular ideologies.

17. These problems take a different form in highly developed societies. Where the society is extremely complex, piecemeal legislation never quite solves problems to anyone's satisfaction. The individual feels lost. He is made trivial in a system, the magnitude of which dwarfs him. The result is a frustrating and continuous search for identity by the members of the society and a lack of solidarity among them.

18. For a discussion of the "bazaar economy," see D. E. Apter, "Political Organization and Ideology," in Moore and Feldman, eds., *Labor Commitment and Social Change in Developing Areas* (New York, 1960), p. 337; see also D. E. Apter, *The Politics of Modernization* (Chicago, forthcoming).

19. Nationalism may be a revolutionary ideology *vis-à-vis* colonialism, but it is not normally so with respect to other aspects of social life. It is largely silent on the forms of economic organization.

20. See David C. McClelland, "The Achievement Motive in Economic Growth," Hoselitz and Moore, eds. *Industrialization and Society* (Paris, 1963), p. 74. McClelland points out that such achievement motivation becomes linked with identity because it is a desire to do well not for the sake of social recognition or prestige but "to attain an inner feeling of personal accomplishment." Ultimately, socialism as an egalitarian system is an effort to induce such achievement motivation.

21. See, for example, Janheinz Jahn, *Muntu: An Outline of Neo-African Culture* (London, 1958), *passim.*

22. M. J. Herskovits, *The Human Factor in Changing Africa* (New York, 1962), p. 467.

23. Robert N. Bellah, *Tokugawa Religion* (New York, 1957), p. 16.

24. *Ibid.,* p. 17.

25. *Ibid.,* p. 20.

26. Robert King Hall, ed., *Kokutai No Hongi, Cardinal Principles of the National Entity of Japan* (Cambridge, Mass., 1949), p. 30.

27. *Ibid.,* p. 94.

28. *Ibid.,* p. 145.

29. A. K. Brzezinski, *Ideology and Power in Soviet Politics* (New York, 1962), p. 115.

30. For a fuller discussion of this aspect of ideology, see D. E. Apter, "Political Religion in the New Nations," in Clifford Geertz, ed., *Old Societies and New States* (New York, 1963).

31. For a discussion of "Robin Hood roles," see D. E. Apter, *Politics of Modernization.*

32. This bureaucratism is another reason for the high emphasis on technical training as preparation for economically significant but politically subordinate positions in the society. The functional roles are open to participants in development. In effect, we have a system in which the hierarchy of roles is functionally validated by the ethics of equality, that is, by socialism.

33. Other examples of interesting hypothetical conditions could be offered to show the dynamic relationships possible between the two sets of factors discussed so far, ideological and functional.

34. See, for example, the study by J. P. N'Diaye, *Enquête sur les étudiants noirs en France* (Paris, 1962).

35. S. N. Eisenstadt, *From Generation to Generation* (New York, 1956), p. 311.

36. This aspect is treated in my article in Geertz, *op. cit.*

37. See S. M. Lipset, "The Sources of the 'Radical Right'—1955," in Daniel Bell, ed., *The Radical Right* (New York, 1963), pp. 260-4.

38. These conditions, increasingly a part of modern life in highly developed communities, did not always prevail. The earlier "technological revolution" was associated with the belief that representative government (the equivalent of consumer's choice in politics) was coterminous with free enterprise. Industrialization was its "natural" product. Such an ideology was remarkable for its consistency and coherence.

39. See Daniel Bell's interesting collection of essays, *The End of Ideology* (New York, 1960), p. 375.

40. Marx's concept of alienation emerged from his analysis of nineteenth-century England at a time when the "British way of life" appeared to outdistance all others in industry and entrepreneurial daring—resulting in a general Victorian smugness.

41. Robert S. Weiss and David Riesman, "Social Problems and Disorganization in the World of Work," in Robert Merton and Robert Nisbet, eds. *Contemporary Social Problems* (New York, 1961), pp. 484-5.

42. One interesting role that combines valuations of superfluousness with an ambiguous but real functional value is that of the salesman. It is recognized that the salesman plays a key role in the success of modern business enterprise, but he is associated with deceit, lack of dignity, and doubtful utility.

43. C. P. Snow, *The Two Cultures and the Scientific Revolution* (New York, 1959); see also D. E. Apter, "New Nations and the Scientific Revolution," *Bulletin of the Atomic Scientists*, XVII (February, 1961), No. 2.

44. See Bryan R. Wilson, "An Analysis of Sect Development," *American Sociological Review*, 24 (February, 1959).

45. Norman Jacobson has argued that American versions of the democratic ideal embodied this norm from the start. See "Political Science and Political Education," *American Political Science Review*, LVII (September, 1963), No. 3.

46. S. M. Lipset has bemoaned the fact that "the very growth of sociology as an intellectual force outside the academy in many western nations is a tribute, not primarily to the power of sociological analysis but to the loss of interest in political inquiry," and he ends his sociological analysis of politics with a note of concern about this trend, since he feels "there is still a real need for polical analysis, ideology, and controversy. . . ." S. M. Lipset, *Political Man: The Social Bases of Politics* (Garden City, 1960), p. 415. More recently, he has also pointed to the application of science to political matters as one of the sources of the "decline of ideologies." *Daedalus*, 93 (Winter, 1964), p. 273.

47. By no stretch of the imagination could one find the opening of a major discourse on revolution by Marx, Lenin, or Sorel, beginning with the words used by Nasser: "Before proceeding with this discourse I would like to pause at the word 'philosophy'. It looks big and sounds grand." Nor would they be able to write, "I do not pretend to be a professor of history. This is the last thing my imagination may entertain. Nevertheless, if I were to attempt to study the story of our struggle like a schoolboy, I would say, for instance, that the revolution of July 23rd is the realization of a hope that the people of Egypt, in modern times, have aspired to since they began to think of governing themselves and since they decided to be masters of their fate." See Gamal Nasser, *The Philosophy of the Revolution* (Buffalo, 1959), p. 25.

48. See Edward Shils's introduction to Georges Sorel, *Reflections on Violence* (New York, 1959), p. 14.

49. Mannheim, *op. cit.,* p. 38.

50. Polanyi, *op. cit.,* pp. 57-8.

51. E. Durkheim, *Professional Ethics and Civic Morals* (New York, 1958), p. 11.

52. One finds evidence for this increasing consumption in the mounting financial support given to universities for social science research and to other bodies. Increasingly, of course, government is undertaking its own research through such organizations as the RAND Corporation for example.

53. Werner Jaeger, *Paideia: The Ideas of Greek Culture,* Gilbert Highet, ed., (2nd ed., New York, 1945), p. xiii.

Ideology as a Cultural System

BY *CLIFFORD GEERTZ*

I.

IT IS one of the minor ironies of modern intellectual history that the term "ideology" has itself become thoroughly ideologized. A concept that once meant but a collection of political proposals, perhaps somewhat intellectualistic and impractical but at any rate idealistic—"social romances" as someone, perhaps Napoleon, called them—has now become, to quote *Webster's*, "the integrated assertions, theories, and aims constituting a politico-social program, often with an implication of factitious propagandizing; as, Fascism was altered in Germany to fit the Nazi *ideology*"—a much more formidable proposition. Even in works that, in the name of science, profess to be using a neutral sense of the term, the effect of its employment tends nonetheless to be distinctly polemical: In Sutton, Harris, Kaysen, and Tobin's in many ways excellent *The American Business Creed,* for example, an assurance that "one has no more cause to feel dismayed or aggrieved by having his own views described as 'ideology' than had Molière's famous character by the discovery that all his life he had been talking prose," is followed immediately by the listing of the main characteristics of ideology as bias, oversimplification, emotive language, and adaption to public prejudice.[1] No one, at least outside the Communist Bloc, where a somewhat distinctive conception of the role of thought in society is institutionalized, would call himself an ideologue or consent unprotestingly to be called one by others. Almost universally now the familiar parodic paradigm applies: "I have a social philosophy; you have political opinions; he has an ideology."

The historical process by which the concept of ideology came to be itself a part of the very subject matter to which it referred has been traced by Mannheim; the realization (or perhaps it was only an admission) that sociopolitical thought does not grow out of disembodied reflection but "is always bound up with the existing life situation of the thinker" seemed to taint such thought with the vulgar struggle for advantage it had professed to rise above.[2] But what is of even more immediate importance is the question whether or not this absorption into its own referent has destroyed its scientific utility altogether, whether or not having become an accusation, it can remain an analytic concept. In Mannheim's case, this problem was the animus of his entire work—the construction, as he put it, of a "non-evaluative conception of ideology." But the more he grappled with it the more deeply he became engulfed in its ambiguities until, driven by the

logic of his initial assumptions to submit even his own point of view to
sociological analysis, he ended, as is well known, in an ethical and episte-
mological relativism that he himself found uncomfortable. And so far as
later work in this area has been more than tendentious or mindlessly empirical,
it has involved the employment of a series of more or less ingenious methodological devices to escape from what may be called (because, like the puzzle
of Achilles and the tortoise, it struck at the very foundations of rational
knowledge) Mannheim's Paradox.

As Zeno's Paradox raised (or, at least, articulated) unsettling questions
about the validity of mathematical reasoning, so Mannheim's Paradox raised
them with respect to the objectivity of sociological analysis. Where, if
anywhere, ideology leaves off and science begins has been the Sphinx's
Riddle of much of modern sociological thought and the rustless weapon of
its enemies. Claims to impartiality have been advanced in the name of
disciplined adherence to impersonal research procedures, of the academic
man's institutional insulation from the immediate concerns of the day
and his vocational commitment to neutrality, and of deliberately cultivated
awareness of and correction for one's own biases and interests. They have
been met with denial of the impersonality (and the effectiveness) of the
procedures, of the solidity of the insulation, and of the depth and genuineness of the self-awareness. "I am aware," a recent analyst of ideological
preoccupations among American intellectuals concludes somewhat nervously,
"that many readers will claim that my position is itself ideological."[3] Whatever the fate of his other predictions, the validity of this one is certain.
Although the arrival of a scientific sociology has been repeatedly proclaimed, the acknowledgment of its existence is far from universal, even
among social scientists themselves; and nowhere is resistance to claims to
objectivity greater than in the study of ideology.

A number of sources for this resistance have been cited repeatedly in
the apologetic literature of the social sciences. The value-laden nature of the
subject matter is perhaps most frequently invoked: Men do not care to have
beliefs to which they attach great moral significance examined dispassionately, no matter for how pure a purpose; and if they are themselves highly
ideologized they may find it simply impossible to believe that a disinterested approach to critical matters of social and political conviction
can be other than scholastic sham. The inherent elusiveness of ideological
thought, expressed as it is in intricate symbolic webs as vaguely defined as
they are emotionally charged; the admitted fact that ideological special
pleading has, from Marx forward, so often been clothed in the guise of
"scientific sociology"; and the defensiveness of established intellectual
classes who see scientific probing into the social roots of ideas as threatening
to their status are also often mentioned. And, when all else fails, it is always
possible to point out once more that sociology is a young science, that it
has been so recently founded that it has not had time to reach the levels
of institutional solidity necessary to sustain its claims to investigatory freedom in sensitive areas. All these arguments have, doubtless, a certain
validity. But what—by a curious selective omission the unkind might well
indict as ideological—is not so often considered is the possibility that a
great part of the problem lies in the lack of conceptual sophistication within

social science itself, that the resistance of ideology to sociological analysis is so great because such analyses are in fact fundamentally inadequate, the theoretical framework they employ conspicuously incomplete.

I shall try in this essay to show that such is indeed the case: that the social sciences have not yet developed a genuinely nonevaluative conception of ideology; that this failure stems less from methodological indiscipline than from theoretical clumsiness; that this clumsiness manifests itself mainly in the handling of ideology as an entity in itself—as an ordered system of cultural symbols rather than in the destination between its social and psychological contexts (with respect to which our analytical machinery is very much more refined); and that the escape from Mannheim's Paradox lies, therefore, in the perfection of a conceptual apparatus capable of dealing more adroitly with meaning. Bluntly, we need a more exact apprehension of our object of study, lest we find ourselves in the position of the Javanese folktale figure, "Stupid Boy," who, having been counseled by his mother to seek a quiet wife, returned with a corpse.

II.

That the conception of ideology now regnant in the social sciences is a thoroughly evaluative (that is, pejorative) one is readily enough demonstrated. "[The study of ideology] deals with a mode of thinking which is thrown off its proper course," Werner Stark informs us; "ideological thought is . . . something shady, something that ought to be overcome and banished from our mind." It is not (quite) the same as lying, for, where the liar at least attains to cynicism, the ideologue remains merely a fool: "Both are concerned with untruth, but whereas the liar tries to falsify the thought of others while his own private thought is correct, while he himself knows well what the truth is, a person who falls for an ideology is himself deluded in his private thought, and if he misleads others, does so unwillingly and unwittingly."[4] A follower of Mannheim, Stark holds that all forms of thought are socially conditioned in the very nature of things; but that ideology has in addition the unfortunate quality of being psychologically "deformed" ("warped," "contaminated," "falsified," "distorted," "clouded") by the pressure of personal emotions like hate, desire, anxiety, or fear. The sociology of knowledge deals with the social element in the pursuit and perception of truth, its inevitable confinement to one or another existential perspective. But the study of ideology—an entirely different enterprise—deals with the causes of intellectual error:

Ideas and beliefs, we have tried to explain, can be related to reality in a double way: either to the *facts* of reality, or to the *strivings* to which this reality, or rather the reaction to this reality, gives rise. Where the former connection exists, we find thought which is, in principle, truthful; where the latter relation obtains, we are faced with ideas which can be true only by accident, and which are likely to be vitiated by bias, the word taken in the widest possible sense. The former type of thought deserves to be called theoretical; the latter must be characterized as paratheoretical. Perhaps one might also describe the former as rational, the latter as emotionally tinged—the former as purely cognitive, the latter as evaluative. To borrow Theodor Geiger's simile . . . thought determined by social fact is like a pure stream, crystal-clear, transparent; ideological ideas like a dirty river, muddied and polluted by the impurities that have flooded into it. From the one it is healthy to drink; the other is poison to be avoided.[5]

This analysis is primitive, but the same confinement of the referent of the term "ideology" to a form of radical intellectual depravity also appears in contexts where the political and scientific arguments are both far more sophisticated and infinitely more penetrating. In his seminal essay on "Ideology and Civility," for example, Edward Shils sketches a portrait of "the ideological outlook," which is, if anything, even grimmer than Stark's.[6] Appearing "in a variety of forms, each alleging itself to be unique"—Italian Facism, German National Socialism, Russian Bolshevism, French and Italian Communism, the Action Française, the British Union of Fascists, "and their fledgling American kinsman, 'McCarthyism,' which died in infancy"—this outlook "encircled and invaded public life in the Western countries during the 19th century and in the 20th century . . . threatened to achieve universal domination." It consists, most centrally, of "the assumption that politics should be conducted from the standpoint of a coherent, comprehensive set of beliefs which must override every other consideration." Like the politics it supports, it is dualistic, opposing the pure "we" to the evil "they," proclaiming that he who is not with me is against me. It is alienative in that it distrusts, attacks, and works to undermine established political institutions. It is doctrinaire in that it claims complete and exclusive possession of political truth and abhors compromise. It is totalistic in that it aims to order the whole of social and cultural life in the image of its ideals, futuristic in that it works toward a utopian culmination of history in which such an ordering will be realized. It is, in short, not the sort of prose any good bourgeois gentleman (or even any good democrat) is likely to admit to speaking.

Even on more abstract and theoretical levels, where the concern is more purely conceptual, the notion that the term "ideology" properly applies to the views of those "stiff in opinions, and always in the wrong" does not disappear. In Talcott Parsons's most recent contemplation of Mannheim's Paradox, for example, "deviations from [social] scientific objectivity" emerge as the "essential criteria of an ideology"—"The problem of ideology arises where there is a *discrepancy* between what is believed and what can be [established as] scientifically correct."[7] The "deviations" and "discrepancies" involved are of two general sorts. First, where social science, shaped as is all thought by the over-all values of the society within which it is contained, is selective in the sort of questions it asks, the particular problems it chooses to tackle, and so forth, ideologies are subject to a further, cognitively more pernicious "secondary" selectivity, in that they emphasize some aspects of social reality—that reality, for example, is revealed by current social scientific knowledge—and neglect or even suppress other aspects. "Thus the business ideology, for instance, substantially exaggerates the contribution of businessmen to the national welfare and underplays the contribution of scientists and professional men. And in the current ideology of the 'intellectual,' the importance of social 'pressures to conformity' is exaggerated and institutional factors in the freedom of the individual are ignored or played down." Second, ideological thought, not content with mere overselectivity, positively distorts even those aspects of social reality it recognizes, distortion that becomes apparent only when the assertions involved are placed against the background of the authoritative findings of social science. "The criterion of distortion is that statements are made about society which by social-scientific methods can be shown to be positively in error, whereas selectivity is involved where the statements are, at the proper level 'true,' but do not constitute a balanced account of the available truth." That in the eyes of the world there is much to choose between being positively in error and rendering an unbalanced account of the available truth seems, however, rather unlikely. Here, too, ideology is a pretty dirty river.

Examples need not be multiplied, although they easily could be. More important is the question of what such an egregiously loaded concept is doing among the analytic tools of a social science that, on the basis of a claim to cold-blooded objectivity, advances its theoretical interpretations as "undistorted" and therefore normative visions of social reality. If the critical power of the social sciences stems from their disinterestedness, is not this power compromised when the analysis of political thought is governed by such a concept, much as the analysis of religious thought would be (and, on occasion, has been) compromised when cast in terms of the study of "superstition"?

The analogy is not farfetched. In Raymond Aron's *The Opium of the Intellectuals,* for example, not only the title—ironically echoic of Marx's bitter iconoclasm—but the entire rhetoric of the argument ("political myths," "the idolatry of history," "churchmen and faithful," "secular clericalism," and so forth) reminds one of nothing so much as the literature of militant atheism.[8] Shils's tack of invoking the extreme pathologies of ideological thought—Nazism, Bolshevism, or whatever—as its paradigmatic forms is reminiscent of the tradition in which the Inquisition, the personal depravity of Renaissance popes, the savagery of Reformation wars, or the primitiveness of Bible-belt fundamentalism is offered as an archetype of religious belief and behavior. And Parsons's view that ideology is defined by its cognitive insufficiencies *vis-à-vis* science is perhaps not so distant as it might appear from the Comtean view that religion is characterized by an uncritically figurative conception of reality, which a sober sociology, purged of metaphor, will soon render obsolete: We may wait as long for the "end of ideology" as the positivists have waited for the end of religion. Perhaps it is even not too much to suggest that, as the militant atheism of the Enlightenment and after was a response to the quite genuine horrors of a spectacular outburst of religious bigotry, persecution, and strife (and to a broadened knowledge of the natural world), so the militantly hostile approach to ideology is a similar response to the political holocausts of the past half-century (and to a broadened knowledge of the social world). And, if this suggestion is valid, the fate of ideology may also turn out to be similar—isolation from the mainstream of social thought.[9]

Nor can the issue be dismissed as merely a semantic one. One is, naturally, free to confine the referent of the term "ideology" to "something shady" if one wishes; and some sort of historical case for doing so can perhaps be made. But if one does so limit it, one cannot then write works on the ideologies of American businessmen, New York "literary" intellectuals, members of the British Medical Association, industrial labor-union leaders, or famous economists and expect either the subjects or interested bystanders to credit them as neutral.[10] Discussions of sociopolitical ideas that indict them *ab initio*, in terms of the very words used to name them, as deformed or worse merely beg the questions they pretend to raise. It is also possible, of course, that the term "ideology" should simply be dropped from scientific discourse altogether and left to its polemical fate— as "superstition" in fact has been. But, as there seems to be nothing at the moment with which to replace it and as it is at least partially established in the technical lexicon of the social sciences, it seems more advisable to proceed with the effort to defuse it.[11]

III.

As the flaws hidden in a tool show up when it is used, so the intrinsic weaknesses of the evaluative concept of ideology reveal themselves when it is used. In particular, they are exposed in the studies of the social sources and consequences of ideology, for in such studies this concept is coupled to a highly developed engine of social- and personality-system analysis whose very power only serves to emphasize the lack of a similar power on the cultural (that is, the symbol-system) side. In investigations of the social and psychological contexts of ideological thought (or at least the "good" ones), the subtlety with which the contexts are handled points up the awkwardness with which the thought is handled, and a shadow of imprecision is cast over the whole discussion, a shadow that even the most rigorous methodological austerity cannot dispel.

There are currently two main approaches to the study of the social determinants of ideology: the interest theory and the strain theory.[12] For the first, ideology is a mask and a weapon; for the second, a symptom and a remedy. In the interest theory, ideological pronouncements are seen against the background of a universal struggle for advantage; in the strain theory, against the background of a chronic effort to correct sociopsychological disequilibrium. In the one, men pursue power; in the other, they flee anxiety. As they may, of course, do both at the same time—and even one by means of the other—the two theories are not necessarily contradictory; but the strain theory (which arose in response to the empirical difficulties encountered by the interest theory), being less simplistic, is more penetrating, less concrete, more comprehensive.

The fundamentals of the interest theory are too well known to need review; developed to perfection of a sort by the Marxist tradition, they are now standard intellectual equipment of the man-in-the-street, who is only too aware that in political argumentation it all comes down to whose ox is gored. The great advantage of the interest theory was and is its rooting of cultural idea-systems in the solid ground of social structure, through emphasis on the motivations of those who profess such systems and on the dependence of those motivations in turn upon social position, most especially social class. Further, the interest theory welded political speculation to political combat by pointing out that ideas are weapons and that an excellent way to institutionalize a particular view of reality—that of one's group, class, or party—is to capture political power and enforce it. These

contributions are permanent; and if interest theory has not now the hegemony it once had, it is not so much because it has been proved wrong as
because its theoretical apparatus turned out to be too rudimentary to cope
with the complexity of the interaction among social, psychological, and
cultural factors it itself uncovered. Rather like Newtonian mechanics, it has
not been so much displaced by subsequent developments as absorbed into
them.

The main defects of the interest theory are that its psychology is too
anemic and its sociology too muscular. Lacking a developed analysis of
motivation, it has been constantly forced to oscillate between a narrow and
superficial utilitarianism that sees men as impelled by rational calculation
of their consciously recognized personal advantage and a broader, but no
less superficial, historicism that speaks with a studied vagueness of men's
ideas as somehow "reflecting," "expressing," "corresponding to," "emerging
from," or "conditioned by" their social commitments. Within such a framework, the analyst is faced with the choice of either revealing the thinness of
his psychology by being so specific as to be thoroughly implausible or con-
cealing the fact that he does not have any psychological theory at all by
being so general as to be truistic. An argument that for professional soldiers
"domestic [governmental] policies are important mainly as ways of retaining
and enlarging the military establishment [because] that is their business; that
is what they are trained for" seems to do scant justice to even so uncomplic-
ated a mind as the military mind is reputed to be; while an argument that
American oilmen "cannot very well be pure-and-simple oil men" because
"their interests are such" that "they are also political men" is as enlightening
as the theory (also from the fertile mind of M. Jourdain) that the reason opium
puts you to sleep is that it has dormitive powers.[13]

On the other hand, the view that social action is fundamentally an unending
struggle for power leads to an unduly Machiavellian view of ideology as a
form of higher cunning and, consequently, to a neglect of its broader, less
dramatic social functions. The battlefield image of society as a clash of
interests thinly disguised as a clash of principles turns attention away from
the role that ideologies play in defining (or obscuring) social categories,
stabilizing (or upsetting) social expectations, maintaining (or undermining)
social norms, strengthening (or weakening) social consensus, relieving (or
exacerbating) social tensions. Reducing ideology to a weapon in a *guerre de
plume* gives to its analysis a warming air of militancy, but it also means
reducing the intellectual compass within which such analysis may be
conducted to the constricted realism of tactics and strategy. The intensity of
interest theory is—to adapt a figure from Whitehead—but the reward of its
narrowness.

As "interest," whatever its ambiguities, is at one and the same time a
psychological and sociological concept—referring both to a felt advantage of
an individual or group of individuals and to the objective structure of
opportunity within which an individual or group moves—so also is "strain,"
for it refers both to a state of personal tension and to a condition of societal
dislocation. The difference is that with "strain" both the motivational background and the social structural context are more systematically portrayed,
as are their relations with one another. It is, in fact, the addition of a

developed conception of personality systems (basically Freudian), on the one hand, and of social systems (basically Durkheimian) on the other, and of their modes of interpenetration—the Parsonian addition—that transforms interest theory into strain theory.[14]

The clear and distinct idea from which strain theory departs is the chronic malintegration of society. No social arrangement is or can be completely successful in coping with the functional problems it inevitably faces. All are riddled with insoluble antinomies: between liberty and political order, stability and change, efficiency and humanity, precision and flexibility, and so forth. There are discontinuities between norms in different sectors of the society—the economy, the polity, the family, and so forth. There are discrepancies between goals within the different sectors—between the emphases on profit and productivity in business firms or between extending knowledge and disseminating it in universities, for example. And there are the contradictory role expectations of which so much has been made in recent American sociological literature on the foreman, the working wife, the artist, and the politician. Social friction is as pervasive as is mechanical friction—and as irremovable.

Further, this friction or social strain appears on the level of the individual personality—itself an inevitably malintegrated system of conflicting desires, archaic sentiments, and improvised defenses—as psychological strain. What is viewed collectively as structural inconsistency is felt individually as personal insecurity, for it is in the experience of the social actor that the imperfections of society and contradictions of character meet and exacerbate one another. But at the same time, the fact that both society and personality are, whatever their shortcomings, organized systems, rather than mere congeries of institutions or clusters of motives, means that the sociopsychological tensions they induce are also systematic, that the anxieties derived from social interaction have a form and order of their own. In the modern world at least, most men live lives of patterned desperation.

Ideological thought is, then, regarded as (one sort of) response to this desperation: "Ideology is a patterned reaction to the patterned strains of a social role."[15] It provides a "symbolic outlet" for emotional disturbances generated by social disequilibrium. And as one can assume that such disturbances are, at least in a general way, common to all or most occupants of a given role or social position, so ideological reactions to the disturbances will tend to be similar, a similarity only reinforced by the presumed commonalities in "basic personality structure" among members of a particular culture, class, or occupational category. The model here is not military but medical: An ideology is a malady (Sutton, *et al.*, mention nail-chewing, alcoholism, psychosomatic disorders, and "crotchets" among the alternatives to it) and demands a diagnosis. "The concept of strain is not in itself an explanation of ideological patterns but a generalized label for the kinds of factors to look for in working out an explanation."[16]

But there is more to diagnosis, either medical or sociological, than the identification of pertinent strains; one understands symptoms not merely etiologically but teleologically—in terms of the ways in which they act as mechanisms, however unavailing, for dealing with the disturbances that have generated them. Four main classes of explanation have been most frequently employed: the cathartic, the morale, the solidarity, and the advocatory. By the "cathartic explanation" is meant the venerable safety-valve or scapegoat theory. Emotional tension is drained off by being displaced onto symbolic enemies ("The Jews," "Big Business," "The Reds," and so forth). The explanation is as simple-minded as the device, but that, by providing legitimate objects of hostility (or, for that matter, of love), ideology may ease somewhat the pain of being a petty bureaucrat, a day laborer, or a small-town storekeeper is undeniable. By the "morale explanation" is meant the ability of an ideology to sustain individuals (or groups) in the face of chronic strain, either by denying it outright or by legitimizing it in terms of higher values. Both the struggling small businessman rehearsing his boundless confidence in the inevitable justness of the American system and the neglected artist attributing his failure to his maintenance of decent standards in a Philistine world are able, by such means, to get on with their work. Ideology bridges the emotional gap between things as they are and as one would have them be, thus insuring the performance of roles that might otherwise be abandoned in despair or apathy. By the "solidarity explanation" is meant the power of ideology to knit a social group or class together. To the extent that it exists, the unity of the labor movement, the business community, or the medical profession obviously rests to a significant degree on common ideological orientation; and the South would not be The South without the existence of popular symbols charged with the emotions of a pervasive social predicament. Finally, by the "advocatory explanation" is meant the action of ideologies (and ideologists) in articulating, however partially and indistinctly, the strains that impel them, thus forcing them into the public notice. "Ideologists state the problems for the larger society, take sides on the issues involved and 'present them in the court' of the ideological market place."[17] Although ideological advocates (not altogether unlike their legal counterparts) tend as much to obscure as to clarify the true nature of the problems involved, they at least call attention to their existence and, by polarizing issues, make continued neglect more difficult. Without Marxist attack, there would have been no labor reform; without Black Muslims, no deliberate speed.

It is here, however, in the investigation of the social and psychological roles of ideology, as distinct from its determinants, that strain theory itself begins to creak and its superior incisiveness, in comparison with interest theory, to evaporate. The increased precision in the location of the springs of ideological concern does not, somehow, carry over into the discrimination of its consequences, where the analysis becomes, on the contrary, slack and ambiguous. The consequences envisaged, no doubt genuine enough in themselves, seem almost adventitious, the accidental by-products of an essentially nonrational, nearly automatic expressive process initially pointed in another direction—as when a man stubbing his toe cries an involuntary "ouch!" and incidentally vents his anger, signals his distress, and consoles himself with the sound of his own voice; or as when, caught in a subway crush, he issues a spontaneous "damn!" of frustration and, hearing similar oaths from others, gains a certain perverse sense of kinship with fellow sufferers.

This defect, of course, can be found in much of the functional analysis in the social sciences: A pattern of behavior shaped by a certain set of forces turns out, by a plausible but nevertheless mysterious coincidence, to serve ends but tenuously related to those forces. A group of primitives sets out, in all honesty, to pray for rain and ends by strengthening its social solidarity; a ward politician sets out to get or remain near the trough and ends by mediating between unassimilated immigrant groups and an impersonal governmental bureaucracy; an ideologist sets out to air his grievances and finds himself contributing, through the diversionary power of his illusions, to the continued viability of the very system that grieves him.

The concept of latent function is usually invoked to paper over this anomalous state of affairs, but it rather names the phenomenon (whose reality is not in question) than explains it; and the net result is that functional analyses—and not only those of ideology—remain hopelessly equivocal. The petty bureaucrat's anti-Semitism may indeed give him something to do with the bottled anger generated in him by constant toadying to those he considers his intellectual inferiors and so drain some of it away; but it may also simply increase his anger by providing him with something else about which to be impotently bitter. The neglected artist may better bear his popular failure by invoking the classical canons of his art; but such an invocation may so dramatize for him the gap between the possibilities of his environment and the demands of his vision as to make the game seem unworth the candle. Commonality of ideological perception may link men together, but it may also provide them, as the history of Marxian sectarianism demonstrates, with a vocabulary by means of which to explore more exquisitely the differences among them. The clash of ideologists may bring a social problem to public attention, but it may also charge it with such passion that any possibility of dealing with it rationally is precluded. Of all these possibilities, strain theorists are, of course, very well aware. Indeed they tend to stress negative outcomes and possibilities rather more than the positive, and they but rarely think of ideology as more than a *faute de mieux* stop-gap—like nail-chewing. But the main point is that, for all its subtlety in ferreting out the motives of ideological concern, strain theory's analysis of the consequences of such concern remains crude, vacillatory, and evasive. Diagnostically it is convincing; functionally it is not.

The reason for this weakness is the virtual absence in strain theory (or in interest theory either) of anything more than the most rudimentary conception of the processes of symbolic formulation. There is a good deal of talk about emotions "finding a symbolic outlet" or "becoming attached to appropriate symbols"—but very little idea of how the trick is really done. The link between the causes of ideology and its effects seems adventitious because the connecting element—the autonomous process of symbolic formulation—is passed over in virtual silence. Both interest theory and strain theory go directly from source analysis to consequence analysis without ever seriously examining ideologies as systems of interacting symbols, as patterns of interworking meanings. Themes are outlined, of course; among the content analysts, they are even counted. But they are referred for elucidation, not to other themes nor to any sort of semantic theory, but either backward to the affect they presumably mirror or forward to the social reality they presumably distort. The problem of how, after all, ideologies transform sentiment into significance and so make it socially available is short-circuited by the crude device of placing particular symbols and particular strains (or interests) side by side in such a way that the fact that the first are derivatives of the second seems mere common sense—or at least post-Freudian, post-Marxian common sense. And so, if the analyst be deft enough, it does.[18] The connection is not thereby explained but merely educed. The nature of the relationship between the sociopsychological stresses that incite ideological attitudes and the elaborate symbolic structures through which those attitudes are given a public existence is much too complicated to be comprehended in terms of a vague and unexamined notion of emotive resonance.

IV.

It is of singular interest in this connection that, although the general stream of social scientific theory has been deeply influenced by almost every major intellectual movement of the last century and a half—Marxism, Darwinism, Utilitarianism, Idealism, Freudianism, Behaviorism, Positivism, Operationalism —and has attempted to capitalize on virtually every important field of methodological innovation from ecology, ethology, and comparative psychology to game theory, cybernetics, and statistics, it has, with very few exceptions, been virtually untouched by one of the most important trends in recent thought: the effort to construct an independent science of what Kenneth Burke has called "symbolic action."[19] Neither the work of such philosophers as Peirce, Wittgenstein, Cassirer, Langer, Ryle, or Morris nor of such literary critics as Coleridge, Eliot, Burke, Empson, Blackmur, Brooks, or Auerbach seems to have had any appreciable impact on the general pattern of social scientific analysis.[20] Aside from a few more venturesome (and largely programmatic) linguists—a Whorf or a Sapir—the question of how symbols symbolize, how they function to mediate meanings has simply been bypassed. "The embarrassing fact," the physician *cum* novelist Walker Percy has written, "is that there does not exist today—a natural empirical science of symbolic behavior *as such* . . . Sapir's gentle chiding about the lack of a science of symbolic behavior and the need of such a science is more conspicuously true today than it was thirty-five years ago."[21]

It is the absence of such a theory and in particular the absence of any analytical framework within which to deal with figurative language that have reduced sociologists to viewing ideologies as elaborate cries of pain. With no notion of how metaphor, analogy, irony, ambiguity, pun, paradox, hyperbole, rhythm, and all the other elements of what we lamely call "style" operate—even, in a majority of cases, with no recognition that these devices are of any importance in casting personal attitudes into public form, sociologists lack the symbolic resources out of which to construct a more incisive formulation. At the same time that the arts have been establishing the cognitive power of "distortion" and philosophy has been undermining the adequacy of an emotivist theory of meanings, social scientists have been rejecting the first and embracing the second. It is not therefore surprising that they evade the problem of construing the import of ideological assertions by simply failing to recognize it as a problem.[22]

In order to make explicit what I mean, let me take an example that is, I hope, so thoroughly trivial in itself as both to still any suspicions that I have a hidden concern with the substance of the political issue involved and, more important, to bring home the point that concepts developed for the analysis of the more elevated aspects of culture—poetry, for example—are applicable to the more lowly ones without in any way blurring the enormous qualitative distinctions between the two. In discussing the cognitive in-adequacies by which ideology is defined for them, Sutton *et al.* use as an example of the ideologist's tendency to "oversimplify" the denomination by organized labor of the Taft-Hartley Act as a "slave labor law":

> Ideology tends to be simple and clear-cut, even where its simplicity and clarity do less than justice to the subject under discussion. The ideological picture uses sharp lines and contrasting blacks and whites. The ideologist exaggerates and caricatures in the fashion of the cartoonist. In contrast, a scientific description of social phenomena is likely to be fuzzy and indistinct. In recent labor ideology the Taft-Hartley Act has been a "slave labor act." By no dispassionate examination does the Act merit this label. Any detached assessment of the Act would have to consider its many provisions individually. On any set of values, even those of trade unions themselves, such an assessment would yield a mixed verdict. But mixed verdicts are not the stuff of ideology. They are too complicated, too fuzzy. Ideology must categorize the Act as a whole with a symbol to rally workers, voters and legislators to action.[23]

Leaving aside the merely empirical question of whether or not it is in fact true that ideological formulations of a given set of social phenomena are inevitably "simpler" than scientific formulations of the same phenomena, there is in this argument a curiously depreciatory—one might even say "over simple"—view of the thought processes of labor-union leaders on the one hand and "workers, voters and legislators" on the other. It is rather hard to believe that either those who coined and disseminated the slogan them-selves believed or expected anyone else to believe that the law would actually reduce (or was intended to reduce) the American worker to the status of a slave or that the segment of the public for whom the slogan had meaning perceived it in any such terms. Yet it is precisely this flattened view of other people's mentalities that leaves the sociologist with only two interpretations, both inadequate, of whatever effectiveness the symbol has: Either it deceives the uninformed (according to interest theory), or it excites the unreflective (according to strain theory). That it might in fact draw its power from its capacity to grasp, formulate, and communicate social realities that elude the tempered language of science, that it may mediate more complex meanings than its literal reading suggests, is not even considered. "Slave act" may be, after all, not a label but a trope.

More exactly, it appears to be a metaphor or at least an attempted metaphor. Although very few social scientists seem to have read much of it, the literature on metaphor—"the power whereby language, even with a small vocabulary manages to embrace a multi-million things"—is vast and by now in reasonable agreement.[24] In metaphor one has, of course, a stratifi-cation of meaning, in which an incongruity of sense on one level produces an influx of significance on another. As Percy has pointed out, the feature of metaphor that has most troubled philosophers (and, he might have added, scientists) is that it is "wrong": "It asserts of one thing that it is something else." And, worse yet, it tends to be most effective when most "wrong."[25]

The power of a metaphor derives precisely from the interplay between the discordant meanings it symbolically coerces into a unitary conceptual framework and from the degree to which that coercion is successful in overcoming the psychic resistance such semantic tension inevitably generates in anyone in a position to perceive it. When it works, a metaphor transforms a false identification (for example, of the labor policies of the Republican Party and of those of the Bolsheviks) into an apt analogy; when it misfires, it is a mere extravagance.

That for most people the "slave labor law" figure was, in fact, pretty much a misfire (and therefore never served with any effectiveness as "a symbol to rally workers, voters and legislators to action") seems evident enough, and it is this failure, rather than its supposed clear-cut simplicity, that makes it seem no more than a cartoon. The semantic tension between the image of a conservative Congress outlawing the closed shop and of the prison camps of Siberia was—apparently—too great to be resolved into a single conception, at least by means of so rudimentary a stylistic device as the slogan. Except (perhaps) for a few enthusiasts, the analogy did not appear; the false identification remained false. But failure is not inevitable, even on such an elementary level. Although a most unmixed verdict, Sherman's "war is hell" is no social-science proposition. Even Sutton and his associates would probably not regard it as either an exaggeration or a caricature.

More important, however, than any assessment of the adequacy of the two tropes as such is the fact that, as the meanings they attempt to spark against one another are after all socially rooted, the success or failure of the attempt is relative not only to the power of the stylistic mechanisms employed but also to precisely those sorts of factor upon which strain theory concentrates its attention. The tensions of the Cold War, the fears of a labor movement only recently emerged from a bitter struggle for existence, and the threatened eclipse of New Deal liberalism after two decades of dominance set the sociopsychological stage both for the appearance of the "slave labor" figure and—when it proved unable to work them into a cogent analogy—for its miscarriage. The militarists of 1934 Japan who opened their pamphlet on *Basic Theory of National Defense and Suggestions for Its Strengthening* with the resounding familial metaphor, "War is the father of creation and the mother of culture," would no doubt have found Sherman's maxim as unconvincing as he would have found theirs.[26] They were energetically preparing for an imperialist war in an ancient nation seeking its footing in the modern world; he was wearily pursuing a civil war in an unrealized nation torn by domestic hatreds. It is thus not truth that varies with social, psychological, and cultural contexts but the symbols we construct in our unequally effective attempts to grasp it. War *is* hell and *not* the mother of culture, as the Japanese eventually discovered—although no doubt they express the fact in a grander idiom.

The sociology of knowledge ought to be called the sociology of meaning, for what is socially determined is not the nature of conception but the vehicles of conception. In a community that drinks its coffee black, Henle remarks, to praise a girl with "you're the cream in my coffee" would give entirely the wrong impression; and, if omnivorousness were regarded as a more significant characteristic of bears than their clumsy roughness, to call a man "an old bear" might mean not that he was crude but that he had catholic tastes.[27] Or, to take an example from Burke, since in Japan people smile on mentioning the death of a close friend, the semantic equivalent (behaviorally as well as verbally) in American English is not "he smiled" but "his face fell"; for, with such a rendering, we are "translating the accepted social usage of Japan into the corresponding accepted social usage of the West."[28] And, closer to the ideological realm, Sapir has pointed out that the chairmanship of a committee has the figurative force we give it only because we hold that "administrative functions somehow stamp a person as superior to those who are being directed"; "should people come to feel that administrative functions are little more than symbolic automatisms, the chairmanship of a committee would be recognized as little more than a petrified symbol and the particular value that is now felt to inhere in it would tend to disappear."[29] The case is no different for "slave labor law." If forced labor camps come, for whatever reasons, to play a less prominent role in the American image of the Soviet Union, it will not be the symbol's veracity that has dissolved but its very meaning, its capacity to be *either* true or false. One must simply frame the argument— that the Taft-Hartley Act is a mortal threat to organized labor—in some other way.

In short, between an ideological figure like "slave labor act" and the social realities of American life in the midst of which it appears, there exists a subtlety of interplay, which concepts like "distortion," "selectivity," or "oversimplification" are simply incompetent to formulate.[30] Not only is the semantic structure of the figure a good deal more complex than it appears on the surface, but an analysis of that structure forces one into tracing a multiplicity of referential connections between it and social reality, so that the final picture is one of a configuration of dissimilar meanings out of whose interworking both the expressive power and the rhetorical force of the final symbol derive. This interworking is itself a social process, an occurrence not "in the head" but in that public world where "people talk together, name things, make assertions, and to a degree understand each other."[31] The study of symbolic action is no less a sociological discipline than the study of small groups, bureaucracies, or the changing role of the American woman; it is only a good deal less developed.

V.

Asking the question that most students of ideology fail to ask—what, precisely, do we mean when we assert that sociopsychological strains are "expressed" in symbolic forms?—gets one, therefore, very quickly into quite deep water indeed; into, in fact, a somewhat untraditional and apparrently paradoxical theory of the nature of human thought as a public and not, or at least not fundamentally, a private activity.[32] The details of such a theory cannot be pursued any distance here, nor can any significant amount of evidence be marshalled to support it. But at least its general outlines must be sketched if we are to find our way back from the elusive world of symbols and semantic process to the (apparently) solider one of sentiments and institutions, if we are to trace with some circumstantiality the modes of interpenetration of culture, personality, and social system.

The defining proposition of this sort of approach to thought *en plein air* —what, following Galanter and Gerstenhaber, we may call "the extrinsic theory"—is that thought consists of the construction and manipulation of symbol systems, which are employed as models of other systems, physical, organic, social, psychological, and so forth, in such a way that the structure of these other systems—and, in the favorable case, how they may therefore be expected to behave—is, as we say, "understood."[33] Thinking, conceptualization, formulation, comprehension, understanding, or what-have-you consists not of ghostly happenings in the head but of a matching of the states and processes of symbolic models against the states and processes of the wider world:

> Imaginal thinking is neither more nor less than constructing an image of the environment, running the model faster than the environment, and predicting that the environment will behave as the model does. . . . The first step in the solution of a problem consists in the construction of a model or image of the "relevant features" of the [environment]. These models can be constructed from many things, including parts of the organic tissue of the body and, by man, paper and pencil or actual artifacts. Once a model has been constructed it can be manipulated under various hypothetical conditions and constraints. The organism is then able to "observe" the outcome of these manipulations, and to project them onto the environment so that prediction is possible. According to this view, an aeronautical engineer is thinking when he manipulates a model of a new airplane in a wind tunnel. The motorist is thinking when he runs his finger over a line on a map, the finger serving as a model of the relevant aspects of the automobile, the map as a model of the road. External models of this kind are often used in thinking about complex [environments]. Images used in covert thinking depend upon the availability of the physico-chemical events of the organism which must be used to form models.[34]

This view does not, of course, deny consciousness: It defines it. Every conscious perception is, as Percy has argued, an act of recognition, a pairing in which an object (or an event, an act, an emotion) is identified by placing it against the background of an appropriate symbol:

> It is not enough to say that one is conscious *of* something; one is also conscious of something being something. There is a difference between the apprehension of a gestalt (a chicken perceived the Jastrow effect as well as a human) and the grasping of it under its symbolic vehicle. As I gaze about the room, I am aware of a series of almost effortless acts of *matching*: seeing an object and knowing what it is. If my eye falls upon an unfamiliar something, I am immediately aware that one term of the match is missing, I ask what [the object] is—an exceedingly mysterious question.[35]

What is missing and what is being asked for are an applicable symbolic model under which to subsume the "unfamiliar something" and so render it familiar:

> If I see an object at some distance and do not quite recognize it, I may see it, actually see it, as a succession of different things, each rejected by the criterion of fit as I come closer, until one is positively certified. A patch of sunlight in a field I may actually see as a rabbit—a seeing which goes much further than the guess that it may be a rabbit; no, the perceptual gestalt is so construed, actually stamped by the essence of rabbitness: I could have sworn it was a rabbit. On coming closer, the sunlight pattern changes enough so that the rabbit-cast is disallowed. The rabbit vanishes and I make another cast: it is a paper bag, and so on. But most significant of all, even the last, the "correct" recognition is quite as mediate an apprehension as the

incorrect ones; it is also a cast, a pairing, an approximation. And let us note in passing that even though it is correct, even though it is borne out by all indices, it may operate quite as effectively to conceal as to discover. When I recognize a strange bird as a sparrow, I tend to dispose of the bird under its appropriate formulation: it is only a sparrow.[36]

Despite the somewhat intellectualist tone of these various examples, the extrinsic theory of thought is extendable to the affective side of human mentality as well.[37] As a road map transforms mere physical locations into "places," connected by numbered routes and separated by measured distances, and so enables us to find our way from where we are to where we want to go, so a poem like, for example, Hopkins's "Felix Randal" provides, through the evocative power of its charged language, a symbolic model of the emotional impact of premature death, which, if we are as impressed with its penetration as with the road map's, transforms physical sensations into sentiments and attitudes and enables us to react to such a tragedy not "blindly" but "intelligently." The central rituals of religion—a mass, a pilgrimage, a corroboree—are symbolic models (here more in the form of activities than of words) of a particular sense of the divine, a certain sort of devotional mood, which their continual re-enactment tends to produce in their participants. Of course, as most acts of what is usually called "cognition" are more on the level of identifying a rabbit than operating a wind tunnel, so most of what is usually called "expression" (the dichotomy is often overdrawn and almost universally misconstrued) is mediated more by models drawn from popular culture than from high art and formal religious ritual. But the point is that the development, maintenance, and dissolution of "moods," "attitudes," "sentiments," and so forth are no more "a ghostly process occurring in streams of consciousness we are debarred from visiting" than is the discrimination of objects, events, structures, processes, and so forth in our environment. Here, too, "we are describing the ways in which . . . people conduct parts of their predominantly public behavior."[38]

Whatever their other differences, both so-called "cognitive" and so-called "expressive" symbols or symbol-systems have, then, at least one thing in common: They are extrinsic sources of information in terms of which human life can be patterned—extrapersonal mechanisms for the perception, understanding, judgment, and manipulation of the world. Culture patterns —religious, philosophical, aesthetic, scientific, ideological—are "programs"; they provide a template or blueprint for the organization of social and psychological processes, much as genetic systems provide such a template for the organization of organic processes:

These considerations define the terms in which we approach the problem of "reductionism" in psychology and social science. The levels we have tentatively discriminated [organism, personality, social system, culture] . . . are . . . levels of organization and control. The lower levels "condition," and thus in a sense "determine" the structures into which they enter, in the same sense that the stability of a building depends on the properties of the materials out of which it is constructed. But the physical properties of the materials do not determine the *plan* of the building; this is a factor of another order, one of *organization*. And the organization controls the *relations* of the materials to each other, the *ways* in which they are utilized in the building by virtue of which it constitutes an ordered system of a particular type—Looking "downward" in the series, we can always investigate and discover sets of "conditions" in which the function of a higher order of organization is dependent. There is, thus, an immensely complicated set of physiological conditions on which psychological functioning is dependent, etc. Properly understood and evaluated, these conditions are always authentic determinants of process in the organized systems at the next higher levels. We may, however, also look "upward" in the series. In this direction we see "structures," organization patterns, patterns of meaning, "programs," etc., which are the focus of the organization of the system at the level on which we have concentrated our attention.[39]

The reason such symbolic templates are necessary is that, as has been often remarked, human behavior is inherently extremely plastic. Not strictly but only very broadly controlled by genetic programs or models—intrinsic sources of information—such behavior must, if it is to have any effective form at all, be controlled to a significant extent by extrinsic ones. Birds learn how to fly without wind tunnels, and whatever reactions lower animals have to death are in great part innate, physiologically preformed.[40] The extreme generality, diffuseness, and variability of man's innate response capacities mean that the particular pattern his behavior takes is guided predominantly by cultural rather than genetic templates, the latter setting the over-all psychophysical context within which precise activity sequences are organized by the former. The tool-making, laughing, or lying animal, man, is also the incomplete—or, more accurately, self-completing—animal. The agent of his own realization, he creates out of his general capacity for the construction of symbolic models the specific capabilities that define him. Or —to return at last to our subject—it is through the construction of ideologies, schematic images of social order, that man makes himself for better or worse a political animal.

Further, as the various sorts of cultural symbol-system are extrinsic sources of information, templates for the organization of social and psychological processes, they come most crucially into play in situations where the particular kind of information they contain is lacking, where institutionalized guides for behavior, thought, or feeling are weak or absent. It is in country unfamiliar emotionally or topographically that one needs poems and road maps.

So too with ideology. In polities firmly embedded in Edmund Burke's golden assemblage of "ancient opinions and rules of life," the role of ideology, in any explicit sense, is marginal. In such truly traditional political systems the participants act as (to use another Burkean phrase) men of untaught feelings; they are guided both emotionally and intellectually in their judgments and activities by unexamined prejudices, which do not leave them "hesitating in the moment of decision, sceptical, puzzled and unresolved." But when, as in the revolutionary France Burke was indicting and in fact in the shaken England from which, as perhaps his nation's greatest ideologue, he was indicting it, those hallowed opinions and rules of life come into question, the search for systematic ideological formulations, either to reinforce them or to replace them, flourishes. The function of ideology is to make an autonomous politics possible by providing the authoritative concepts that render it meaningful, the suasive images by means of which it can be sensibly grasped.[41]

It is, in fact, precisely at the point at which a political system begins to free itself from the immediate governance of received tradition, from the direct and detailed guidance of religious or philosophical canons on the one hand and from the unreflective precepts of conventional moralism on the other, that formal ideologies tend first to emerge and take hold.[42] The differentiation of an autonomous polity implies the differentiation, too, of a separate and distinct cultural model of political action, for the older, unspecialized models are either too comprehensive or too concrete to provide the sort of guidance such a political system demands. Either they trammel political behavior by encumbering it with transcendental significance, or they stifle political imagination by binding it to the blank realism of habitual judgment. It is when neither a society's most general cultural orientations nor its most down-to-earth, "pragmatic" ones suffice any longer to provide an adequate image of political process that ideologies begin to become crucial as sources of sociopolitical meanings and attitudes.

In one sense, this statement is but another way of saying that ideology is a response to strain. But now we are including *cultural* as well as social and psychological strain. It is a loss of orientation that most directly gives rise to ideological activity, an inability, for lack of usable models, to comprehend the universe of civic rights and responsibilities in which one finds oneself located. The development of a differentiated polity (or of greater internal differentiation within such a polity) may and commonly does bring with it severe social dislocation and psychological tension. But it also brings with it conceptual confusion, as the established images of political order fade into irrelevance or are driven into disrepute. The reason why the French Revolution was, at least up to its time, the greatest incubator of extremist ideologies, "progressive" and "reactionary" alike, in human history was not that either personal insecurity or social disequilibrium were deeper and more pervasive than at many earlier periods—though they were deep and pervasive enough—but because the central organizing principle of political life, the divine right of kings, was destroyed.[43] It is a confluence of sociopsychological strain and an absence of cultural resources by means of which to make (political, moral, or economic) sense of that strain, each exacerbating the other, that sets the stage for the rise of systematic (political, moral, economic) ideologies.

And it is, in turn, the attempt of ideologies to render otherwise incomprehensible social situations meaningful, to so construe them as to make it possible to act purposefully within them, that accounts both for the ideologies' highly figurative nature and for the intensity with which, once accepted, they are held. As metaphor extends language by broadening its semantic range, enabling it to express meanings it cannot or at least cannot yet express literally, so the head-on clash of literal meanings in ideology—the irony, the hyperbole, the overdrawn antithesis—provides novel symbolic frames against which to match the myriad "unfamiliar somethings" that, like a journey to a strange country, are produced by a transformation in political life. Whatever else ideologies may be—projections of unacknowledged fears, disguises for ulterior motives, phatic expressions of group solidarity—they are, most distinctively, maps of problematic social reality and matrices for the creation of collective conscience. Whether, in any particular case, the map is accurate or the conscience creditable is a separate question, to which one can hardly give the same answer for Nazism and Zionism, for the nationalisms of McCarthy and of Churchill, for the defenders of segregation and its opponents.

VI.

Though ideological ferment is, of course, widespread in modern society, perhaps its most prominent locus at the moment lies in the new (or renewed) states of Asia, Africa, and some parts of Latin America; for it is in these states, Communist or not, that the initial steps away from a traditional politics of piety and proverb are just now being taken. The attainment of independence, the overthrow of established ruling classes, the popularization of legitimacy, the rationalization of public administration, the rise of modern elites, the spread of literacy and mass communications, and the propulsion willy-nilly of inexperienced governments into the midst of a precarious international order that even its older participants do not very well understand all make for a pervasive sense of disorientation, a disorientation in whose face received images of authority, responsibility, and civic purpose seem radically inadequate. The search for a new symbolic framework in terms of which to formulate, think about, and react to political problems, whether in the form of nationalism, Marxism, liberalism, populism, racism, Caesarism, ecclesiasticism, or some variety of reconstructed traditionalism (or, most commonly, a confused melange of several of these) is therefore tremendously intense.

Intense—but indeterminate. For the most part, the new states are still groping for usable political concepts, not yet grasping them; and the outcome in almost every case, at least in every non-Communist case, is uncertain not merely in the sense that the outcome of any historical process is uncertain but in the sense that even a broad and general assessment of overall direction is extremely difficult to make. Intellectually, everything is in motion, and the words of that extravagant poet in politics, Lamartine, written of nineteenth-century France, apply to the new states with perhaps even greater appropriateness than they did to the dying July Monarchy:

> These times are times of chaos; opinions are a scramble; parties are a jumble; the language of new ideas has not been created; nothing is more difficult than to give a good definition of oneself in religion, in philosophy, in politics. One feels, one knows, one lives, and at need, one dies for one's cause, but one cannot name it. It is the problem of this time to classify things and men. . . . The world has jumbled its catalog.[44]

This observation is no truer anywhere in the world right now than it is in Indonesia, where the whole political process is mired in a slough of ideological symbols, each attempting and so far each failing to unjumble the Republic's catalogue, to name its cause, and to give point and purpose to its polity. It is a country of false starts and frantic revisions, of a desperate search for a political order whose image, like a mirage, recedes more rapidly the more eagerly it is approached. The salving slogan amid all this frustration is, "The Revolution Is Unfinished!" And so, indeed, it is. But only because no one knows, not even those who cry most loudly that they do, precisely how to go about the job of finishing it.[45]

The most highly developed concepts of government in traditional Indonesia were those upon which the classic Hinduized states of the fourth to fifteenth centuries were built, concepts that persisted in somewhat revised and weakened form even after these states were first Islamicized and then largely replaced or overlaid by the Dutch colonial regime. And of these concepts the most important was what might be called the theory of the exemplary center, the notion that the capital city (or more accurately the king's palace) was at once a microcosm of the supernatural order—"an image of . . . the universe on a smaller scale"—and the material embodiment of political order.[46] The capital was not merely the nucleus, the engine, or the pivot of the state; it *was* the state.

In the Hindu period, the king's castle comprehended virtually the entire town. A squared-off "heavenly city" constructed according to the ideas of Indic metaphysics, it was more than a locus of power; it was a synoptic paradigm of the ontological shape of existence. At its center was the divine king (an incarnation of an Indian deity), his throne symbolizing Mount Meru, seat of the gods; the buildings, roads, city walls, and even, ceremonially, his wives and personal staff were deployed quadrangularly around him according to the directions of the four sacred winds. Not only the king himself but his ritual, his regalia, his court, and his castle were shot through with charismatic significance. The castle and the life of the castle were the quiddity of the kingdom, and he who (often after meditating in the wilderness to attain the appropriate spiritual status) captured the castle captured the whole empire, grasped the charisma of office, and displaced the no-longer-sacred king.[47]

The early polities were thus not so much solidary territorial units as loose congeries of villages oriented toward a common urban center, each such center competing with others for ascendency. Whatever degree of regional or, at moments, interregional hegemony prevailed depended, not on the systematic administrative organization of extensive territory under a single king, but on the varying abilities of kings to mobilize and apply effective striking forces with which to sack rival capitals, abilities that were believed to rest on essentially religious—that is, mystical—grounds. So far|as the pattern was territorial at all, it consisted of a series of concentric circles of religio-military power spreading out around the various city-state capitals, as radio waves spread from a transmitter. The closer a village to a town, the greater the impact, economically and culturally, of the court on that village. And, conversely, the greater the development of the court— priests, artisans, nobles, and king—the greater its authenticity as an epitome of cosmic order, its military strength, and the effective range of its circles of outward spreading power. Spiritual excellence and political eminence were fused. Magical power and executive influence flowed in a single stream outward and downward from the king through the descending ranks of his staff and whatever lesser courts were subordinate to him, draining out finally into the spiritually and politically residual peasant mass. Theirs was a facsimile concept of political organization, one in which the reflection of the supernatural order microscopically mirrored in the life of the capital was in turn further and more faintly reflected in the countryside as a whole, producing a hierarchy of less and less faithful copies of an eternal, transcendent realm. In such a system, the administrative, military, and ceremonial organization of the court orders the world around it iconically by providing it with a tangible paragon.[48]

When Islam came, the Hindu political tradition was to some extent weakened, especially in the coastal trade kingdoms surrounding the Java Sea. The court culture nevertheless persisted, although it was overlaid and interfused with Islamic symbols and ideas and set among an ethnically more differentiated urban mass, which looked with less awe on the classical order. The steady growth—especially on Java—of Dutch administrative control in the mid-nineteenth and early twentieth centuries constricted the tradition still further. But, since the lower levels of the bureaucracy continued to be manned almost entirely by Indonesians of the old upper classes, the tradition remained, even then, the matrix of supravillage political order. The regency or the district office remained not merely the axis of the polity but the embodiment of it, a polity with respect to which most villagers were not so much actors as audience.

It was this tradition with which the new elite of republican Indonesia was left after the revolution. That is not to say that the theory of the exemplary center persisted unchanged, drifting like some Platonic archetype through the eternity of Indonesian history, for (like the society as a whole) it evolved and developed, becoming ultimately perhaps more conventional and less religious in general temper. Nor does it mean that foreign ideas, from European parliamentarianism, from Marxism, from Islamic moralism, and so forth did not come to play an essential role in Indonesian political thought, for modern Indonesian nationalism is very far from being merely old wine in a new bottle. It is simply that, as yet, the conceptual transition from the classic image of a polity as a concentrated center of pomp and power, alternately providing a cynosure for popular awe and lashing out militarily at competing centers, to one of a polity as a systematically organized national community has, for all these changes and influences, still not been completed. Indeed, it has been arrested and to some extent reversed.

This cultural failure is apparent from the growing, seemingly unquenchable ideological din that has engulfed Indonesian politics since the revolution. The most prominent attempt to construct, by means of a figurative extension of the classic tradition, an essentially metaphoric reworking of it, a new symbolic framework within which to give form and meaning to the emerging republican polity, was President Sukarno's famous Pantjasila concept, first set forth in a public speech toward the end of the Japanese occupation.[49] Drawing on the Indic tradition of fixed sets of numbered precepts—the three jewels, the four sublime moods, the eightfold path, the twenty conditions of successful rule, and so forth—it consisted of five (*pantja*) principles (*sila*) that were intended to form the "sacred" ideological foundations of an independent Indonesia. Like all good constitutions, the Pantjasila was short, ambiguous, and impeccably high-minded, the five points being "nationalism," "humanitarianism," "democracy," "social welfare," and (pluralistic) "monotheism." Finally, these modern concepts, set so nonchalantly in a medieval frame, were explicitly identified with an indigenous peasant concept, *gotong rojong* (literally, "the collective bearing of burdens"; figuratively, "the piety of all for the interests of all"), thus drawing together the "great tradition" of the exemplary state, the doctrines of contemporary nationalism, and the "little traditions" of the villages into one luminous image.[50]

The reasons why this ingenious device failed are many and complex, and only a few of them—like the strength in certain sectors of the population of Islamic concepts of political order, which are difficult to reconcile with Sukarno's secularism—are themselves cultural. The Pantjasila, playing upon the microcosm-macrocosm conceit and upon the traditional syncretism of Indonesian thought, was intended to contain within it the political interests of the Islamic and Christian, gentry and peasantry, nationalist and communist, commercial and agrarian, Javanese and "Outer Island" groups in Indonesia; to rework the old facsimile pattern into a modern constitutional structure in which these various tendencies would, each emphasizing one or another aspect of the doctrine, find a *modus vivendi* at each level of administration and party struggle. The attempt was not so totally ineffective nor so intellectually fatuous as it has sometimes been painted. The cult of the Pantjasila (for that is what it literally became, complete with rites and commentaries) did provide for a while a flexible ideological context within which parliamentary institutions and democratic sentiments were being soundly, if gradually, forged at both local and national levels. But the combination of a deteriorating economic situation, a hopelessly pathological relationship with the former metropole, the rapid growth of a subversive (in principle) totalitarian party, a renascence of Islamic fundamentalism, the inability (or unwillingness) of leaders with developed intellectual and technical skills to court mass support, and the economic illiteracy, administrative incapacity, and personal failings of those who were able (and only too willing) to court such support soon brought the clash of factions to such a pitch that the whole pattern dissolved. By the time of the Constitutional Convention of 1957, the Pantjasila had changed from a language of consensus to a vocabulary of abuse, as each faction used it more to express its irreconcilable opposition to other factions than its underlying rules-of-the-game agreement with them, and the Convention, ideological pluralism, and constitutional democracy collapsed in a single heap.[51]

What has replaced them is something very much like the old exemplary center pattern, only now on a self-consciously doctrinaire rather than an instinctive religion-and-convention basis and cast more in the idiom of egalitarianism and social progress than in that of hierarchy and patrician grandeur. On one hand, there has been, under President Sukarno's famous theory of "guided democracy" and his call for the reintroduction of the revolutionary (that is, authoritarian) constitution of 1945, both an ideological homogenization (in which discordant streams of thought—notably those of Moslem modernism and democratic socialism—have simply been suppressed as illegitimate) and an accelerated pace of flamboyant symbol-mongering, as though, the effort to make an unfamiliar form of government work having misfired, a desperate attempt to breathe new life into a familiar one was being launched. On the other hand, the growth of the political role of the army, not so much as an executive or administrative body as a backstop enforcement agency with veto power over the whole range of politically relevant institutions, from the presidency and the civil service to the parties and the press, has provided the other—the minatory—half of the traditional picture.

Like the Pantjasila before it, the revised (or revivified) approach was introduced by Sukarno in a major speech—"The Rediscovery of Our Revolution"—given on Independence Day (August 17) in 1959, a speech that he later decreed, along with the expository notes on it prepared by a body of personal attendants known as The Supreme Advisory Council, to be the "Political Manifesto of the Republic":

> There thus came into existence a catechism on the basis, aims and duties of the Indonesian revolution; the social forces of the Indonesian revolution, its nature, future and enemies; and its general program, covering the political, economic, social, mental cultural, and security fields. Early in 1960 the central message of the celebrated speech was stated as consisting of five ideas—the 1945 constitution, Socialism à la Indonesia, Guided Democracy, Guided Economy, and Indonesian Personality—and the first letters of these five phrases were put together to make the acronym USDEK. With "Political Manifesto" becoming "Manipol," the new creed became known as "Manipol-USDEK."[52]

And, as the Pantjasila before it, the Manipol-USDEK image of political order found a ready response in a population for whom opinions have indeed become a scramble, parties a jumble, the times a chaos:

> Many were attracted by the idea that what Indonesia needed above all was men with the right state of mind, the right spirit, the true patriotic dedication. "Returning to our own national personality" was attractive to many who wanted to withdraw from the challenges of modernity, and also to those who wanted to believe in the current political leadership but were aware of its failures to modernize as fast as such countries as India and Malaya. And for members of some Indonesian communities, notably for many [Indic-minded] Javanese, there was real meaning in the various complex schemes which the President presented in elaboration of Manipol-USDEK, explaining the peculiar significance and tasks of the current stage of history. [But] perhaps the most important appeal of Manipol-USDEK, however, lay in the simple fact that it promised to give men a *pegangan*—something to which to hold fast. They were attracted not so much by the content of this *pegangan* as by the fact that the President had offered one at a time when the lack of a sense of purpose was sorely felt. Values and cognitive patterns being in flux and in conflict, men looked eagerly for dogmatic and schematic formulations of the political good.[53]

While the President and his entourage concern themselves almost entirely with the "creation and recreation of mystique," the army concerns itself mainly with combating the numerous protests, plots, mutinies, and rebellions that occur when that mystique fails to achieve its hoped-for effect and when rival claims to leadership arise.[54] Although involved in some aspects of the civil service, in the managing of the confiscated Dutch enterprises, and even in the (nonparliamentary) cabinet, the army has not been able to take up, for lack of training, internal unity, or sense of direction, the administrative, planning, and organizational tasks of the government in any detail or with any effectiveness. The result is that these tasks are either not performed or very inadequately performed and the supralocal polity, the national state, shrinks more and more to the limits of its traditional domain, the capital city—Djakarta—plus a number of semi-independent tributary cities and towns held to a minimal loyalty by the threat of centrally applied force.

That this attempt to revive the politics of the exemplary court will long survive is rather doubtful. It is already being severely strained by its incapacity to cope with the technical and administrative problems involved in the government of a modern state. Far from arresting Indonesia's decline into what Sukarno has called "the abyss of annihilation," the retreat from the hesitant, admittedly hectic and awkwardly functioning parliamentarianism of the Pantjasila period to the Manipol-USDEK alliance between a charismatic president and a watchdog army has probably accelerated it. But what will succeed this ideological framework when, as seems certain, it too dissolves, or from where a conception of political order more adequate to Indonesia's contemporary needs and ambitions will come, if it does come, is impossible to say.

Not that Indonesia's problems are purely or even primarily ideological and that they will—as all too many Indonesians already think—melt away before a political change of heart. The disorder is more general, and the failure to create a conceptual framework in terms of which to shape a modern polity is in great part itself a reflection of the tremendous social and psychological strains that the country and its population are undergoing. Things do not merely *seem* jumbled—they *are* jumbled, and it will take more than theory to unjumble them. It will take administrative skill, technical knowledge, personal courage and resolution, endless patience and tolerance, enormous self-sacrifice, a virtually incorruptible public conscience, and a very great deal of sheer (and unlikely) good luck in the most material sense of the word. Ideological formulation, no matter how elegant, can substitute for none of these elements; and, in fact, in their absence, it degenerates, as it has in Indonesia, into a smokescreen for failure, a diversion to stave off despair, a mask to conceal reality rather than a portrait to reveal it. With a tremendous population problem; extraordinary ethnic, geographical, and regional diversity; a moribund economy; a severe lack of trained personnel; popular poverty of the bitterest sort; and pervasive, implacable social discontent, Indonesia's social problems seem virtually insoluble even without the ideological pandemonium. The abyss into which Mr. Sukarno claims to have looked is a real one.

Yet, at the same time, that Indonesia (or, I should imagine, any new nation) can find her way through this forest of problems without any ideological guidance at all seems impossible.[55] The motivation to seek (and, even more important, to *use*) technical skill and knowledge, the emotional resilience to support the necessary patience and resolution, and the moral strength to sustain self-sacrifice and incorruptibility must come from somewhere, from some vision of public purpose anchored in a compelling image of social reality. That all these qualities may not be present; that the present drift to revivalistic irrationalism and unbridled fantasy may continue; that the next ideological phase may be even further from the ideals for which the revolution was ostensibly fought than is the present one; that Indonesia may continue to be, as Bagehot called France, the scene of political experiments from which others profit much but she herself very little; or that the ultimate outcome may be viciously totalitarian and wildly zealotic is all very true. But whichever way events move, the determining forces will not be wholly sociological or psychological but partly cultural—that is, conceptual. To forge a theoretical framework adequate to the analysis

of such three-dimensional processes is the task of the scientific study of
ideology—a task but barely begun.

VII.

Critical and imaginative works are answers to questions posed by the situation in
which they arose. They are not merely answers, they are *strategic* answers, *stylized*
answers. For there is a difference in style or strategy, if one says "yes" in tonalities
that imply "thank God!" or in tonalities that imply "alas!" So I should propose an
initial working distinction between "strategies" and "situations" whereby we think
of . . . any work of critical or imaginative cast . . . as the adopting of various
strategies for the encompassing of situations. These strategies size up the situations,
name their structure and outstanding ingredients, and name them in a way that contains
an attitude toward them.
    This point of view does not, by any means, vow us to personal or historical sub-
jectivism. The situations are real; the strategies for handling them have public content;
in so far as situations overlap from individual to individual, or from one historical
period to another, the strategies possess universal relevance.
                                    Kenneth Burke, *The Philosophy of Literary Form*

As both science and ideology are critical and imaginative "works" (that
is symbolic structures), an objective formulation both of the marked
differences between them and of the nature of their relationship to one
another seems more likely to be achieved by proceeding from such a concept
of stylistic strategies than from a nervous concern with comparative episte-
mological or axiological status of the two forms of thought. No more than
scientific studies of religion ought to begin with unnecessary questions about
the legitimacy of the substantive claims of their subject matter ought scientific studies of ideology to begin with such questions. The best way to deal
with Mannheim's as with any true paradox is to circumvent it by reformu-
lating one's theoretical approach so as to avoid setting off yet once more down
the well-worn path of argument that led to it in the first place.

The differentiae of science and ideology as cultural systems are to be
sought in the sorts of symbolic strategy for encompassing situations that they
respectively represent. Science names the structure of situations in such a
way that the attitude contained toward them is one of disinterestedness. Its
style is restrained, spare, resolutely analytic: By shunning the semantic
devices that most effectively formulate moral sentiment, it seeks to maximize
intellectual clarity. But ideology names the structure of situations in such a
way that the attitude contained toward them is one of commitment. Its style
is ornate, vivid, deliberately suggestive: By objectifying moral sentiment
through the same devices that science shuns, it seeks to motivate action.
Both are concerned with the definition of a problematic situation and are
responses to a felt lack of needed information. But the information needed
is quite different, even in cases where the situation is the same. An ideologist
is no more a poor social scientist than a social scientist is a poor ideologist.
The two are—or at least they ought to be—in quite different lines of work,
lines so different that little is gained and much obscured by measuring the
activities of the one against the aims of the other.[56]

Where science is the diagnostic, the critical, dimension of culture,
ideology is the justificatory, the apologetic, one—it refers "to that part of
culture which is actively concerned with the establishment and defense of

patterns of belief and value."[57] That there is natural tendency for the two
to clash, particularly when they are directed to the interpretation of the same
range of situations, is thus clear; but that the clash is inevitable and that
the findings of (social) science necessarily will undermine the validity of
the beliefs and values that ideology has chosen to defend and propagate
seem most dubious assumptions. An attitude at once critical and apologetic
toward the same situation is no intrinsic contradiction in terms (however
often it may in fact turn out to be an empirical one) but one sign of a certain
level of intellectual sophistication. One remembers the story, probably *ben
trovato,* to the effect that when Churchill had finished his famous rally of
isolated England, "We shall fight on the beaches, we shall fight on the
landing grounds, we shall fight in the fields and in the streets, we shall fight
in the hills . . ." he turned to an aide and whispered, "and we shall hit them
over the head with soda-water bottles, because we haven't any guns."

The quality of social rhetoric in ideology is thus not proof that the
vision of sociopsychological reality upon which it is based is false and
that it draws its persuasive power from any discrepancy between what is
believed and what can, now or someday, be established as scientifically
correct. That it may indeed lose touch with reality in an orgy of autistic
fantasy—even that, in situations where it is left uncriticized by either a
free science or competing ideologies well rooted in the general social structure, it has a very strong tendency to do so—is all too apparent. But however interesting pathologies are for clarifying normal functioning (and however common they may be empirically), they are misleading as prototypes of
it. Although fortunately it never had to be tested, it seems most likely
that the British would have indeed fought on the beaches, landing grounds,
streets, and hills—and with soda-water bottles too, if it came to that—for
Churchill formulated accurately the mood of his countrymen and, formulating
it, mobilized it by making it a public possession, a social fact, rather than a
set of disconnected, unrealized private emotions. Even morally loathesome
ideological expressions may still catch most acutely the mood of a people or
a group. Hitler was not distorting the German conscience when he rendered
his countrymen's demonic self-hatred in the tropological figure of the magi-
cally corrupting Jew; he was merely objectifying it—transforming a prevalent
personal neurosis into a powerful social force.

But though science and ideology are different enterprises, they are not
unrelated ones. Ideologies do make empirical claims about the condition
and direction of society, which it is the business of science (and, where
scientific knowledge is lacking, common sense) to assess. The social function
of science *vis-à-vis* ideologies is first to understand them—what they are, how
they work, what gives rise to them—and second to criticize them, to force
them to come to terms with (but not necessarily to surrender to) reality. The
existence of a vital tradition of scientific analysis of social issues is one of
the most effective guarantees against ideological extremism, for it provides
an incomparably reliable source of positive knowledge for the political
imagination to work with and to honor. It is not the only such check.
The existence, as mentioned, of competing ideologies carried by other powerful groups in the society is at least as important; as is a liberal political
system in which dreams of total power are obvious fantasies; as are stable

social conditions in which conventional expectations are not continually frustrated and conventional ideas not radically incompetent. But, committed with a quiet intransigence to a vision of its own, it is perhaps the most indomitable.

NOTES

1. F. X. Sutton, S. E. Harris, C. Kaysen, and J. Tobin, *The American Business Creed* (Cambridge, Mass., 1956), pp. 3-6.
2. K. Mannheim, *Ideology and Utopia* (Harvest ed.; New York, n.d.), pp. 59-83; see also R. Merton, *Social Theory and Social Structure* (New York, 1949), pp. 217-20.
3. W. White, *Beyond Conformity* (New York, 1961), p. 211.
4. W. Stark, *The Sociology of Knowledge* (London, 1958), p. 48.
5. *Ibid.*, pp. 90-1. Italics in the original. For approximation of the same argument in Mannheim, formulated as a distinction between "total" and "particular" ideology, see *op. cit.*, pp. 55-59.
6. E. Shils, "Ideology and Civility: On the Politics of the Intellectual," *The Sewanee Review*, 66 (1958), 450-80.
7. T. Parsons, "An Approach to the Sociology of Knowledge," *Transactions of the Fourth World Congress of Sociology* (Milan and Stressa, 1959), pp. 25-49. Italics in the original.
8. R. Aron, *The Opium of the Intellectuals* (New York, 1962).
9. As the danger of being misinterpreted here is serious, may I hope that my criticism will be credited as technical and not political if I note that my own general ideological (as I would frankly call it) position is largely the same as that of Aron, Shils, Parsons, and so forth; that I am in agreement with their plea for a civil, temperate unheroic politics? Also it should be remarked that the demand for a nonevaluative concept of ideology is not a demand for the nonevaluation of ideologies, any more than a nonevaluative concept of religion implies religious relativism.
10. Sutton, *et al., op. cit.*; White, *op. cit.*; H. Eckstein, *Pressure Group Politics: The Case of the British Medical Association* (Stanford, 1960); C. Wright Mills, *The New Men of Power* (New York, 1948); J. Schumpeter, "Science and Ideology," *American Economic Review*, 39 (1949), 345-59.
11. There have been in fact, a number of other terms used in the literature for the general range of phenomena that "ideology" denotes, from Plato's "noble lies" through Sorel's "myths" to Pareto's "derivations"; but none of them has managed to reach any greater level of technical neutrality than has "ideology." See H. D. Lasswell, "The Language of Power," in Lasswell, N. Leites, and Associates, *Language of Politics* (New York, 1949), pp. 3-19.
12. Sutton, *et al., op. cit.*, pp. 11-12, 303-10.
13. The quotations are from the most eminent recent interest theorist, C. Wright Mills, *The Causes of World War Three* (New York, 1958), pp. 54, 65.
14. For the general schema, see Parsons, *The Social System* (New York, 1951), especially Chaps. I, VII. The fullest development of the strain theory is in Sutton, *et al., op. cit.*, especially Chap. XV.
15. Sutton, *et al., op. cit.*, pp. 307-8.
16. Parsons, "An Approach."
17. White, *op. cit.*, p. 204.
18. Perhaps the most impressive *tour de force* in this paratactic genre is Nathan Leites's *A Study of Bolshevism* (New York, 1953).
19. K. Burke, *The Philosophy of Literary Form, Studies in Symbolic Action* (Baton Rouge, 1941). In the following discussion, I use "symbol" broadly in the sense of any physical, social, or cultural act or object that serves as the vehicle for a conception. For an explication of this view, under which "five" and "the Cross" are equally symbols, see S. Langer, *Philosophy in a New Key* (4th ed.; Cambridge, Mass., 1960), pp. 60-6.
20. Useful general summaries of the tradition of literary criticism can be found in S. E. Hyman, *The Armed Vision* (New York, 1948) and in R. Welleck and A. Warren, *Theory of Literature* (2nd ed.; New York, 1958). A similar summary of the somewhat more diverse philosophical development is apparently not available, but the seminal works are C. S. Peirce, *Collected Papers*, C. Hartshorne and P. Weiss, eds. (8 vols.; Cambridge, Mass., 1931-58); E. Cassirer, *Die Philosophie der symbolischen Formen* (3 vols.; Berlin, 1923-9); C. W. Morris, *Signs, Language and Behavior* (Englewood Cliffs, 1944); and L. Wittgenstein, *Philosophical Investigations* (Oxford, 1953).
21. W. Percy, "The Symbolic Structure of Interpersonal Process," *Psychiatry*, 24

(1961), 39-52. Italics in the original. The reference is to Sapir's "The Status of Linguistics as a Science," originally published in 1929 and reprinted in D. Mandlebaum, ed., *Selected Writings of Edward Sapir* (Berkeley and Los Angeles, 1949), pp. 160-6.

22. A partial exception to this stricture, although marred by his obsession with power as the sum and substance of politics, is Lasswell's "Style in the Language of Politics," in Lasswell, *et al., op. cit.,* pp. 20-39. It also should be remarked that the emphasis on verbal symbolism in the following discussion is merely for the sake of simplicity and is not intended to deny the importance of plastic, theatrical, or other nonlinguistic devices—the rhetoric of uniforms, floodlit stages, and marching bands—in ideological thought.

23. *Op. cit.,* pp. 4-5.

24. An excellent recent review is to be found in P. Henle, ed., *Language, Thought and Culture* (Ann Arbor, 1958), pp. 173-95. The quotation is from Langer, *op. cit.,* p. 117.

25. W. Percy, "Metaphor as Mistake," *The Sewanee Review,* 66 (1958), 79-99.

26. Quoted in J. Crowley "Japanese Army Factionalism in the Early 1930's," *The Journal of Asian Studies,* 21 (1958), 309-26.

27. *Op. cit.,* pp. 4-5.

28. K. Burke, *Counterstatement* (Chicago, 1957), p. 149.

29. *Op. cit.,* p. 568.

30. Metaphor is, of course, not the only stylistic resource upon which ideology draws. Metonymy ("All I have to offer is blood, sweat and tears"), hyperbole ("The thousand-year Reich"), meiosis ("I shall return"), synechdoche ("Wall Street"), oxymoron ("Iron Curtain"), personification ("The hand that held the dagger has plunged it into the back of its neighbor"), and all the other figures the classical rhetoricians so painstakingly collected and so carefully classified are utilized over and over again, as are such syntactical devices as antithesis, inversion, and repetition; such prosodic ones as rhyme, rhythm, and alliteration; such literary ones as irony, eulogy, and sarcasm. Nor is all ideological expression figurative. The bulk of it consists of quite literal, not to say flat-footed, assertions, which, a certain tendency toward *prima facie* implausibility aside, are difficult to distinguish from properly scientific statements: "The history of all hitherto existing society is the history of class struggles"; "the whole of the morality of Europe is based upon the values which are useful to the herd"; and so forth. As a cultural system, an ideology that has developed beyond the stage of mere sloganeering consists of an intricate structure of interrelated meanings—interrelated in terms of the semantic mechanisms that formulate them—of which the two-level organization of an isolated metaphor is but a feeble representation.

31. W. Percy, "Symbolic Structure."

32. G. Ryle, *The Concept of Mind* (New York, 1949).

33. E. Galanter and M. Gerstenhaber, "On Thought: the Extrinsic Theory," *Psychological Review,* 63 (1956), 218-27.

34. *Ibid.* I have quoted this incisive passage before, in a paper attempting to set the extrinsic theory of thought in the context of recent evolutionary,. neurological, and cultural anthropological findings. See C. Geertz, "The Growth of Culture and the Evolution of Mind, in J. Scher, ed., *Theories of the Mind* (New York, 1962).

35. W. Percy, "Symbol, Consciousness and Intersubjectivity," *Journal of Philosophy,* 55 (1958), 631-41. Italics in the original.

36. *Ibid.*

37. S. Langer, *Feeling and Form* (New York, 1953).

38. The quotations are from Ryle, *op. cit.,* p. 51.

39. Talcott Parsons, "An Approach to Psychological Theory in Terms of the Theory of Action," in S. Koch, ed., *Psychology: A Study of a Science* (New York, 1959), Vol. III. Italics in the original. Compare: "In order to account for this selectivity, it is necessary to assume that the structure of the enzyme is related in some way to the structure of the gene. By a logical extension of this idea we arrive at the concept that the gene is a representation—blueprint so to speak—of the enzyme molecule, and that the function of the gene is to serve as a source of information regarding the structure of the enzyme. It seems evident that the synthesis of an enzyme—a giant protein molecule consisting of hundreds of amino acid units arranged end-to-end in a specific and unique order—requires a model or set of instructions of some kind. These instructions must be characteristic of the species; they must be automatically transmitted from generation to generation, and they must be constant yet capable of evolutionary change. The only known entity that could perform such a function is the gene. There are many reasons for believing that it transmits information, by acting as a model or template." N. H. Horowitz, "The Gene," *Scientific American* (February, 1956), p. 85.

40. This point is perhaps somewhat too baldly put in light of recent analyses of animal learning; but the essential thesis—that there is a general trend toward a more

diffuse, less determinate control of behavior by intrinsic (innate) parameters as one moves from lower to higher animals—seems well established. See Geertz, *op. cit.*, where the whole argument, here strenuously compressed, is developed in full.

41. Of course, there are moral, economic, and even aesthetic ideologies, as well as specifically political ones, but as very few ideologies of any social prominence lack political implications, it is perhaps permissible to view the problem here in this somewhat narrowed focus. In any case, the arguments developed for political ideologies apply with equal force to nonpolitical ones. For an analysis of a moral ideology cast in terms very similar to those developed in this paper, see A. L. Green, "The Ideology of Anti-Fluoridation Leaders," *The Journal of Social Issues,* 17 (1961), 13-25.

42. That such ideologies may call, as did Burke's or De Maistre's, for the reinvigoration of custom or the reimposition of religious hegemony is, of course, no contradiction. One constructs arguments for tradition only when its credentials have been questioned. To the degree that such appeals are successful they bring, not a return to naive traditionalism, but ideological retraditionalization—an altogether different matter. See Mannheim "Conservative Thought," in his *Essays on Sociology and Social Psychology* (New York, 1953), especially pp. 94-8.

43. It is important to remember, too, that the principle was destroyed long before the king; it was to the successor principle that he was, in fact, a ritual sacrifice: "When [Saint-Just] exclaims: 'To determine the principle in virtue of which the accused [Louis XVI] is perhaps to die, is to determine the principle by which the society that judges him lives,' he demonstrates that it is the philosophers who are going to kill the King: the King must die in the name of the social contract." A. Camus, *The Rebel* (New York, 1958), p. 114.

44. Alphonse de Lamartine, "Declaration of Principles," in *Introduction to Contemporary Civilization in the West, A Source Book* (New York, 1946), II, 328-33.

45. The following very schematic and necessarily *ex cathedra* discussion is based mainly on my own research and represents only my own views, but I have also drawn heavily of the work of Herbert Feith for factual material. See especially *The Decline of Constitutional Democracy in Indonesia* (New York, 1962), and "Dynamics of Guided Democracy" in R. McVey, ed., *Indonesia* (New Haven, 1963), pp. 309-409. For the general cultural analysis within which my interpretations are set, see C. Geertz, *The Religion of Java* (New York, 1960). The ideas compressed here and the history abbreviated here will be re-expanded to something closer to their normal size in a forthcoming work on the development and present condition of Indonesian civilization.

46. R. Heine-Geldern, "Conceptions of State and Kinship in Southeast Asia," *Far Eastern Quarterly,* 2 (1942), 15-30.

47. *Ibid.*

48. "The whole expanse of Yawa-land [Java] is to be compared with one town in the Prince's reign.

By thousands are [counted] the people's dwelling places, to be compared with the manors of Royal servants, surrounding the body of the Royal compound.

All kinds of foreign islands; to be compared with them are the cultivated land's areas, made happy and quiet.

Of the aspect of parks, then, are the forests and mountains, all of them set foot on by Him, without feeling anxiety."

Canto 17, stanza 3 of the "Nagara-Kertagama," a fourteenth-century royal epic

(Translated in Th. Piegeaud, *Java in the 14th Century* (The Hague, 1960), III, 21. The term *nagara* still means, indifferently, "palace," "capital city," "state," "country," or "government"—sometimes even "civilization"—in Java.

49. For a description of the Pantjasila speech, see G. McT. Kahin, *Nationalism and Revolution in Indonesia* (Ithaca, 1952), pp. 122-7.

50. The quotations are from the Pantjasila speech, as quoted in *ibid.*, p. 126.

51. The proceedings of the Convention, unfortunately still untranslated, form one of the fullest and most instructive records of ideological combat in the new states available. See *Tentang Negara Republik Indonesia Dalam Konstituante* (3 vols.; n.p. [Djakarta?] n.d. [1958?]).

52. Feith, "Dynamics of Guided Democracy," p. 367. A vivid, if somewhat shrill, description of "Manipol-USDEKism" in action can be found in W. Hanna, *Bung Karno's Indonesia* (New York, 1961).

53. Feith, "Dynamics of Guided Democracy." 367-8. *Pegang* literally means "to grasp"; thus *pegangan,* "something graspable "

54. *Ibid.*

55. For an analysis of the role of ideology in an emerging African nation, conducted along lines similar to our own, see L. A. Fallers, "Ideology and Culture in

Uganda Nationalism," *American Anthropologist,* 63: 677-86. For a superb case study of an "adolescent" nation in which the process of thoroughgoing ideological reconstruction seems to have been conducted with reasonable success, see B. Lewis, *The Emergence of Modern Turkey* (London, 1961), especially Chap. 10.

56. This point is, however, not quite the same as saying that the two sorts of activity may not in practice be carried on together, any more than a man cannot, for example, paint a portrait of a bird that is both ornithologically accurate and aesthetically effective. Marx is, of course, the outstanding case, but for a more recent successful synchronization of scientific analysis and ideological argument, see E. Shils, *The Torment of Secrecy* (New York, 1956). Most such attempts to mix genres are, however, distinctly less happy.

57. Fallers, *op. cit.* The patterns of belief and value defended may be, of course, those of a socially subordinate group, as well as those of a socially dominant one, and the "apology" therefore for reform or revolution.

National Loyalties in a
Newly Independent Nation

BY *JOSEPH W. ELDER*

I. The Problem

THE POST-WORLD-WAR-II era has witnessed the struggle for survival of a number of newly independent nations—a struggle often directed less against hostile external powers than against schismatic internal groups. The autocratic governments that have emerged in Pakistan, Burma, and Ghana have tried to justify their abrogation of earlier rights by pointing to "antinational" factions threatening to their country's integrity. Even countries, like India, that have managed to retain their democratic structure have openly expressed concern over disunity and factionalism.

During the past decade, a number of scholars has examined the question of national loyalty.[1] How do national loyalties develop? In any given country at any particular time who are the ones with the most national loyalty? Has it been necessary for them to abandon their loyalties to lineage, caste, tribe, village, and ethnic group in order to be loyal to their nation? Or have they retained these loyalties and merely capped them with loyalty to the state? Are the nationalistic sentiments aroused during a nation's struggle for independence useful once a nation has achieved independence? Or does the struggle for independence require one type of national loyalty, while the participation of citizens in a self-governing nation requires another?

II. The Research

The field work on the basis of which this paper tries to answer the above questions was carried out in India between April and September, 1963. In view of the diversity of language and cultural heritage in different parts of India, I selected two widely separated areas from which to gather my data: the Hindustani-speaking state of Uttar Pradesh bordering the Himalayas in the North and the Tamil-speaking state of Madras approximately 1000 miles away at the southern end of India. My sampling units were intact nuclear families (fathers and mothers alive and in residence) of eleven-year-old boys. In both north and south India I drew random samples of approximately 100 families from a major city (Lucknow in Uttar Pradesh and Madurai in Madras)—100 families from a town, and 100 families from villages.

Uttar Pradesh (North India)
  City: Lucknow, population 656,000
  Town: Malihabad (15 miles west of Lucknow), population 8000
  Villages: Utraitia and vicinity (8-12 miles east of Lucknow), population
      of each less than 2000

Madras State (South India)
  City: Madurai, population 425,000
  Town: Melur (20 miles east of Madurai) population 15,000
  Villages: Chittampatti and vicinity (9-11 miles east of Madurai) popula-
      tion of each less than 1000

I selected this particular research design in order to study the relative amounts of influence of the two parents on the formation of their son's attitudes in a variety of fields, as well as to study changes in these attitudes over three generations (in each nuclear family, I interviewed any resident grandparents as well.) My research design automatically excluded, however, certain categories of respondents who might have been most useful in a study exclusively of national loyalties—for example, college students and young men who have left their village homes to work in cities.

In both north and south India, I hired teams of interviewers to do the actual fieldwork. I observed the local proprieties by having women interview the eleven-year-old boys, their mothers, and their grandmothers while men interviewed the fathers and grandfathers. With minor variations in its three versions (sons, mothers-grandmothers, fathers-grandfathers), the interview schedule contained about seventy-five items, including two based on the Kluckhohn values questionnaire[2] and (in the adult schedules) an F-scale[3] modified for the Indian setting. In both the Hindi and Tamil translations of the schedule, I went to considerable effort to have the questions put in normal, conversational language, so that a minimum of reinterpretation by the interviewers would be necessary in the field.[4] In both the North and the South, the translations were tested in the field for clarity before they were turned over to the printers to be included in the final version of the interview schedule. Despite all these precautions, the possibility remains that the dual-language research design may have distorted some of my findings.

My interview schedule contained nine items directed at general attitudes toward government and the political process in India. It included, however, no specific questions aimed at determining "national loyalty." My first indication that I might be able to operationalize "national loyalty" came during the fieldwork in north India. The day my interviewers began working in the city of Lucknow, after having completed the work in Malihabad and the villages, a number of them commented, "The people in Lucknow are answering the questions so differently from the people in Utraitia and Malihabad." Two open-ended questions seemed to elicit the most noticeable differences. Question 76 asked, "If you had some extra money, what would you use it for?" Question 77 asked, "What is the best and finest thing you could do in your life?" The typical village and town responses included buying land, building a brick house, educating the children, arranging a daughter's or sister's marriage, building a temple (for Hindus), going on the Haj (for Muslims), contributing to charities, and caring for aged relatives. In Lucknow, the answers included "serve my country," "give to the national defense fund," "help my country any way I can," and "join the army and defend India's borders."[5]

It occurred to me that these two questions might be used as an operational index of "national loyalty." In view of the fact that these questions were not phrased in ways that normally evoked patriotic replies, we might assume that those from whom these questions elicited patriotic replies do indeed have greater awareness of "nation-ness" and greater commitment to the continuity and improvement of the nation. In short, we might assume that these respondents are more "nationally loyal" than those who replied in the more typical fashion.

Lucknow, however, had been singularly close to the Himalayan fighting half a year earlier and had served as headquarters for the Eastern Command. Numerous battle casualties had been brought down to the large military hospital in the cantonment. During the critical months, the city had been dimmed out at night, and trenches had been dug in the public parks. Possibly the degree of "national loyalty" I was discovering in Lucknow was more a reflection of the recent crisis than of continuing, stable sentiments. The only way in which I could check on this possible distortion was to see what responses these questions elicited in south India, far from the Himalayan fighting and the atmosphere of emergency.

The south Indian picture proved reassuring. Within each category of my sample, the relative frequency of "nationally loyal" responses was practically identical with those in the North:

TABLE I — Percentage of Respondents Giving "Nationally Loyal" Replies

North Indian sons	8%	(N = 436)
South Indian sons	8%	(N = 365)
North Indian fathers	5%	(N = 410)
South Indian fathers	4%	(N = 347)
North Indian mothers	2%	(N = 444)
South Indian mothers	1%	(N = 362)

If there was distortion in the North because of the Himalayan crisis, I found no clear-cut evidence of it. To the contrary, my evidence suggests that Questions 76 and 77 tapped a fairly stable attitude—an attitude one might describe as "national loyalty."

III. The Parameters of National Loyalty

Assuming that our operational index is a valid one, who are the people who are "nationally loyal"?

Boys (8%) and fathers (5%) are more "nationally loyal" than grandfathers (2%), mothers (1%), and grandmothers (0%).[6] In fact, there were so few "nationally loyal" responses from mothers, grandfathers, and grandmothers that I analyzed them no further, since my internal comparisons would have been statistically insignificant. All the subsequent parameters of the "nationally loyal" refer only to boys and fathers.

That men exceeded women in national loyalty is not surprising. In most societies men have more contacts outside the kin groups, and such is certainly the case in India. That boys exceeded fathers in "national loyalty"[7] may be explained in a variety of ways—perhaps by their lesser involvement in the problems of supporting and providing for kin groups, by the relatively greater "idealism" of the young, or by the greater and continuing exposure of the boys to "nationally loyal" sentiments taught in the schools.

The "nationally loyal" are more educated (see Table II). For the schoolboys in my two research areas, education meant exposure to textbook patriotism ("Our National Anthem," "Our Tricolor," "Jawaharlal Nehru," "Our Land of India," "Forward, O Courageous Ones"), accounts of the glorious days of the *Ramayana* and *Mahabharata* and of India's cultural heritage ("Three Indian Saints," "Shah Jahan," "Three Immortal Poets"), and descriptions of India's most recent struggle for independence ("The First War of Independence," "The Indian National Congress," "The Father of Our Country").

For the fathers in my two research areas literacy meant the possibility of reading daily newspapers and government bulletins, as well as of being exposed to the written propaganda of political parties. All these media presumably would heighten their awareness of the nation and its problems.

Since I was aware that education might be a critical factor in the formation of so many of the attitudes I was interested in exploring and since I had noted in my own sample the high correlation between national loyalty and education, I decided to introduce a control for education.

TABLE II — Education and National Loyalty

	No schooling	Some primary schooling	Some secondary schooling	Some college	
Nationally loyal fathers	12%	35%	35%	18%	100% (N = 34)
Other fathers	33%	38%	23%	6%	100% (N = 723)

	0—3 years of schooling	4 or more years of schooling	
Nationally loyal sons[a]	9%	91%	100% (N = 65)
Other sons[a]	37%	63%	100% (N = 736)

a. χ^2 significant at the .001 level.

On all subsequent parameters of national loyalty I compare only the educated nationally loyal and the educated others.[8]

The nationally loyal are more concentrated in towns and cities (Table III). Malihabad and Melur are *tahsil* (*taluk*) headquarters (county seats), as well as block headquarters for the community development program. Madurai serves as headquarters for Madurai District and, in certain departments, for Ramanathapuram District as well—one of the few double-district centers in India. The city of Lucknow is headquarters for Lucknow District, as well as capital of the State of Uttar Pradesh. In addition to their political importance, all four localities are strategically located on main lines of bus or train transportation. Living in these centers implies greater exposure to travelers from other districts and their views of what the government is or is not doing. Living in these centers also implies wider exposure to the mass media—the radios in the tea and coffee shops, the newsreels in the cinemas—

TABLE III — The Educated by Place of Residence

	Villages	Towns and cities	Total
Nationally loyal fathers[a]	10%	90%	100% (N = 30)
Other fathers[a]	27%	73%	100% (N = 484)
Nationally loyal sons[b]	14%	86%	100% (N = 59)
Other sons[b]	24%	76%	100% (N = 462)

a. χ^2 significant at the .05 level.
b. χ^2 significant at the .15 level, below the .05 level usually considered significant.

as well as to such less formal sources of information as political arguments in front of neighborhood stores. Finally, living in these centers implies first-hand exposure to government in action: tax offices, municipal council halls, legislative assembly buildings, building of new roads, government industrial estates rising on the edge of the cities, political rallies, and the coming and going of jeeps stenciled "Planning Commission," "Public Works Department," "Malaria Control" or "Ministry of Education."

The nationally loyal are more highly concentrated in the white-collar, proprietary, and professional occupations (Table IV). This observation may be viewed as a case of the more general proposition that, the higher the status a group enjoys in a society, the greater is its commitment to the maintenance of that society.[9] In this case, the white-collar and professional groups earn more income, are able to purchase more of the amenities, and enjoy

TABLE IV — The Educated by Occupation

	Unskilled and manual occupations[c]	White-collar and professional occupations[c]	Total
Nationally loyal fathers[a]	25%	75%	100% (N = 32)
Other fathers[a]	52%	48%	100% (N = 482)
Nationally loyal sons[b]	30%	70%	100% (N = 53)
Other sons[b]	54%	46%	100% (N = 427)

a. χ^2 significant at the .01 level.
b. χ^2 significant at the .02 level.
c. For sons, occupations of their fathers were recorded.

higher degrees of status than do the unskilled and manual groups. Insofar as the white-collar and professional groups recognize that their own well-being is interlocked with the well-being of the nation, it is not surprising that they are more nationally loyal than the unskilled and manual workers.

Among the Hindus, the nationally loyal are more concentrated in the higher castes (*Brahmans, Kshatriyas, Vaishyas, and Kayasthas*) (Table V). This observation may also be viewed as a case of the more general proposition that the higher-status groups have greater commitments to the maintenance of their society. In this case, however, the covariance of high caste with national loyalty is especially interesting, in view of the present government's avowed policy of reducing distinctions among classes and castes. The higher castes might legitimately be less loyal to the government because of the threat to their present high status. My own interpretation, however, is that the government's pronouncements speak more softly than its actions.

TABLE V — The Educated by Caste

	Twice-born castes	Other castes	Total
Nationally loyal fathers[a]	67%	33%	100% (N = 24)
Other fathers[a]	40%	60%	100% (N = 359)
Nationally loyal sons[b]	63%	37%	100% (N = 51)
Other sons[b]	36%	64%	100% (N = 347)

  a. χ^2 is significant at the .02 level.
  b. χ^2 is significant at the .001 level.

Higher castes still hold a disproportionate number of positions in government service and will probably continue to do so for some time. As with the higher occupational classes, the higher castes may recognize that, at least for the time being, their well-being is interlocked with the well-being of the nation.

In addition to sex, residence, education, occupation, and caste, the nationally loyal respondents shared a number of attitudinal parameters.

The nationally loyal are more oriented toward the future (Table VI).

TABLE VI — The Educated by Orientation in Time[a]

	Past	Present	Future	Total
Nationally loyal fathers[b]	27%	13%	60%	100% (N = 30)
Other fathers[b]	32%	26%	42%	100% (N = 480)
Nationally loyal sons[c]	19%	19%	62%	100% (N = 59)
Other sons[c]	28%	27%	45%	100% (N = 461)

  a. This table is based on answers to Question 44 in our questionnaire: One man says, "The things of the present are best. Things of the past are forgotten, and nobody can tell what the future holds." A second man says, "The practices and customs of our fathers and grandfathers are best. The modern age is not good." A third man says, "The future is what is important. That is what we must prepare for." Which of these three men do you think is correct?
  b. χ^2 is significant at the .08 level.
  c. χ^2 is significant at the .01 level, below the .05 level usually considered significant.

Perhaps this linking of national loyalty with future orientation is a characteristic of newly independent nations rather than of nations already possessing several centuries of national history. There has been some discussion[10] of how much present nationalism in India draws upon religio-political ideologies or loyalties to ancient India, when kings revered Brahmans and Brahmans upheld the fourfold divisions of society. Our own evidence suggests that most national loyalty in India today does not look backward to the glorious days of the kingdom of Ayodhya so much as it looks forward to the future—a future for which one must prepare.

One of the questions in which I was most interested involved the degree to which it was necessary for a man to abandon his loyalties to kin, caste, tribe, village, or ethnic group in the course of developing loyalty to his nation. One could argue, on one hand, that loyalty to one's nation is merely an extension of loyalty to groups contained within it. In such a case, national loyalty could be village loyalty or caste loyalty "writ large." On the other hand, one could argue that tribal, caste, or ethnic loyalty *impedes* the development of national loyalty. In fact, national loyalty can be defined in such a way as to require the subordination of all other loyalties to that of the nation-state.[11] My study produced several bits of evidence relevant to the problem of national *versus* subnational loyalties.

On a scale designed to test adherence to caste taboos,[12] both the nationally loyal sons and the nationally loyal fathers appear to adhere significantly *less* to caste-avoidance taboos than do those who are not nationally loyal. As soon as I introduced the control variable "education," however, the apparent correlation disappeared. Educated people abandon caste taboos more readily than uneducated people—regardless of whether or not they are nationally loyal.

On a question designed to test relative civic-mindedness—sense of responsibility to neighbors rather than to relatives—the nationally loyal sons and fathers indicated a deeper sense of responsibility to neighbors (Table VII). This correlation remained even when controlled for education. One could argue, however, that, to a certain extent, this question is a reformulation of Question 76, one of the questions used initially to distinguish between those who are and those who are not nationally loyal. In other words, this correlation could have been predicted almost by definition.

On two other questions, designed to test relative weakening of the sense

TABLE VII — Civic-Mindedness among the Educated[a]

	Help neighbors	Help relatives	Total
Nationally loyal fathers and sons[b]	91%	9%	100% (N = 89)
Other fathers and sons[b]	80%	20%	100% (N = 936)

a. This table is based on answers to Question 75 in our questionnaire: A man whose children were grown was asked by his panchayat for some money for a new school. The panchayat said, "You will be helping your neighbors' children and your village if you give some money for the school." The man said, "I need that money for my daughter's marriage and for assisting my relatives. I must help them first." Who do you think was right?

b. χ^2 is significant at the .02 level.

of responsibility for one's kinfolk, there is no apparent correlation between weaker kinship ties and stronger national loyalty.[13]

On one question, designed to test respect for traditional religious authority, there is no apparent correlation between less respect for traditional religious authority and more national loyalty.[14]

In short, one can apparently *add* national loyalty to one's other loyalties without detracting from those other loyalties. A good family man and a devout follower of his religion can still be nationally loyal.

IV. Two Types of National Loyalty: Nationalism and Patriotism

While I was viewing the surface dimensions of national loyalty, one observation kept stubbornly bobbing to the surface, disturbing the otherwise symmetrical pattern of findings. With chance distributions, it was to be expected that on certain answers the nationally loyal sons might differ significantly from other sons while the nationally loyal fathers would not differ from other fathers. On a number of questions, however, the replies of the nationally loyal sons and fathers were both significantly skewed from the replies of their peers *but in opposite directions*. Given the general parameters of national loyalty already described, there seem to be two varieties of national loyalty—one for the fathers and the other for the sons.

Because of the relationship between the nature of my sample design, the date of my study, and the date of India's independence, the fathers in my study had been young men at the time of India's final struggle for independence. These men had developed their earliest concepts of national loyalty during the course of that struggle. The sons, however, had been born five years after independence. By the time they became aware of concepts like "nation," India was a going concern. Their national loyalty was the product of training both inside and outside school—some of it directed quite consciously at making them responsible citizens of an independent state.

One might label these two types of national loyalty in a number of ways: "adult loyalty" and "youth loyalty"; "preindependence loyalty" and "post-independence loyalty"; "first-generation loyalty" and "second-generation loyalty"; or "the loyalty of external struggle" and "the loyalty of internal cohesion." How one labels the phenomena affects (in fact, may even in a sense determine) the generalizations one bases upon them. Let us, for the sake of convenience, arbitrarily label the loyalty of the fathers "nationalism" and the loyalty of the sons "patriotism." Hopefully, we may thus avoid premature definition of the limits of any generalizations we may wish to make.

The Nationalists

Nationalists are more authoritarian (Tables VIII and IX).

TABLE VIII — Educated Fathers by General Attitudes toward Exercise of Authority[a]

	Low authoritarian			High authoritarian		Total
	0—2	3	4	5	6—7	
Nationally loyal fathers[b]	0%	13%	47%	30%	10%	100% (N = 30)
Other fathers[b]	24%	19%	24%	19%	14%	100% (N = 482)

a. This table is based on answers to Question 37 in the questionnaire, a seven-point scale that includes the following items: An insult to one's honor should always be punished; human nature being what it is, there will always be wars and conflicts; people can be divided into two classes, the strong and the weak; it is not good to think too much; a great many things can be predicted by astrology; there are so many evil people nowadays that it is dangerous to go out alone; nowadays the courts don't give as severe punishments to lawbreakers as they ought to.

b. χ^2 is significant at the .01 level. For χ^2 purposes, categories 0–2, 3–4, and 5–7 were used.

TABLE IX — Educated Fathers by Attitudes toward Exercise of Authority over Sons[a]

	Should obey	Should think for self	Total
Nationally loyal fathers[b]	90%	10%	100% (N = 30)
Other fathers[b]	77%	23%	100% (N = 480)

a. This table is based on answers to Question 35 in the questionnaire: One man says, "The most important thing an eleven or twelve-year-old boy should learn to do is always obey the wishes of his elders." Another man says, "The most important thing a boy should learn is to think for himself." Which man do you think was correct?

b. χ^2 is significant at the .07 level. Ordinarily a significance at this low a level means that a hypothesis of no association cannot be rejected. In conjunction with the F-scale score above, however, this covariance seems relevant.

Nationalists are more fatalistic (Table X). In view of the demonstrated relationship between nationalism and authoritarianism and the generally close link between authoritarianism and fatalism, we could expect a close relationship betwen nationalism and fatalism.

Nationalists have higher aspirations, which have not been realized (Table XI). If one can assume that unrealized aspirations are a source of frustration, this finding may be interpreted as support for the hypothesis that personal frustration is linked with authoritarianism and fatalism.

TABLE X — Relationship between Nationalism and Fatalism among the Educated[a]

	Results follow work	Results in God's hands	Total
Nationally loyal fathers[b]	33%	67%	100% (N = 30)
Nationally loyal sons[b]	56%	44%	100% (N = 59)
Other fathers and sons[b]	49%	51%	100% (N = 946)

a. This table is based on answers to Question 46 in the questionnaire: One man says, "One must work hard in order to have better results." A second man says, "One must work hard but the results are in God's hands." A third man says, "One need not work hard, because the results are in God's hands." Which of these three men do you think is correct?

b. χ^2 is significant only at the .17 level. Ordinarily a significance this low means that the hypothesis of no association cannot be rejected. Because of the direction of the skew, however, and because of the frequent conjunction of authoritarianism and fatalism, this covariance seems relevant.

TABLE XI — Educated Fathers Measured by Unrealized Aspirations[a]

	No more	High school	College	Post-graduate	Total
Nationally loyal fathers[b]	33%	7%	10%	50%	100% (N = 30)
Other fathers[b]	31%	26%	20%	23%	100% (N = 481)

a. This table is based on answers to Question 48 in the questionnaire: If you had the opportunity . . . up to what class would you have liked to study?

b. χ^2 is significant at the .01 level.

Nationalists are more satisfied with the nation's progress since independence (Table XII). This finding may be interpreted in at least two ways. First, it may indicate that the nationalists feel a greater obligation to shut their eyes to their nation's defects. Second, it may indicate that the nationalists choose the winning of independence as their standard for "progress." Once India had gained her independence, rapid national progress was guaranteed, in their eyes, virtually by definition.

TABLE XII — Educated Fathers' Estimates of National Progress since Independence[a]

	No or some progress	Rapid progress	Total
Nationally loyal fathers[b]	30%	70%	100% (N = 30)
Other fathers[b]	51%	49%	100% (N = 481)

a. This table is based on answers to Question 57 in the questionnaire: Please tell which of these statements you think is true:

1. Since independence the country has not progressed at all.
2. Since independence the country has progressed somewhat.
3. Since independence the country has progressed rapidly.

b. χ^2 is significant at the .01 level.

Nationalists feel that progress comes more through struggle and less through moral suasion and priestly encouragement (Tables XIII and XIV). This finding is also in line with the general authoritarian syndrome.

TABLE XIII — Attitudes toward Relationship between Competition and Progress among the Educated[a]

	Competition beneficial	Competition harmful	Total
Nationally loyal fathers[b]	90%	10%	100% (N = 30)
Nationally loyal sons[b]	59%	41%	100% (N = 59)
Other fathers and sons[b]	67%	33%	100% (N = 941)

a. This table is based on answers to Question 62 in the questionnaire: One learned man says, "When people compete with each other, they work harder and do their best, and there is progress." Another learned man says, "When people compete with each other, they become enemies, and progress becomes impossible." Which of these learned men do you think is correct?

b. χ^2 is significant at the .02 level.

TABLE XIV — Educated Fathers' Attitudes toward Role of Priests in Progress[a]

	Priests help	Priests impede	Total
Nationally loyal fathers[b]	31%	69%	100% (N = 23)
Other fathers[b]	63%	37%	100% (N = 337)

a. This table is based on Question 66 (asked of Hindus only) in the questionnaire: One man says, "Priests and purohits are helping our nation progress." Another man says, "Priests and purohits are an obstacle to our nation's progress." Which of these two men do you think is correct?

b. χ^2 is significant at the .05 level.

Nationalists exhibit less concern over the maintenance of harmonious relations within the nation (Tables XV, XVI, and XVII).

TABLE XV — Respect for Others' Religions among the Educated[a]

	Don't respect	Do respect	Total
Nationally loyal fathers[b]	17%	83%	100% (N = 29)
Nationally loyal sons[b]	0%	100%	100% (N = 59)
Other fathers and sons[b]	9%	91%	100% (N = 942)

a. This table is based on answers to Question 32 in the questionnaire: Two men are watching members of another religion worshipping together. One man says, "Their religion is a hypocritical show; so we should not be respectful while they are worshiping." The other man says, "Their religion may be false, but *they* believe it is true. Therefore, we should be respectful while they are worshiping." Which man do you think was correct?

b. χ^2 is significant at the .03 level.

TABLE XVI — Attitudes toward Belligerence among the Educated[a]

	Take insulter to court	Forget insult	Total
Nationally loyal fathers[b]	37%	63%	100% (N = 30)
Nationally loyal sons[b]	12%	88%	100% (N = 59)
Other fathers and sons[b]	21%	79%	100% (N = 945)

a. This table is based on answers to Question 41 in the questionnaire: A man severely insulted two clerks in front of a large crowd. One clerk said, "I will take you to court. You have insulted me, and I must remove the dishonor from my name even if I must spend much money." The other clerk said, "Your insults are only words. I shall forget the matter." Which clerk do you think was correct?

b. χ^2 is significant at the .02 level.

TABLE XVII — Relative Value of Group Harmony among the Educated[a]

	Complain about election	Accept election	Total
Nationally loyal fathers[b]	52%	48%	100% (N = 29)
Nationally loyal sons[b]	32%	68%	100% (N = 59)
Other fathers and sons[b]	37%	62%	100% (N = 939)

a. This table is based on answers to Question 73 in the questionnaire: A club once held an election. One candidate lost by only a few votes. One friend told him, "Complain about the election and make them count the votes again." Another friend told him, "Do not complain about the election. It will only make disharmony in the club." Which of these friends do you think was correct?

b. χ^2 is significant at the .20 level, below the .05 level usually considered significant.

The over-all picture of the nationalist, then, is that of a nationally loyal father, more satisfied with the country's progress than most fathers, more frustrated in his own career ambitions, more authoritarian, more convinced of the part fate plays in the outcome of men's actions, more doubtful that religious leaders contribute to national progress, more convinced of the benefits of struggle and competition, and less committed to the maintenance of social harmony and mutual give-and-take.

The Patriots

Patriots are no more authoritarian than other sons (see Table XVIII).

Patriots are no more fatalistic than other sons (see Table XIX). In fact they tend to be less fatalistic.

TABLE XVIII — Attitudes toward Filial Obedience among the Sons[a]

	Obey	Think for self	Total
Nationally loyal sons[b]	85%	15%	100% (N = 59)
Other sons[b]	85%	15%	100% (N = 459)

a. This table is based on answers to Question 35 in the questionnaire: One man says, "The most important thing a boy should learn is always to obey the wishes of his elders." Another man says, "The most important thing a boy should learn is to think for himself." Which man do you think is correct?

b. χ^2 is not significant; the null hypothesis cannot be rejected.

TABLE XIX — Fatalism among the Sons[a]

	Results follow work	Results in God's hands	Total
Nationally loyal sons[b]	56%	44%	100% (N = 59)
Other sons[b]	50%	50%	100% (N = 462)

a. This table is based on answers to Question 46 in the questionnaire: One man says, "One must work hard in order to have better results." A second man says, "One must work hard, but the results are in God's hands." A third man says, "One need not work hard, because the results are in God's hands." Which of these three men do you think is correct?

b. χ^2 is not significant; the null hypothesis cannot be rejected.

Patriots have higher educational expectations than other sons (Table XX).

Patriots have higher professional expectations than other sons (Table XXI). Perhaps between high educational expectations and high professional expectations one can find a clue as to why the patriots feel as they do toward their nation. The patriot expects to go far. Optimism about his own future may facilitate broader concerns for the welfare of his fellow countrymen. Or the very optimism he feels about his own future plans may have been derived from the same process of socialization through which he acquired his patriotic perspective.

TABLE XX — Sons' Educational Expectations[a]

	Primary or secondary	College or technical	Total
Nationally loyal sons[b]	17%	83%	100% (N = 59)
Other sons[b]	43%	57%	100% (N = 460)

a. This table is based on answers to Question 49 in the questionnaire: Up to what level do you expect to study?
b. χ^2 is significant at the .001 level.

TABLE XXI — Sons' Professional Expectations[a]

	Unskilled, white-collar, and owner	Manager and professional	Total
Nationally loyal sons[b]	17%	82%	100% (N = 52)
Other sons[b]	41%	54%	100% (N = 449)

a. This table is based on answers to Question 51 in the questionnaire: What do you think you will do to earn a living when you grow up?
b. χ^2 is significant at the .01 level.

Patriots expect the government to do less for the citizens and the citizens to do more for themselves (Table XXII).
Patriots exhibit more concern over the maintenance of harmonious relations within the nation (Table XXIII; see also Tables XV, XVI, and XVII).

TABLE XXII — Attitudes among the Educated toward Self-Help[a]

	Government help	Self-help	Total
Nationally loyal fathers[b]	80%	20%	100% (N = 30)
Nationally loyal sons[b]	64%	36%	100% (N = 59)
Other fathers and sons[b]	77%	23%	100% (N = 940)

a. This table is based on answers to Question 61 in the questionnaire: One boy says, "The government should do more to raise the standard of living of the people." Another boy says, "The government should not do so much for the people, because in this way the people will become lazy and do nothing for themselves." Which of these two boys do you think is correct?
b. χ^2 is significant at the .01 level.

TABLE XXIII — Sons' Concern for National Harmony[a]

	General societal integration	Other reason	Total
Nationally loyal sons[b]	17%	83%	100% (N = 59)
Other sons[b]	6%	94%	100% (N = 458)

a. This table is based on answers to Question 19 in the questionnaire: Why do you enjoy (your favorite) festival?
b. χ^2 is significant at the .02 level.

Patriots are more willing than other sons to abandon restrictions on inter-caste marriages (Table XXIV).

In short, our picture of a patriot is that of a boy who has developed a broadly based sense of identification with the people of his country, who believes that fate plays a somewhat smaller part in man's affairs than the nationalists believe, who is less likely than the nationalists or other sons to insist on having his own way, who is willing to play the election game according to the rules, who recognizes his responsibility as a citizen to inaugurate improvements without waiting for the government, and who is more willing to abandon one of the most central tenets of the caste system—the restriction of marriage to those within the same caste.

In his discussion of the circulation of political elites, Vilfredo Pareto describes two types of personality, the Lions and the Foxes.[15] The Lions are the men of "persistence" who use force and direct appeals to sentiments that they themselves share. The Foxes are the men of "combinations" who employ ruse and appeals to sentiments that they themselves do not share. Pareto observed that during times of revolution the Lions came into power, only—inevitably—to be followed by the Foxes.

TABLE XXIV — Willingness among Sons to Abandon Caste Restrictions on Marriage[a]

	Approve	*Disapprove*	*Total*
Nationally loyal sons[b]	27%	73%	100% (N = 51)
Other sons[b]	10%	90%	100% (N = 349)

a. This table is based on answers to Question 69 (asked of Hindus only) in the questionnaire: If your older brother or sister were to marry someone from a low caste, would you—Approve? Disapprove?

b. χ^2 is significant at the .001 level.

My study was certainly not a study of elites. On the contrary, it was a study of a deliberately selected cross-section of the total society. Nonetheless, an analogy between my nationalists and patriots and Pareto's Lions and Foxes is not altogether inappropriate. It was the Lions who struggled to rid India of the English. It is the Foxes who are being trained today in the schools to identify their interests with those of their fellow countrymen, to respect the beliefs of all, and to work through the democratic machinery with its inevitable give and take. Suggestive of the difference between the nationalists and the patriots (or the Lions and the Foxes) is the fact that, in my study, I could find no significant covariance between a father's national loyalty and his own son's national loyalty. Empirically, as well as analytically, they seem to be two different things.

While indulging in speculation, we may note that, from India's point of view, the national loyalty of the nationalists was appropriate in the days of British domination. With their authoritarianism, their belief in the guiding hand of fate, their chip-on-the-shoulder approach to personal relations, their willingness to contest rights imaginary or real, and their lack of respect for people of different faiths, the nationalists were the very people to engage in a scrappy fight for independence from the great power. With the coming of independence, however, those same qualities may have become liabilities. Perhaps the new nation needs patriots—not nationalists.

It is not too presumptuous to suggest that one of the problems the newly independent Pakistans and Burmas, Congos and Ghanas have had to face is the type of national loyalty predominant among its citizens. When compromise has been called for, jealousy has been forthcoming. When tolerance has been needed, there has been intolerance. Quite possibly, any recently liberated colony must pass through a peculiarly vulnerable historical period (similar to that in the United States between the acceptance of the Articles of Confederation and the ratification of the Constitution) while the nationalists are being replaced by the patriots. If the transition can be made successfully, then perhaps something like a political "take-off" point can be reached, at which patriots train new patriots until the basic loyalties of citizens to their nation's political process are no longer problematic but have become one of the factors that can be presumed.

NOTES

1. See, for example, Karl Deutsch, *Nationalism and Social Communication* (Cambridge, Mass., 1956); Thomas Hodgkin, *Nationalism in Colonial Africa* (New York, 1957); James Coleman, *Nigeria: Background to Nationalism* (Berkeley, 1958); Daniel Lerner, *The Passing of Traditional Society* (New York, 1958); Rupert Emerson, *From Empire to Nation* (Cambridge, Mass., 1960); Hans Kohn, *The Idea of Nationalism* (New York, 1961); Lucian Pye, *Politics, Personality, and Nation Building: Burma's Search for Identity* (New Haven, 1962); Seymour Lipset, *First New Nation* (New York, 1963); and Fred von der Mehden, *Religion and Nationalism in Southeast Asia* (Madison, 1963).

2. F. Kluckhohn and F. Strodtbeck, *Variations in Value Orientations* (New York, 1961).

3. See T. W. Adorno, *et al., The Authoritarian Personality* (New York, 1950), Chap. 7.

4. Only those familiar with the gulf between the spoken and the written languages in most of India can fully appreciate how difficult it was to convince both translation assistants and printers that I wanted to *write* the language *spoken* in normal conversation!

5. It was six months after the fighting on the Sino-Indian border.

6. χ^2 difference significant at the .001 level.

7. χ^2 difference significant at the .05 level.

8. In effect, I dropped out of my sample all sons with three years of schooling or less and all fathers with no schooling at all.

9. For a discussion of related propositions concerning stratification, see Edward A. Shils, "Class," *Encyclopedia Britannica*, 5 (1960), pp. 766-8.

10. See D. Mackenzie Brown, *The White Umbrella: Indian Political Thought from Manu to Gandhi* (Berkeley, 1953).

11. See, for example, Hans Kohn, *Nationalism, its Meaning and History* (Princeton, 1955), p. 9.

12. These questions were asked of all Hindus:

Question 67. Would you be willing to be friends with someone from a low caste?

Question 68. Would you be able to eat food prepared by someone from a low caste?

Question 69. (Fathers) Would you be able to marry your son or daughter to a boy or girl from a low caste?

(Sons) If your older brother or sister were to marry someone from a low caste, would you approve or disapprove?

13. Question 28. Relatives came to two men asking for money and help. One man felt this was a burden. The other man did not feel this was a burden. Which of these two men do you think was correct?

Approximately 7% of the sons and 5% of the fathers felt that it was a burden, with no significant difference between the nationally loyal and their peers.

Question 29. One man says, "My family gets along with its relatives better than other families do." A second man says, " My family gets along with its relatives about as well as most families do." A third man says, "My family gets along with its relatives worse than most families do." Which of these three men is most like you?

Approximately 6% of the sons and 2% of the fathers felt that they got along with their relatives worse than most families, with no significant difference between the nationally loyal and their peers.

14. Question 36. One man says, "Priests and sacred books contain all truth. We must always do whatever they tell us to do." Another man says, "Priests and sacred books may be true, but we must do what our consciences tell us." Which of these two men do you think was correct?

Approximately 67% of the sons felt that they should obey the priests, with no significant difference between the nationally loyal and their peers. Approximately 47% of the fathers felt that they should obey the priests, with no significant difference between the nationally loyal and their peers.

15. Vilfredo Pareto, *The Mind and Society,* ed. by Arthur Livingstone, transl. by Andrew Bongiorno and Arthur Livingstone (New York, 1935), para. 2170-220.

Ideology and Modernization—
The Japanese Case

BY *ROBERT A. SCALAPINO*

JAPAN IS a fascinating society in which to study the relationship between social change and ideology, partly because the process of Japanese modernization, extending over a period of more than 100 years, is sufficiently lengthy to provide us with a meaningful perspective. Today, Japan must be considered an advanced—albeit very special—industrial society. In both its classical and modern periods, furthermore, Japan has had a significant intellectual tradition and one directly related to politics. Few political elites in the premodern era were as consciously influenced by and committed to ideology as were the Japanese. A pervasive, systemized value-institutional structure guided each successive generation of rulers, maintaining the boundaries within which they could legitimately operate, perpetuating the central beliefs that governed and rationalized political behavior. The Japanese "way of life," known in modern times as *kokutai*, was a uniquely powerful force in the traditional era.

I. Classicism and Japanese Ideological Proclivities

The very richness of the traditional ideological heritage presented in one sense, a formidable challenge to "Western-style modernization." Japan, unlike some parts of the non-Western world, did not come into the modern world *tabula rasa*, and therefore the legacies of the past were certain to color the new order. But if this situation represented a challenge, in another sense it also represented an opportunity. The experience of working with complex and sophisticated abstractions, of being influenced by them and of using them for manipulative purposes was in itself invaluable preparation for the massive adjustments that modernity required. Among the resources that Japan could bring to the modernization process, a conscious intellectual tradition was certainly one of the most impressive.

In its initial phases, modernization meant Westernization. Thus, what was *new* was also *foreign*—perhaps the most important single fact that can be cited in connection with the problem of Japanese modernization. As we shall note repeatedly, the most basic intellectual responses to the modernization process were of two types: on one hand, the gradual movement from rejection to acceptance; on the other hand, a pendulum-like swing between two polar positions—extensive adherence to the indigenous value-institutional structure and wholehearted commitment to Westernism. Each of these responses fundamentally involved a complex attempt to resist or adjust to the ever-changing realities of a great transitional era.

The confrontation between Japan and the modern West must be dated from the second half of the nineteenth century. Dutch learning had had some influence prior to the arrival of Commodore Perry and his "black ships" in Edo Bay in 1853. It is only after the Perry Expedition, however, that Japanese society was forced into massive, sustained contact with the West. Only after the mid-nineteenth century was Japan pushed into the universal stream. To appreciate fully the significance of this event, one must understand the intellectual essence of the old era. What was the dominant ideological tone of Tokugawa Japan?

Japanese Confucianism, substantially affected by Shinto, Buddhism, feudal-military society, spelled out the nature of man, society, and the state in comprehensive fashion.[1] The major themes can be set forth succinctly as follows:

1. Human nature is potentially good, but man is easily corrupted. One of the primary purposes of the state is to cultivate the better aspects of human nature and to curb digressions from the proper path. In short, the function of the state is to develop the good man.

2. To be legitimate, political authority must rest upon a moral-ethical base.

3. Familial relations should serve as a model for political relations, for the family is the primary unit of society and the fundamental basis of social order. Proper relations between ruler and subject are thus to be drawn from relations between parent and child.

4. The best government is a government of wise men who, by their exemplary conduct, establish the permanent values of the society. The relationship between superior and inferior is like that between the wind and the grass. When the wind blows, the grass must bend down.

5. The state is properly concerned about every aspect of society. Art, music, literature, social relations—all affect the character and the values of man and are therefore subject to regulation and control.

6. Social distinctions must be maintained if propriety and order are to be preserved. With each class, each age, each category go certain specific obligations. Correct relations among groups must be upheld if the society is to be harmonious and well ordered.

7. To covet material gain is productive of evil. To separate the individual from society is the essence of selfishness. Society is an organism the interactive parts of which are delicately balanced but susceptible to permanent functioning if basic values can be maintained and change or disruption prevented.

Despite its traditional cast, Japanese Confucianism provided some assistance to modernization quite apart from its general representation of a powerful intellectual heritage. Central to Confucian doctrine was the idea of tutelage, the concept that an intellectual elite should guide the "backward masses" toward certain pre-established goals. The strictures upon the ruling class, moreover, were substantial. The Japanese elite was burdened with moral obligations quite as burdensome, if fulfilled, as the Protestant ethic. Indeed, it is crucial to realize that in a society like Japan there could be a counterpart to the Protestant ethic that performed the same basic function in connection with modern economic development. Conditions in Japan were conducive to the emergence of a modernizing oligarchy, an "enlightened conservatism."

Such a development was further abetted by the strictly hierarchial nature of Japanese society and the strong ideological defense of hierarchy. According to the Confucianists, stability and indeed morality demanded a proper ordering of society on the basis of birth, age, and sex. Upon all of the governed lay stern injunctions to live in conformity with status and to obey superiors in unswerving fashion. The traditional Japanese family system, with its emphasis upon paternal absolutism, even undermined to some extent the type of contractual theory of reciprocal duties and rights so prominent in Western feudalism. In feudal Japan, rights were more precarious, duties more absolute.

England and Japan, however, are both good examples of the fact that hierarchy can serve the cause of modernization well. The notion that modern economic development can only be advanced through a rapidly increasing degree of egalitarianism is not borne out by the facts. Limited social mobility first contributes to political stability, an indispensable prerequisite for economic growth. In addition, it makes possible a high level of commitment to the whole range of differentiated tasks upon which the industrial revolution depends. One should distinguish clearly between two types of mobility. Horizontal movement like transfer from farm to factory may be aided by a strong hierarchical tradition. Certainly, such movement does not necessarily require or involve vertical movement, the type most often associated with the term "social mobility."

In many respects, to be sure, Confucianism represented a powerful obstacle to modernization. Even in methodology, its conservatism cast a long shadow over the modern era. To the Confucianist, the function of the scholar was not to be creative but to understand and interpret correctly the "truths" contained in the classics. Appeal to authority rather than experimentalism was the primary method. The premium was upon orthodoxy, not iconoclasm; upon the well-trod paths, not the unknown frontiers. Paradoxically, the later influence of Marxism upon Japanese intellectuals was clearly related to some aspects of this tradition.

Contrary intellectual currents, however, also operated in traditional Japan. The very fact that Japanese Confucianism had a significant admixture of Shintoism, Buddhism, and other doctrines indicated the important strain of eclecticism that runs through Japanese cultural history. Lying on the peripheries of Asia and possessed of a less mature civilization than existed on the mainland, the Japanese from earliest times had borrowed unabashedly from China and Korea in the realm of both ideas and institutions.

The difficulty of making these ideas and institutions operative in a different cultural context represented the great historical problem for Japan. The problems implicit in confrontation with the West were therefore not new ones.

Indeed, it might be said that the Japanese elite, in addition to being armed with authority and a sense of responsibility, was also psychologically prepared for the task of synthesis.

In truth, two conflicting intellectual traditions exist, each having deep roots in Japanese society. One is represented by the scholar, who retires into his study, keeping aloof from either social participation or empirical research, holding firmly to cosmic truth or "pure theory." The other is represented by the scholar-bureaucrat or policy scientist, who holds certain abstract values but is experimental and pragmatic by necessity and who is also sufficiently uncertain of the superiority of his methods (sometimes read "culture") to be receptive toward others. The making of modern Japan and the as yet unresolved conflict within it are intimately connected with these two strikingly contradictory, competitive, and powerful intellectual traditions within the society.

Certain negative factors of importance that relate to premodern Japanese thought have not been mentioned. The Japanese tradition was essentially, although not wholly, a secular one. After due homage is paid to the role of Shintoism and Buddhism in Japanese political theory, one finds most of the central themes articulated in secular form. More importantly, perhaps, there is no heritage of an organized, politically powerful church. As a result, the state has had only limited competition in its drive for loyalty and commitment, primarily from the family. But in Japan, as has been noted, the family was more integrated than competitive with the state. The absence of a powerful doctrine of limitations on state power is undoubtedly due to the absence of any great institutional struggle for power. The Japanese state came down to the modern era with an almost unchallenged supremacy.

There also existed in Japanese tradition a singular lack of emphasis upon the individual. Perhaps it would be misleading to say that individualism was denied. It was never discovered. Japanese political theory traditionally considered the family to be the atom in human society, the elemental unit that could not be split. The individual was thus a part, never a whole. When this assumption is connected with the antimaterialist tone natural to an agrarian society, "conservatism" and "radicalism," in their broad Western senses, become terms of dubious meaning applied to modern Japan. Against the background of Japanese tradition, a liberal, individualist philosophy is truly radical, and all statist doctrines are basically conservative. Indeed, it is wrong to assume that such concepts as "private enterprise" and "private initiative" have had the same meaning in modern Japan as in the West. In most of what is called "private," the proportion of group, communal, or public elements is much higher. Under all these circumstances, doctrines of socialism in general and Marxism in particular represented hybrid radical-conservative movements. The inner significance of this fact has escaped many modern Japanese intellectuals.

In sum, when Japanese society came into confrontation with the modern West, certain powerful political proclivities had already been firmly established. The table of probability was steeply graded in the direction of elitist tutelage; purposeful, responsible leadership and structured, committed followers; statism of a more or less authoritarian type, moderated by the pluralism implicit in family and other small-group organizations; definition of political problems in ethical-moral terms; primary support for the harmonist, organic theory of state; and decision-making on the basis of consensus—or strife. Some of these principles were common to all "backward" societies; others were to be found throughout the Confucian orbit; still others were uniquely the products of the Japanese environment. The intermixture, in any case, represented a statist ideology with power and depth.

II. Challenge and Response

The great motive force in Japanese modernization was the threat of absorption or destruction by the West. After the mid-nineteenth century and for at least fifty years, this threat dominated policy-making in Japan. Because of it, an essentially conservative elite abandoned earlier theories and turned with great seriousness, if not total enthusiasm, to the task of modernizing the nation. Naturally, conservative control of the modernization process in Japan, together with the particular timing of that process, vitally affected its character. Under these circumstances, it was easier to restructure certain aspects of traditionalism, making it serviceable for the modern era. The distinctive quality of Japanese modernization was the extraordinary degree to which the past could be adapted to the needs and purposes of the present. Conservative leadership made maximal use of the resources that were built into their society—values, institutions, and men.

In its approach to the West, Japan went through the same three broad stages characteristic of much of the non-Western world. At first, the dominant attitude was one of total rejection. It was followed by an attempt to make a distinction between Japanese values and Western technology. Finally, the search began for a synthesis that would fit all "necessary" or "desirable" aspects of Westernism to the needs and nature of Japanese society. Let us note briefly the unfolding of these three stages.

Naturally, the interaction between Japan and the West was an extraordinarily complex matter because it involved dynamic forces. The West itself was constantly changing and capable of discarding one fashion just as it was being "discovered" in Japan. What is more, sometimes the West perversely showed an inferior or insignificant side of itself thereby causing precious time and effort to be wasted. At times, the "advanced" West seemed to move closer to Japan; at other times, further away. It was Germany, or more precisely Prussia, with its similar timing of political and economic modernization, that provided the most appropriate model, as the Meiji leaders were quick to learn. But if the West was constantly changing, so was Japan. Thus, "Japonism," in whatever form, was itself increasingly adulterated with Western accretions, as it had been in earlier times with Chinese and Korean ones. It had no claim to purity.

We can still refer to the great pendulum swings between Westernism and Japonism discussed earlier. In a certain sense, these two forces represented a continuation of the historic elements *yin* and *yang,* so prominent in the background of Sinic culture, symbolizing black and white, male and female, the union of opposites that was the essence of creativity and life. Through its congeniality with these concepts, Hegelianism came to have a special meaning to the modern Japanese intellectual, whether or not he was conscious of that fact. Thesis—antithesis—synthesis constituted the ultimate approach of Japan to the challenge of Westernism and lay at the heart of modern Japanese ideology.

That the Japanese intellectual should initially reject the West is hardly surprising. Man's first impulse is almost always to reject the unknown and usually to fear or hate it. The Japanese intellectual tradition, moreover, had been sufficiently influenced by the Chinese classics to make a sharp distinction between the civilized man and the barbarian. The former had acquired the culture of the Confucian world, while the latter lay outside that world. Like the ancient Greeks and the modern French, the people of northeast Asia believed that a truly enormous gap existed between civilization (their way of life) and barbarism (all others).

Thus, when the Tokugawa government was put under increasing pressure by the Russians, British, and finally Americans to open up the country, it faced a serious dilemma. As more information was acquired, Tokugawa officials came to realize that Japan did not have the power to exclude the West. Furthermore, that power could only be obtained with Western assistance. Yet the government faced major opposition from a provincial military elite, which, having little contact with the West and little responsibility for national defense, could afford to hold to its classical position. It was natural that this provincial, agrarian-based military elite would champion the cause of traditionalism and view with alarm the crumbling of an old way of life. How could it rest satisfied with current trends? Through their slogan, *Sonno-joi* ("Revere the Emperor, Oust the Barbarian!") the members of the elite proposed a restoration of Imperial rule, a return of Japan to some mythical, golden age in which *samurai* and peasant would be harmoniously (but unequally) united.

Such a primitivist response to the Western threat has been characteristic of many, perhaps most, non-Western societies at some early stage in the confrontation process. Examples can be seen in India (the Mutiny), China (the Boxer Rebellion), Burma (the Saya San Rebellion), Kenya (Mau Mau), and Indonesia (Darul Islam), to cite only a few instances. But invariably, the thrust of such movements has changed, or they have gone down to defeat. After the early nineteenth century, there was no long-range hope for primitivist victory over the forces of modernism, be these forces essentially foreign or indigenous. Yet the primitivist answer was so natural, so deeply reflective of grass-root mores, that it often received first priority. Only after it had been tried and had failed, could other, more rational responses receive support.

So it was in Japan. The initial struggle was one between an ideology consonant with the past and the harsh, unyielding realities of the present. But in the exciting decade beginning in 1860, many members of the provincial elite, including some of the most fanatic young *samurai*, were forced to change their views as a result of events. By the time of the Meiji Restoration in 1867, the cry of "Oust the Barbarians!" had begun to fade. The *samurai* of Choshu and other fiefs had been forced to recognize the fact of Western power after Western ships had sailed with impunity along their shores and Western cannons had levelled many of their coastal forts. And the men most responsible for signaling this first major retreat from traditionalism were those who had seen the West in person, participants in the initial expeditions abroad. The view of England, France, and the United States in the 1860s produced a revolution in the thinking of even the most antiforeign *samurai*. One might say that empirical research—concrete experience in the Western world—first toppled certain basic premises in traditional thought, leaving the way open for the subsequent influence of more abstract Western ideas.

Primitivism, however, was not completely vanquished. Rather, it took new forms, implanting itself deeply into the "new" nationalist ideology that was being fashioned, as well as reasserting itself from time to time in frontal assaults upon the whole modern movement. Still, after the 1860s, the major trend was away from primitivism, away from the blind xenophobia, the wholesale opposition to modernism. The new era, however, in no way altered the conviction of the overwhelming number of political leaders and intellectuals that their own set of ethical political values, not only had greater validity for them, but was infinitely superior to other value-institutional systems. This conviction was the key to that stage broadly described as one of "Japanese values-Western technology."

While this second stage was soon to give way to the search for a more integral synthesis, it has continued to have a certain meaning throughout the modern period. The technological discovery of the West, it should be noted, preceded by some decades a more comprehensive intellectual discovery, and, in any case, it was always much easier to borrow foreign technology than to adopt successfully a foreign ethical-political system. The former contains a high quotient of universalism, while the latter is strongly particularistic because of the myriad of variables out of which it is constructed. Like other follower societies, Japan did not escape the basic problem of how satisfactorily to integrate rapid economic, social, and political changes, all of which were more or less stimulated by and modeled after foreign examples.

The pioneer societies of the West had no extraordinary problem of integration. Theirs was a relatively "natural" development, in which political change had a close interrelation with socioeconomic advance. The problem of timing did not occur, and no basic evolutionary stages were skipped. In the late-developing societies, it has been different. In both the economic and the political fields, stages can be skipped, and indeed, if one is taking Western experience as a guide, some stages cannot be reproduced. One result is the grave problem of keeping a logical, working relationship among culture, economic institutions, and polity.

Culture represents the iceberg so much of which lies beneath the surface of a society undergoing rapid change. Economic institutions, as noted earlier, are subject to relatively fast, predictable development under conditions such as prevailed in Japan, benefiting from the high universalist quotient in modern technology. The polity—that complex of political institutions and ideology—may also be susceptible to substantial changes as a result of large-scale borrowing or revolution. In both intellectual and operational terms, however, political institutions and values are vastly more difficult to assimilate. Most important, to keep them in phase with the socioeconomic changes taking place represents a supreme challenge under these particular conditions.

To illustrate this problem, let us take one specific example from modern Japanese history. After a period of hectic political debate among a small elite, the Emperor was led to bestow a Constitution upon his people in 1889.[2] With this action, Japan was thrust into the era of constitutional, representative government. Clearly, the Meiji Constitution was ambivalent on certain critical issues. In some respects it was more logically the instrument for an emperor-centered, organic state than for a parliament-centered, democratic one. Nevertheless, in 1889 the Meiji Constitution was generally ahead of, rather than behind, the political capacities of its society. It would be impossible to argue that the Japan of this period could have achieved this form of constitutionalism "naturally" as a result of its socioeconomic development. For the moment at least, political institutions and ideas lacked the socioeconomic underpinnings necessary for their successful operation.

By 1920, however, socioeconomic change had begun to overtake the Meiji Constitution and the value system that underlay it. Japan had entered an era of large-scale industrialization, competitive pressure groups, and increasing diversity—centrifugal tendencies of many types. Meiji-style constitutionalism rapidly became anachronistic. The gap between polity and society widened, bringing increased political unrest in its wake. Indeed, the militarist era that followed may be viewed in certain respects as a product of that widened gap, as a period when a new effort was made to reintegrate polity and society.

After World War II, another set of political institutions and values anticipating rather than mirroring the socioeconomic order was established. Once again, the problem of imbalance, along with that of adaptability, has occupied the center of the stage. Are the rapid socioeconomic changes now taking place in Japan bringing *society* abreast of *polity*? Are Western-style institutions and values susceptible to adaptation in Japan; can they be made to fit the contours of Japanese society?

The issue of synthesis thus continues to be central to Japanese political thought in these two fundamental areas: proper meshing of the social, economic, and political factors involved in rapid modernization; and harmonization of exogenous and indigenous value-institutional complexes. It is no exaggeration to assert that the critical issues involving ideology in modern Japan have revolved around these two basic problems.

III. National Unification

Against this background, let us now explore in greater detail the relationship between ideology and modernization, taking each successive phase of modern Japanese evolution into account. For each phase, one or two problems were critical. There was a natural tendency for political debate to center around these critical problems. It is thus important first to identify the basic issue of the times and then to examine the varying ideological adjustments to it.

The first great issue was that of national unification. As noted earlier, a strongly unified, relatively centralized state was essential if the Western threat was to be met. The burning issue of the late Tokugawa and early Meiji periods therefore, was how best to unify the nation, and in many respects that remained the critical question until nearly the end of the nineteenth century. Only with the Japanese victory over China in 1895 and the abolition of the unequal treaties in 1899 did new issues come to the fore.

What approaches to the problem of Japanese unification were advanced? The earliest debate was related to the question of isolation *versus* foreign involvement, as has already been noted. Those who took the position, "Revere the Emperor, Oust the Barbarian!" believed the only answer to the Western threat was the re-establishment of the ancient way of life and the maintenance of a rigid exclusion policy. They blamed the troubles of the times primarily upon the fact that there was no longer a proper relationship between classes and functions. At the top, power had been usurped from the rightful ruler by the Tokugawa family. The military class, moreover, had become increasingly separated from the soil and from the peasants. And among the people, the merchant class was gaining in wealth and power, despite the fact that it occupied a low social position. Only a restitution of the "proper order," with the emperor in his rightful place and the various classes in theirs, could unify the people and re-establish social order.

The *Sonno-joi* position, of course, contained a basic paradox that could not be resolved. On the one hand, it reflected the yearnings of an agrarian-based, feudal elite for a system that would guarantee its functions and prestige. In these terms, it was localist, hierarchical, exclusionist, and strongly anti-modern. On the other hand, it sought to use the Emperor as a symbol, as a unifying force in time of trouble. In this sense, it anticipated modern Japanese nationalism and carried within it the potentials for centralism, egalitarianism, international involvement, and modernization.

Even before the Western impact was felt, Japanese intellectuals were already wrestling with the problem of exogenous *versus* indigenous factors. The *Mito* school that emerged during the Tokugawa period and represented the avant-garde of the *Sonno-joi* movement was a center of early nationalism. Its writers carefully scrutinized Confucianism, challenging those aspects they regarded as inapplicable to Japan and strongly asserting both the uniqueness and the superiority of the *true Japanese way*. China and Japan were proclaimed to be very different societies, with the solutions of the former not necessarily applicable to the latter. Almost everywhere, modern Asian nationalism has been exclusively or extensively a reaction to the modern West. Japanese nationalism represents a partial exception. In its earliest forms, it was a reaction to a set of borrowed values and institutions predating Western ones, namely the Chinese Confucian legacy.

The most clear-cut opponents of the *Sonno-joi* position were those espousing the course of *Sabaku-kaikoku,* "Protect the Military Government, Open the Country!" Supporters of the Tokugawa regime took the position that Tokugawa rule was in line with Japanese political tradition and that the legitimate role of the emperor had been maintained. They argued, furthermore, that trade and commerce would benefit the people and strengthen the state, giving it a more adequate base from which to defend itself.

As in so many cases in politics, the Tokugawa government executed a necessary policy at the cost of its own existence. Over the violent objections of many within the military class, Japan was opened to foreign intercourse. A decade later, the Tokugawa regime gave way to an imperial restoration, and political power gravitated into the hands of a small number of court nobles and younger *samurai,* many of them men of relatively low rank.

The issue of unification now became even more critical, and a complex medley of theses was voiced. The primitivists, with their arguments about unity via the pure Japanese route, continued to make themselves heard and felt, but they were no longer dominant. The ideological "main stream" that now developed might be labeled "enlightened conservatism." The leading slogan was, "A Powerful Military Force—A Rich Country." And how to achieve this goal? Out of a process of trial and error and with reliance upon a basically pragmatic approach, the ruling elite gradually developed a philosophy that interwove traditional and modern elements with considerable skill.

There was much that was sweeping, daring, and new in the programs that followed the Meiji Restoration. As in most revolutions (and despite the opinion of many scholars, we are inclined to regard the Restoration as a revolution), the first-generation revolutionary elite was essentially composed of young intellectuals, men bold in conceptualizing the basic problems and prone to accept major risks. By necessity, they were also broadly capable, since specialized skills—and the inevitable compartmentalization that accompanies them—were not yet available. The professional bureaucrats who generally compose the second-generation revolutionary elite in modern times were to come upon the scene at a later point. In this earlier era, indeed, there was an extraordinary interplay between the official and the intellectual —as a combination of functions in the same individual or an open dialogue between two individuals who had come to diverge functionally but who had the same class and intellectual antecedents. Such an interplay was not to recur in modern Japan, for as we shall note later, the "official" and the "intellectual" became separate and largely antagonistic categories. The former continued to carry the "main stream" ideology of "enlightened conservatism" forward; the latter operated increasingly as social critics, dissidents who advanced a variety of reformist or revolutionary creeds. The separation of the officials and the intellectuals after the early Meiji period did much to shape the ideological trends of the modern era. It provided the structural-functional basis for the great debates that were to follow.

The essential elements in the Meiji ideology of enlightened conservatism were nationalism, mass mobilization, and modern economic development. The first commitment was to a centralized nation-state, with the emperor serving as a primary symbol and source of unity. Initially, to be sure, there was some bold and unsuccessful experimentation with Western-style constitutionalism. In the years immediately after the Restoration, the ideas embodied in the American Constitution and in other documents of the "advanced" West were temporarily regarded as the secrets of Western power. In 1868, the first Japanese "constitution" was promulgated, a charter owing much to Western examples. Like the newly independent Asian states after World War II, however, Japan could not adapt Western political institutions to her requirements at that point. Failure was swift, and the first retreat from Westernism toward Japonism ensued less than a decade after the Restoration. The parallel between the Japanese experience in the 1870s and the broader Asian experience of the 1950s is a striking and significant one.

Japanese adjustment to this initial failure, however, was relatively rapid. Within a short time, a form of political modernization more appropriate to Japan was being fashioned. The first phase involved the creation of a more powerful central administration at the expense of the old feudal units. The progressive withering away of local autonomy was one of the most pronounced characteristics of the Meiji era. By World War I, local government in Japan had become an impotent adjunct of the national bureaucracy. This centralization of power was not accomplished without opposition. From the Satsuma Rebellion of 1877 to the Young Officers' Movement of the 1930s, protests were launched against the whittling away of local autonomy and on behalf of localist, agrarian values. Japanese modernization, however, dictated that the philosophy of centralism had to triumph.

Critical in its triumph was the institutionalized imperial court. There is no evidence that the Meiji leaders initially had a clear idea of the role of the throne despite their earlier loyalism. For a time, they even allowed public discussion of the respective merits of monarchism and republicanism. Gradually, however, the value of developing the imperial institution was appreciated. To use the throne as the center of loyalty, while keeping it relatively divorced from active politics had many advantages. It provided Japan with a permanent, untarnished father figure, a true link with the past who provided comfort and security at a time when many elements of the past were being torn loose from their moorings. Traditionalism, including the deepest reaches of the mythical past, could thus be brought to the service of the modern state. The emperor became a substitute for the charismatic leader so prominent in the modernization of most non-Western societies of a later period, a substitute that was more permanent, more deeply rooted in the culture, and more invulnerable to attack. The emperor represented the great triumvirate: father of his people, head of his nation, and benefactor of the world. Meanwhile, the real political genius of Japan was well served. That genius lay in oligarchy, not monarchical absolutism, and it had always been so. As the emperor cult was advanced, the modernizing oligarchy was given a powerful shield behind which to operate.

Only when these facts are fully appreciated can the existence of a "divine right of kings" theory in twentieth-century Japan be understood.[3] It is wrong to assume, as have some foreign observers, that Japanese conservative theory posited the existence of a living god. Whatever the ancient ties between Shintoism and a theocracy like that of Tibet, modern Japanese theory had somewhat different connotations. The Japanese term *kami,* which is translated as "god," cannot be equated precisely with that Western word. *Kami* means "a superior being," not a being who is omnipotent, omniscient, and omnipresent. Japanese conservative-nationalist thought, relying heavily upon the Shintoist classics, advanced the thesis that *all* Japanese were descendants of *kami* of various levels and that the emperor was descended from the Sun Goddess, highest on the hierarchical ladder. But if he differed in degree, he did not differ in kind from his people.

The concept of a chosen people was central to the conservative-nationalist ideology developed in the Meiji era. Certainly, such a concept was not unique to Japan. Indeed, most late-developing societies or emerging powers were in need of some such theory. The European states in their rise to global domination had their "white man's burden"; America had its "manifest destiny"; Germany its doctrine of Aryan supremacy. The emperor-people myth of modern Japan unquestionably advanced the basic goals of the political elite: The destruction of feudalism was rendered easier; the nation-state was created with speed and sureness; official exhortations for public sacrifices could be issued in the name of the emperor and thereby given added solemnity; and a doctrine of racial superiority helped to combat the inferiority complex that was always close to the surface of Japanese life, steeling the people for the enormous changes through which they had to pass.

It is sometimes asked, "How could so primitive a myth and so absolutist a doctrine have received the necessary support—both from the masses and from the elite—to have been serviceable in the twentieth century?" Those who ask such a question fail to understand the nature of our times. The advance of "science" and the development of "rational man" have been paralleled by the continuation of all manner of myths and by levels of irrationality at least equal to those of the past. In a period of unprecedented strain resulting from incredibly rapid change and from the first full-fledged introduction of the masses to politics, is this parallel not completely understandable? In the case of Japan, the emperor-people myth was so eminently suited to the initial stage of modernization, so easily applied, and so successful that political realism dictated "belief" on the part of the elite. Nor did one have to accept the same primitive level of interpretation as existed among the peasant class. As in the case of religion, the range of sophistication could be great. The emperor could be accepted as the symbol of a culturally advanced, homogeneous people, a representation of their lengthy historical traditions and their essential unity.

The emperor myth had its primary function in facilitating mass mobilization. Perhaps the most striking adjustment on the part of the Meiji leaders—themselves almost exclusively from the military class—was the acceptance of the common man as an integral part of state power. No doubt this acceptance was a result of observing the contemporary West, coupled with certain internal pressures that we shall shortly discuss. Whatever its wellsprings, however, the early acceptance and utilization of mass mobilization represent the true hallmarks of "enlightened conservatism." Within several years after the Restoration, the conscription system had replaced the old elitist system of *samurai* recruitment; land tax reforms had been carried out; compulsory primary education had been inaugurated; and other means had been found to involve the common man in the purposes of state. By means of elitist tutelage, the average Japanese was made aware of his obligations to throne and to country and was equipped in a variety of ways to carry out these obligations.

It was in connection with mass mobilization that the conservative-nationalist ideology incorporated certain egalitarian notes. The old feudal hierarchy had to be broken if the tasks of modern economic and political development were to be fulfilled. As a result, the new conservative theme became, "All are equal under the Emperor." It was argued that the emperor was father of *all* the people and that he could not possibly have gradations of love or concern for them—nor could they stand in differing degrees of responsibility before him. Everyone was equal before the throne. In such fashion, did Japanese conservatism accommodate itself to the requirements of a modern, mass society and succeed in injecting a strong egalitarian strain into what had been a theory of rigid hierarchy.

Modern economic development was the third commitment of the enlightened conservatives of the Meiji era. Once again, it is fascinating to study the transformation of an ideology that had been attuned to an agrarian, static society. Retaining much of the old system, the conservatives nevertheless managed to accommodate themselves to the concepts of industrial primacy and limitless economic growth. The old theory of static society, the endless wheel of life, was replaced by a doctrine of dynamic progress—and with this new doctrine, a true revolution had been wrought. What was the path by which this transformation could take place? Once again, the force of nationalism can scarcely be overestimated. *Samurai* and others were exhorted to enter industry and commerce "to save the nation." This patriotic appeal counteracted the social stigma that had long been attached to "the merchant" and softened the antimaterialist bias that was so prominent in traditional thought.

By the same token, the continuing role of the state in supervision of fiscal and economic policies could never be challenged. Not only was it sanctioned by the past, but it had current justification in the primary function that economic development was supposed to fulfill: a powerful military force —a rich country. Over time, a gradual metamorphosis took place. State enterprise shared the scene with private enterprise, and *laissez-faire* became a respectable concept, albeit one never fully applied. Most significantly, materialism penetrated the ethic of Japanese life, and the time would come when the concept of "a rising standard of living" would vie with that of "a rich country." But that development awaited the enlightened conservatism of the 1960's.

If conservatism in these forms constituted the main stream of Meiji ideology, we should not ignore the emergence of a "liberal" opposition that was more important than the retreating primitivist movement. It is not necessary here to chronicle the details of the power struggle that abetted the liberal cause within the Meiji oligarchy. Suffice it to say that one portion of the younger *samurai* group that came to power in 1868 adopted Western liberalism as its primary weapon in that power struggle, committing itself to some of its central themes and publicizing them to the nation at large.

Perhaps nothing fascinated Japanese intellectuals traveling abroad more than the workings of representative government. Men like Fukuzawa Yukichi and many others have recorded their amazement at this unique institution.[4] The Japanese, to be sure, had had experience with consultative councils composed of *daimyo*, but the idea of a parliament or congress based upon fairly extensive suffrage and having true legislative powers was quite novel. Consequently, it is not surprising that some Japanese observers suspected that such institutions held the real secret of Western power. By the early 1870s, moreover, the writings of John Stuart Mill, Rousseau, and Locke had become known to a small number of Japanese intellectuals, who eagerly translated them and made them available to the entire political elite.

In the course of the next decade, a movement known in Japan as the *jiyuminken undo* or "popular rights movement" spread throughout the prefectures, reaching its climax in the period 1880-1884. This period, incidentally, was one of severe deflation and economic troubles, circumstances that stimulated political unrest. In earlier times, traditional peasant riots and military campaigns by disaffected *samurai* to topple the government might well have been the primary responses. Indeed, both did occur in this general period. The Satsuma Rebellion of 1877, representing the last major effort of the feudalists to stem the tide of modernization, had been a serious threat to the central government, and, in the years of deflation, peasant riots were not uncommon. But a new element had been added. The Western ideology of liberalism had made an impact upon some of the dissidents, causing their protest movement to take a new form. In such a case one can see the creative role of a foreign ideology in influencing the nature of protest and response and thus in affecting the entire modernization process.

The central appeals of the Meiji liberals were for constitutionalism and representative government. Denied what they considered to be a legitimate share of power and deeply troubled by certain trends (feudal values died hard), they used the liberal creed as a weapon with which to attack the "monopoly of power" held by a small oligarchy. Their primary arguments were twofold: First, Western-style liberalism represented the wave of the future, and a society would be judged as civilized or backward depending upon its adjustment to the most advanced political forms; second, only an enlightened, participating people could make possible a powerful, wealthy state.

Both of these arguments are extremely revealing. The discussion of "What is civilized?" and "What is modern?" presaged a broader, more complex debate that would take place later. Of necessity, the Japanese intellectual wanted desperately to discern the future and catch up with the *avant-garde* of the world. Only then could he attain a basic intellectual equality, an opportunity to be creative on the furthest frontiers of man's knowledge, along with the intellectuals of the "advanced" world. (He was loathe to recognize the types of creativity open to the intellectual in a late-developing society.) We may define one special problem of the intellectual in a follower society as that of "teleological insight." Teleological insight is the capacity or, more accurately, the *assumed* capacity—to discern the future of one's own society by projecting it in accordance with conditions and trends in the "advanced" world. The impact of teleological insight upon creativity, political-social interrelation, and timing in the ideological development of the "emergent" world can scarcely be exaggerated.

In the second argument, the Meiji liberals were adjusting perforce to the central problem of their times, that of national unity. Against the conservative charge that it was too soon for representative government and that political parties were divisive instrumentalities, factions that would perpetuate the old personal and sectional differences, the liberals answered with the strongest argument they could muster: *Only* through constitutional, representative government could a nation become strong. Taking selected passages from Mill and others, they insisted that the most effective unity is achieved by an educated and participating people, that a citizenry involved in the political process is capable of establishing a far more meaningful national consensus than a small oligarchy that seeks to impose its will upon an ignorant, uninspired mass.

The Meiji liberals were divided into two main groups. The group led by Itagaki Taisuke and including such political theorists as Ueki Emori and Nakae Chomin were generally typed as the more radical elements. Their nucleus was composed of Tosa *samurai,* many of whom found the problems of transition extremely difficult, but from Tosa the movement spread to other prefectures, especially to areas of rural unrest. The patron saint of the Itagaki liberals was Rousseau. The more moderate wing of the Meiji liberal movement was led by Okuma Shigenobu, and Fukuzawa was its chief mentor. The Okuma faction included many young urban intellectuals from such schools as Keio and looked primarily to the British utilitarians for ideological guidance.[5]

It is interesting that Rousseau had an immediate appeal to a large number of Japanese intellectuals because of his ambivalence toward individualism, his emphasis upon the general will, his Janus-faced approach to democracy and modern totalitarianism. Above all, it was the age of nationalism for Japan, and the Meiji liberals along with other elements of Japanese society could not escape being influenced by this fact. Naturally, the emphasis was upon liberalism as a method of acquiring "civilization," national prestige, and power. The same stress was not placed upon the right of dissent, protection of minority rights, and the importance of the individual.

Nor was the imperial institution challenged. Liberal spokesmen contented themselves with arguing that, since the emperor always wanted what was good for his people, he would naturally favor constitutionalism and popular rights. The issue was not monarchy *versus* republicanism but rather monarchical absolutism *versus* constitutional monarchy. Even here, the liberals gave much ground. They did not openly question the imperial myth, and the very terms in which they put the issue—that the emperor, as father of his children, naturally desired their good—was a weak basis upon which to rest the liberal cause. In fact, the key issue quickly became not one of imperial powers but one of whether or not a given group was interposing itself between the emperor and his people, preventing the sovereign from knowing the truth, usurping his powers, and misruling.

This issue had recurrent echoes in modern Japan. It was an eminently logical part of the ideological pattern that was being formed. By definition, the emperor was "all-good" and had only the best interests of his people and his nation at heart. To him could be assigned no blame, and in fact he did not exercise political power without advice and consent. Those who were in power bore responsibility to him (not to the Diet) and ruled in his name. In actions where they were "wrong," therefore, they could be accused of interposing themselves between the throne and the people, keeping the former ignorant and blocking the legitimate rights of the latter. This charge provided the most convenient expression of dissidence in Japan throughout the entire period before World War II. To the liberals, it represented a cry for responsible government and party supremacy; to the radical right, it represented the appeal for another restoration and, in some extreme cases, the romantic notion of direct imperial rule.

That the issue should ultimately be framed in this manner suggests certain broader considerations of interest. Japan was the last of the "classical" modernizing states, the first of the "new" modernizers. This transitional status can be noted in both ideology and institutions. At the time of Japan's emergence into the universal stream, there was only one basic model of modernization—the classical, Western model. That model, to be sure, had significant variations. The advanced or emerging societies of Western Europe—notably Prussia but, in certain respects, England also—represented the more conservative types of the model, with monarchy, hierarchy, and other feudal legacies still prominently displayed. America represented the more radical type, with a high level of egalitarianism and social mobility, reflecting the absence of a feudal tradition. Naturally, Japan, her own feudal traditions so pervasive and so recently abandoned, turned to the more conservative variants of the classical model. But the Japanese problem remained essentially one of timing. In connection with the monarchical institution, for example, which she found so conducive to the unification process, Japan had only a few decades in which to cover the ideological ground that England had taken centuries to traverse. Even Prussia, with its more compressed time schedule, shared in the Western heritage sufficiently to make possible a transition to political modernism that was not too jarring. But Japan was forced by circumstances to move from a "divine right" theory to one of constitutional monarchy in a space of time far too brief to make an easy adjustment possible. At certain points in her modern history, indeed, there was probably a wider ideological spread in Japan than in any society of the so-called civilized world. Modernity was being encompassed in all of its reaches at a point when medievalism—even primitivism—was still very much alive.

Today the basic models of modernization are more numerous and more widely varied than when Japan first entered the universal stream. Whatever the variation between late nineteenth-century Prussia and America, it was scarcely as great as that represented by the Soviet Union and the United States today. Nor do these two societies exhaust the alternatives—or even the extremes. The current range reflects multiple differences in cultural antecedents, in timing of development, and in total resource patterns of the societies involved. One generalization seems possible, however: The classical political route starting with monarchical absolutism is now archaic. Nor is the main stream of the modernization movement flowing via the constitutional-democratic state at present. Obviously, if Japan were entering the process of modernization at this point in history, both ideology and institutions would take a radically different course from the one they took in the late nineteenth century, even if past traditions had somehow remained the same. Ideology is a product of the times. The timing of Japanese modernization dictated a modified classical approach, greatly complicated both by the speed of the required transition and by the emergence of new, rival ideologies reflecting the twentieth century while the Japanese modernization process was still in its initial stages.

Before turning to the second stage of Japanese modernization, let us suggest several other intriguing aspects of the relationship between ideology and modernization as revealed by the Meiji era. The early Meiji liberal movement clearly indicates some of the complexities involved in borrowing a foreign ideology. In the first place, certain key words must be selected, and there is always the possibility that for some reason these words will bear different connotations from those in the place of their origin. The combination of Chinese characters used to represent the term "political party," for example, included a character formerly associated with the idea of faction, clique, or band and having strong pejorative connotations. There were similar problems with a great many other concepts in the new ideology.

Another difficulty lay in the fact that ideas did not necessarily come in sequence, and, of course, there was the omnipresent gap between ideas and the social environment to which they had been brought. Certain intellectual complications were inevitable in discovering Mill before Rousseau and Bluntschli before both. The problem of distinguishing immediately between important and trivial Western thinkers was also difficult. Names and ideas flooded into Japan at a very rapid rate after 1870. Some men affixed themselves permanently to a given foreign writer, serving as his translator and "sponsor," rising or falling in accordance with his prestige. With careers at stake, new types of rigidity were created.

Despite these problems, however, it is inaccurate to suggest, as is often done, that the Meiji intellectuals (or those who followed) did not understand the essential elements of the foreign theories with which they sought to deal. Rarely was that the case. When they diverged in terms of emphasis or interpretation, it was ordinarily a conscious or unconscious effort to meet the demands of indigenous conditions. Another positive point is in order here. The Japanese intellectual and political elites were forced into the world stream at a relatively early point in the course of Western modernization, in comparison with African and other Asian societies. Consequently, they had a relatively long time in which to adjust to the successive waves that emanated from the Western modernization process. To put the matter simply, the Japanese intellectuals were allowed some three decades to conjure with Mill and Locke before they met Marx. Their counterparts in China and elsewhere did not have the same opportunity.

IV. Progress—Which Route?

At the beginning of the twentieth century, Japan could legitimately claim to have achieved unification, and indeed she had begun to exercise some hegemony over northeast Asia. China and Russia had been defeated militarily, and Korea was moving into the Japanese orbit. The concept, "A powerful military force—a rich country," seemed to be approaching reality, at least in statist terms. In a variety of other ways, Japan was also entering the charmed circle of "civilized, advanced" nations. In this era, the West had made universal its own broad definition of civilization and advancement: Science, economic development, and democracy—these elements at least were indispensable. *Progress* was to be measured for the *avant-garde* in these terms. For Japan, as for other "advanced" nations, the primary issue thus became, What is the best route toward achieving these goals, and what are their most superior forms?

The second era of Japanese modernization can be dated from approximately the First World War to the Manchurian Incident of 1931. Some brief setting must be provided for the ideological currents that flowed during this period. With respect to the criteria of progress noted above, Japan made substantial gains. World War I provided the opportunity for extremely rapid economic growth, and, at the close of that war, Japan had shifted from being predominantly an agrarian nation; industrial production henceforth accounted for more of the gross national product. And while the 1920s were uncertain and troubled in economic terms, industrial efficiency, technology, and production all increased. In part, this increase was due to the rapid absorption of science and its practical utilization: Technical education, all forms of mass media, and greatly improved communications were only a few of the methods by which the scientific revolution was put to the service of Japanese progress, with almost no obstacles and few delays.

In politics also, it could be argued that the trend was away from oligarchy and toward democracy. The *Genro*, the small group of early Meiji leaders that in later life served as an informal co-ordinating and supreme decision-making body, faded away as death overtook the first-generation revolutionaries. No similar body took its place. Instead, a working agreement of sorts had to be established among the parties, the civil bureaucracy, and the military. Such an agreement was almost always uneasy and was frequently upset. "Democracy" under the Meiji Constitution thus produced a fairly high level of political instability and popular discontent. Nevertheless, the political parties did establish themselves in a position of quasi-supremacy in the mid-20s, universal manhood suffrage was achieved, and civil liberties, while still limited in certain respects, became fuller than at any time in Japanese history. Indeed, the political trends involved multiple centrifugal tendencies that once again threatened, if they did not destroy, the organic unity so integral to the value-institutional system of the Meiji era. As this phase of modernization came to a close, an air of political disquiet hung heavily over Japan.

In this period, the political spectrum was broad indeed. Despite the general acceptance of "progress," the primitivists had not been totally vanquished. Indeed, stimulated by various economic and political problems involved in modernization, they returned to the struggle with renewed vigor, although they were never more than a small minority in terms of articulate elements.[6] In some of their positions, the primitivists resembled our own populists of the late nineteenth century. To them, the corruption and inequities of urban, industrial life were signs of the decadence inherent in modernism. They were quick to decry the materialism implicit in both capitalism and socialism and to assert that such groups as the politicians, the big businessmen, and the officials around the throne were all guilty of self-seeking, antisocial actions. In their view, the primary fault lay in the fact that Japan was following the false doctrines of the West, having forsaken the values and the way of life that were true to the Japanese spirit. By the close of this second phase of modernization, a small group of young

military officers and peasant lads had committed themselves to these doctrines with sufficient fervor to rock Japan in a series of assassinations and
attempted *coups d'état*. Their hope was a second restoration, with re-establishment of agrarian-military supremacy and purification of the Japanese people
through a purge of the old, corrupt elements and the full commitment of
everyone to the throne.

Since Japan was scarcely a generation away from feudalism, such
sentiments could still strike a responsive chord, especially among the rural
elements, who were often the victims of social injustice and whose education
generally went no further than the primary level. It was at this level that
neo-Confucian, nationalist indoctrination took its most intensive forms.
Japanese education operated on a simple plan: basic literacy and loyalty for
the lower levels, technical skills for the higher levels. But for all its vigor,
the primitivist movement had to be modified by some concessions to modernity
before it could be made acceptable to any significant number of the elite,
even the military elite. Power, after all, could not be built entirely out of
faith in the ancient way.

The more powerful sweep of the conservative movement, however, led
in other directions. The "right" wing of the conservative movement continued to resist democracy, while still committing itself to state power via
centralization, modern economic development, and mass involvement. In the
early part of this period, the central issue to which the right-wing conservatives
addressed themselves was that of imperial sovereignty. Men like Hozumi
Yatsuka and Uesugi Shinkichi, professors at Tokyo University, staunchly
insisted that the Meiji Constitution had to be interpreted literally and that the
emperor was a personal sovereign with unlimited powers.[7] They argued that
"progress" consisted in the perfection of the emperor's administration rather
than in any restrictions placed upon him. Men like Minobe Tatsukichi were,
in the right wingers' opinion, totally wrong in advancing an "organ" theory of
state in which the emperor became merely a part of the organism, bound by
the very charter that had been his gift to the people.

Nevertheless, it was the "enlightened" conservatives of this era who set
the basic tone, and, in their positions, they were moving toward a modernist
line. Indeed, by the close of World War I, many of this group had accepted
the "organ" theory of state set forth by Minobe. According to this theory,
sovereignty rested with the state itself, rather than with any individual or
collectivity like "the people." The state was a legal person in whom was
vested ultimate sovereign powers, with the emperor serving as an organ of
the state. This concept, derived essentially from German legalism, was
scarcely revolutionary, despite the bitter attacks launched upon it by the
fundamentalists. It was, however, a position that could conveniently serve
conservatives and liberals alike as a transitional movement away from a
"divine right" theory. It was a possible interpretation of the Meiji Constitution, an interpretation that could be defended against charges of *lèse
majesté* yet one that might ultimately be fitted into a system of parliamentary
supremacy. Thousands of young students aspiring to be officials were
taught the Minobe doctrine after 1910, and it figured prominently in the
civil-service examinations. The term "democracy," *minshushugi*, was not
used, even by the liberals, because it involved risk of a frontal challenge to

the imperial institution, but the enlightened conservatives of the Taisho period had begun to modify their earlier, more rigid notions.

It is also interesting to note the changes that were taking place in the interpretation of *kokutai*. For the conservatives, the Japanese way had come to encompass the concept of private property, as well as a centralized state unified by the imperial institution. It involved an ever increasing commitment to industrial, urban life and to the advancement of state power. In politics, the premium was upon a careful balancing of powers and responsibilities among the coequal elements of the polity—the parties, bureaucracy, and military services. Some conservatives, however, were prepared to accept party and parliamentary supremacy, and, in reality, a fierce power struggle within the conservative camp ensued after World War I. It was during this era that Japan had her closest rendezvous before World War II with constitutional, parliamentary government. She was hobbled, however, by a parliamentary tradition that was both too brief and too weak. The balance of power within the conservative movement was thus soon to change. But for this period, the enlightened conservatives defined progress in terms of mixed neo-Confucian, liberal values; a harmonious, organic society; and continued emphasis upon the industrial, technological revolution.

The outstanding exponent of democratic liberalism in this period was Yoshino Sakuzo, Professor of Political Science at Tokyo University.[8] It was Yoshino who advanced the thesis of *mimponshugi*, a concept of democracy that avoided the dangerous word "sovereignty" and could be translated literally as "the principle of the people being the base." Yoshino argued that the essence of constitutionalism throughout the world was respect for the people and the guarantee that government would be dedicated to their interests. He was certainly not alone in advancing the cause of human rights. In this era, a portion of the liberal movement began to shift from the earlier emphasis upon unity, power, and nationalism. Expressions like "self-respect, self-consciousness, and self-realization" flooded liberal writings. In this age, the liberal *avant-garde* sought to make individualism an acceptable and meaningful concept. Progress, for such liberals, was defined in terms of freedom, human dignity, and social justice.

It is most significant, however, that men like Yoshino and the hundreds of young intellectuals strongly influenced by his group were dedicated to democratic socialism. The discovery of the individual almost immediately led to a concern about social and economic justice. Some intellectuals approached this problem via the route of the German school of *Sozialpolitik,* but Yoshino and many others were attracted to the doctrines of Fabian socialism. Dedicated to parliamentary government, civil liberties, and political competition, they also regarded the capitalist system as basically exploitative and incompatible with the democratic creed. They saw Japanese capitalism, in particular, as monopolistic in character and closely wedded to the old sociopolitical order. Consequently, they equated democracy with "social democracy" and insisted that it was the only modern system for the twentieth century.

In this second phase of modernization, the radical "Left" emerged. The Anarchists constituted the spearhead and they represented a tiny but vocal contingent even before World War I. The advent of the Bolshevik

Revolution stimulated an interest in Marx, and, after the early 1920s, the Marxists became the primary representatives of the radical Left. In numerical terms, the influence of Marxism and Marxism-Leninism was not great. Such doctrines appealed only to a small number of individuals, almost wholly intellectuals. These particular intellectuals, however, often happened to be in strategic positions in the academic, literary, or journalistic world. Within a few years, Marxism was a force to be reckoned with in Japan. There was little likelihood that the Marxists would succeed politically, but they were having a pronounced influence on theory and criticism within the ranks of the intelligentsia.

What were the main sources of Marxian appeal?[9] Earlier remarks should be recalled here. In functional terms, the Japanese intellectual was now cast as a social critic, and Marxism was an excellent weapon of social criticism. Marxism, moreover, bore the label "scientific," and, in comparison with earlier methodologies in vogue, it offered certain central explanations for economic, social, and political phenomena that seemed to many to be "the truth." Contemporary liberal theory, in comparison, seemed old-fashioned—out of date and not attuned to "late-developing" societies. In addition to representing "science" and "truth," Marxism was also a philosophy of optimism. It promised that Japan would indeed catch up with the West, that it would go through the same stages and arrive at the same end —thus joining the advanced world. Many intellectuals were desperately anxious to end their sense of isolation, particularization, and "backwardness." Under such circumstances, the dialectic could be extremely comforting.

Furthermore, to the Japanese, Marxism was rich in theory, *pure* theory. Steeped as the Japanese intellectual often was in German philosophy, Marxism had a familiar ring. Indeed, one is tempted to suggest an admittedly risky thesis: In the very structure of the Japanese and German languages and the thought processes involved, there are some striking similarities. But in any case, the Meiji era was increasingly marked by the prominence of German philosophy, and, at the end of this era, Tokyo University had become a great citadel of German thought. The extensive interest of the Japanese intellectual in theory, however, does not need to be explained upon grounds of affinity to German philosophy or to abstractions in general. The factor of timing was also involved. Terribly conscious of being "behind," many Japanese intellectuals sought to catch up by borrowing "the latest, most advanced" ideology, especially one that provided cosmic explanations. There was, after all, no time for empirical research.

Traditionalism also aided the cause in certain respects. Not only did Japanese traditional thought have certain built-in anticapitalist, antiliberal biases. It also involved one attractive type of intellectual process: the appeal to authority and extensive textual criticism. The Marxist, like the Confucianist, could concentrate upon what the creators really meant and debate endlessly the precise meaning of words, phrases, and abstract concepts in the Marxian classics.

Even in this quasi-liberal era, the Marxist was often under heavy official pressure. Writing was relatively free, but action—as might have been expected—was carefully circumscribed. But in this period as in others, the dedicated Marxist was a true believer. His concept of progress was not difficult to define: the acceptance of Marxism as the only "scientific" methodology/ideology for Japan; the substitution of socialism for capitalism; and the movement from bourgeois democracy to dictatorship of the proletariat.

These concepts were the primary ideologies that vied for position and influence during the second phase of Japanese modernization. Perhaps the most impressive general trend was the great sweep toward Westernism that characterized this period. From "enlightened" conservatism to Marxism, borrowings from the West were extensive and sustained. Even on the Right, multiple evidences of Western penetration could be found. Except for a few scattered elements, Japan had accepted the Western concept of progress and had accepted also its hallmarks: science, modern economic development, and democracy. Perhaps the last principle was in greatest debate, but most conservatives accepted at least the idea of constitutional government. Acceptance of these broad principles, however, only opened the debate. "Science" had one meaning for the conservatives, quite another for the Marxists. There was a wide difference of opinion also on the meaning of "democracy" and on the appropriate economic system. Because the "enlightened" conservatives were dominant in this period, theirs was the prevailing ideology: a concept of *kokutai* that sought to retain as much of the familial, paternal ethics as possible; that conceived of the state in organic terms; that accepted the free-enterprise system without abandoning the notion of the state as an over-all supervisory, regulatory body; and that espoused a modified parliamentary system.

V. Identification and Acceptance

The third phase of Japanese modernization began about the time of the Manchurian Incident in 1931. In the background lay a protracted and serious economic crisis. By 1930, agrarian debt had reached nearly six billion *yen*. Distress in the rural areas was widespread. Urban unemployment was also a serious problem. As a result of recurrent difficulties, a program of industrial rationalization had been undertaken. Many small and medium industries had been amalgamated or eliminated. Naturally, these developments had their political repercussions. A heavy assault upon the "old order" was underway even before the opening of Japan's undeclared war upon China. Parties and parliament were repeatedly denounced as corrupt and decadent. Political leaders were sharply criticized, and a series of assassination attempts took place, some of them successful. Japan was involved in a mounting political storm, and soon the trend toward militarism became apparent.

In this third phase, the primary political issues might be termed those of identification and acceptance. Since the Restoration, the Japanese had been under a forced march; for its time, Japanese modernization was the most rapid and extensive change in the world. Furthermore, it had involved a severe wrenching process for many, despite the remarkable degree to which traditional elements had been adapted to new requirements. In recent decades particularly, "Westernism" in all its forms had poured into Japan. In the *après-guerre* period of the early Twenties, even the flapper had made an appearance in Tokyo. The "modern *giru*" was symptomatic of the deep cultural impact of contemporary Western fads, especially in urban centers.

When the excesses of this era had accumulated and Western institutions showed signs of weakness or failure, a sharp reaction was inevitable. Once again, the pendulum swung away from the West. Once again, a search was undertaken for a "true" and "valid" indigenous ideology that would give the Japanese people renewed confidence in themselves, halt dangerous divisive trends, and "solve" the burning problems of the times. In one sense, this search was a quest for identity. The questions, "Who are we? What are our values and our purposes?" were repeatedly raised, and, as we have indicated, there was a pronounced retreat from Westernism, an insistence that Japanese *integrity* had to be recaptured. Out of the compartmentalized man, who was one-third Western, one-third Japanese, and one-third hybrid, had to be built a whole man, integrated around genuine, internalized values.

A central paradox, however, was involved in this era. On the one hand, a renewed nationalist thrust dominated the period, with Japan turning inward upon herself, looking back to her own history for a satisfying ideology. On the other hand, Japan sought, by making use of her accumulated power, to play a more important role, particularly in Asia. In ever increasing degree, therefore, she looked outward and, not content with mere power, sought acceptance from other peoples, especially peoples of the "have-not" world. This drive for acceptance and hegemony in Asia ran concurrently with the quest for identity, and both figured prominently in the ideological struggles of the militarist era.

In many respects, this period was suited to the resurgence of traditionalism in "pure" or "modified" forms. Perhaps the traditionalists may be divided into two or three basic categories. First, there were the true primitivists who represented thoroughgoing antimodernism. They wanted to strike out against the whole complex of industrialization, urbanization, and liberalization that served as the core of the modernization process. To them, this complex, so long the dominant trend in Japanese society, was at the root of such problems as disunity, corruption, and massive insecurity. Modernism was a Western-derived concept, incompatible with the basic nature of Japan and fundamentally immoral. The primitivists were not in complete agreement about patron saints or solutions, however. Interestingly enough, some of their leading spokesmen sought answers outside the framework of Japanese culture alone, looking elsewhere in Asia. Men like Gandhi were often praised as representatives of nonmaterialistic ideologies that drew their main sources of support from indigenous cultures. Gandhi's championing of cottage industry, rural self-sufficiency, and political decentralization was hailed as a position in basic conformity with the great Asian tradition.[10] Not all primitivists, however, were Pan-Asiatic. Many found support for these same concepts in the recesses of Japanese history. Insisting upon a second restoration, they called for the re-establishment of the soldier-peasant alliance that had carried within it the essence of Japanese uniqueness and the well-springs of Japanese greatness. Attacking all "foreign" ideologies as deficient in qualities of "spiritualism," they called for a sacred war against the corruption of the Japanese soul.[11]

Defeat for the primitivist ideology was inevitable because the primitivists could never come squarely to grips with the realities of power in the modern

world. Their own literature revealed the central paradox, as we have suggested. Recognizing the indispensable need for unity and strength, they
insisted upon complete and unswerving allegiance to the throne, yet, in
socioeconomic-political terms, they proposed to undermine unity and power
with a system that would have divorced their society completely from all
important aspects of modernity. Their influence, however, made itself felt
in the more realistic and dominant conservative ideology of this period, as
we shall note.

Another ideology carrying extensive traditional overtones was that of
national socialism. The most famous national socialist of this period was
Kita Ikki.[12] His *Outline of Principles for the Reconstruction of Japan,* originally written in 1919, became a bible for the so-called radical Right. The Young
Officers Movement, which disrupted Japanese politics repeatedly in the
period between 1930 and 1936, probably owed more in ideological terms, to
Kita than to any other individual. Kita's basic goal was to combine nationalism and socialism in such fashion as to enable Japan to lead a revolutionary
new Asia that could stand against Western imperialism. This leadership, in
Kita's mind, was not to take "old, imperialist" forms but was to be based
upon the stimulus of a national socialist movement. Asia could not be
liberated from Western imperialism without also being liberated from the
Western value-institutional structure that had been imported with Western
power. But while Kita decried imperialism, his doctrines fitted in with the
general concept of internal reform-external expansion that had been the hallmark of the "radical Right" since Meiji days.

Kita's ideas upon *kokutai* and the emperor system were sufficiently unorthodox at one point to cause him to be labeled "subversive" by the conservative elite. He regarded the state as a "living organism," an entity
transcending others, and the only legitimate source of sovereign power.
He believed that the emperor and the people should be on equal footing
with respect to rights and powers, although the former should be the great
symbol of unity and continuity. "Socialism in one state" expressed Kita's
objective in one sense, for he believed that Japanese socialism should reflect
the unique historical traditions and current conditions of Japan and should
pay homage to the fact that *national* competition was at least as potent as
class competition in the modern world. Yet at the same time, Kita did
see a successful Japanese revolution as a model—and a shield—for the
rest of Asia.

Like the primitivists, the national socialists were defeated, although not
without a serious struggle. To many younger elements of Japanese society,
particularly those from agrarian or military backgrounds, the idealism implicit
in national socialism provided a substitute for the idealism involved in
Marxism. The concepts of Pan-Asianism were more meaningful than the
earlier, vaguer doctrines of internationalism. And here was a socialist movement that did, indeed, concentrate upon capturing and using nationalism.
Unquestionably, racial issues were also involved. Two words went together
in the vocabulary of the radical Right—white imperialism. The call for the
advance of the yellow and brown races aimed at the undercurrent of racial
prejudice that always lay near the surface of Japanese society, especially in
periods of trouble.

The national socialists, however, were entrapped in several paradoxes not easy to resolve. Despite the strong antiwhite, anti-Western element that could be found in their doctrines, they, like the liberals before them, had borrowed heavily from the West. German Nazi doctrine had a pronounced influence in this period, as German constitutional and social doctrines had had in earlier times. Such concepts of the national socialists as "the uniqueness of the Japanese polity," glorification of war and the spartan life, and racial superiority all found support in fascist doctrine quite as much as in traditional thought. Fascism also lent negative support: It proclaimed the decadence of Western liberalism and thereby encouraged the Japanese national socialists in their belief that Europe itself was abandoning liberalism and turning to a new ideology.

The process of "catching up" still preoccupied many Japanese intellectuals, including some of those who figured prominently in the national socialist movement. Yet it was not possible to duplicate the Italian or German fascist experience. The very emperor system that the radical Right ultimately had to uphold made this duplication impossible. No *Führer* could emerge, gathering unto himself the masses, eclipsing the emperor in symbolism and power. Under such conditions, the creation of a true mass movement was almost impossible. Ironically, in the final analysis, the national socialists found the throne as much an obstacle to their basic goals as had the democratic liberals before them. But, like the primitivists, the national socialists also made their imprint upon Japanese thought in this period. Conservatism was forced to accommodate itself to the pressures from the Right.

This analysis leads us to the dominant ideology of the times, a refurbished conservatism that sought to protect itself against socialist onslaughts by retreating from Westernism and taking refuge in neoclassical doctrine, while at the same time retaining a full commitment to the vital economic components of modernization. Increasingly, the great Confucian values were stressed: the superiority of an ethical system drawn from familial relations and the importance of stressing "proper conduct" over self-gain, morality over materialism. In politics, an effort was made to return to the "true meaning" of the Meiji Constitution. The Minobe thesis was rejected as false. Sovereignty lay with the emperor, and all organs of government existed to assist him in his rule. Parliamentary supremacy and the competitive party system thus became incompatible with Japanese constitutionalism and the unity of the Japanese people. At the same time, the conservatives forwarded the process of turning Japan into a mass society. Acknowledging the supreme importance of popular loyalty and support, they did not rely solely upon Confucian rescripts or imperial New Year's Day proclamations. Going back into the ancient roots of their society, they reconstructed "neighborhood associations," small group organizations that could serve as vehicles for the execution of national policy. In such movements as the Patriotic Labor Movement for the workers and the Imperial Rule Assistance Association, the common man of Japan found himself more involved in politics and organization, more part of a mass movement than at any time in his history.[13]

Clearly, the conservatives of this era did not subscribe to antimodernism in economic terms. While some decentralization of industry was carried out for strategic and economic reasons, the general trend toward industrialization and urbanization continued. Heavy industry was naturally emphasized because of the need to augment state power. And in the international arena, Japan concentrated upon two objectives: leadership in Asia and alliance with the Axis powers. It was in this area that the conservatives accepted many of the radical Right's theses. Japan was a victim of Western white imperialism, a member of the great "have-not" portion of the world. Its logical mission was to lead the Asian world in an assault upon Western control, and, for these purposes, it could align itself with those powers in Europe who were seeking to topple the old order and to preserve the new one against communism. Since Japan was an Asian nation, its mission was to save Asia both from communism and from Western imperialism.

Japanese conservative ideology in this period was largely fashioned by senior military and bureaucratic representatives, with a small number of quasi-intellectuals in their service. The preponderance of intellectuals, however, remained silent or confined itself largely to narrow, technical matters. Liberalism and Marxism were forced into precipitous retreat. In vain the liberals argued that Japan risked isolation from the Western world and ultimately defeat. In vain they insisted that modernism and progress could not be served by premodern political values, by myths that defied science and logic. In a curious way, the liberals suddenly found themselves labeled "out-of-date," passé. In addition, they were frequently regarded, along with the Marxists, as unpatriotic or subversive. In this period, when Japanese nationalism carried all before it, the antiliberal wing of the conservatives maintained secure control of nationalist symbols. It was they who determined the line between patriotism and antinational acts, between support for *kokutai* and attempts to undermine it. Both liberals and Marxists fought a losing battle against the nationalist tide, and a number ended by joining it.

In retrospect, it is easy to discern the dominant answer of this era to such questions as "Who are we? What are our values and our purposes?" As spelled out by the military-bureaucratic conservatives, the answer could be outlined: "We are an Asian people who have much in common with other peoples of the Far East. Yet we are also unique, molded by a lengthy historical tradition that is fully shared by no one else. To be ourselves, we must be true to that tradition. In recent times, many Japanese have become superficial, fragmented, and confused because they have sought to forsake their own traditions and follow various foreign innovations. Inevitably, they have failed because, in the final analysis, ideology cannot be separated from way of life, and this integrity relates to the whole cultural complex that shapes national character and capacity. We can only follow an ideology that conforms to our national character. Theories like Marxism that posit universal identities and ignore cultural differences are basically false. We must not be subverted by Westernism in any form, be it liberalism, communism, or fascism. Our genius lies in perfecting the harmonious interrelation of all groups and classes under the throne, of applying familial ethics to state relations. This way is the only way in conformity with our traditions and character. At the same time, we must continue to harness Western-style technology to the support of our way of life. In advancing this combination lies our potential contribution to an independent Asia. Our primary international goal must be acceptance by our fellow Asians through our championing of the cause of the colored races of the world."[11] (It is interesting to note that Communist China has currently undertaken this role, since Japan's power has faded.)

In essence, the conservative doctrine of the military era reverted to the principle of Western technology combined with Japanese values. Oblivious to the fact that many of its "Japanese values" were themselves impregnated with Westernism, the conservatives stressed neo-Confucianism, cultural relativism, and the importance of restoring "genuineness" to Japanese thought and character. This era represented another great pendulum-swing away from Westernism and an attempt to rely anew upon traditional values. Indeed, the supreme paradox of the conservatives during this period was their simultaneous stress upon uniqueness and superiority—their high quotient of particularism—and the ardent quest for Asian leadership, their obsession with acceptance.

In all these matters, Japan was scarcely alone among the nations of the world, which makes the paradox even more interesting and complex. Modernization had everywhere reached a stage in which the liberal ideology was being subjected to an unprecedented attack. In many cases, that attack had a strong nationalistic and particularistic flavor. Japan, for all her "uniqueness," was thus an inextricable part of the universal stream she had joined more than a half-century earlier. It is intriguing to note that her primary Asian opponents of this period—Chiang Kai-shek and his Kuomintang— were engaged in a similar retreat from Westernism and a similar return to Confucianism, an attempt to find unity and security in the indigenous past after a period of extensive Westernization. But neither Tojo's Japan nor Chiang's China could escape from the compelling requirements of the modern world. Survival demanded acceptance of "progress," and progress involved at the least science, modern economic development, and political power based upon the effective mobilization of the masses. And because they could not meet these requirements either in ideological or technical terms, Tojo and Chiang were both to disappear shortly from the world stage, as their particular forms of conservatism passed from the scene.

VI. Democracy

All events after 1945 conspired to make democracy the primary political issue of the times for Japan, the topic around which basic ideological disputation took place. For the first time in her history, Japan was a subjugated nation. The primary victor, furthermore, was the United States, the vital center of the world liberal movement. The occupation was almost wholly an American one, and one of its basic objectives was the establishment of Japanese democracy. The atmosphere was conducive to change. Immediately after the war, old leaders and institutions were subjected to an unprecedented attack. They had failed and in their failure had been revealed as shallow and "backward." Misery was rife, and the appalling conditions could only be blamed upon those who had misled the people in the past. The stage was set for a new era of extensive Westernization.

Perhaps the key question was, "What kind of democracy is appropriate for

Japan?" Despite the fact that the United States controlled Japan in this era, the Left took a strong initiative in shaping the initial ideological trends. Both consciously and unconsciously, America promoted a radical tide, as she had done earlier in the Meiji era. Marxism enjoyed a rapid rise in popularity, especially among the intelligentsia. Who had a better claim to omniscience concerning the fate of Japanese militarism than the Marxists, it could be argued, and who had a greater purity with which to enter the postwar political arena? The Marxists were the only group that had opposed militarism and the conservative-nationalist doctrines of the prewar period completely and without quarter. What is more, Marxism could now operate in an environment of unparalleled freedom upon a people made desperate by economic conditions and the collapse of old values. When these facts are added to the intellectual appeal of Marxism suggested earlier, the rise of the Left can be understood.

How did the Marxists regard the problem of Japanese democracy? Within Marxian circles, there were a number of ideological differences, some of them significant. Such groups as the Left Socialists, the *Rono* faction of Yamakawa Hitoshi, and the Communists (themselves divided on occasion) all claimed to be Marxists, yet they rarely agreed on specific policies, and there were also important doctrinal differences among them. In general terms, however, the Marxian view of Japanese democracy may be set forth as follows: As a result of American tutelage, Japan has been projected into the bourgeois stage of democracy more fully than was possible in the prewar period. At the same time, however, Japan is not a truly sovereign nation, for it must be considered either an American colony (Communists) or heavily under the influence of American policy (Left Socialists).

This analysis provides the base from which Marxian policies develop. The need is to combine a movement from bourgeois to proletarian democracy with a national liberation movement that will eliminate American control or authority. The first movement, that of establishing proletarian democracy, can best be achieved according to the Communists by a United Front of all "progressive" elements, including the proletariat, the peasants, and the national *bourgeoisie*. Whether evolutionary or revolutionary tactics are necessary can only be determined by events. In the meantime, the Diet should be used along with all other opportunities granted by the Constitution of 1947 to forward the Communist cause. The Left Socialists are much more ambivalent with respect to both tactics and strategy. The continuing Marxist influence upon them causes them to define democracy in class terms and to regard this period as one of "bourgeois democracy." They regard the only appropriate democracy for Japan as one led by the working class and involving a socialist economy. They are committed to parliamentarism, however, and oppose both a United Front with the Communists and any forcible overthrow of the existing political structure. In transition at the moment, the Left Socialists can be regarded as Marxist revisionists.

Nearly two decades after World War II, Marxism remains a formidable ideological force in Japan, both in academic and political terms. While the Communist movement is weak and divided, the Socialist Party is still under the control of Marxist revisionists, and it garners close to one-third of the vote in national elections. Marxian influence is also appreciable in *Sohyo*, the dominant trade union federation, and it is still to be seen in a variety of forms in academic circles. Despite these facts, however, the signs are now clear that Marxism as an ideological force in Japan has passed its peak and is in decline. There may be many twists and turns, some temporary revivals, and, if world conditions were to move decidedly in the direction of Communist power, conceivably a reversal of the present trend. But if internal conditions remain the controlling factor, it is very unlikely that Marxism will recapture its former peak strength.

What is the reason for the decline of Marxism as an ideological influence? In the broadest sense, the answer lies in the fact that Japan has reached a stage of modernization that makes her a post-Marxist society. Marxism-Leninism has now evolved a tactics and strategy that, together with its underlying ideological principles, give it maximum applicability both *intellectually* (in terms of its relative truth) and *tactically* at a given stage in the development of a given society. In these terms, each society of the "emerging" world has a pre-Marxist, potential-Marxist, and post-Marxist era. The pre-Marxist era is that period when, for a variety of reasons, internal conditions are not suitable for Marxism to constitute a major influence—as for example, the absence of a modern-educated, dissident intelligentsia. The period of potential Marxism is that period when internal conditions are most conducive to the maximum impact of Marxism or, more precisely, when the combination of indigenous-exogenous factors is most conducive. It is possible that, in some societies, indigenous conditions will reach the point of maximum receptivity at a moment not propitious from an international standpoint and therefore that Marxism will fail in its thrust toward power because of an imbalance of indigenous-exogenous elements.

But why can Japan be considered a post-Marxist society? In the last ten years, Japanese society has enjoyed phenomenal economic growth. Poverty has ceased to be a class problem, and social mobility, while still limited, has greatly increased. As one consequence, the simplistic theories of Marxism have come to have progressively less validity in a socioeconomic structure marked by growing complexity. In sheer methodological terms, new techniques emanating from Western social science are vastly more "scientific," "advanced," and appropriate to the emerging problems than the approaches or answers that Marxism can provide. This fact has psychological implications for a Japanese intelligentsia that is increasingly sophisticated and specialized. To be Marxist is to be old fashioned, and now, as always, the Japanese intellectual wants to catch up, to join the *avant-garde*.

It is conceivable that Marxism may at some point undertake a massive restructuring of its basic political and methodological tenets—a modernization program of its own—in order to come abreast of the advanced society. Indeed, the Italian Communist Party in particular is making such an attempt. But *Asian* Marxism, dominated currently by the Chinese Communists, is still the "science" of revolution and the first climb out of backwardness. To this fact must be added the fact that Japanese Marxists, largely undefiled by power, continue their quest for "pure theory," showing little interest in adjustment to the realities of the new Japan. So far as most Japanese Marxists are concerned, the gap between ideology and reality must be bridged by faith, a faith so long held in most cases as to have acquired the force of tradition.

It is in this sense among others that the "pure" Marxists take on a strongly conservative hue.

If the "radical Left" is not in the ascendancy, neither is the "radical Right." It too has seen history move away from it as the modernization process has advanced. Some would argue that no portion of the radical Right could long have maintained itself in power and that its periodic surges forward were merely short-term responses to desperate conditions, responses that, viewed in historical perspective, could only be regarded as momentary, transitional interludes. The inexorable demands of modernity, it is argued, serve in the final analysis to defeat a force so encrusted with irrationality and tradition. But this argument is debatable. Ours is an era of unprecedented pressure and tension, one in which the premium upon speed and change is enormous. Many of the old forms of solace or security, such as those provided by religion or the family, have been seriously eroded. There is ample room for a dramatic secular doctrine geared to the most deeply rooted fears, prejudices, and myths of the common man and closely identified with his folk-culture. Modern politics has demonstrated conclusively that mass mobilization is essential to success, and few methods of mobilization are more effective than those that aim for the emotions and cater to kin-tribal patterns of identification. However extreme the particular forms these appeals took in prewar Japan, their impact cannot be denied.

The demise of the radical Right is directly connected with a drastic shift in the foreign and domestic conditions that previously had fostered it. On the international scene, fascism has been destroyed as a major world force, and there has been a general trend away from the type of race-culture-tradition oriented ideologies so prevalent before 1945. Nationalism remains strong everywhere, but it is now forced to take on a much stronger commitment to universalism, "science," "democracy," and modernity. When this fact is coupled with events in Japan, the decline of the radical Right is completely understandable. Defeat was itself associated primarily with this group, and myths so gross could only be perpetuated in the context of success. There was little "come-back" capacity in such doctrines as "divine right."

But in addition, the entire institutional structure of the Japanese polity has shifted away from the radical Right. Its major pillars of support have been smashed; its line of argument rendered totally meaningless and obsolete. The fact that the revolution was conducted under American auspices made it none the less telling. The imperial institution has been restructured beyond repair, and consequently the elaborate mythology surrounding it has been obliterated. The educational system, beginning at the all-important primary level, has been turned against the very ideology it once underwrote. A new generation of Japanese has grown up emphatically disbelieving the doctrines so fundamental to the primitivists and the conservatives of the militarist era.

Indeed, postwar Japanese conservatism faced an initial crisis: What was it to conserve? Conservative ideologies of the immediate past had been antidemocratic and were now passé. The old pressure groups, which had supported the primary conservative themes, had either been restructured or drastically reduced. The military had disappeared as a social class. Land reform—and subsequent agrarian prosperity—had greatly altered the character and proclivities of the rural classes. In sum, both the political and the socioeconomic underpinnings of the radical Right had been destroyed.

Ideological disputation in postwar Japan has thus taken place within a gradually narrowing range, with the radical Right in oblivion and the radical Left in decline. This narrower range of disputation is not the product of coercion but the result of the advancing modernization process. Marx's dictum that a heightened class struggle would accompany modern economic development has once again been challenged by events. Taking a longer perspective, one can say that Japan has moved from an era when ideological disputation was contained through state power and other "artificial" means to an era when it can be contained through "natural" developmental processes. At the same time, the role of ideology in society is also changing. The old tendency to conceive of ideology as a total way of life or an abstract cosmic theory into which all phenomena should be fitted has begun to fade away. Only among the Marxists and a few conservatives does this concept remain strong. In this sense, it is possible to speak of the decline of ideology in Japan, as elsewhere in the "advanced" world.

It is doubtful, however, that ideological decline is a proper conceptualization of these continuing trends. The primary political questions that occupy attention on the domestic front may be defined as operative, procedural ones: How should the government act toward the opposition? What are the legitimate boundaries of minority action? What constitutes free and fair elections? How are the political parties to be brought closer to the people? Yet these "procedural" problems lie at the very heart of the great political issue—What is democracy, and how can it be made meaningful for Japan? Once again, after a period of excessive Westernization, Japanese society is experimenting with the supremely difficult task of shaping and integrating largely exogenous institutions and ideas with her indigenous society. The problem of Japanese democracy is in large measure the problem of the gap between *politics* and *society,* the gap between the principle of majoritarianism and the practice of decision-making through consensus, between the principle of open political organizations available to the masses and the practice of closed leader-follower factional groups, between the principle of political competition and the practice of a one-and-one-half party system with a permanent majority and minority. Under these circumstances, technical, "procedural" issues are central to ideological confrontation.

In the area of foreign policy, ideology in its more classical forms prevails, for in this area it is easier to argue in terms of comprehensive belief-value patterns at an abstract or at least a generalized level. The issue, for example, of whether one best upholds democracy by joining "the free world" or by standing aloof from alliance with either "camp" in the Cold War can be developed into a general debate on universal values. Suddenly one finds the "great issues" being argued: the "new" *versus* the "old" democracy; statism *versus* individualism; welfare *versus* freedom. It is understandable that the foreign-policy arena is the last stronghold of classical ideology, for it is precisely in this arena that the cultural-developmental range is greatest and consequently that the "way of life" issue transcends "procedural" issues.

A new conservatism is rapidly being fashioned in Japan. It is being shaped by modernists who are increasingly aware of the new science of power and its dictates. With a few reservations, they accept constitutional, representative government, political competition, and substantial civil liberties. In pragmatic fashion, they operate in such a manner as to stay in power. This pragmatism has required them to pay increasing attention to public opinion and, on occasion, to be bound by it even when it does not conform to their own desires. The quotient of statism in the philosophy of the modern Japanese conservative remains relatively high, yet this statism does not interfere basically with support for "private enterprise." In economic affairs, the role of government is to promote, to supervise, and to protect the vital industrial sector of the economy. The fiscal and economic powers of the state should be used to the extent necessary to maintain rapid economic development. At the same time, modern conservatives are committed to the principle of the welfare state, albeit on a much more modest and gradual scale than their socialist opponents. Government *for* the people, as we have noted, is sanctioned by Japanese tradition, as well as by necessity for political survival in the contemporary world. In the area of politics, as suggested earlier, there remains a gap between commitment and practice. Bureaucratic officiousness, elitist tutelage of the "masses," closed political associations, and contempt for the opposition all remain in some degree as legacies of the past. Yet none of these concepts or practices is defended intellectually. Conservative ideology currently lies on the side of democracy.

The socialist opposition today is deeply divided. A minority adheres fully to social democracy and is strongly influenced by trends in the British Labour Party and similar movements. To this group, democracy must be defined in social, economic, and political terms. The "new" democracy is humanistic, socialist, and parliamentary. The majority of the socialists, as noted earlier, can be classified as Marxist revisionists at present, with the trend away from many central Marxian positions. With considerable reservations, the Marxist revisionists, like the conservatives, accept constitutional, representative government, political competition, and substantial civil liberties. There remains a significant ambivalence, to be sure. As noted earlier, the old Marxian concept of "class" lingers on, as do abstractions like capitalism and socialism, "bourgeois democracy" and "proletarian democracy." Some Left Socialists seem committed to the use *and* abuse of parliament in the same fashion as the Communists. There can be no question also that the Left, having been continuously out of power and faced with no legacy of policy responsibility, finds it more tempting and more possible to be ideologically "pure." In this sense, the Left Socialists have remained more committed to ideology in its classic form—an identification of ideology with the way. They have therefore been less susceptible to public opinion, less flexible, and less capable of attuning themselves to the rapidly changing society in which they live.

The concern of the Left Socialists with ideology helps to explain the heavy emphasis they place on the issue of foreign policy. Here the broad issue has been alliance with the West *versus* neutralism. In contrast to the conservative desire for identification with the "advanced" world, the socialists have sought their primary identification with the Afro-Asian world. Both of these positions, as we have noted, have had a lengthy tradition in modern Japan, and both are susceptible to ideological "classification." In policy terms, of course, Japan is best served currently by extensive identification with both worlds.

Whatever their ambivalence, however, the Socialists have, in recent years, repeatedly averred their philosophic commitment to evolution rather than to revolution. They have pledged full support to the parliamentary system, and they have abjured any United Front with the Communist Party. While continuing to adhere to the idea of a "class" party in theory, they have begun to re-examine the role, status, and structure of the party, probing the possibilities of a broader, national base. In sum, despite a gap between performance and theory and some theoretical ambivalence, the primary intellectual commitments of the Socialists are increasingly in the direction of constitutional, representative government. To a greater extent than at any time in Japanese history, the ideological gap between major contending forces has narrowed.

VII. Conclusion

There is no intention here to assert that every aspect of the Japanese experience with ideology and modernization will find parallels in the experiences of other follower societies. On the contrary, at one level, the differences are likely to be much more striking than the similarities. The importance of Japan, however, is to indicate the type of logical relationship between ideology and modernization that tends to accompany the modernizing process. In conclusion, let us set forth briefly some of the salient points suggested in this essay:

1. At all stages, ideology has played a dynamic and creative role in the Japanese modernization process. Tradition supported this role, and successful modernization demanded it. Schooled in Confucianism, the modernizing oligarchy of Meiji Japan had been trained to justify and relate policies to a way of life, and ideology took on this connotation in their minds. Naturally, Japan entered the universal stream with certain ideological proclivities drawn from the past. The degree to which new ideas from abroad caused a restructuring of the value-institutional system of the Meiji era, however, is striking. The attitudes and policies of both the government and the opposition were dramatically affected. Whatever its links with the past, the Meiji Constitution was the first great monument to the impact of exogenous ideas and to the supreme importance that Japanese leaders attached to providing their people with a way of life properly adjusted to accommodate the new goals.

2. The timing of the entrance of Japan into the universal stream had an effect upon her interrelated ideological development and modernization that can scarcely be exaggerated. Japan entered the world at a time when there was only one basic model of modernization, the classical liberal model. It was thus necessary to attempt adaptation of that model. Inevitably, Japan found that the modification of the model most suited to her own conditions was that of the Prussian system because of a broad similarity of timing and problems.

At a relatively early point in her modernization process, however, Japan began to feel the impact of the forcible, new challenges that were being raised against classical liberalism. Many of these challenges coincided with the natural points of resistance implicit in Japanese tradition or current circumstances. Thus—in rough conformity with the world pattern—she began an ideological retreat from liberalism after a relatively brief and partial experimentation. The stimulus of Western fascism replaced that of Western liberalism in the militarist era.

After World War II, every significant elite in the world paid homage to "democracy." It remained only to define the term and to defend one's definition. Once again, Japan followed or was forced to follow the universal stream. At this point, however, Japan was no longer a "backward" nation just emerging into independence and beginning the process of economic development. She had a legacy of nearly 100 years' modernization, and consequently her ideological proclivities were vastly different from those of "democratic Africa."

3. Each broad phase of modernization produced a central issue or closely related cluster of issues around which ideological disputation tended to center and that shaped, in considerable measure, the characters of all competitive ideologies. The issue of unification thus dominated most of the Meiji era, and conservative and liberal doctrines alike were attuned primarily to it. The issue of progress—quite possibly the most revolutionary Western idea to be introduced in Asia—was a key to the second phase of Japanese modernization, and widely divergent answers were provided, indicating the increasingly centrifugal tendencies that were now developing as a result of the modernization process. The deep insecurities and the rising problems of this period led to the issue of identification and acceptance that colored the militarist era. It was via this route that, after defeat, Japan came to the issue of democracy.

4. Like all follower societies, Japan faced a number of added complications in her modern ideological development. Throughout the entire period, she was engaged in a great pendulum-like swing toward and away from Westernism, a movement interactive with, yet in some degree separate from, specific idcological trends. In her broadest reactions to the West, Japan followed the historic stages characteristic of most other non-Western societies: rejection, selection, and synthesis. But within the latter two stages, there was much oscillation. Periods of extensive Westernization were followed by periods of retreat during which "excesses" and "incongruities" were violently attacked and the quest for "the true Japanese way" undertaken. One can discern at least four great swings of the pendulum in the hundred years that followed 1860.

Meanwhile, the task of synthesis posed enormous problems, for an attempt was being made to adjust borrowed values and institutions to a complex of indigenous conditions and to keep their movement more or less synchronized. The problem was multifaceted: Speed and degree of absorptive capacity varied from institution to institution, and this variation, quite as much as the relationship between foreign and domestic elements, made matters difficult. In general, the political value-institutional system, resting upon the most intricate mosaic of supporting factors, proved the most difficult to borrow and synchronize. It had a relatively higher particularist quotient than the purely technological facets of Westernism.

To the special complications, one must add that of "teleological insight," the apparent capacity of the intelligentsia to foresee its future mirrored in the development of other societies and the impact this "ability" has upon creativity, timing of ideological movements, and even methodology.

5. Today Japan belongs *ideologically* to the ranks of the "advanced" societies. In its later stages, modernization tends to reduce the ideological gaps among the more significant disputants. It also tends to raise the importance of so-called technical, procedural issues and to orient ideological debate increasingly around "specific," as opposed to "cosmic," issues, particularly in the domestic arena. Some regarded this process as the decline of ideology, but it is more properly viewed as adaptation to new stages of development. That Japan is now approaching the *avant-garde* stage reflects primarily the phenomenal success of her modernization during the past decade and the 100 years' experience with the universal world stream that she has now enjoyed.

NOTES

1. For one analysis of Japanese Confucianism see Marayama Masao, *Nihon seiji shisho shi kenkyu, Studies in the History of Japanese Political Thought* (Tokyo, 1952).

2. For details, see Robert A. Scalapino, *Democracy and the Party Movement in Prewar Japan* (Berkeley, 1953), pp. 82 ff.; and George M. Beckman, *The Making of the Meiji Constitution* (Lawrence, Kansas, 1957).

3. For a general discussion of Shinto and its ideological implications, see Daniel C. Holton, *Modern Japan and Shinto Nationalism* (Chicago, 1943).

4. See *The Autobiography of Fukuzawa Yukichi,* translated by Eiichi Kuyooka (Tokyo, 1934).

5. There is a great volume of literature on the Meiji theorists, including many collections of the leading writings of this period. One recent and varied collection of essays is *Kindai Nihon shiso shi koza, (Series on the History of Japanese Thought)* (5 vols.; Tokyo, 1959-60). See also Kosaka Masaaki, ed., *Japanese Thought in the Meiji Era,* translated by David Abosh (Tokyo, 1958).

6. Two English-language studies offer detailed evaluations of the prewar ultra-nationalist movements: Delmer M. Brown, *Nationalism in Japan* (Berkeley, 1955); and Richard Storry, *The Double Patriots* (London, 1951).

7. For a valuable monographic exposition of the theories of Hozumi and Minobe, see Frank O. Miller, *Minobe Tatsukichi: Interpreter of Constitutionalism in Japan* (Unpublished doctoral dissertation, University of California, 1961).

8. For one recent study of Yoshino, see Moriya Masomichi, "Yoshino Sakuzo," in *Nihon jinbutsu shi tai kei (A Compilation of Japanese Leaders),* Vol. 7 (Tokyo, 1960).

9. For a further evaluation of this question, see Scalapino, "The Left Wing in Japan," *Survey,* (August 1962), No. 43, 102-111.

10. Okawa Shumei, for example, was a strong admirer of Gandhi.

11. See Gondo Seikyo, *Juji minpan (Popular Rules of Self-Government)* (Tokyo, 1932).

12. See Tanaka Sogoro, *Kita Ikki Nihon teki Fashisuto no schocho (Kita Ikki, Symbol of Japanese Fascists)* (Tokyo, 1959); and Kuno Osamu, "A Prototype of Ultranationalism —The Case of Kita Ikki," in *Kindai Nihon shiso shi koza,* Vol. 4.

13. See Storry, *op. cit.*

Ideological Foundations of
Egyptian-Arab Nationalism

BY *LEONARD BINDER*

I.

"EVERY NATIONALIST movement must have an ideology," states one Egyptian writer, thus boldly expressing the intellectual confusion by which Arab nationalist writers have been able to avoid their responsibility for critically examining the values upon which political legitimacy and policy are said to rest.[1] We need not lose sight of the fact that such phrasing suggests the primacy of action and sentiment and the merely secondary quality of verbal explication and elaboration in noting that the search for an ideology is one of the central themes of contemporary Arab nationalist writing.[2] Nationalism, and Arab nationalism in particular, is itself ideology and therefore has to be explained outside the framework of its own component ideas. The tests of language, historical consciousness, and the rest are applications of the idea of nationalism and depend upon prior acceptance of the nation as the determinant of the political community. For the examination of diverse applications of this sort, important though they may be, there is a relatively easy method. When faced with such questions as whether or not a Lebanese Maronite is an Arab or a Karaite Jew an Arab, we know that the answers have but the remotest connection to any truly objective order of the universe. But nationalism itself as a general principle raises questions of another magnitude.

Our problem here is not an examination of the ideology of Arab nationalism in the sense of the value consequences of some historically objective fact like the existence of an Arab nation. Our concern is rather with the more striking transformation of the ultimate value from which all others are derived, from revelation to the postulate of nationality.

II.

Regardless of what else is claimed for modern nationalism, the single objective ideological consequence of nationalism on which there can be near unanimous agreement is that it delimits the political community.[3] Arguments for the need to add ideology to nationalism merely take nationalistic goals as a basic premise and attempt to derive from it certain consequences for political organization. This procedure is followed by nationalist writers who must accept this "ought" on the basis of faith alone, for it has no rational basis and only the cloudiest of experiential referents.

The subjective, nonrational core of nationalism is beclouded by alternative arguments that stress objective characteristics like language, geographical proximity, and the like, but even these arguments degenerate quickly into postulations of the existence of common historical memory, common destiny, and common interest.[4] Nevertheless, the objective argument reveals some of the philosophical heritage of nationalism and some of the inherent difficulties of the concept as an ultimate value.

If the essence of nationalism is subjective and even personal, it follows that nationality, when not completely identical with citizenship and language, is a categorical quality that can become socially and politically relevant only on the basis of conventional agreement, similar to our agreement that red is red. Hence the penetrating insight of Michel Aflaq's argument that nationalism is like one's name or physiognomy.[5] But if that is true, then surely no social consequences can be derived from such a concept unless they are put into it from the beginning.

Our two assertions, that nationalism deals only and essentially with delimiting the political community and that it is inherently a subjective sentiment from which nothing further may be logically derived, are both resisted if not denied by a great many nationalist writers. Furthermore, search though we may for really significant discussions of the first assertion as a critical problem in political theory before the rise of nationalism, we find next to nothing. How is it possible that so central a problem of modern politics was so neglected in earlier times? How can we explain the emergence of this question from an intellectual climate dominated by universalism?

While not entirely neglected, the problem of delimiting the political community received little serious philosophical attention because it did not demand any. In Islam as in Christianity, society came to be viewed separately from polity. Princes governed a part of the whole, and all princes were supposed to do the same thing anyway. It hardly mattered who was prince over how much territory. All Muslim rulers jointly executed the holy law throughout the abode of Islam, and foremost among them were those who carried out the general responsibilities of the Jihad and the defense of Islam. In Christian Europe, the device of the Holy Roman Empire did much to paper over the issue. To some extent, Ottoman suzerainty and the investiture of Sunni rulers had a similar effect. Nevertheless both Muslim and Christian writers were wont to discuss the responsibilities of the ruler, meaning all rulers, somewhat in contradiction to the dedications of their works to "the ruler of the world," as caliphs, padishahs, and shahinshahs might be addressed. Quite justifiably, as it appears to us, the rationalism of the Enlightenment and of the French Revolution was universalist. If it admitted the reality of separate states or political communities, it did not attempt to justify them.

In fact it did not need to justify political boundaries because it was primarily concerned with political relationships within existing boundaries. The only body of thought that concentrated on the order of relations among states and therefore with political boundaries was international law.

But the very concepts of that discipline clouded the issue even more by providing the ready device of transferring the base of sovereignty from rulers to subjects. The implication of this qualitative change from subject to citizen-sovereign has brought forth no response from international law, other than to sustain the anti-individualistic notion of the general will embodied in the concept of a collective and still indivisible sovereign.

There were two ideas offered by political philosophy to fill the gap between universalist ideology and the existence of delimited states. Rousseau presented both ideas, the social contract and its all but contradictory complement the general will. The idea of the general will does not necessitate a natural conception of political society as opposed to the convention of the social contract, but the moral character of the general will if the idea is based only on the social contract becomes contingent and positivist. Either morality was impossible outside civil society, or, if the general will could exist in the absence of the social contract, civil society itself as concretely constituted must depend upon nature. Rousseau posed the dilemma and did not resolve the issue of the natural or conventional basis of the polity.[6]

III.

The really surprising thing about the development of nationalist thought in the nineteenth century was the near abandonment of the rationalist argument for nationalism based on the conventional character of civil society. In its stead, there emerged a decided preference, although not a universal one, for the natural conception of the polity, as expressed in romantic nationalism. How did romantic nationalism derive from revolutionary rationalism? The inherent difficulty of this problem at the theoretical level is too easily glossed over by the historians. That such a shift occurred is admitted, but the task of understanding so complex a development requires more than the mere assertion of fact or simplistic explanations in terms of inevitability, dialectic, or the changed spirit of the times.

In order to explain this change, we must explain certain philosophical contradictions: Herder's nationalism and his universalistic cosmopolitanism, for example, or Rousseau's rationalism and his romanticism,[7] Fichte's shift from welcoming the French Revolution to opposing it, or even Burke's continued concern with both individuality and virtue.[8]

To get at the philosophical basis of these contradictions and therefore at the pattern of ideological dynamics, we can trace the connection in ideas from Condillac's (or Locke's) science of ideas as the basis of a new interpretation of reason through Kant's and Fichte's subjective conceptions of reality and especially Kant's postulate of the will as the basis of morality.[9] It must be remembered, however, that the relationship between reason and ultimate value was not the creation of the Age of Reason but its heritage. Reason was already a conceptual receptacle into which a new content was put. Romanticism could arise from reason only when reason itself was made to stand on a subjective foundation. But the changed basis of reason is only a condition of such a derivation, and the existence of such an "idea-slot" is but a permissive circumstance—for to derive romanticism from a critique of reason as a criterion for determining reality is an extremism.

On the other hand, we note the concern of thinkers to sustain a rational political order by the use of nonrational and nonuniversal symbols—or to buttress romantic or idealistic notions with positivist-rational argument. At another level, goddesses of reason are set up, and historical rationalizations are used to sustain nonrational legitimacy. In an era of mass political participation, in which the relatively uneducated citizen has a large part to play, it does not seem paradoxical that rational and romantic symbols are appealed to simultaneously. The contradictions we find in philosophical works are not so much the consequences of muddled thinking as evidences of a clear grasp of political reality. The difficulty lies in the inherent incongruence of logical thought and human behavior, and one need not be a materialist to hold such a position. In any case, the capacity for logical thought does not exhaust the resources of the human mind, nor does it comprehend the only conceivable basis for discovering the ultimate good.

Our conclusion is that there was terminological "space" for the development of new concepts of reason during the Enlightenment, that the treatment of reason by philosophers at the end of the eighteenth century was not wholly free of nonrational elements, and that the supposed contradictions in the thought of such philosophers are to be explained by reference to their own experiences and to their striving to put their notions of reality into words; it is not to be explained away. At the very least, we may say that those thinkers who contributed most to the origins of nationalism believed in the nonrational as a practical necessity for any polity.

Nor was practical necessity new to political philosophy at that time; it was rather part of the baggage of medieval thought. Practical necessity was the corollary of the views that held politics to be a practical art, a result of the fall of man, or, later still, dependent upon reason of state rather than on pure reason. It remained, however, for the rise of the nation-state as the ultimate value in itself for reason of state to become the particular form of association between reason and nonrational symbol.

IV.

In this sense, the rational and the romantic are not wholly alternative or antagonistic but are at least in some measure complementary. The former is concerned with the conventional aspects of community, the latter with the nonrational elements of identity. From this point of view, there is little wonder that the two forms are not separated by centuries or class differences, that they emerge continuously out of one another, and that they can be completely intertwined in a single piece of ideological writing.

The romantic form is essential to the solution of the problem of identity, for its content can only be categorical. Islam on the one hand and Arab Islam on the other are not simply the forms into which the real *Weltanschauung* of romanticism is placed. It is not romanticism that is essential to a view of reality; the real problem is posed by the question, Who am I? The answer usually involves an examination of experience and sentiment, the justification for which can hardly be rational.

That the problem of identity is real is obvious to anyone who has had first-hand experience in the emerging countries. The following general causes are usually suggested for the disturbance of previous identity solutions: geographical mobility, involving separation from both locality and family; education, which has weakened religious practices and sometimes religious belief itself and has provided a new sense of history and a new perspective of the self as part of an abstract state community; the new occupational structure involving organizational membership, new formal rules, and new social-competitive norms; the emergence of a new prestige-power hierarchy and the decline of the old statutes. Regardless of how we explain these and, doubtless, other changes, there is no gainsaying their effectiveness in producing an identity crisis. As we have attemped to show elsewhere, nationalist ideologies in the Middle East have a false ring about them precisely because they are largely imitative and because identity or the psychological self is a culturally taboo subject in Islam.[10] But these circumstances should not lead us to believe that the Arab is either incorrigibly romantic or that the notion of his search for new identity through nationalism is wholly fictitious.

As for community, is it essentially of a rational, conventional nature or only the sum of individuals sharing common identity? The idea of nation is a romantic one postulating the "natural" unity of a number of persons. According to the romantic idea, the political and social arrangements of the nation are or ought to be an expression of reason in history.

There is an essential difference between this romantic idea of the community as an extension of individual identities and the idea of the *ummah* in Islam. On one hand, the *ummah* is the whole body of true believers, and, on the other, it has continuity in history quite apart from its component individuals. Of course, there is a clear and sensible recognition of the generational basis of continuity in Islam, but it is not considered a very efficient way of providing for the spiritual continuity of the community, in marked contrast to nationalist theory in which the generational process is a central operating mechanism rather than a deficiency producing but necessary material process.

The Islamic view of the community was strengthened rather than weakened by the philosophical view that the nature of the state was dependent upon the ideas of the citizens. Nationalism has modified this notion of the *ummah*, but it has not really been effective in eliminating the Islamic faith as a characteristic of full membership in the Egyptian or Arab nation.[11] Furthermore and despite the legalistic treatment of the office of the caliph in both classical and modern times, the utilitarian aspect of the specific political and social arrangements of the Islamic community was never wholly lost from view. It is, of course, characteristic of modern nationalist theory that attempts are made to relate these utilitarian and programmatic ideas to the "spirit of the nation." Nevertheless, the mode of thought by which these programmatic ideas are put forward is rationalistic and utilitarian—all the way from al-Afghani to Gamal Abd-al-Nasir. Means-end rationalism is being associated paradoxically with a romantic conception of the nation, although rationalism may be applied to any political community regardless of how constituted. Furthermore, the current emphasis upon economic development, technological advance, rational planning, political equality and participation, education, bureaucratization, and so forth by radical-reform governments hardly permits us to treat these goals as simple derivatives of nationalism.

Let us see if we cannot elucidate somewhat the ideological connection between the romantic idea of identity and the conventional idea of the community. In nationalism, membership in the nation is absolute, categorical, and unchangeable. But any conventional solution to the problem of community that involves political values and specific allocation of influence and rewards may, perhaps must, raise the question of whether generationally produced members of the nation are "true" members. Are reactionaries, the current enemies of Arab socialism, true Arabs? Are those who were subject to the land reform laws true Egyptians? Are those who help currency smugglers true nationalists?

In addition to this difficulty, a truly rational means-end approach to policy involves some trial and error, some shifting of emphasis and priorities. In the face of such pragmatic searching, the definition of the "true" member of the nation must also shift. Rationalization, therefore, conflicts with certain elements of identity, and, where no fixed formula has been worked out or where excessive rationalism attempts to keep the society completely fluid and mobilizable, the result approaches the pure form of mass society.[12] This sort of result has nowhere been achieved among the new nations, nor is rationalist sentiment so strong and dangerous among the political leaders of these countries.

The "mass" idea is clearly related to the problem of identity, for identity is essentially an individual problem. Masses do not become "available" until identity becomes a widespread problem. The mass movement is therefore an irrational approach to the problem of community, in the sense that the search for support in any chosen identity resolution through generalizing that concept of identity for others is substituted for the search for a rational and conventional basis of co-operation with others in a political community. The attempt to resolve the problem of community through nonrational ideology or by treating it as a residue of identity, is not only irrational philosophically but practically.

V.

In the Arab East, nationalism was borrowed from the West as a means of entering into the modern world—as that world was defined by the dominant West. It may or may not be true that such acceptance was a matter of life or death, but many thought it was. Nevertheless, the minds of Arab intellectuals, particularly those who knew something about traditional learning, were not *tabulae rasae*. They had ideas of their own, mostly derived from a system of thought that was in the main hostile to modern Western ideas but that, when broken down into its component elements, seemed to comprehend a number of ideas of particular relevance to those of the West. At least, they seemed to provide a means of understanding (or misunderstanding) the terms in which Western thought was couched.

In addition to the divergent intellectual background into which national ideas came, the political, economic, and social contexts also differed appre-

ciably from those that nourished nationalism in Europe. This paper is not
the place to attempt an elaboration of these differences, and it would be misleading to suggest that adequate historical research is at our disposal so
that we may do so. What is clear is that, at the end of the nineteenth
century, Europe was already, for the most part, comprised of self-conscious
nation states, while the Arab East was not; Western Europe was already
industrialized, while the Arab East was not; Europeans thought in terms of
a neat three-class social structure, while Arabs thought in terms of millets first
and a more complex occupational gradation second. The nations of which
Europeans were speaking had already emerged as politically tangible entities,
while in the Arab East the nation was a remote abstraction at best and even
the notion of an Arab nation lacked all clear definition at the time.

The particular way in which Arab, and especially Egyptian, nationalist
thought developed may be understood against the background of these two
elements—the Islamic influence on the understanding of Western ideas and
the concrete problems of social structure, community, and national interest
that arose once these Western ideas began to be incorporated into Arab
thought. It may be argued that it is too mechanistic to attribute all ideological consequences to these forces and none to genuine intellectual inspiration, but we do not deny the possibility of such insight; we merely deny
that it occurred. That there has been considerable artistic achievement
and more scholarship cannot be gainsaid, but our concern here is with
ideology and its adaptation to material circumstances, and that has been
almost wholly derivative.

VI.

Superficially, the social circumstances surrounding the rise of Egyptian
nationalism appear similar to those of Europe in the nineteenth century, but
certain points of difference must be borne in mind. These points should
prevent us from making too facile generalizations about the direction of
both material and ideological development. Consider especially that Islamic
civilization was a defeated civilization; that no part of Islamic thought
allowed for a situation in which whole countries would be under alien, that
is, non-Islamic rule; that Europeans had already gone through many of the
changes affecting Egypt, so that modernized groups acquired their modern
ways of thinking more rapidly and more self-consciously; that modernization was "imported" only into certain social sectors so that there remains
a sharp discontinuity in society between the old and the new; that Europeans
already had ideas and a ready terminology to explain what was happening
in the Middle East; that the period during which Egyptian nationalist thought
developed was one of foreign domination and its aftermath, a domination
that was accompanied at times by severe attacks on Islam; and that Egypt
did not share the Western European heritage of an independent ecclesiastical
structure, free cities, the early rise of a *national* bourgeoisie, and the unified,
bureaucratized, monarchial state of the enlightened, benevolent despot.

When we compare Egypt and Western Europe, therefore, and find that it
was similarly "clerks" and those who had left the "vicarage" (that is, ex-
ulama) who developed nationalist thought, we must bear in mind that these

Egyptian clerks, who could so easily identify their European counterparts, did not until recently discover a clientele for their writing as had the Europeans. Instead of an historically rooted bourgeoisie to consume their product, Egyptian intellectuals wrote for and co-operated politically with a town-dwelling agrarian middle and upper class, most of whom were absentee landlords and only a few of whom were business-oriented.

At the same time, we note the disturbance of the traditional pattern of local ties and primary-group loyalties. Exactly how much and where has not been documented, but we know that in nineteenth-century Egypt an entirely new pattern of land tenure, cropping, irrigation, marketing, and taxation was developed. We also know that there was a change in the social composition of the group of largest landowners and a similar change in the means of acquiring large estates.[13] There was a gradual decline in the size of middle holdings and in the political influence of one class of local notables and a probable increase in the influence of another group that, in terms of individual families, became partially modernized. It is also argued that agricultural changes brought in their wake a reduction of the traditional level of peasant co-operation in the villages, but the extent of this reduction is less well known. Of greater importance is the increase of rural population, which has by far outrun the increases in crop area. Concomitantly with these changes, rapid urbanization has occurred, and more recently there is evidence of the growth of a literate public for whom modern technical and language skills (in the special use of Arabic too) are of central importance.[14]

The development of a press, the cheaper printing of books, an increasing number of translations of foreign works, government-financed education abroad, and an increasing number of foreign visitors parallel the communications and information revolution that occurred in nineteenth-century Europe.[15] In the Middle East, it has still not reached the proportions it had reached in England in the 1870s, but it is sufficient to sustain a new class of literate and popular writers and to give them at once a medium of expression and a small audience. But these writers are communications specialists. Professional philosophers, in the Middle East, remain strictly within the framework of the academic study of the classic Western or Islamic philosophers, leaving to civil servants, military officers, secondary-school teachers, and journalists the task of writing ideological tracts.

The spread of education, although still limited by comparison with the West, had certain similar effects. It produced a larger audience for nationalist writings and a bureaucratic middle class desirous of political recognition and social change. But in Egypt there was little vocational education, nor was there until recently a serious effort to educate the masses.[16] Education meant a change in social structure, a change in cultural orientation, and above all an increase in the number of aspirants for "clerical" occupations. There is no real educational, cultural, or social difference between writers and readers. Amateurs and specialists write for one another. All education in Egypt is geared to higher education and is nearly useless unless capped by university training.

We can further contrast the class origins of the nationalist groups in Europe and in Egypt. In Europe, it was the urban bourgeoisie, the younger sons of the aristocracy, the guilds, and offshoots of the clergy who contributed most to the growth of nationalism. These groups were all urban groups and part of the rational and more or less workable order of medieval corporativism. In Egypt it is the urbanized segments of the agrarian middle class, faced with the anarchy of the Islamic city, that have led the nationalist "struggle."[17]

The hold of religion has also declined in Egypt but for additional and complex reasons, among which we note the weakness of the religious institution (the *ulama*) *vis-à-vis* the government; the administrative inroads into *waqf*-religious endowments for the support of religious education and *ulama;* the higher prestige accorded those who hold jobs that require a Western type of education, as a consequence of the greater influence and higher salaries associated with such jobs compared to the influence and salaries associated with jobs held by the average graduates of religious institutions; the irrelevance of religion to the problems facing a country challenged by Western technology and power; the growth of a contrary philosophy of reason and naturalism;[18] and the alliance of the *ulama* with the throne.[19]

This last factor would have meant little had not traditional legitimacy in Egypt, as in Europe, become undermined. But it must be remembered that the Egyptian monarchy was never fully legitimate in Islamic terms. It could only represent a compromise with necessity contingent upon adequate performances. The Muhammad Ali dynasty had been established within recent memory; it had itself attempted to bring about modernization, thus shaking its own social roots; through its efforts, foreign advisers and administrators were introduced into Egypt; and when the time came it failed to defend the country against foreign occupation. Later on when nationalism grew, Faruk failed dismally to give his leadership any nationalist character.[20]

There has been in Egypt, as in parts of Europe, a rediscovery of the peasant as the symbol of the nationalist spirit and nationalist solidarity, but the theme is much weaker and does not account for the more important cultural and social differences between the impoverished peasant and the *kulak*.

A further element of outstanding importance for the understanding of Egyptian nationalism, an element that was not present in western Europe though of some importance in eastern Europe, was the special and enviable status of the minorities under colonialism. These people not only dominated the modern commercial field but competed effectively for many of the administrative jobs that were the only goal of the educated Egyptian Muslims.[21] Egyptian social structure was thus doubly distorted when viewed by the educated Muslim.

VII.

The problem of the limits of the national community, seldom a matter of major dispute on the objective plane in Europe, has no such simple solution for the Arabs and particularly for Egypt. In Europe, the composition of the national community was usually not so controversial a question, although the disposition of border areas led to many disputes and much violence. In the Arab East, the limits of the national community are a question that involves the subjective identities of whole peoples. Persians and Turks have been clearly and willingly separated from their Arab fellow Muslims since World War I, although the question of the disposition of Mosul and Hatay or Alexandretta demonstrates that it was not a wholly clean break.

Despite this schism in the Islamic community (Iran had to all intents and purposes been separated since the year A.D. 1500), it is still impossible to separate Islam from the sentiment of national identity. One of the central questions of Arab nationalism remains the position of the Christian Arab minority. Paradoxical as it may seem, the Christian Arabs of the Levant were the initiators of the Arab nationalist movement, although primarily through literary and intellectual pursuits.[22] One of their major goals was to find a basis of closer co-operation with their Muslim neighbors. The only element they shared in full measure was the Arabic language. The early Christian overtures came to little, and later, when the Muslims aroused themselves to nationalism, it was a nationalism so heavily laden with Islamic sentiment that it has made both the Christians of the Levant and the Copts of Egypt somewhat apprehensive about their status in an Arab nationalist state. Nevertheless, Christian Arabs are active in nationalist activities but tend to prefer smaller political units to what is called "comprehensive" Arab nationalism—which seeks unity from the Persian Gulf to the Atlantic. This attitude is particularly strong among Lebanese Christians and to a lesser extent among Syrian Christians since the separation of Syria and Egypt.

Among the Muslims, Arab nationalism was not the immediate response to Western pressures. Instead there was first an attempt at Islamic political revival and then an attempt to reform Islamic legal theory and philosophy to accommodate the requirements of a modern society, economy, and military establishment. Jamal al-Din al-Afghani is associated with the first, or Pan-Islamic, movement; his disciple, Muhammad Abduh of Egypt, is most closely associated with the second. The views of both, but especially of the former, were reinterpreted with some distortion and under a certain vague influence from the puritanical Wahhabism of Arabia by Rashid Ridha, who may be regarded as the leading light of fundamentalist Islamic reaction. The goal of all three movements was to reinvigorate Muslims and to create in them a self-conscious desire for dignity, modernity, solidarity, and the preservation of religious values. In the face of European nationalism, these leaders of Islamic modernism wished Islam to fulfill the functions of nationalism among all Muslims.

Their efforts failed for many reasons: the demise of the Ottoman caliphate, the ambition of various Arab rulers, the British occupation of Egypt, and —perhaps most important—the cleavage of outlook between the traditional elites, including the *ulama*, who were the main support of religion, and the Western-educated moderns. Pan-Islam did not get off the ground, but its various exponents did succeed in producing a number of new interpretations of Islam that render it compatible with a modern outlook and hence dignify the Islamic identity to the point where it is nowadays frequently written about by both Muslims and Christians as an integral part of Arab nationalism.

Egyptian ideas have undergone the greatest transformation during the last century, although the situation in other Arab countries has been similar if less ambiguous. As a "vassal" of the Ottoman sultan-caliph, the Pasha of Egypt aspired simply to greater independence and to the elevation of his status to that of kingship.[23] These ambitions, which were behind much of the nineteenth-century modernization of Egypt, were transformed during the British occupation into a desire to achieve independence from the British through the action of the Ottoman sultan. After the turn of the century, it seems that the khedive entertained certain hopes of acquiring the dignity of an Arab caliph. The first Egyptian "nationalists" or patriots aimed at getting rid of foreign influence and limiting the powers of the khedive. The first party of the same name was founded by Mustafa Kamil, and it was pro-Ottoman.[24] The partition of the Arab lands of the Fertile Crescent by British and French mandates discouraged any thought of co-operation with other Arab countries for most of the interwar period, and Egyptian nationalist leaders looked elsewhere for assistance. It was not until World War II, when it became clear that the Arab states would achieve independence and would be organized in some form of league or federation through the agency of Great Britain, that Egyptian leaders felt the need of entering into Arab politics. They took this action to prevent any of the other Arab leaders, especially the Hashemites, from forming a united Arab state that might serve as a counterweight to Egypt and weaken Egyptian efforts to be free of British occupation. Egyptian leadership of the Arab League and the nearly unaccountable entry of Egypt into the Palestine war sealed the identification of Egypt as an Arab country at the political level but certainly not at the psychological level.

During the interwar years, Egyptian writers and intellectuals sought a suitable symbol of Egyptianism. They fumbled at one point with a Pharaonic revival that is now much condemned.[25] There followed Taha Hussain's now rejected assertion that Egypt formed part of a much broader Mediterranean civilization.[26] In the mid-Thirties, however, there was a much more powerful turn toward romantic Islamic symbols through the medium of biographical writings on the Prophet and his successors.[27] Lately, these themes have been not so much abandoned as subordinated to Pan-Arab symbols. There is, however, a certain uneasiness about these symbols as well, for despite Egypt's clear cultural leadership among the Arabs of both the East and the West, there appears to be too much political manipulation of Arab symbols and too little real empathy. On their own part, Sunni Arabs outside Egypt have been too willing to use Egyptian power to settle their own domestic scores and too reluctant to work out the basis of a real union. Part of the difficulty is, of course, that Egypt's population is greater than that of the rest of the eastern Arab states combined and that there is no leader of stature comparable to President Nasir. Despite these difficulties, the nationalist die has been cast, and Egypt has come, by a devious process, to be an unequivocally Arab country. Not even the traumatic separation of Syria can change this fact, although there have been a few recent evidences of a revival of Pharaonic symbols and some comparisons of the progressive Arab West and the reactionary Arab East.[28]

The Hashemite dynasts, of whom only King Hussain of Jordan is now left, lay claim to the leadership of the Arab national movement. This claim is of course based upon the role of Sharif Hussain of Mecca in the Arab revolt of 1916, which T. E. Lawrence has made famous.[29] After the assassination of his cousin King Faisal II of Iraq in 1958, the possibility of a Hashemite state, unifying the whole Fertile Crescent and possibly the Hejaz in accordance with the early aspirations of the long deceased Sharif, is all but nonexistent. Nevertheless there appears to be some sentiment for this type of more limited unity.

Islamic and Christian sectarianism has also played an important role in limiting for some Arabs the territorial scope of their ideal Arab state. The Parti Populaire Syrien, which failed in an attempted *coup* in Lebanon in early 1962, had a program of unifying the Fertile Crescent and Cyprus in an Arab nation-state. Many of its members were Greek Orthodox in religion. Nearly 40% of the population of Syria is either non-Sunni or nomadic, and this fact has certainly been partially responsible for the absence of political unity in Syria. It also, no doubt, lies behind the separation from Egypt. But the most outstanding case of the effect of minorities and sectarianism is demonstrated in the incapacity of Egypt and Iraq to agree on procedure toward Arab unification. Less than half the population of Iraq is Sunni, the remainder is Shi'ite. Somewhat less than a quarter of the population of Iraq is Kurdish, with its own national aspirations. Under Qasim, the consequences of these divisions were some tentative but largely unsuccessful attempts to create an Iraqi nationalism, while attempting to stave off union by using both sectarian and leftist sentiments against the Sunni minority.

The foregoing discussion has offered only the briefest suggestions of the magnitude of the concrete problems involved in welding a common national identity for only the eastern Arab peoples. In the latter half of the twentieth century, Arabism has been accepted in its broadest form, but it is clear that its psychological essence varies still from country to country on the basis of the particular experience, social structure, and ethnic and religious composition of each. Ideological efforts in writings and speeches, propaganda and songs have done much to bridge the gap, but the persistent demand for an ideology for Arab nationalism suggests that the path ahead is long. Nevertheless, so compelling is the idea of Arab nationalism itself and so insistent is its normative claim, that few may admit adherence to it in limited or conventional form.[30] Arab nationalism and Arab unity are now one aspiration. Advocacy of federative unity is suspect.

VIII.

It is apparent that Arab nationalism has been accepted, at least by the intellectuals of the Arab world, as an ideology, but it has not yet been applied in any meaningful way to everyday political life. Ideology may serve as a link between two kinds of meaning, philosophical and psychological. It can also serve to help bring about change. The problem of Arab nationalism is not that it has no ideology but that the link between abstract ideas and identity sentiments has not been fully forged. The weakness of this link, however, is less evident between Islamic philosophy and nationalism than between nationalism and historically defined personal identity.

Islamic philosophy was brought into accord with nationalism by an ideological process that we shall shortly describe. In the accomplishment of this task, however, Muslims also became heirs to all of the ideational tensions of modern nationalism. It is not an easy matter to join Arab identity and Islamic community ideologically. It is not at all self-evident that the romanticism involved in the rejection of recent history and the rationalism by which that history is to be changed are ideologically compatible. "Will," "reason," "history," and "nature" are the philosophical terms that have been used to bridge the gap between Islamic philosophy and the nationalist idea. The resulting weaknesses of Arab nationalism are the weaknesses of all nationalisms, caused by the intrinsic duality of identity and community, of subjective sentiment and the conventional order of human society.

The most imposing problem of all is to explain how a people imbued with belief in a divinely ordained ultimate revealed in holy writ could transfer its loyalty to a pantheistic notion like nationalism. As we have seen, this transfer was not complete, nor has it extended to all Muslims—but the intellectual issue is not diminished by these qualifications. Nor will all the evidence of social and economic change tell us why this particular ideological change came about in Egypt any more than the same changes explain ideological change in Europe without reference to the limiting channels of existing ideas. In the West, the gradual development of nationalist ideas depended upon the transformation of a conception of natural law. The association between reason and nature was an ancient heritage, and we recall that, without the new rationalism based on a new concept of nature, we could not have achieved the romanticism of the nineteenth century.

But Islam was also heir to Greek reason. It is true that "orthodox" Ash'arism succeeded in defeating the rationalist theology of the Mu'tazilah at an early stage in Islamic history; but it is apparent that the Mu'tazilites were not fully in control of the Greek philosophical tradition. The introduction of this tradition into Islamic intellectual circles in its most influential form was the work of al-Farabi.[31] The "philosophic" tradition in Islamic thought that was thus introduced was highly suspect in the eyes of traditional, orthodox theologians, because it raised the controversial issue of the relationship between reason and revelation—an issue that penetrated into Western Christianity. The "philosophers," as the exponents of the received Greek tradition were called, were not immediately nor widely influential. Nevertheless, for all their fear of persecution and for all the abstruseness of their expression, their works have been accepted into the Islamic corpus of learning, and their central postulate of the rationality of the universe and of revelation has been adopted.

The philosophical position that aroused the ire of the Ash'arites was the assertion that the universe could be comprehended through reason, as well as through revelation. If pushed to its logical conclusion, this view reduces the miracle of the Qur'an, which is itself the proof of its own authenticity and of the truth of Muhammad's prophecy, to the work of a philosopher. The opposing positions were reconciled by adding that human reason was nevertheless not so nearly perfect as divine reason. Revelation was therefore necessary to provide for the true guidance of mankind. Despite the verbal acceptance of this compromise, the sincerity of the philosophers was still suspect; even when formalized into a standard Islamized philosophic tradition, tension persisted between the legists and the specialists in divine philosophy. But the revised tradition was popularized and became widely available to intellectuals, especially in the work of al-Dawwani. Significantly, Dawwani's *Ethics*, a sort of compendium of true knowledge, combines, among other things, this watered-down philosophic tradition and the Iranian tradition of practical statecraft.[32]

There was a further complication, however, in the relationship between reason and revelation. If the limitations upon reason were a matter of dispute, the difficulty of the Qur'an was a matter of general agreement. Of course, the obscurity of certain verses was attributed to the passage of time and the loss of live contact with the Prophet himself. Dependence upon *hadith* or traditions of the Prophet's words and actions was thus justified. But these traditions are themselves subject to much suspicion of forgery. In addition to this basic difficulty, there are also passages in the Qur'an that are said to contradict other passages or to permit reconciliation only by the most complicated means. In other words, instead of revelation completing reason, the issue might well have been put quite the other way around. But it is not the same thing to declare that reason may attain all the truth that is revealed in the Qur'an and that the difficulties of interpreting the obscurities of the Qur'an may be resolved through the application of reason. Even the latter more limited position was further restricted by making such use of reason dependent only upon certain rational techniques, like grammatical analysis, analogy, and the reconciliation of divergent texts. The really critical problem is what is meant by reason.

Despite the fact that such matters were the concern of only a small group of traditional intellectuals, the same themes were rapidly taken up by Westernized writers after having been applied to the problem of the suitability of Islam to the modern age by Afghani and more especially by Abduh. Afghani's position on the matter is not at all clear, but two of his most important statements permit us to make some suggestions about the effects of his teaching. His attack on the Naitchuri movement among Indian Muslims demonstrates his opposition to a materialistic solution of the problem of reason.[33] He insisted on the importance of will and spiritual strength in human affairs. This attitude is indicative, to some extent, of an inclination toward the traditional Islamic "philosophical" school. His reply to Renan's lecture on religion and science appears to contradict his writings aimed at Muslim audiences, for in that letter he asserts that all religions stand in the way of scientific progress and that the problem of scientific progress is not resolved through a compatible religion but through devices for mitigating religious influence.[34] One hardly knows what to make of this position unless it can be shown that Afghani's notion of science was that of traditional philosophy, in the sense that knowledge is not essentially empirical but the product of speculative reason. Reason and religion would then always be in conflict, in the sense of the medieval controversy over whether or not revelation is necessary to complete reason. Eventually reason would prevail over revelation, but for the time being religion would be necessary. Religion was to serve the function of political myth.

Abduh was also exposed to the teachings of the traditional "philosophical" school, but he was more deeply influenced by the conciliatory efforts of Ibn Khaldun. Abduh held that reason and revelation could not be in conflict. Islam and only Islam among the religions accords fully with reason. If reason and its product, science, had declined among Muslims, the cause was not Islam but the misrule of sultans and the fanatical conservatism of the *ulama*.

Abduh thus attempted, without immediate success, to restore reason to a
position of respect among the orthodox. His more immediate accomplishment was to convince a small group of Western-educated laymen of the
harmony of reason and religion in Islam.

As Safran has shown, it is probable that Abduh's concept of reason did
not differ much from that of al-Afghani.[35] That is, he probably thought of
reason as the mechanism of speculative philosophy. Nevertheless, he was
not wholly consistent in his various references to reason, philosophy, and
science or knowledge. One of the most interesting peculiarities of Abduh's
thought is his equation of speculative reason with science and practical reason.
It would seem that he reversed the philosophic tradition that tended to place
the religious sciences among the practical sciences and speculative reason
apart from them and presumably higher. In this manner, science and speculative philosophy are assimilated to politics, ethics, and the productive arts.[36]
Philosophy may concern itself also with the laws of existence but not with
the core of religion, that is, with the nature of God.

It is not at all clear that Abduh rested his notion of reason upon nature as
revealed in history, a transformation necessary to the development of
nationalist ideology. Nevertheless, his treatment of the problem of reason
and its relation to his understanding of modern science permitted others to
draw timely conclusions. He argued that Islam encouraged man to use his
reason to discover the laws of existence. Although religion and not reason
must be the basis of the ideal state, nearly everything else related to politics
is in the sphere of reason, according to Abduh. Material and scientific
progress was associated with the application of reason to Islamic law (but
not to theology). Reason and free will were materially conditioned by the
order of created existence, and they were sufficient for man's earthly needs.
Intellectual order and harmony or their reverse determine the course of
history.

By these means, Abduh reasserted the relationship between reason and
nature that had been all but eliminated by Islamic occasionalism and legal
theory. In effect, Abduh approached a reconciliation of the views of al-
Afghani and of the Indian Naitchuri movement, which al-Afghani had so
bitterly attacked. But, in medieval philosophic fashion, Abduh set reason in
opposition to history—or at least to Islamic history. The explanation of why
reason had not manifested itself in history is based on the rigid acceptance
of traditional authority. It is in his rejection of *taqlid* or traditional authority
that Abduh comes closest to rendering reason, and consequently Islamic law,
dependent upon history. Had he carefully distinguished between speculative
reason and practical reason or had his followers a better understanding of
medieval philosophy, his solution of the problem of *taqlid* would not appear
so revolutionary. After all, both politics and religious law (in Islam) had been
considered by Muslim philosophers to belong to the realm of practical
wisdom.

On the problem of history, Safran has again shown that Abduh had a
dualistic view.[37] Abduh saw human history up to the time of the Islamic
revelation as steady progress and maturation. Thereafter, political cleavages
caused the decline of Muslim society, and the decline was proportional to the
passage of time from the appearance of the Prophet. Abduh thus accepts

history as the product of reason until the appearance of revelation—after which, history represents unreason. It is further significant that Abduh attributes part of the reason for the Muslim decline to misunderstanding of the Qur'an—a misunderstanding caused, in some degree, by the rapid conversion of non-Arabs.[38]

IX.

The most characteristic feature of reformist Islam, in all its varieties, is the rejection of *taqlid* or the doctrine of required acceptance of received authority. All reformers insist that the force of earlier consensus (*ijma*) be limited or subject to review in the light of new criteria. As the concomitant of this view, they also hold that the use of independent judgment (*ijtihad*) to initiate new interpretations of the law is permitted for those who have the requisite qualifications of learning and piety.

The primary emphasis of Abduh's critique of *taqlid* and *ijma* was on rejection of the historical consensus of the Islamic community and on insistence that only the consensus of reason was valid.[39] *Ijtihad was to be based on reason.* The controversy over the binding nature of *taqlid*, thus joined, was not a new one in Islam. For example. the Shi'a have always held that "consensus" means consensus of the judgments of the imams and that the "gate of *ijtihad*" remains open for the practice of qualified *mujtihads*. One of the four "roots" of the law for the Shi'a is *'aql* or reason (intelligence), though there are diverse interpretations of its application. *Taqlid* for the Shi'a means only that certain *ulama* and laymen choose to accept the authority of a particular *mujtihad*, generally one with whom they may have some personal contact, that is one who is living and resident in their locality. There were also, from time to time, Sunni *ulama*, bent on reform, who denied the extreme form of *taqlid* that had become the single most important constitutional feature of the religious institution of Islam. But these few, like Ibn Taiymiyya, are outstanding exceptions; while the differences with the Shi'a are of the most critical importance in understanding the theoretical centrality of *taqlid* and *ijma* to the Sunni position.

As Abduh mentions with some regret, opposing views of the caliphate became mixed up with various theological positions.[40] In his general avoidance of the question of Islamic government, he follows the spirit of al-Ghazali in the latter's doubts about the significance of the doctrine of the caliphate for Islamic theology.[41] Ali Abd al-Raziq pressed this attitude too far in arguing that it was incorrect to insist that Islamic law dealt with the state as well as with religious matters, thus demonstrating once again how Abduh's use of traditional ideas was distorted by his eager followers.[42] Regardless of this revised assessment, it is true that doctrines of legitimate government were intimately bound up with theological considerations. The Shi'a claimed that the imams, who were the best qualified and impeccable beside, should have been the caliphs and that only they had the right of *ijtihad* during their respective lives. In their view, the Islamic community has been misguided in its majority and throughout the great bulk of its history. The Sunni argument was that those who had actually served as caliphs, especially before Ali, were sufficiently qualified and did not need to be impeccable. Their proof for this claim was the *ijma* or consensus of the community. According to the Sunni view, the Islamic community was still divinely guided, not so much by its caliphs as through the immanence of divine will in the community itself.

The fundamental religious attitude toward history in Islamic civilization is bound up with this position in the politico-theological controversy. There were, of course, many divergent schools of historiography, but we are here concerned with the one that accords most closely with the Sunni theological orientation. From this point of view, the purpose of writing history was essentially didactic, to show the consequences and explain the nature of good and evil acts.[43] It was also a continuation of the religious work of describing in detail the life of the Prophet and of his companions, in the sense of extending the narrative of God's intervention in human affairs: *gesta dei per musulmanos*. But the subject matter of history is divided generally into political annals and biographical works, the former reporting the deeds of both good and bad rulers and the latter primarily the works of pious men, poets, learned scholars, and the like. Hence Islamic historiography recorded the decline of the community, from the perfection attained under Muhammad and the first four, the "rightly guided," caliphs, on the one hand, and the admirable upholding of the Islamic tradition by individual members of the community, on the other. The caliph, as the Sunni theologians insisted, need not be impeccable, nor was he. The Shi'a by contrast insisted that this approach provided a dreary history of sin and that, if the Islamic community had been divinely guided through the imams, the perfection attained under Muhammad could have been maintained. In effect, the Shi'a challenged all Muslims to reachieve that past perfection. The challenge of the West was not really much different.

To rephrase these generalizations, we may say that history represented a decline from a past apex of ethical achievement. In one sense and one temporally restricted to early Islam, history was derivatively constitutive. In another sense, history represented the baneful effect of the interposition of an increasing number of generations between those who knew Islam at first hand from the Prophet and living Muslims who know it only by the handing down of tradition. This last view lay behind the later doctrine that the true caliphate lasted only thirty years, the view of some reformers that only the *ijma* of the generation of the Prophet was to be accepted as binding. Only a certain period of history was constitutive of law in the later religious view.

Abduh did not oppose this view. In fact his whole outlook on the decline of Islam is permeated by it, but, in rejecting a *taqlid* that emerged out of particular historical controversies, he argued that the nearest approximation to reachieving the heights of early Islam might be attained by the application of reason to the law. Furthermore, as we have seen, he freely mixed experimental science, speculative philosophy, and practical reason in his notion of reason. The door was therefore open to a blending of his rejection of *taqlid* with that of the Naitchuris. The view that emerged most strongly in India was that *taqlid* must be rejected and the gate of *ijtihad* opened because *ijma* was valid only for particular times and particular places. When material circumstances changed, the interpretation and application of the law must change. This argument was Iqbal's "principle of movement" in Islam.[44] Nor was Abduh explicitly uncongenial to this point of view. "Indeed, the later generations have a knowledge of past circumstances, and a capacity to reflect upon them, and to profit by the effects of them in the world, which have survived until their times, that the fathers and forefathers who preceded them did not have."[45] The temporal and geographical limitation of *ijma* was particularly agreeable to the nationalist idea; but it also led directly to a new view of history. History now became, in a certain sense, truly constitutive, but the dictates of historical circumstances had to be interpreted by *ijtihad*, a striving to grasp their true meaning. *Taqlid* had prevented Muslims from adapting Islam and their own social and political arrangements to historical circumstances in the past.

It is significant that the new historical outlook permitted the early glories of Islam to be preserved in order to inspire the present. There was general agreement that the long middle stage of Islamic history was characterized by a decline—which was variously interpreted. The contemporary stage is viewed as one of awakening.

X.

Obviously there was some ambiguity in the orthodox religious attitude toward history. On one hand, we have determination to maintain the idea of the divine guidance of the Muslim community and, on the other, the difficulty posed by the actual shortcomings of Islamic government. These shortcomings were treated in the writings of the legists but generally without specific reference, so that they appeared in the guise of recurring conditions. This treatment was a result of the style of legal writing, which aimed at the theoretical resolution of every problem as part of a general case rather than providing for discretionary powers on the part of the judge. Hence we find al-Baqillani discussing the problem of the simultaneous existence of two legitimate caliphs, al-Mawardi discussing the "amirate by seizure" and the problem of heretical practorianism, and al-Ghazali discussing the problem of an unqualified caliph.[46]

In order to cope with such situations and the doctrinal compromises in which they resulted, al-Ghazali employed the concept of necessity.[47] In the sense in which he used the term, "necessity" meant a general condition of social and political relations. There is a clear connection here between this doctrine and the philosophical doctrine of understanding sensible historical reality. We must, however, distinguish between the notion of *Sunnat Allah* and this concept of necessity.[48] *Sunnat Allah* or the "way of God" was used as an explanation of man's ability to make sense out of sensible reality; the doctrine of necessity explained the deviation of that reality from the Islamic ideal in such a manner as to render the validity of orthodox doctrine independent of sensible reality.

The connection between the two concepts results from their resolution of the problem of the origin of evil. If all human acts are created by God, then evil acts are also created by God. Necessity and *Sunnat Allah* cannot therefore be fully separated. There were various devices for coping with this difficulty that do not here concern us, for none mitigated the basic principle. It is this connection that permitted Ibn Khaldun to use the idea of *Sunnat Allah* to explain his theory of historical causation.

But we must bear in mind that there is an important distinction between a perceived causal relationship between two objects (*Sunnat Allah*) and the total societal configuration of such relationships (necessity) that al-Ghazali believed conditioned the morality of certain political acts. The justification of this transformation of necessity into political right was significantly based on the good of the community.

We have already noted the influence of al-Ghazali on Abduh, and the doctrine of necessity offers another example. In this instance, however, we note a substantial departure on Abduh's part, perhaps under the influence of Ibn Khaldun, from al-Ghazali's use of the term "necessity." Abduh denied that Islam had been spread by the sword and explained that Muslim conquests were prompted by self-defense. "Thus the beginning (of conversion) was a consequence of the necessity of political society."[49] Here, it is apparent that "necessity" takes on a broader meaning, involving, instead of a detraction from an ethical ideal, a highly desirable consequence from the Muslim point of view. Necessity is no longer something with which the human conscience must wrestle but a general condition of morality. The implications of this view for the development of a relativist morality and the material conditioning of values is great indeed, even though Abduh did not push it very far. It was left to his successors to twist the notion even further, as in a recent work on Arab nationalism in which the expulsion of all non-Muslims from Arabia is justified by reference to the security of the fledgling Islamic state.[50] In this manner, Abduh's "necessity of political society," which referred to the natural order of human society, was transformed into material-istic prudence and self-interest. Necessity was now used to justify acts of government instead of to explain its failings and to serve as a warning to truly pious men to steer clear of political affairs. Al-Ghazali's concept of neces-sity now evolved into the equivalent of "reason of state," through the medium of a reformulation based on Western influences.

XI.

Romanticism and vitalism are characteristic features of contemporary Arab nationalist thought. The foundation of these themes in nationalist literature is insistence on the freedom of the human will. Without this link, all interpre-tations of the various historical stages through which Muslims have passed would be meaningless, for they all conclude with various reasons for the present decline. The true spirit of the Arab nation was revealed in history but must be discovered by an inner act of recognition, and the true place of the Arab nation among the peoples of the civilized world must be attained by an act of will.

The surprising thing about this romantic view, which parallels the ideology of many an European nationalism, is, not that it contradicts the sort of rationalism that we have found in reformist Islam, but that it so flagrantly contradicts the Ash'arite-orthodox position on God's creation of human acts and man's mere acquisition of those acts. Presumably the Ash'arite doctrine of perpetual creation should have stood in the way of such a transformation, but there were other elements in Islam that, when stressed, opened a direct path to romantic vitalism. We have already pointed out where even the orthodox conception of history departed from the strict influence of Ash'arite occasionalism. We have also noted the distinction between the use of the terms *Sunnat Allah* and "necessity." And then we have the obscure Ash'arite device for reconciling occasionalism and responsibility—acquisition. Man acquired his acts by virtue of accepting them as his own, that is, by willing them. This act of will, which is essential to all nonmaterialist rational philosophy, is also the foundation of modern nationalist romanticism. History determines the identity of the individual, and he "acquires" this identity by consciously willing it.

If orthodox Islamic thought did not completely suppress the notion of will, the Islamic philosophical school preserved the idea of the rational will as received from classical philosophy. It was this idea, rather than the Ash'arite view, that Abduh passed on, and we take note of the amazing paradox by which the modernization of Islamic thought is made easier by drawing upon a secondary tradition. But Abduh's treatment of the will and its freedom, whether because of his prudent desire to limit discussion or because of his alleged "empiricism," accords very well with a romantic nationalism.[51]

According to Abduh, the Necessarily Existent or God necessarily has will, and this will is a characteristic that informs the actions of the Knowing One in any one of His possible manifestations. All things created are thus in accordance with divine wisdom and will. "Will" implies that all creatures have specific attributes and positions in time and place that characterize them as distinct from all other possible creatures. The question of decision or choice does not apply to God, who acts out of knowledge and will. But this question does affect created beings in whom knowledge (reason?) is imperfect. Will is contingent upon knowledge. When there is complete knowledge, only one decision can be forthcoming, and in God the will and the deed are one. The meaning of "power" in the sense of "God's power" over man is nothing but God's control over the act of creation, that is creation in accordance with His knowledge and will. Choice or freedom of the will is nothing but the effect produced on "power" (ability to act) by the measure of knowledge and the determination of the will. That is, freedom of the will is contingent only upon human knowledge or reason. Man does not act without sense or will, nor is it beneficial to him to believe that he is compelled to act as he does, for such a view relieves him of responsibility. Rather the welfare of man and the order of creation are determined by the fact that they have been effected by the most perfect of beings, and the (degree of approximation to?) perfection of the created follows from the perfection of the Creator, in Whom there is both complete knowledge and absolute will.[52]

From the foregoing paraphrase of Abduh's views on freedom of the will, knowledge, and choice, we can see that classical occasionalism is not permitted to affect human responsibility. There is a parallel here between the position of Abduh and that of Aquinas, a parallel going all the way back to the idea of the creation of man in the image of God. But there is no grace in Abduh's system; there is no transcending of the human condition. Material reality does not determine the will; it is the condition of the possibility of choice. Knowledge, will, and choice are at once free and contingent upon the order of creation. The contingency of will upon the natural order is the condition of its variability, and variability is the definition of freedom. The limitation of knowledge or reason proceeds beyond this point so that either correct or incorrect decisions may be made even within the framework of the created order. There is still some distance between this view and the doctrine that the true spirit of the Arab people has revealed itself in history and that the recognition of such reality depends upon an act of will by the right-thinking vanguard of the nation; nevertheless, this doctrine is one of the ways in which the groundwork was laid.

There were other themes that contributed to the same end and are presently at the root of Arab nationalist romanticism and vitalism. These contributory themes will not long detain us, although it is well to bear in mind that there was more than a single ideological influence. One of the sources of such ideas is the concern with prophecy in Islamic theology, which produced the terms *ilham* and *wahy*, both referring to inspiration—the former emphasizing its human instinctive aspect and the latter the act of God in instilling an idea in a human being. Another impetus to "vitalism" lies in the mystic tradition of Islam, which tended to stress the importance of immediate religious experience above legal conformity. Nor should we overlook the implications of the Naitchuri argument that contributed to Iqbal's reconstruction of *ijma* as the "principle of movement" in Islam. Afghani's own antimaterialism is yet another source of vitalism, one that is particularly important in view of his emphasis upon spiritual values as the source of political solidarity and social stability.

Not less important than these ideas and in some cases contributing to their interpretation was the revival of Ibn Khaldun's concept of *asabiyyah* or social solidarity. Ibn Khaldun's theory was based in part on his observation of the effects of the decline of tribal solidarity in urban surroundings. *Asabiyyah* meant this sort of prescriptive solidaristic norm but was also used to refer to parochial fanaticism. Abduh substituted for this idea the theory that love held social units together and motivated their mutual assistance.[53]

The passage in which Abduh refers to love as the basis of the political community is interesting in itself, but it also has important implications for the subsequent development of Arab nationalist thought. Readers who are at all familiar with the ideas of Michel Aflaq of the Ba'ath Party of Syria will immediately recognize the contribution of the love theme to his alternatively subjective and natural-historical conception of the basis of the Arab political community.[54] In Abduh's treatment, however, the main aim is to prove the necessity of prophecy. Prophecy, particularly the prophecy of Muhammad, it is implied, is the functional substitute for love. Abduh does not deny that mutual affection can remain the basis of the polity; in fact, he does not work out the precise relationship between prophecy and love. He is at pains rather to prove that the basis of the political community cannot be rational. Perhaps he believed that mutual affection could prevail only after a messenger had been sent by God.

Of the need which each member of a society has for his fellows there can be no doubt . . . as a consequence whereof there is the link extending from the family to the tribe then to the nation (ummah) and to all mankind . . . the form which these needs take, particularly within nations worthy of the name, that is those characterized by relationships and ties which distinguish them from others, are the need to subsist, the need to enjoy the advantages of life, the need to acquire the things desired, and the need to fend off all sorts of adversities . . . if human affairs proceeded according to the methods of the rest of creation, then these needs would be among the most important factors producing love among human beings . . . it is of the nature of love that it maintains within nations and inspires their subsistence, and it is of the nature of love that it is closely connected to human needs in accordance with the determination of the laws of existence . . . there is no doubt that the persistence of a society under these conditions (the breakdown of love because it is not instinctive in mankind) is impossible, for it is necessary for humankind to preserve itself through love or some substitute . . . At various times certain thinkers resorted to justice . . . thinking that justice might take the place of love . . . but who will lay down the rules of justice? Do they say that reason will do it? . . . but has it ever been heard of in the history of mankind and does it accord with human behavior that a whole society or its majority should submit to the opinion of a wise man simply because it is correct? . . . No. Such has never been heard of in the history of man and such is not in accord with his nature.[55]

The influence of Ibn Khaldun upon Abduh is apparent even from this omission-scarred quotation. Ibn Khaldun's *asabiyya* was a natural solidarity, found among tribal peoples and subject to decline with the civilization of nomadic conquerors by their victims. Ibn Khaldun held further that Arab *asabiyya* was greatly enhanced by the admixture of religious *asabiyya* after the mission of the Prophet. Abduh, however, adds another term between natural *asabiyya* and religious solidarity: "subjective sentiment." It was in stressing this subjective sentiment rather than in his rejection of the historical possibility of the rule of philosopher-kings that Abduh departed from Ibn Khaldun and the medieval philosophers. In rejecting the rational basis of the political community, Abduh attempted to stress the subjective religious sentiment that remains so important a factor in the contemporary solidarity of Muslim Arabs.

XII.

In the preceding sections, we have been concerned to elaborate a few of the Islamic ideas that were susceptible of adaptation to meet the social and ideological crisis confronting Egyptians and all Muslims at the end of the nineteenth century. We have not argued that today's nationalism is the outgrowth of these ideas alone nor even of these ideas in a social context. The task of ideological analysis does not end with pointing out the parallelism of certain ideas. Explanation born only of parallelism leads to the Starkian notion of social knowledge and to the language of the "spirit of the age."[56] Not only does such language in itself lack meaning, but it also fails to answer such significant questions as why Muslims did not, as many Christian observers hoped and expected they would, merely accept Christian values and Christianity. Can one argue that the form of ideas is important and the content merely epiphenomenal, the reverse of the way in which the national question was dealt with by Stalin? That is, can we hold that it is the romantic or rational form that is significant rather than the specific Islamic content of these ideas? Is *Weltanschauung* form or substance? If substance, how can we explain the persistence of both rational and romantic ideas among the same people, even in the writings of the same person, at the same time in history?

Or is it preferable to argue with Stark that this contingent content is ideological, while the *Weltanschauung* is a form of knowledge in some sense? What, then, is our own age—the age of rationalism or the age of romanticism?

It is remarkable that the major works on ideology pay so little attention to nationalism. I think there is no good explanation for this omission other than the kinds of theory with which the subject matter of the sociology of knowledge has been associated and the universalistic biases of its exponents. One of the principal points of departure for such theory appears to have been lack of concern with ultimate values and disproportionate interest in programmatic ideology.

As is well known, the study of ideology received its greatest impetus from Marx, but ultimately the central idea behind the sociology of knowledge goes back to Montesquieu and beyond. These two lines of thought, which have contributed so much to modern sociology and anthropology, have also inspired two somewhat divergent kinds of analysis and theoretical approach to the study of ideology. The first attempts to explain ideology as a condition of the social position of the individual, primarily his social class; the second leans more heavily upon explanations based on stages of intellectual growth, maturation, or modernization. Mannheim, with his conservative-radical dichotomy and ideology-utopia distinction, is an exponent of the first tendency. Dilthey and Weber follow the second tendency, the former in his types of *Weltanschauung* and the latter in his types of authority and types of rationality. But ideologies (whether or not one insists that ideology distorts) differ in their evaluations of events even under the common intellectual umbrella of a single ontology. The difficulty is illustrated by these two tendencies in the sociology of knowledge. Marx considered ontology to be dependent upon ideology, but Dilthey, Weber, and Stark have all tried to establish the dependence of ideology on ontology. When we examine nationalism in the light of these considerations, especially in the light of the European nationalism to which these writers were exposed, we find that it does not appear to fit into either category. European nationalism has cut across class lines, has been now the cry of radicals and now of conservatives. It has affected a large group of nations of roughly equal intellectual maturity in Europe with diverse ideological results, while it has affected peoples of quite disparate cultures outside Europe with amazingly similar results in our own day.

The tendency of the sociology of knowledge has therefore been to regard the nationalist idea itself, that is the ultimate value to which the programmatic is attached, merely as an epiphenomenon. Surely the absence, even unintentional, of any serious treatment of the core idea itself has led to explanations of nationalism that leave unanswered the question of why such a "meaningless" ultimate has been so widely chosen when other notions might serve equally well to mask the class interests of the rising bourgeoisie or working-class intentions to preserve hard-won benefits. Nor—and this point is crucial—would any serious person argue that nationalism represents a higher stage of intellectual maturity.

Thus the study of nationalism poses an enigma matched only by the nationalist's claim that his nationalism is *sui generis* and cannot be understood by reference to any other idea calling itself nationalism. As a consequence of such theoretical neglect, nationalism has become a subject for the discipline of the unique *par excellence,* that is, for history. The best works on nationalism are by historians, who trace the intellectual and political sequences by which modern nationalism has risen supreme and who have been able to point out how the shape of international politics has changed as a consequence. When statements are made about all nationalisms or even a group of nationalisms, no theoretical or ideological characterizations are usually given. Nationalism is either condemned for leading to political excesses domestically and internationally or praised for leading to the cultural enrichment of the world and as a way station on the road to universal harmony. It is explained in terms of its origins or its ends, but almost never in terms of its essence. That essence is either affirmed as unique by nationalists or rejected as nonexistent by historians who well know of cases in which nationalism itself was nonexistent.

Perhaps indeed there is no special essence, but even then existing explanations raise more problems than they solve. It appears that the nationalist classes have changed over time, and that such social change, rather than resulting in greater maturity of thought or rationalism, has resulted in a nationalist shift more and more toward romanticism. These changes are amply highlighted by comparison of Kohn's characterization of the nationalist class and Benda's characterization of that same class in France.[57] We may also contrast the rationalism of the French Revolution with the romanticism of German nationalism.

It is instructive to compare Kohn's presentation with Benda's critique. Kohn holds that the national awakening in each case has resulted in the integration of the dominant ideology or "philosophy" of the period into the more widely participant politics that has been the consequence of admitting the bourgeoisie as citizens as well as subjects. He therefore finds within the same framework of nationalism distinct national ideologies—not national character but national values.[58] The emergence of nationalism is, for him, an ideological cutoff point, at which social processes fix a particular value configuration. For Benda, however, nationalism is inextricably bound up with positivism and the conquest of French intellectuals by German romantic philosophy.[59] While, for Kohn, French rationalism and nationalism go together, for Benda, nationalism is unreason and represents the politicization of philosophy.[60] For Kohn, it is almost the reverse: the philosophizing of politics.

It is significant that Kohn does not argue, as do some others, that the pattern of nationalist thought is everywhere the same. In fact, for him a national ideology is the same as a nationalist ideology: French nationalism was rationalist, and German nationalism was romantic. But Benda might argue that French rationalism was not nationalist as was French romanticism. Kohn does consider the romantic and self-regarding aspects of national ideologies, but these aspects are looked upon as more truly ideological, that is, as mere justifications of the cores of national ideologies.

To contrast Kohn with Marx, it may be said that Kohn finds that ideology is determined by vertical divisions (not class or occupational divisions) within the bourgeoisie, while Marx finds the essential divisions to be horizontal within the socioeconomic structure as a whole. It is, however, clear that Kohn does not argue that social position determines ideology; it determines only that there will be an ideology. It may be added that it is not at all clear that this ideology must be nationalistic, although historically it appears that it must assume nationalistic features as a matter of self-defense. What was to be defended, of course, was the right to a national ideology.

Now the justification of the right to a national ideology may be called "nationalism." Kohn was not primarily concerned with the connection between ideology and ontology, but the right to a national ideology surely calls into question the unity of mankind, the essential rationality of mankind, and the possibility of a wholly rational basis for the political community. Nationalism demands an historical ontology. Such an ontology was provided by the works of Dilthey, Weber, Mannheim, and Stark, to leave out of account the historians themselves. All four argued that ideology was based on ontology, while ontology itself changed with historical conditions. What is the more remarkable is that all these students of ideology believed that the spirit of the modern age is rationalist and therefore diametrically opposed to nationalist thought. One might then expect, in Kohn's terms, that all national ideologies would be rationalist, that none would develop nationalistic elements, and that no ideational barriers of an ontological nature would be put up against the creation of a world state. Nevertheless, the very relativism with which they treated the rationalism of the modern age contributed to the strengthening of romantic nationalist ideas.

The crux of the problem is really the relationship between identity and community. In a purely analytical sense, we may agree that identity is irrational and community necessarily rational. It may even be agreed that identity is "natural" in the historical sense, while community is "conventional." Analysis aside, experience strongly urges upon us the conclusion that both irrational and rational needs must be satisfied for the maintenance of a stable polity. Viewed in this light, both identity and community determine the political function of ideology; but this function is itself defined philosophically, that is, by our ideas of the nature of the political community. The democratization of political life entrained the politicization of identity in place of its functional equivalent: divine right. The politicization of identity in Europe has so far been more significant than the rise of industrialism in determining the nature of political cleavages. Vertical cleavages have been more important than horizontal ones.

Ideally, a national ideology (in Kohn's terms) ought to include symbols that fulfill both functional requisites of identity and community. The existence of a vertical cleavage is empirical evidence of the failure to satisfy identity needs, whatever their historical origins may be. This failure is one source of nationalist ideologies (in our terms). Political communities exist within a context of other political communities, and their separate existences may be challenged by their neighbors. This possibility is a second source of nationalist ideologies. The justification of a challenge to the separate existence of another political community may be the antithesis of a nationalist ideology, that is, it may be an argument for the essentially rational basis of the community. Similarly, the justification for refusal to recognize the existence of a vertical political cleavage may be that the conventional community determines identity. These incomplete generalizations are not very important for European history, but they are essential for an understanding of the rise of

nationalism in the underdeveloped areas. The imperialistic argument justi-
fying the subjection of colonial peoples was an argument from the rational
and conventional basis of the political community. It was argued, for example, that European administration was better than native administration.
European imperialists were inconsistent, of course, for in Europe they argued
that identity determined community, while in Africa and Asia they argued that
community ought to determine identity.

The rise of colonial nationalism may be attributed, in part, to the outcome
of this simple debate. Still, if there was inconsistency on the imperialist side,
there was incongruency on the colonial side. Nationalist modes of thinking
developed without the prior appearance of national ideologies. There were
occurrences of this kind in Europe too, and Kohn takes pains to point out
the differences.[61] But the important point is that the converging processes
described by Kohn and Deutsch[62] had not yet taken place when the vertical
political cleavage between colonial and imperialist became too manifest to be
resisted. The search for an Arab nationalist ideology expresses this deficiency.
Instead of a western European type of combination of national ideology and
nationalist-historical ontology, we find in the Middle East, as elsewhere
among the new nations, a traditional often religious ideology sustained by a
nationalist ontology that has been evolved from the theological. Perhaps a
national ideology is in the process of being created. We may even begin to
suggest from where these incipient ideas will come. But for the time being,
the really significant element in the study of Arab nationalist ideology is the
means by which the philosophical foundations were provided for nationalist
modes of thought. The essential consequence of this ideological process has
been insistence upon the natural basis of the political community.

NOTES

1. Ibrahim Gum'ah, *Idiyulujiyyah al-Qawmiyyah al-'Arabiyyah* (Cairo, 1960), p. 25.
2. See N. Rejwan, "Arab Nationalism," in W. Z. Laqueur, *The Middle East in Transition* (New York, 1958).
3. E. Kedourie, *Nationalism* (Revised ed., New York, 1960), p. 9.
4. For example, Muhammad al-Ghazali, *Haqiqat al-Qawmiyyah al-'Arabiyyah* (Cairo, n.d.), p. 149.
5. See Leonard Binder, "Radical Reform Nationalism in Syria and Egypt," *Muslim World* (April and July, 1959).
6. See the discussion of Rousseau in L. Strauss, *Natural Right and History* (Chicago, 1953), pp. 252f.
7. A. Cobban, *Rousseau and the Modern State* (London, 1934).
8. Strauss, *op. cit.*, p. 323.
9. Kedourie, *op. cit.*, pp. 32f.
10. This problem is treated in Binder, "The Modernization of Egyptian Political Culture," a paper prepared for the SSRC Comparative Politics Summer Institute, 1962.
11. See L. Gardet, *La cité musulmane* (Paris, 1954).
12. W. Kornhauser, *The Politics of Mass Society* (New York, 1959).
13. See G. Baer, *A History of Landownership in Modern Egypt, 1800-1950* (London, 1962).
14. D. Lerner, *The Passing of Traditional Society* (New York, 1958), pp. 251f.
15. N. Safran, *Egypt in Search of Political Community* (Cambridge, 1961), pp. 57f.
16. Kamal al-Din Husain, *Al-Tarbiyyah wa'l-Ta'lim fi Khamsah Sanawat* (Cairo, 1957).
17. See X. de Planhol, *Le monde islamique* (Paris, 1957), pp. 5f., on the anarchy of the Islamic city.
18. Safran, *op. cit.*, pp. 85f, 129f.
19. M. Colombe, *L'Évolution de L'Egypte, 1924-1950* (Paris, 1951), p. 68 *et passim*.

20. *Ibid.*, pp. 270-1 *et passim.*
21. M. Berger, *Bureaucracy and Society in Modern Egypt* (Princeton, 1957), pp. 13-14, 22, 63.
22. G. Antonius, *The Arab Awakening* (London, 1938). The importance of these pursuits should not be exaggerated, however. See S. G. Haim, *Arab Nationalism* (Berkeley, 1962), p. 4.
23. H. A. B. Rivlin, *The Agricultural Policy of Muhamad Ali in Egypt* (Cambridge, 1961), pp. 250-4.
24. J. M. Landau, *Parliaments and Parties in Egypt* (New York, 1954), p. 114.
25. Colombe, *op. cit.*, pp. 167f.
26. *Ibid.*, p. 124.
27. *Ibid.*, p. 147; see also W. C. Smith, *Modern Islam in India* (London, 1947), pp. 64f.
28. *The Charter* (Draft), May 21, 1962, Information Department, U.A.R., pp. 18, 19; M. H. Haikal, editorial, *al-Ahram,* September 14, 1962.
29. See letter of King Husain to President Nasir, *al-Ahram,* March 31, 1961; see also C. E. Dawn, "The Amir of Mecca al-Husayn ibn Ali and the Origin of the Arab Revolt," *Proceedings of the American Philosophical Society,* 104/1 (February, 1960).
30. The fate of more recent discussions of Arab unity (since April, 1963) sustains the point.
31. M. Mahdi, *al-Farabi's Philosophy of Aristotle* (Arabic text) (Beirut, 1961) p. ix.
32. E. I. J. Rosenthal, *Political Thought in Medieval Islam* (Cambridge, 1958), pp. 210f.
33. Jamal al-Din al-Afghani, *Refutation des Materialistes,* A.-M. Goichon, ed. and tr. (Paris, 1942).
34. *Ibid.*, pp. 174f.
35. Safran, *op. cit.*, p. 69.
36. M. Abduh, *Rissalah al-Tawhid* (17th ed.; Cairo, 1960), p. 20.
37. *Op. cit.*, pp. 72-3; see also G. E. von Grunebaum, *Islam* (2nd ed.; London, 1961), pp. 189f.
38. Abduh, *op. cit.*, p. 14.
39. Safran, *op. cit.*, p. 65.
40. Abduh, *op. cit.*, p. 16.
41. *Ibid.*
42. Ali Abd al-Raziq, *al-Islam wa-Usul al-Hukm* (Cairo, 1925); see Colombe, *op. cit.*, p. 127.
43. H. A. R. Gibb, "Tarikh," *Studies on the Civilization of Islam* (Boston, 1962), p. 121.
44. M. Iqbal, *The Reconstruction of Religious Thought in Islam* (London, 1934); Gibb's treatment of Iqbal in his *Modern Trends in Islam* (Chicago, 1947) is most relevant here.
45. C. C. Adams, *Islam and Modernism in Egypt* (London, 1933), p. 132.
46. Gibb, *Studies,* pp. 151f.
47. L. Binder, "al-Ghazali's Theory of Islamic Government," *Muslim World* (July, 1955).
48. M. Mahdi, *Ibn Khaldun's Philosophy of History* (London, 1957), pp. 257 (n. 7), 258. Safran also treats this problem but somewhat less satisfactorily, *op. cit.*, p. 68.
49. Abduh, *op. cit.*, p. 191.
50. Ibrahim al-Basati, *Wahdat al-'Arab* (Cairo, 1960), p. 36. The term used is "the supreme interest of the state."
51. Safran, *op. cit.*, p. 64; J. M. Ahmed, *The Intellectual Origins of Egyptian Nationalism* (London, 1960), p. 43.
52. Abduh, *op. cit.*, pp. 40-1.
53. *Ibid.*, pp. 98f.
54. Haim, *op. cit.*, p. 242.
55. Abduh, *loc. cit.*
56. W. Stark, *The Sociology of Knowledge* (London, 1958).
57. H. Kohn, *The Idea of Nationalism* (New York, 1961), pp. 3, 345, *et passim.* J. Benda, *The Betrayal of the Intellectuals* (Boston, 1955), p. 19.
58. Kohn, *op. cit.*, pp. 9, 273, 276, *et passim.*
59. Benda, *op cit.*, p. 21 *et passim.*
60. Kohn, *op. cit.*, p. 259; Benda, *op. cit.*, p. 77 *et passim.*
61. Kohn, *op. cit.*, p. 457.
62. K. Deutsch, *Nationalism and Social Communication* (New York, 1953).

Democracy and Socialism: Ideologies of African Leaders

BY *CHARLES F. ANDRAIN*

I. Introduction

African socialists, like European socialists before them, claim that democracy and socialism are inseparable; without socialism there can exist no true democracy. As Kwame Nkrumah, President of Ghana, has stated, "Democracy, for instance, has always been for us not a matter of technique, but more important than technique—a matter of socialist goals and aims. It was, however, not only our socialist aims that were democratically inspired, but also the methods of their pursuit were socialist."[1] In one sense, the African interpretations of democracy and socialism are closely related. Both concepts imply an absence of conflict. Socialists have historically aimed to secure the abolition of conflict over economic matters. They fought against economic poverty and moral injustice. The demands for "justice" (the elimination of exploitation) and "bread" (the achievement of economic abundance) have long rallied men to the socialist cause. Public ownership of the primary means of production and communal ownership of land have constituted the major means to secure a socialist society.[2] Africans also interpret democracy to mean equality, solidarity, and pursuit of the general interest. Yet from another standpoint, democracy presupposes conflict rather than its abolition. According to Joseph Schumpeter, "democracy" means free competition among would-be leaders for the votes of the electorate. All groups have freedom to compete for leadership, and freedom of discussion, a free press, and the right of the electorate to vote a government out of office exist as a result.[3] Democracy and socialism thus do not always have similar meanings.

Despite a certain disparity between the concepts of democracy and socialism, however, they are clearly interrelated in practice, for they reflect the desire for African independence. In this sense, "democracy" means African control of political life, rather than competition among groups. "Socialism" refers to African operation of the economy. The leaders articulate a theory of African democracy that posits different institutions from those of Western parliamentary democracy. Elaborating their ideas about African socialism, most leaders point out that the economic system must be adapted to African realities and not to an imported theory like bourgeois capitalism or Marxism-Leninism.

The sources of African leaders' ideologies arise from European theories and African traditional beliefs. From European thought, the ideas of Rousseau, Marx, and Lenin have probably had the greatest influence. Through universities in East Europe and the Soviet Union; Marxist study groups in London and Paris; *groupes d'études communistes* established in Dakar, Conakry, Abidjan, and Bamako; the Rassemblement Démocratique Africain associated from 1946 to 1950 with the French Communist Party; and the Communist-led Confédération Générale du Travail, the ideology of Marx and Lenin has become part of the Africans' intellectual heritage, especially in French-speaking West Africa. The themes of egalitarianism and humanism have constituted the primary Marxist contributions. The stress on party organization and the interpretation of European imperialism reflect the dominant Leninist influence. Education in French schools introduced Africans to the thinking of Jean-Jacques Rousseau. The African focus on egalitarianism, general will, and community solidarity expresses this intellectual debt.

Besides reflecting the ideas embodied in European theories, African political beliefs also express values of the African *milieu*. The concepts of democracy, socialism, and independence are partly based on certain attributes of pre-colonial culture. African democracy conceived of discussion and consensus-building in the context of the village and tribe. Custom, an "unwritten constitution," usually restrained arbitrary political power. Furthermore, traditional African life was "socialistic." The individual lived in close interrelationship with other members of his group; he felt a collective concern for his family, extended family, and tribe. In the economic sphere, there were no classes based on capital accumulation, although there were social categories based on functional differentiation—masons, blacksmiths, and warriors, for example. All property was held in common by the family or village. In most areas, Africans practiced communal landholding and land cultivation. When African leaders put forward their demands for independence, they invoke memories of the great states of pre-colonial history—Mali, Ghana, Songhai—and the Africans who initially resisted European intrusion—Almamy Samory, El Hadj Omar, Chaka Zulu.

In general, African political leaders have not formulated a clearly defined ideology, in the sense of a comprehensive, consistent, and carefully elaborated system of beliefs. Especially in English-speaking Africa, the pragmatic empiricism of British thought has influenced nationalist ideas. In former French West Africa, however, the greater abstractness of the French intellectual tradition has led such politicians as Léopold Senghor, Mamadou Dia, and Sékou Touré to define more systematic intellectual doctrines. This paper examines the meanings African leaders give to general concepts like democracy, socialism, and independence.

II. The Concept of Democracy

All African leaders, whether of populist or traditionalist orientation, emphasize the distinctiveness of African democracy. Arguing that democracy was an integral element of traditional African society, they hold that contemporary African states embody the essence of democracy. For example, President Nkrumah has written:

Ghana society is by its own form and tradition fundamentally democratic in character. For centuries our people gave great powers to their chiefs but only so long as they adhered to the rules and regulations laid down by the people; the moment they deviated from these rules, they were deposed . . . . I have no doubt that in time we in Africa will evolve forms of government rather different from the traditional western pattern but no less democratic in their protection of the individual and his inalienable rights.[4]

Even conservative monarchs like Emperor Haile Selassie find democratic values in the historical tradition of Ethiopia: "Democracy as the share of the people's voice in the conduct of their own affairs is not foreign to Ethiopia; the democratic Spirit is not new to Us. It is only that Ethiopia's traditional democratic concepts and convictions have now taken on new expression and fresh forms."[5]

In the view of most African leaders, this "democratic spirit" must not be considered synonymous with certain institutional forms of democracy found in Western parliamentary regimes. Such institutional features as a two-party system, a loyal opposition, an independent judiciary, and a neutral civil service constitute the "circumstantials," rather than the "fundamentals," of democracy. While all African societies embody the universal spirit of democracy, the democratic institutions will vary according to the social conditions of each particular country. Prime Minister Abubakar Balewa of Nigeria has cautioned Western critics about confusing the essential spirit of democracy with certain imported institutions: "The Westminster brand of democracy . . . is one method of ensuring democracy as a form of government. If that method fails, another might succeed."[6] All African leaders agree that the essence of democracy consists in the promotion of the people's welfare, discussion, equality, and respect for the general interest. The democratic spirit does not extend to anarchy and license, to activities threatening the stability of the new states. According to President Léopold Senghor of Senegal, who has an intellectual commitment to diversity and decentralization, the role of the opposition "is to criticize. But criticism means critical spirit, not spirit of criticism, systematic carping. In democracy, criticism must be constructive and serve the general, not factional, interest."[7] For all African leaders, order and authority constitute part of the essence of democracy.

Despite this unanimous verbal attachment to African democracy, African leaders have formulated three somewhat different ideological interpetations of a democratic society. Sékou Touré, Kwame Nkrumah, and Julius Nyerere express a monistic interpretation. A second theory, best stated by Nigerian leaders, is based on a pluralistic model, in which larger institutionalized groups compete for influence. A third model, a variant of the pluralistic interpretation, expresses the individualistic revolt against racial groupism in East, Central, and South Africa. Most explicitly defined by Albert Luthuli of South Africa and Tom Mboya of Kenya, this theory stresses individual, rather than group, rights.

The Monistic Model

The monistic, populist concept of democracy, expressed mainly by Sékou Touré, Kwame Nkrumah, and Julius Nyerere, emphasizes the values of popular sovereignty and political equality. According to this interpretation, the social structure must maximize equality. Decision-making must function on the basis of consensus, not on formal votes. Decisions should be unanimous. The individual must subordinate his desires to the group interest. The leaders attempts to minimize conflict and "deviant" behavior; they postulate an identical group goal, which all members should pursue. They stress the need for cohesion, co-operation, and consensus.[8]

The ideology of Sékou Touré best exemplifies the monistic ideal of democracy. For the Guinean President, there exists only one popular will, one general interest. Democracy connotes the subordination of individual interest to the general interest. In a democratic state, the interests of the more general group take precedence over the interests of the more particular. In hierarchial fashion, the interests of the family, then the village, district, and nation have priority over the interests of the individual.[9] At the highest, most general level, citizens in democratic Guinea ought to achieve a consciousness of the universal interests of Africa. Beyond the contradiction between African and imperialist interests, Africans in all sectors of life share an identity of interests: "This democracy, both mother and daughter of that liberty which denotes the constant objective of the P. D. G. [Parti Démocratique de Guinée], again enables us to transcend all which appeared as divergent or factional interests and to consider and ensure that only the sole interests of Africa constitute our common platform. . . ."[10]

Consistent with this stress on the dominance of the general interest, the ideology of Touré condemns both individualism and liberalism. Instead of individualism, the Guineans must focus on the solidarity and sovereignty of the people. Since the distinctive African philosophy affirms collective values, "if it is necessary we do not hesitate to sacrifice the individual for the good of the community."[11] As Touré equates individualism with selfishness, he identifies liberalism with compromise, anarchy, and the reign of individual and group interests:

The enemy of revolutionary firmness is liberalism which from compromise to compromise drives a party into incriminations and anarchy. The best arrangements and the most clever compromises only lead to general discontent and could not possibly preserve the higher interests of the people since they subordinate them, wholly or partly, to the selfish interests of groups or individuals; they could only maintain inequalities and increase antagonisms.[12]

In accordance with his interpretation of democracy as the expression of the general interest, Touré also equates democracy with the dominance of the popular will. African democracy is based on egalitarian relations; there are no privileged groups. The leaders exercise power in the interests of the whole people, rather than of a class or faction of the population. Since Africa has no antagonistic social classes, she can construct a democracy founded on the unanimous will of the people, rather than on a social class as in bourgeois or proletarian democracy, on a religous conception as in Christian or Islamic democracy, or on a political system as in parliamentary or presidential democracy.[13]

By stressing the participation of all the people in political affairs, Sékou Touré formulates a theory of "popular dictatorship." According to this interpretation, "dictatorship" means the exercise of authority, the power of direction over men and things. Democracy implies popular participation in government, as well as respect for the authority of the whole people. In Guinea the dictatorship will be democratic, for the major political principles are defined in party congresses and assemblies, and popular, for its decisions will safeguard the rights of the people.[14] In this "popular dictatorship," formal rules do not constitute the source of authority. Political officials must obey the popular interest, the law of the people, rather than invoke a formal law to justify an action contrary to the interests of the nation.[15]

For President Touré, the single political party, the Parti Démocratique de Guinée, assumes the dominant political position in the state. Since there exists only one general interest, one unanimous popular will, and one pre-eminent thought, only one political party must carry out political activities. The PDG defines the general interest, serves as the custodian and depository of the popular will, and embodies the collective thought of the whole Guinean people. By defining the general policies of all sectors of life, the PDG guides, directs, and controls activities in the state.

> On the human plane, nothing can exist without having been previously conceived, evaluated, and directed by a thought. The Party constitutes the thought of the people of Guinea at its highest level and in its most complete form. The thought of the Party indicates the orientation of our actions; the thought of the Party specifies the principles which ought to direct our behavior, our collective and individual attitude.[16]

Hence the PDG, according to Touré, does not resemble a European political party. Where European parties represent the partial interests of either workers or capitalists, the PDG refuses to become the political expression of a given social class; rather it embodies the common, indivisible interest of all African social strata.[17]

We can better understand the pre-eminent role of the party by examining the relation of the PDG to the masses and the government and the relationship between party leaders and militants. In his attitude toward the masses, Touré shows the same ambivalence characteristic of leaders influenced by Leninist ideology. On one hand, Touré holds that the party must be both in the vanguard of the masses and in their midst. In the vanguard, the PDG defines the meaning and objectives of the political struggle; it raises the level of consciousness of the people; it educates the masses and improves their character.[18] Working in the midst of the masses, the good party leader participates in all political activities; he serves as a good example to the masses; he demonstrates superior organizational and mobilizing talents and encourages a spirit of struggle and sacrifice. Touré writes, "Everywhere, the Party is pre-eminent; everywhere it must think, act, direct, and control the action of the toiling masses. . . ."[19] On the other hand, besides assuming that the party must control the masses, Touré looks favorably on the creative ability of these same masses. The party must also be behind the masses, as well as in the vanguard and in their midst. Expressing his regard for the worth of the common people, Touré observes, "There is a simple way of narrowing this gap between the needs and the methods placed at our disposal—that is to remain in contact with the masses, and the secret of the masses lies more in the feeling of justice, of dignity, than in all that we can offer them in the field of technology or science."[20]

In contrast to the communist parties, the PDG is a mass rather than an elite organization. Bernard Charles estimates that more than 50% of the Guinean population belongs to the PDG, compared with 5% party membership in most communist states. This 50% figure is of particular significance because 40% of the Guinean population is under fifteen years old.[21]

In the Guinean government, the party exercises supremacy over administrative organs. The PDG is the brain, or conscience, of the society, while the state is the executive part. As embodiment of the collective conscience, the PDG directs all state organs:

> At the level of each group, the Party assumes this organization and orientation. At the village level, it is the committee; at the level of the district, it is the section. At the level of the nation it is the mass of the Party. Thus, the Party determines and directs the action of the nation, the action of the districts, the action of the villages, the action of each group and the action of the mass of groups. Beginning from this fundamental idea, we have adapted the political and administrative structures to the democratic structures of the Party.[22]

Consistent with this view of party hegemony over government, Sékou Touré's ideology opposes the concepts of both an omnipotent state and a representative government based on parliamentary supremacy. He identifies both these concepts of the state with political practices under colonial administration. But while supremacy of government and administration implies domination by alien forces, the pre-eminence of the party connotes supremacy of the people. By reasoning based on Rousseauean principles, Touré holds that even a parliamentary regime does not ensure popular sovereignty. Where parliament is supreme, the voters become slaves of the elected representatives, and the deputies assert the dominance of partial interests. Only on election days do the people under a parliamentary system regain their sovereignty.[23] Thus in Guinea all representatives to the National Assembly are elected on a single national list; they do not represent the more partial interests of geographic regions. Unlike its counterparts in West European democracies, the civil service is not politically neutral *vis-à-vis* the party in office. Touré insists that political office must be granted on the basis of loyalty to party tenets and not according to class origin, wealth, education, or technical knowledge.[24]

In regard to party militants and supporters, the party leaders tend to emphasize the need for discipline. Within the PDG, Secretary-General Touré has opposed all factions based on self-interest. Like Lenin, on whose ideas of organization the PDG is largely based, Touré articulates the doctrine of democratic centralism, a blend of free discussion and unity in action. Democracy operates when the party militants choose the leaders and freely discuss various policy decisions. The emphasis on discipline and unity in action reveals the centralization principle. After a majority vote decides a course of action, both leaders and supporters must obey that decision. Furthermore, responsibility for leadership, in contrast to responsibility for decision, cannot be shared. Violation of party discipline is forbidden.[25] But Touré cautions that the practice of democratic centralism does not mean bureaucratic centralization, the dominance of individual authoritarianism. Rather, there must be spontaneous co-operation and understanding between party leaders and militants.[26] The leaders select the appropriate tactics and decide the best ways to apply them. In turn, the supporters have the responsibility to discuss problems and choose solutions for them.

In light of Touré's conception of the relationship between the party leaders, the militants, and the masses, the commitment in practice to freedom of expression and legitimate opposition becomes doubtful. The stress on discipline, unity, absolute authority of the party, and antifactionalism makes difficult the voicing of disagreement over policies. The establishment of many organizations affiliated to the party—the Jeunesse du Rassemblement Démocratique Africain and the Confédération Nationale des Travailleurs de Guinée—not only provides for popular participation in political life but also facilitates party control over the populace. The characteristic attempt of a monistic body to secure cohesion, consensus, and unanimous opinions tends to result in pseudo-participation, in which the party leaders merely communicate goals to members. The party and affiliated organizations may thus serve to persuade the masses to accept and endorse decisions already made by the leaders. For effective popular participation and influence over decisions, there must exist some institutionalized means by which the members can challenge policy both before and after it is made. In addition to a variety of autonomous organized centers of power, there should also be relative equality of access to the means of influence.

The hierarchial structure of the PDG, the hostility to factions within the party, and the absence of autonomous organizations outside party control hinder the development of legitimate conflicts. From top to bottom, the party structure on the executive level consists of the Bureau Politique National, the *sections,* and the *comités de village et de quartier;* on the legislative level, there are the National Congress, regional congresses, and general assemblies. In this structural arrangement, the Bureau Politique controls the government and party. As Secretary-General of the PDG and President of the Republic, Sékou Touré appoints ministers and heads of departments who are responsible to the party. Diallo Saïfoulaye, the political secretary of the party, wields the most political influence after Touré. These leading politicians, along with the other members of the Bureau Politique, make crucial policy decisions. The PDG controls the villages through local committees and agricultural cooperatives. In general, the party leaders designate candidates for office, although, at the lowest levels, the number of candidates may exceed the number of positions.[27]

Under these conditions, the opportunities for effective popular participation seem limited. In a sense, Touré's concept of democracy resembles Bonapartist ideology. As defined by Robert Michels, "Bonapartism does not recognize any intermediate links. . . . The power of the chief of state rests exclusively upon the direct will of the nation."[28] In Guinea, however, there is not so much a charismatic leader as a charismatic party. Not Sékou Touré but the PDG possesses extraordinary qualities and powers. Although the individual may commit errors, the party as an institution never errs.[29] Touré frequently reiterates the necessity for the individual personality to become submerged in the personality of the party: "No responsible political man, whatever the authority he represents, could substitute himself for the Party. If he emanates from it, if he is its speaker, he can only act as a reflecting instrument, not of his own personality, but of the Party which alone can express the will, the aspirations, the needs, and the hopes of our people."[30]

This faith in the virtues of organization has led Touré, like Lenin, to overlook the fact that an organization can be only as virtuous as its leaders.

Already within Guinea, the pressure toward total politicization has resulted in the bureaucratization of social life. In contrast to the Weberian model, the party has tended to produce a rather inefficient, instead of a rationally efficient, bureaucracy. Although certain aspects of PDG practice may further democracy —the encouragement of popular discussion of issues, allowance for disagreement within the party, the value placed on social equality—the extent to which PDG leaders allow legitimate opposition depends, in the long run, on the degree of control exercised by the party over sociopolitical life.

The political beliefs of President Kwame Nkrumah reveal the same emphasis on simplicity that characterizes a monistic group. Inherent in monistic processes is the tendency towards homogeneity, toward reducing differences and trying to eliminate "deviant" behavior and attitudes. Nkrumah's concept of democracy, like that of Touré, illustrates a centralist and populist bias. Rather than stressing the values of diversity and complexity, the Ghanaian leader upholds the need for simple structures. He opposes the complicated system of checks and balances. "A parliamentary system of the Western type . . . is a subtle and sophisticated type of administration full of balances and checks. This by its very nature is a very difficult and cumbersome system to apply to our traditional pattern of government."[31] Consistently with his stress on simplicity, Nkrumah tends to equate democracy with centralization. He opposes the federal system of government, not only because the maintenance of both central and regional governments absorbs greater man power and economic resources than does a unitary form, but also because federalism confuses the locus of power and thus becomes too complex a system to operate. Threatened by neocolonialism, nuclear imperialism, and balkanization, the nations of modern Africa require strong central governments.[32]

President Nkrumah holds a less monistic theory of political reality than does Sékou Touré. While Touré believes that only one organization—the Parti Démocratique de Guinée—can legitimately embody the general interest and the people's will, Nkrumah feels that three agencies—the national parliament, the party, and the president—embody popular sovereignty: "We have adopted a people's democracy in which the sovereign will of the people is exercised through Parliament, a President and a party."[33] Since Ghana received its independence in 1957, the Convention People's Party has assumed a more and more dominant role over parliament. In a speech delivered to the Ghanaian legislative assembly in November, 1956, Nkrumah defined "democracy" as the provision of rights for the opposition and minority parties. The opposition should receive guaranteed representation on assembly committees, as well as equal rights with the government to communicate through the State Broadcasting Committee.[34] At that time, Nkrumah's political beliefs reflected more closely the influence of British parliamentary traditions. He felt that all political parties should have freedom to operate and to recruit members. Four years later, however, when Ghana became a republic, President Nkrumah spoke in more sweeping terms of the supremacy of the party: "The Convention People's Party . . . is the uniting force that guides and pilots the nation and is the nerve center of the positive operations in the struggle for African irredentism. Its supremacy cannot be challenged. The Convention People's Party is Ghana, and Ghana is the Convention People's Party."[35]

Party membership now takes precedence over parliamentary membership.

With the decline of the opposition United Party after 1960, the constituency and branch organizations of the CPP began to express a pronounced localism. The local party leaders voiced many of the demands formerly made by the United Party. To combat this challenge to the party's National Secretariat, Nkrumah affirmed the dominance of party representation over geographic representation:

> Members of Parliament must remember at all times that they are representatives of their constituencies only by reason of their Party membership and that on no account should they regard constituency representation as belonging to them in their own right. In other words, constituencies are not the property of Members of Parliament. It is the Party that sends them there and fights for them to become Members of Parliament.[36]

Party membership becomes not only more important than parliamentary status but also more politically significant than holding a governmental ministerial position. "Since the Party forms the Government, the members of the Central Committee, the leading directorate of the Party, will in future take precedence over non-Central Committee Ministers at all Party ceremonies and at all public and civic functions. . . . It is the Convention People's Party which makes the Government and not the Government which makes the Convention People's Party. . . ."[37]

This monistic interpretation of democracy coincides with the increasing dominance of the CPP over all aspects of Ghanaian life. Few organizations have remained free from party control. Nkrumah views the party in terms of an organic analogy: "Our Party is likened to a tree—a huge and mighty tree with great branches sticking out elsewhere. The trunk and the branches form the tree. It is a single unit, living a single life and when it dies, it dies a single death."[38] Nkrumah considers the various organizations attached to the CPP as branches of the party. Groups like the Trade Union Congress, the United Farmers' Council, and the National Council of Ghana Women are not "affiliates" of the party but "integral elements." Various youth groups, particularly the Ghana Young Pioneers Movement, have also come under direct party control. In short, party leadership of the communications media and trade-union, farmers', youth, and women's groups has tended to hinder the expression of nonviolent opposition. The demands for order and the desire to bind leaders and masses closely together do not allow for the spontaneous operation of intermediary groups between the central government and the citizens.

The role of personal leadership assumes greater prominence in the political beliefs of Kwame Nkrumah, in contrast to those of Sékou Touré. Not only the parliament and party but also the president expresses the people's will. Although Touré rarely speaks of his personal life, family, or early career, Nkrumah has written widely of the major events in his life. He regards himself as the living embodiment of the national legitimacy of Ghana. His autobiography is entitled *Ghana: The Autobiography of Kwame Nkrumah*. Within Ghana, the press and political subordinates most frequently refer to Nkrumah as "Osagyefo," the Victorious Leader. Party leaders take an oath of personal loyalty to Nkrumah. Those who deviate from the party line are accused of insubordination and rebellion toward the President, not of disobedience to collective decisions made by the party organs.[39] Kofi Baako, Reverend Dzirasa, and other close lieutenants of Nkrumah have tried to make out of such ideas a philosophy of "Nkrumaism." According to Baako,

"In whatever we do, we must be guided by the policy statements of our great leader, whose ideas and ideals constitute Nkrumaism."[40] This view of leadership reveals the monistic concept of democracy held by the Ghanaian President. As in a small group, no intermediary associations intervene between the leader and members. Nkrumah favors a unicameral legislature, a unitary form of government, one party, and one leader. "Democracy" does not imply disorder or anarchy, and it does not mean supporting multiple factions "warring within the bosom of a divided nation."[41] The demand for order in a stable democracy thus takes priority over factional competition.

Julius Nyerere, President of Tanganyika, holds a more pluralistic interpretation of democracy than does either Nkrumah or Sékou Touré. If Sékou Touré proceeds in the tradition of Rousseau, focusing on the general will, cohesion, and community solidarity, Nyerere has elaborated a democratic model that stresses the reconciliation of differences through discussion. He thus reiterates values held by the Athenians, who carried on lively debates in the small Greek *polis*. According to Nyerere, "The African concept of democracy is similar to that of the ancient Greeks. . . . To the Greeks, democracy meant simply 'government by discussion among equals.' "[42] Like Aristotle, Nyerere sees the family, the most significant small group in society, as the basis of the state. The feeling of democratic equality arises from the sense of belonging to a community, brotherhood, or family. Traditional African polities formed a society of equals; the individual felt integrated into a cohesive community rather than separated from it:

> In his own traditional society the African has always been a free individual, very much a member of his community, but seeing no conflict between his own interests and those of his community. This is because the structure of his society was, in fact, a direct extension of the family. First you had the small family unit; this merged into a larger "blood" family which, in its turn, merged into the tribe. The affairs of the community . . . were conducted by free and equal discussion. . . . [43]

Although Nyerere recognizes that free discussion operates best in such small communities as the Greek city-states or African tribal settings, he hopes that the ideal can also be realized on a national level within the single party and parliament.

President Nyerere accepts the widely held distinction between the essence and institutions of a democratic state. As a state of mind, an attitude, a universal essence, democracy must be distinguished from its machinery and structure, which vary from country to country.[44] Free discussion in a "society of equals" constitutes the essence of democracy, but this process of discussion or "talking until you agree" does not require organized opposition parties. The two-party system is not synonymous with democracy. Contrary to Western opinion, which sees democracy as a conflict between competing, institutionalized groups, Nyerere argues that a single-party state like Tanganyika will promote greater democracy and freedom of expression than does the two-party system of Great Britain. In England, the leaders of each party impose a rigid discipline on the members. At election time, all members must support the candidate selected by the organization's leadership. During parliamentary debates, the backbenchers must follow the policy line dictated by the party's parliamentary leaders. In contrast, the Tanganyika African National Union provides greater freedom for its members. During the elections, voters in each constituency can choose from among several candidates. Elections occur more often than every five years. Whenever the people become dissatisfied with a leader, he can be voted out of office at any time. National leadership is therefore constantly changing.[45] During the decision-making process, conflicting arguments should be heard in parliament. The public must have the relevant information to understand these political decisions. Within party circles as well as in the legislature, TANU leaders must ensure that members have the right to challenge policy decisions. Policies ought not to become dogma: "Dogmatism and freedom of discussion do not easily go together."[46]

Nyerere also justifies the one-party system by identifying the single party with the national interest. Like Sékou Touré, he equates the two-party system with class politics. Applying Marxist analysis to the African context, Nyerere sees the two parties in England and the United States as reflections of divergent classes:

> There was a struggle between the "haves" and the "have-nots"—each of whom organized themselves into political parties. . . . Thus the existence of distinct classes in a society and the struggle between them resulted in the growth of the two-party system. . . . With rare exceptions the idea of class is something entirely foreign to Africa. Here in this continent the nationalist movements are fighting a battle for freedom from *foreign* domination, not from domination by any ruling class of our own. To us "the other party" is the colonial power.[47]

While European parties were formed to oppose antagonistic economic groups, African parties arose to challenge foreign rulers. Since these latter parties embody the national interest, Nyerere prefers to call them "national movements." They represent whole nations, rather than parts or sections of communities.[48] The "national movement" has an open membership. Politics is of concern to the whole community in Tanganyika, and all citizens are free to participate in the party. This situation contrasts with those in both Western democracies and Communist states. In the latter, elites or "vanguard aristocracies" run political affairs. In the two-party states, factions predominate; this "politics of groups" involves only a minority of the people.[49]

Both Sékou Touré and Julius Nyerere strongly attack factionalism and individualism. Nyerere's opposition stems from his identification of factionalism with self-interest or selfishness. Like Touré, he criticizes the antisocial character of a faction; its goals may conflict with the good of the community. The self-interest of a faction will prove even more harmful than the self-interest of an individual, for a group is more powerful than an individual, and its motives are more difficult to recognize.[50]

Even though Nyerere opposes factionalism, he seems more willing than Touré to encourage compromise. But such compromise must occur between individuals rather than groups or factions:

> In any human society compromise between individuals is not only necessary but desirable; for it is the only means of arriving at the common denominator without which the very idea of society would be impossible. But, if compromise is desirable, what makes it so is the common good—not sectional interests. Individualism, therefore, should be tempered with, or subjected to, the good of society as a whole, not merely to the good of a part of society. . . . In a society which is united, which is like a family, the only differences will be those between individuals.[51]

In line with this desire to establish a polity based on family-like relations, Nyerere assumes that Africans have a personal rather than institutional concept of government. A democratic society must function under personal rather than impersonal authority. He is opposed to an institutionalized system of checks and balances and favors strong personal leadership by the president. The chief executive must control the civil service and also appoint the judges; these two agencies must not operate as neutral forces to check the leaders. They must demonstrate rather their total commitment to accomplishing the tasks set by the government. As in a family, the agent of authority must not be separate from the source of authority. In declaring for a republican form of government, Nyerere stated his preference for a president with both real and symbolic authority.[52]

According to Nyerere's monistic concept of noninstitutionalized democracy, the distinctions between the party and the government and between politicians and civil servants have little relevance to Tanganyika. In a multiparty system, a neutral civil service provides continuity of public administration against a background of changing parties that exercise governmental power on a temporary basis. But in a single-party state, the party *is* the government. When making policies therefore, the politicians ought to have available the resources of an intelligent and able civil service.[53]

In practice, the Tanganyikan political system has provided channels for egalitarian participation and discussion. At the local level, the village *baraza,* or general discussion, forms the center of party life. Here every member of the village has the opportunity to discuss and voice grievances. In local elections, more than one TANU candidate often stands for a single seat. The major decision-making body of the party, the National Executive Committee, includes representatives of such diverse groups as trade unions, youth leagues, co-operatives, ethnic associations, and lower party organs. Compared with many other African states, the central legislature, which Nyerere calls a "discussion-house," has independent authority apart from TANU agencies.[54] In actuality as in theory, therefore, the Tanganyikan political institutions provide means for the discussion of major issues.

The Pluralistic Model

In contrast to Touré, Nkrumah, and Nyerere, the pluralists regard democracy as a framework within which institutionalized groups compete for power. Recognizing the need for checks against majority or minority-group tyranny, the pluralists hold that intermediary or secondary associations between government and populace can preserve liberty. The basic goal is to prevent the accumulation of all power in one group. Individual attachments to various subnational groups can not only prevent concentration of power but also bind the members more firmly to the society. Various citizens have a diversity rather than an identity of interests. The various social groups must secure unity rather than uniformity. The basic problem facing the pluralists involves the need to induce loyalty to the nation and to ensure that loyalties to subnational groups do not lead to disintegration of the state. The political actors must share a consensus on the "rules of the game," a consensus that will mitigate intense group conflict and encourage citizens to support the national regime.

Throughout most of French-speaking Africa, groups operate as factions within a coalitional single party. For example, in Senegal the party organizers, young intellectuals, Moslem *marabouts,* and civil servants form strong factions within the ruling Union Progréssiste Sénégalaise. President Senghor believes that too great a political centralization will engender bureaucratization. Traditional African society was based on a pluralistic unity. Contemporary African states must aim to secure unity in diversity instead of unanimity.[55] Dahomey and the Ivory Coast are undergoing similar attempts to construct democratic states based on traditional diversity. In Dahomey, the governing Parti Dahoméen de l'Unité is a coalition of two regional-religious factions: the northern, Moslem wing and the southern, Catholic wing. In the Ivory Coast, President Houphouët-Boigny has tended to include potential opposition—notably ethnic leaders, students, and trade unionists—in the party and government.

In contemporary Africa, Nigeria represents the best example of pluralism. Here ethnic groups are institutionalized within the federal system. Three Nigerian leaders, Obafemi Awolowo of the Western Region, Nnamdi Azikiwe of the East, and Tafawa Balewa of the North, all tend to argue for a pluralistic concept of democracy. As the political beliefs of these three leaders indicate, the pluralists do not usually articulate an elaborate, systematic, or explicit ideology. The need to make frequent compromises among diverse group pressures exercises a strong pragmatic influence on the leaders' thinking. Political beliefs tend to be flexible and adaptive. A federal system, moreover, discourages ideologism or focus on substantive goals—and encourages legalism, the concern with procedures.

Of all Nigerian politicians, Chief Obafemi Awolowo, a Yoruba and principal opposition leader to the federal coalition of the Northern People's Congress and the National Convention of Nigerian Citizens, best expresses the pluralistic interpretation of democracy. The traditional Yoruba political system resembled a constitutional monarchy, characterized by checks against the arbitrary exercise of power. The value Awolowo places on checks and balances, on federalism, and on traditional elements within the government reveals a pluralistic view of democracy. Opposing parties, ethnic groups, and their traditional leaders must find institutionalized places within the political structure. In contrast to Nkrumah and Nyerere, Awolowo looks favorably upon a system of checks and balances: "The beauty and the essence of democracy, in spite of its known and admitted imperfections, lie in the checks and balances which it provides among the members of a community. By means of these devices, no one citizen is in a position to lord it over his fellow citizens, or to deprive others of their fundamental rights."[56] Consistent with this stress on the need for diversity, Chief Awolowo attacks the idea of a one-party state. The existence of several parties is necessary to express the divergence of opinions found in every society and to prevent a monopoly of power:

> Whenever there are two or more persons, divergence of opinion is bound to exist.
> . . . The people are entitled as of right to be given the chance to examine all sides of
> the problems confronting them, before expressing their majority will at the polls. Such
> an examination, however, will be possible only where people who hold different shades
> of opinions are allowed to organise themselves into parties if they wish, and are also free
> to explain their respective points of view to the electorate. . . .[57]

Awolowo has often voiced the need for a strong opposition in all regions of

Nigeria. During his conflict with Chief Akintola, Prime Minister of the Western Region, Awolowo argued that the Action Group should not remain a regional, Yoruba-based party. Rather it should campaign in the North and East to maintain a parliamentary opposition to the NPC and NCNC.

According to Awolowo, both powerful opposition parties and strong regional governments are needed to preserve the delicate balance of power within a democratic state. Federal systems must reflect the ethnic diversity of Nigeria. Writing immediately after World War II, Awolowo held that each state in the Nigerian federal union should contain a separate ethnic group; a future United States of Nigeria could thus have as many as thirty or forty states: "It is essential that each ethnical group be constituted into a separate Province or number of Provinces. . . . Under a true federal constitution each group, however small, is entitled to the same treatment as any other group, however large. Opportunity must be afforded to each to evolve its own peculiar political institution."[58] Awolowo's position on federalism is motivated by a desire not only to preserve ethnic diversity but also to maintain a power equilibrium within Nigeria. A federal government may prevent the potential tyranny of stronger groups like the Hausa-Fulani of the North. The federal form will also reduce the tyranny of the state by providing for the development of strong intermediate groups between the central government and the masses. The Action Group did not strongly support the creation of the new Mid-West Region. It is committed to the creation of new regions out of a redivision of all the present regions, especially the North—but the Mid-West region reduced the Western Region by nearly one-third in population and area.[59]

Besides strong regional governments, sufficient power for traditional groups is required to preserve the delicate power balance within a democratic state. These traditional groups form significant intermediary powers to preserve freedom. Futhermore, the chiefs can provide greater stabilization in an era of change and conflict. Chiefs can also serve as an effective agent of modernization. Awolowo has written:

> The office of Chiefs will continue to have incalculable sentimental value for the masses in Western and Northern Nigeria. This being so, it is imperative, as a matter of practical politics, that we use the most effective means ready at hand for organizing masses for rapid political advancement. . . . The masses revere the office, and regard it as divine. They look upon Chiefs . . . as the representatives of God on earth.[60]

In accordance with these views, Awolowo wants to democratize the role of the chiefs. In order to make both the chiefs and the people jointly responsible for all governmental acts, he instituted reforms in the Western Region to make the *obas* more responsible to the electorate. Awolowo has shown a desire to bring traditional elements into the authoritative decision-making processes. While serving as minister of local government in the Western Region, he established a system of local councils, with seats reserved for the chiefs. In the spring of 1960, he favored for governor-general, not a party politician like Nnamdi Azikiwe, but a paramount chief. According to his logic, paramount chiefs were regarded as kings before the British came and are thus "true representatives of the British monarchy."[61] Recently, however, Awolowo has moved to weaken ties with the Yoruba traditional rulers. At the time of the 1962 emergency in Western Nigeria caused by the dismissal of Chief Akintola, Awolowo turned for support to the young intellectuals, while Akintola found his greatest following among Lagos businessmen and traditional Yoruba leaders.

Other Nigerian leaders also agree with Awolowo that democracy requires competition among several organized groups. But transcending the group struggle there must be a common loyalty, agreement on procedures and broad goals, and a spirit of reconciliation. President Nnamdi Azikiwe and Prime Minister Abubakar Tafawa Balewa stress the values of tolerance and the need for a common Nigerian nationality. Balewa plays the role of the great reconciler, the evoker of toleration and national consensus. In his view national unity and toleration are prerequisites for a democratic state.[62] Similarly, Dr. Azikiwe sees the necessity for a co-ordinated, rather than an imposed, unity. Federalism, the democratic mechanism to maintain peace among diverse units, must be pervaded by the feeling of community: "A nation is not necessarily racial or tribal, but a historically constituted community of people based on community of interests with which are interwoven community of race, community of language, community of religion, geographic unity, and common political aspirations."[63]

In summary, all three Nigerian leaders hold a pluralistic concept of democracy, an interpretation that connotes a pragmatic, empirical spirit. Within a federal system, institutionalized groups compete for influence. Opposition parties, strong local governments, and traditional authorities help to maintain diversity and to check concentrated power. Participation in local or other subnational groups will, hopefully, give the citizen a feeling of attachment to the national system. In contrast to Nkrumah and Touré, the Nigerians expect that a feeling of community will arise from diversity. The heterogeneity of Nigeria requires that the Nigerian leaders recognize the need for overlapping loyalties in a democratic regime. The current danger to political stability involves the absence of national loyalty and the concentration of one dominant ethnic group in each region. The disintegrating effects of tribalism and regionalism may overcome their stabilizing values. While each of the three parties remains largely confined to one region and while the North remains under authoritarian religious rule, the operation of democratic group pluralism will be stunted in practice. The dangers to national stability may impel the federal government to suppress democratic freedoms in the regions, as happened for a time during 1962 in the Western Region.

The Individualistic Model

In the multiracial states of Kenya and South Africa, African leaders oppose the group theory of democracy and focus instead on the rights of the individual. Especially in South Africa, the racial communities are closed, exclusivist groups. The individual's status depends ultimately on his birth. The darker his skin, the lower his position in the power and prestige hierarchy. The whites —Afrikaners and Englishmen—fill the top positions, although they make up only 20% of the population. In descending order in the caste hierarchy come the Indians and then the colored population. At the bottom are the Africans, who in the last century have been largely excluded from top positions in the political and industrial life of the country. In their attack on these racial castes, Albert Luthuli of South Africa and Tom Mboya reject racial exclusiveness, preferring to evoke the right of each individual to participate in political life. For them, individual merit rather than race must be the determining factor of the right to share in sociopolitical benefits.

In South Africa, the repressive policies of the Afrikander Nationalist government, coming after a long period of industrialization, have largely disintegrated African group loyalties. The forced separation of husbands and wives has led to disintegration of the African family. In the urban areas, the African child lacks the protection of the extended family group. Individualism, the placing of self-interest above family or larger groups, has increased among these Africans.[64] These conditions have influenced the political beliefs of Albert Luthuli, the leader of the African Nationalist Congress. For him, democracy must be based on criteria of merit; group exclusiveness must end, and the government should allow all those qualified by talent to share in decision-making. Merit, not race, ought to fix the position of the individual in society: "We do not desire to dominate but to share as between brethren, basing our hierarchy on ability, not colour."[65] In an ideal future South African government, individual ability will determine the political position of an official. The state will protect the rights of the individual rather than promote the exclusiveness of racial groups: "Within the orbit of my State, the individual will remain cardinal, for 'the state exists for the individual,' and not 'the individual for the state.'"[66] In this regard, Luthuli fundamentally challenges the official Calvinist ideology of the Afrikänder government, which holds that the state has been created by God to counteract the effects of the fall of man and exists independently of its citizens. For the Afrikander Calvinists, the authority of the state is unlimited and indivisible; it possesses a monopoly of force.

In the view of Chief Luthuli, the slogan "Africa for the Africans" illustrates the current objectionable stress on race. He says, instead, "I do not cherish such expressions as 'The All-Black Government,' 'The African majority.' I like to speak about a 'democratic majority,' which should be a non-racial majority, and so could be multi-racial or not. My idea is a non-racial government consisting of the best men—merit rather than colour."[67] Thus the term "African" refers not to race but to territorial residence. The concept of citizenship for all will transcend the caste hierachy of South Africa.

> To me, the expression "Africa for Africans" is valid in a non-racial democracy, only if it covers all, regardless of color or race, who qualify as citizens of some country in Africa. . . . The question of reserving rights for minorities in a non-racial democracy should not arise. It will be sufficient if human rights for all are entrenched in the constitution.[68]

Luthuli's devaluation of the racial factor does not mean elimination of individual diversity. Individuals can differ as much as they desire in habits of life and cultural ways. In the political and economic spheres, however, the racial factors must become irrelevant.[69]

Luthuli not only opposes the racial group theory of democracy; he also attacks the divisive effects of tribal groupism. The forced alliance between chiefs and the Afrikander government has destroyed the latter's claim to legitimacy. Tribes should fulfill functions in the ceremonial aspects of social life but not in the political sphere. "Tribalism as such will have no place in the new South Africa, for by its narrow outlook it has been used as a means to divide and rule by the Whites. But tribal traditions that have promoted African stability will be encouraged so long as they are not in conflict with the civilized standards of living in the modern world."[70] In contrast to many other parts of Africa, where ethnic groups want to maintain their separate identity, in the Republic of South Africa the Nationalist government has tried forcibly to restore the tribal spirit among both rural and urban Africans. The stress Luthuli places on individualism and loyalty to South Africa as a whole illustrates his revolutionary challenge to the existing stratification and governmental systems. But, in South Africa today, leadership has passed from the peaceful revolutionaries like Luthuli to more violent leaders oriented toward black, rather than nonracial, supremacy. Because of the deteriorating position of the Africans, Luthuli's focus on nonracial, individual rights will become increasingly subordinate to the assertion of a collective black African solidarity.

With their triumph over the white settlers, Kenya's African leaders have been more successful than the South Africans in realizing the individualist conception of democracy. Like Chief Luthuli, Tom Mboya focuses on the theme of individual rights as the essence of democracy. Democracy means equality of individual citizens rather than of racial groups. According to Mboya,

What is important is the grant of citizenship rights, and here the non-Africans and the Africans have got to learn to talk of individuals instead of groups. So far, it is only the Africans who advocate the need for getting away from communal group identity to democratic individual citizenship. . . . Democracy would recognize the individual as against the present groups. . . . It would accord individual citizenship rights and protections instead of minority safeguards and group privileges.[71]

Mboya interprets democracy to include the elimination of privileges for racial groups. A democratic Kenya must be based on human equality and recognition of individual merit. Mboya objects to multiracialism because of its stress on maintaining the identities of separate racial groups. He focuses on merit rather than race: "Racial privilege can have no place in a democratic society. As an individual the European will be accepted for what he himself is; he will be judged according to his merits and rewarded according to his individual contribution to the society in which he lives."[72] Like Luthuli, Mboya also rejects the slogan "Africa for the Africans"; it negates the democratic principle of equality for all people regardless of race.

In Northern Rhodesia, Kenneth Kaunda's writings reveal a similar emphasis on individual rights. Both Kaunda and Luthuli have come under the influence of Protestant missions. For Kaunda, Europeans and Africans deserve treatment as individual human beings rather than as members of separate races: "We are to build a non-racial society and meet within that society not as Africans and Europeans but as human beings. . . . We are not concerned solely with the rights of Africans, we are struggling for human rights—the inalienable rights of all men."[73] Striving for political equality in multiracial societies, Luthuli, Mboya, and Kaunda call upon nonracial, individualist principles. As opponents of the colonial or white settler governments, they urge racial equality and individual rights. For them, the individual's status depends on his contribution to society rather than his birth within a tribal group or racial caste.

III. The Concept of Socialism

The interpretations of both democracy and socialism embody the distinctiveness of the African style of life. In warning against "blind imitation" of other socialist countries, Africans seek to adapt their political and economic systems to peculiarly African conditions. For example, President Nkrumah insists that socialism must fit the African situation:

> Our road to socialism must be a road designed and charted in accordance with the conditions of Ghana and the historical and social conditions and circumstances of Africa as a whole. We do not therefore seek to copy the methods by which other countries have achieved socialism within their own States. Indeed, the path to socialism followed by many countries has not been one worked out in accordance with a pre-conceived plan.[74]

Neither bourgeois capitalism nor proletarian communism is appropriate for Africa. Rather than stressing metaphysics, these leaders concentrate on concrete realities and flexible plans for economic development. Instead of complete nationalization, a mixed economy is preferred by most Africans.

These leaders also focus on the ethical-humanistic principles of socialism; their theoretical goals emphasize the satisfaction of simple human needs and the welfare of the community more than rapid industrialization. In contrast to the Russians and Chinese, Africans pay most attention to raising the living standards of the farmers. Rapid industrialization and the organization of the working class assume less importance. In accordance with this more humanistic, less doctrinaire bent, African leaders deny the relevance to the African situation of the class struggle between the bourgeoisie and the proletariat. For them, the real struggle lies between the exploiting colonialists and the exploited Africans.

We can best understand African socialism as fulfilling the same functions as did the Protestant ethic for Western capitalist development. The language of African socialist beliefs sounds very much like that of Puritanism. Max Weber noted the pietist stress on the virtues of the dignity of work, frugality, austerity, and discipline. He wrote, "Labour must . . . be performed as if it were an absolute end in itself, a calling. But such an attitude is by no means a product of nature. It . . . can only be the product of a long and arduous process of education."[75] In the opinion of leaders like Sékou Touré, socialism becomes an ethical imperative to work; the party carries out the process of socialist education. For Touré and many other leaders of French-speaking Africa, the policy of *l'investissement humain* seeks to make use of "human capital" to modernize society. Under this program, "voluntary" unpaid labor is encouraged to build roads, plant trees for conservation purposes, and construct schools and dispensaries. In English-speaking Africa, leaders like Julius Nyerere also identify socialism with the ethic of work:

> There is no such thing as socialism without work. A society which fails to give its individuals the means to work, or having given them the means to work, prevents them from getting a fair share of the products of their own sweat and toil, needs putting right. Similarly, an individual who can work—and is provided by society with the means to work—but does not do so, is equally wrong. He has no right to expect anything from society because he contributes nothing to society.[76]

Although agreeing on the need for a humanistic socialism adapted to African realities, African leaders differ in their interpretations of socialism itself. These interpretations range from African Marxism, characterized by political control of the economy, with a high degree of public ownership; through humanistic, "middle of the road" socialism that stresses spiritual and cultural values; to a welfare-state type of socialism that articulates more pragmatic, non-Marxist principles like equality of distribution of wealth, joint partnership between African and foreign firms, and government aid to indigenous entrepreneurs.

African Marxism

Of all African heads of state, Sékou Touré has been most strongly influenced by Marxian socialism and Leninist principles of organization. The political thought of Touré, however, does not slavishly copy Marxist-Leninist theories; rather, it posits the need to combine Marxism with a uniquely "communaucratic" socialism indigenous to Africa. In what respects do the political beliefs of Touré resemble the theories of Karl Marx? First, following Marx, Touré seeks to unify thought and action. According to Marx, theoretical philosophy and concrete human activities are closely related. The proletariat, discovering its "conceptual weapons" in philosophy, provides philosophy with its "material weapons." The principles of philosophy are thus realized through the action of the proletariat.[77] Marxism also contains a strong pragmatic streak. Contemptuous of merely speculative knowledge, Marx held that all theory must serve as a basis for control of the human and physical environment. The truth of a theory lies in its usefulness as a guide for successful actions.

These Marxian themes reappear in the thought of Sékou Touré. In his view, the action and thought of the party should become unified: "We are engaged in a revolution which has no historical precedent and which must result in a radical transformation of our conditions of life. But if the revolution is directed by thought, it is by acts that it operates. The putting into practice of our ideas assures its development."[78] We find a similar focus on reality and concrete needs, the same disdain for abstract speculative knowledge unrelated to action. For Touré, as for Marx, theoretical speculation separated from concrete human needs results in a "false consciousness." Rather than become immersed in sterile polemics, African Marxists must constantly adapt their thought and actions to the real social context. In the opinion of Touré, Africans should apply the "science" of Marxism to society instead of imposing pure Marxist theory on inappropriate conditions:

Society is not made for principles, for a philosophy, for a doctrine, for a given science. But, on the contrary, science, philosophy, and principles of action must be determined for the people and as a function of the realities of the people. Instead of applying society to science, we must apply science to society. Thus, Marxism, which has served to mobilize the African peoples and particularly the working class and to lead the working class toward success, has been shorn of those characteristics which do not correspond to African reality.[79]

Second, in his focus on man, Touré reveals a debt to Marxist humanism. According to Marx, the capitalist world of mid-nineteenth-century Europe had become oriented to objects and abstractions. Man was subordinated to machines. The triumph of the proletariat would, however, redeem suffering humanity. Man would once more conquer nature. Touré believes that the colonialists' economic plans failed because they neglected the human factor. In their concern to reap profits and increase efficiency, the colonialists considered only the technical aspects of economic operations: "Our Plan will succeed because it has the People for its center of interest, because it will be conceived by the People and realized for the People."[80] "Socialism" essentially means concern for the welfare of the people, the well-being of collective humanity.

Third, Touré follows Marx in upholding social values over purely economic considerations. Marx believed that, after the abolition of capitalism, man would revert to his natural status as a social being. Social solidarity and fraternal community would replace the acquisitive, self-interested calculations of the market place. For Touré too economic development must serve as an instrument of social development. The principle of solidarity constitutes the fundamental basis of socialist action in the Guinean Republic.[81] But Touré follows Lenin in asserting the dominance of the political. Although Marx hoped that socialism would transcend politics, Touré wants to make the economy a function of social demands, which are in turn oriented toward politics.[82]

Fourth, like Marx, Touré strikes an optimistic note. Dialectical movement will result in spiraling progress. Touré sees continual progress and evolution ahead for Africa. Unlike Marx, however, the Guinean President does not envision a final state in which the dialectic will cease to operate. Even when totally free, Africa will have to adapt to new forms, conditions, and objectives.[83]

Fifth, although Touré and Marx share a notion of contradictions, their interpretations of the nature of these contradictions differ somewhat. For both, the contradictions convey moral indictment of the economic *status quo*. Karl Marx assumed that at a certain stage of capitalist development, the relations of production (organization of industry, the institution of private property, class relations) come to hinder the forces of production (natural resources, physical equipment, technological skills, and division of labor). The primary contradiction revolves around the disparity between theory and practice. While in theory the relations of production are based on private property, in actuality the forces of production are socialized. Touré reiterates this notion of contradiction between the productive forces and relations of production. For productive development to occur, the productive forces, especially the working masses, must determine the relations of production.[84] Touré, however, does not stress this form of contradiction, which exists principally at a higher stage of economic development than Africa has so far attained. Instead, he sees the primary contradiction as one between the African people and the European colonialists. The colonialists are the capitalists hindering the productive forces, the African masses. The contradictions among Africans, among different social strata, result from lack of political maturity. These contradictions remain secondary to those separating the African and colonial interests.[85] The contradictions within African society resemble "cultural discontinuities," rather than impediments to the working out of the logic of productive forces. Contradictions still remain in Guinea among the various ethnic groups, religions, regions, young men and young women, intellectuals and illiterates, urban workers and peasants, and youth and parents.[86] Without changing the structure left by the colonialists, the Guineans cannot resolve these basic contradictions and realize the general interest.

Touré's concentration on the general political interest, rather than on a more particular class or economic interest, marks his main departure from Marxian theory. For Touré, as for Lenin, "socialism" means a form of political economy; the economic domain constitutes one aspect of the political realm: "Political economy is not the adaptation of political action to economic action; on the contrary, it is the use of economic activities for political ends."[87] The given economic conditions are not purely "independent variables" but must be manipulated by political organization.

In stressing the general interest, Touré denies the relevance of the class struggle to Africa. Since the instruments of production belonged to society, Africa experienced no class antagonisms until the coming of the foreign occupation. Within African society, there exists only one class—that of the dispossessed united by their common misery. Among the social strata, the women and peasants rather than the workers have been the most exploited.[88] Marx had shown contempt for the peasantry. In contrast, Touré believes that Guinean socialism must be primarily concerned with the peasants, who comprise more than 90% of the population. Essentially an agricultural region, Africa should place maximum emphasis on agricultural production and should consider industry a complementary factor of economic development.[89]

In his attempt to articulate an ideology appropriate to the African *milieu*, Sékou Touré attempts to blend Marxism with the "communaucratic" values of precolonial African society. Since Guineans are a proletarian people, Marxism offers more useful possiblities to Africans than does bourgeois capitalism. Yet Africans live under conditions transcending the class struggle. The term "socialism" might give outside observers misleading impressions Touré told a reporter:

> Your question implies that we have defined what you call "African socialism" and that we are making our political orientation and our principles of action dependent on that definition. That is not true. . . . We use the expression "communaucratie" precisely in order to avoid all equivocation and all false analogies. . . . Our solidarity, better known under its aspects of social fraternity, the preeminence of group interests over the personal interest, the sense of common responsiblities, the practice of a formal democracy which rules and governs village life—all of which constitute the base of our society—that is what forms what we call our communaucratic realities.[90]

This stress on communaucracy reflects Touré's concern to achieve an economic policy independent of both European capitalism and communism. Since Africa has neither a bourgeoisie nor a large accumulation of capital, capitalism is not appropriate to the present stage of Guinean development. Touré further attacks capitalism for the individualism, egotism, and anarchy it exemplifies. As he opposes a multiparty regime because of its disorder, so he criticizes liberal capitalism for a similar anarchy of economic forces.[91] President Touré also rejects the East European and Russian brands of socialism, for he feels that communism resembles a collective form of national capitalism. In a capitalist regime, the workers' surplus value goes to the capitalists. In a communist country, the state recovers all or part of the workers' profits. Since both Russia and West Europe are highly industrialized, both systems use similar technical means. Neither communism nor capitalism is therefore applicable to Africa because the Soviet Union, as well as Europe and America, is far more highly developed than African states. "Thus, when people ask us if we are for capitalism or for socialism, for the East or for the West, we invariably answer that what we consider first and above all is the Africa we intend to liberate from foreign domination, sickness, misery, and ignorance."[92] In short, the desire for independence is reflected not only in foreign relations but also in economic policy. For Touré, Africa constitutes a third force, an undeveloped area between the communist and capitalist camps.

The "non-atheistic socialist" beliefs of Kwame Nkrumah also express the urge to formulate a distinctive economic program independent of both capitalism and communism. Compared with Touré, Nkrumah has failed to elaborate a systematic African Marxist theory; the influence of Marx on Nkrumah remains largely at the level of slogans. The mobilization of the masses for the "socialist reconstruction of Ghana," the second revolution after political independence, requires a simplified form of communication. Socialist slogans appropriated from Marx and Lenin outline some economic goals for Ghana. The following four quotations illustrate how Nkrumah has lifted some popularized slogans from the writings of Marx:

"The aims and objectives of the Party, among other things, are the building of a socialist pattern of society in which the free development of each is the condition for the free development of all. . . ."
"Freedom connotes necessity."
"The workers could do without capitalists, but capitalists cannot do without workers. For labour is the source of all wealth. . . ."
"We aim at creating in Ghana a socialist society in which each will give according to his ability and receive according to his needs."[93]

In his conception of Marxism as a guide to action and his interpretation of imperialism, Nkrumah follows Leninist teaching. While a student in London after the Second World War, he wrote, in 1947, a pamphlet entitled *Towards Colonial Freedom: Africa in the Struggle Against World Imperialism,* which rather literally applies the Leninist theory of imperialism to the African scene. Lenin's notions about colonialism as monopoly finance capitalism, the uneven development of capitalism, the inevitability of war under imperialism, the creation of a class-conscious working class, and the need to form an alliance between the colonial peoples and the European proletariat all reappear in this pamphlet designed to foment the "organization of the colonial masses." According to Nkrumah, the colonial liberation movement received its main impetus from "the amalgamation of the first two fronts against imperialism, namely the front of the working class of the capitalist countries and of the front of the toiling masses of the colonies for colonial emancipation."[94] Although Nkrumah has in recent years abandoned many of these Leninist principles, he still believes that imperialism is identical with finance capitalism and that an alliance between the African anti-colonialists and some sections of the European working class and intelligentsia will hasten the downfall of colonialism.[95]

Despite these Leninist themes, Nkrumah has tended toward a mixed economy rather than complete state ownership. The Marxian slogans refer mainly to humanistic aspirations. For the Ghanaian leader, socialism means such general goals as a welfare state; equal opportunities for all citizens; the absence of individual, tribal, and class exploitation; and economic production benefiting the whole community rather than individual profiteers.[96] In theory, socialism means economic egalitarianism; in practice, the means of reaching these goals is a mixed economy. The seven-year plan aims for a balance between public and private investments. Nkrumah recognizes five sectors operating within the Ghanaian economy. The state enterprises and co-operatives are public forms. Private enterprise will function through foreign firms and small-scale Ghanaian businesses. The Ghana government and foreign private companies will work together in jointly owned state-private enterprises.[97] The government has banned all firms owned jointly by foreign companies and individual Ghanaians. Ghanaian citizens will have exclusive control of the small-scale private enterprise sector; foreign firms will control larger economic enterprises. This stress on African control of the economy reflects a form of economic nationalism more than the originally more universalistic Marxian socialism. Through public ownership and control of the economy, restrictions on foreign private investors, and increased trade with Communist nations, Ghana hopes to end European domination and create an independent, industrialized state.

Socialist Humanism

Although Touré and Nkrumah both stress the humanistic aspects of socialism, they tend to subordinate these spiritual values to the demands of political mobilization. The two leaders of Senegal, President Léopold Senghor and former Prime Minister Mamadou Dia, in contrast, have elaborated a model of socialism that integrates the humanistic values of traditional African society and pre-1848 Marxism. Subordinating economics and politics to culture, Senghor and Dia stress ethical and spiritual principles, with equilibrium as a goal of economic development. This model exemplifies a "middle of the road" approach between the political economy of Touré and the pragmatic welfare state ideas of Azikiwe and Nyerere. Senghor has written, "We stand for a middle course, for a democratic socialism, which goes so far as to integrate spiritual values, a socialism which ties in with the old ethical current of the French socialists."[98]

The socialist humanism articulated by Senghor and Dia reconciles the ethical-spiritual, "communitarian" values of African life with the humanistic appeals of Karl Marx. According to Dia, the traditional African economy had a socialistic or communitarian nature. African thought was based on a collective mentality. Those humanistic values expressed in precolonial African societies included co-operation, solidarity, altruism, harmony between the individual and general interest, a spirit of simplicity, and an equal sharing of goods that forbade surpluses and luxurious tastes.[99] For Senghor too, African society revealed a communal solidarity, with man at the center of the universe. In comparison with European collectivism, African socialism focuses more on the group than on the individual, more on the communion of persons than on their autonomy, more on the *person* than on the *individual*. While in European societies the individual demands autonomy from the group in order to affirm his identity, in an African communitarian society the person feels that he can develop his original virtues only in and through society.[100] Because of this community-based solidarity, this spiritual nature of African life, Seneghor believes that socialism will come easily to Africa: "Negro African society is collectivist, or, more exactly, communal because it is rather a communion of souls than an aggregate of individuals. . . . We had already realized socialism before the coming of the European. . . . Our duty is to renew it by helping it to regain spiritual dimensions."[101]

In their desire to formulate a socialist humanism, Senghor and Dia focus on the early humanistic Marx who wrote of the need for ethical, as well as economic, redemption. For Marx, the proletariat symbolized the fate of suffering humanity; the triumph of socialism would redeem humanity from the tyranny of material things and philosophical abstractions. In the opinion of Dia and Senghor, Marx made his most valuable contribution in stressing the effect of industrial economy on modern man. As a science of economics, Marxism has limited usefulness, for it is historically relative to mid-nineteenth-century capitalism. In particular, the theory of the class struggle is not relevant to Africa. Although there may exist castes or stratification based on religion, traditional Negro African society has no classes founded on wealth. Whereas European workers experienced class subjugation, the mass of African peoples came under racial domination. The major aim of African socialism therefore must be to abolish the inequalities arising from the Colonial Pact.[102] In contemporary African society, social groups in a struggle for influence have supplanted warring classes. Class warfare will result, however, if the intellectuals—liberal professionals, functionaries, employers, even workers—are allowed to oppress the peasants, shepherds, and artisans.[103] Because of this potential tendency toward class formation, Africans must seek to restore the communal values of Negro African society and to revive the humanism of Marx.

The Marxian concept of human alienation has a central place in Senghor's theory of socialist humanism. According to him, capitalism brought economic, political, and cultural alienation to Africa. In the economic sphere, capitalism alienated man from his work and the products of his labor; it also dehumanized workers. In the political arena, the result was domination of one country by a foreign power. In the social and cultural realms, one racial group became subject to another; the system of economic and political alienation was thus colored by racism.[104]

Mamadou Dia also emphasizes the humanistic contributions of Marx. Economics, originally designed to serve men, has become the study of products, techniques, calculations of interest, and quantitative factors. Socialist economy must make of man an end, not a means. Although criticizing, like Senghor, the Marxian ideas of violence, atheism, and philosophical materialism, Dia praises Marx's condemnation of the exploitation of man by man and his recommendation for how governmental action can equalize relations between the world's dominant and dominated economies. Like Marx, Dia wants man to become the active conqueror of nature, rather than to remain the passive subordinate of exterior mechanical forces.[105] Although Dia supports the humanistic principles of Marxism, he rejects certain other ideas of Marx, especially the labor theory of value. An economy that worships work risks becoming an inhuman civilization. The economy of human costs transcends the notion of work, which, in the contemporary mechanized world, leads to alienation.

Since the socialist revolution posits the revolt of each man rather than the revolt of the masses, the ideas of classes and nations have become outmoded. Dia believes that, rather than concentrating on how to increase the prosperity of a particular nation, African socialists must discover how to secure a more equitable sharing of wealth so that all humanity will benefit.[106] Beyond the enrichment of African culture lies the task of elaborating a new universal humanism that transcends all national frontiers. He hopes that socialist intervention in the economy will raise African societies to the technical level obtained by West Europe while ensuring the flowering of African culture. In short, economics is not an end in itself. The economy is merely an instrument for building a new African and universal humanism. It will fulfill this task only by safeguarding African values and the personality of the black man.[107]

In the thought of Dia and Senghor, there recurs the value of equilibrium. A socialist society should help to secure a balance of human and societal needs, an equilibrium between technical, materialistic values and cultural, spiritual values. According to Dia, in African agrarian societies there was a harmonious equilibrium between land and labor and between the individual and the general interest. The village formed a group in which the interest of each peasant agreed with the interest of all.[108] Modern African economies must achieve an equilibrium between the public and private sectors and between industrialization and agricultural development.

Both Dia and Senghor argue for coexistence between the private and public sectors and against total nationalization. Senghor's economic theory postulates three sectors in the economy. The free or private sector will comprise banks, commerce, and industry, all of which must be oriented toward development-plan objectives. The mixed or semipublic sector includes public utilities like transport and power. The agricultural sector will be socialized, for it has been traditionally communal. This development plan does not require nationalization. From Senghor's perspective, nationalization would discourage investment and provoke internal conflicts. Furthermore, Senegal lacks the trained personnel to administer nationalized industries. Most important, when foreign capitalists train African personnel for employment, reinvest part of their profits, and pay taxes, they directly benefit Africa.[109]

Mamadou Dia believes that African socialists need to develop simultaneously both the industrial and agricultural sectors. Modernization of the African economy without industrialization is inconceivable in today's world, since industrialization brings necessary technical advantages to man. Similarly, a a solid agricultural infrastructure must sustain industrial development.[110] Although agricultural production will help industrialization, African states must not make of industrialization an end in itself: "By principally stressing heavy industry, massive industrialization tends to depress the standard of living and to lower real wages by forcing an increase in importation of equipment and machines at the expense of agricultural commodities and consumer goods. . . ."[111] African nations should realize instead a synthesis between the agricultural and industrial solutions. The policy of equilbrium rejects all extreme or dogmatic approaches.

Dia and Senghor evaluate the contributions of various economic systems according to how well they fulfill humanistic values. As a method of analysis, socialism is open, flexible, and undoctrinaire. Senghor values socialism as an open method of empirical investigation. Under the open dialectical method, the encounter between theory and experience leads to "objective truth." From European socialism, Africans must borrow the methodology of carefully analyzing the realities of a country or area and then adapting institutions expressing these realities to the demands of the modern world.[112]

Dia agrees with Senghor that the socialist economic plan must be open and flexible, rather than abstract, doctrinaire, and rigid. Since the plan must be adaptable to unforeseen demands, it should embody a continuous creation rather than a precise, unchangeable act.[113] Since socialism must continuously adapt itself to African realities, it must not attempt to copy the economic experiences of the Western capitalist democracies, the Communist states of Russia and China, or India. Capitalism in Africa has neglected human needs and African values. Capitalism is based on greed and exploitation; it has failed to satisfy man's fundamental needs: "Since economy is essentially based on human and social relations, since it is in essence socialistic, in the broadest sense of the term, the rule of the accumulation of money—the foundation of capitalism—cannot be the law that will determine the formation of structures in such civilizations."[114] Besides sacrificing basic human needs to the desire to maximize profits, European capitalism neglected the artistic, religious, literary, and philosophical values of Negro Africa. The capitalist philosophy of assimilation assumed that only the European incarnated human values. Even from an economic point of view, capitalism failed to bring benefits to Africans. Since the capitalists wanted African territories to serve as outlets for European industries, they refused to undertake industrialization. Sacrificing agricultural development for mining industries, capitalism did not improve the conditions of the peasant masses.[115] What is more, the capitalist states of West Europe and the United States enjoyed two conditions absent in Africa—abundant capital and a bourgeois class willing to take risks. Neither precolonial African economies nor colonial capitalism favored the formation of a middle class or indigenous capital. In actuality, European capitalism created in most areas of Africa a "subproletariat," rather than an African bourgeoisie.[116]

If the experiences of capitalism do not have too much relevance for African economies, neither do the autocratic communist examples of the Soviet Union and China, both of which have used state authority to increase economic development. In the view of Dia, communism, like capitalism, neglects human needs, for its autocratic methods subject the individual person to state power. In contrast to Russia and China, the traditional African community excluded totalitarianism. Dia admires the Chinese experiment more than the Russian. While the Soviet leaders sacrificed the peasants for rapid industrialization and capitalist profits, China pays greater attention to agricultural development and the need to harness the faith and enthusiasm of the people. In contrast, India lacks the enthusiasm that possesses China. The pursuit of concrete social objectives does not suffice. Indian economic development is too slow; it needs a doctrine to provide the requisite "soul enthusiasm" and purpose.[117]

President Senghor also shows concern for the effect of the economy on the human soul. The Communist countries have repudiated the Marxian concern for human dignity. By making the state an "omnipotent, soulless monster," the Bolsheviks have stifled the expression of artistic values. What is more, African communalism rejects communist violence and prefers to reconcile differences through mutual consultation and co-operation.[118] Rather than following the examples of either communism or capitalism, both of which curtail freedom of thought and art, African socialists must encourage the expression of a socialist humanism sensitive to original African conditions, a humanism safeguarding human spontaneity and traditional cultural values.

The Social-Welfare State

The social-welfare state model represents a still more pragmatic and even less theoretical brand of socialism than either African Marxism or socialist humanism. For the welfare statists, "socialism" means general, vague aspirations like social justice, equality of distribution of wealth, equal opportunity, and satisfaction of basic human needs. There is little attempt to formulate explicit, systematic socialist philosophy as Sékou Touré, Senghor, and Dia have done. The welfare-state model of socialism reveals little influence of Marx, Lenin, or other European socialists. Compared with African Marxism, social-welfare beliefs stress agricultural development over rapid industrialization and political control of distribution of resources over public ownership of the means of production. In contrast to the socialist humanists, the welfare statists pay less attention to ethical and spiritual principles and concentrate more on economic factors. The businessman has greater opportunity to pursue strictly economic ends free of political control. For most of the welfare statists, the government functions mainly as the financial support of private indigenous firms. Foreign investment is welcomed, but overseas businessmen should enter into joint partnership with African agencies, either public or private. Public control with private ownership is the most widespread economic form in these states.

Leaders from English-speaking Africa most frequently espouse this pragmatic welfare-state approach to socialism. Julius Nyerere, Nnamdi Azikiwe, and Obafemi Awolowo all express beliefs about the need for a humanistic, expedient, untheoretical approach to economics. Both Nyerere and Azikiwe equate socialism with a distributive principle of sharing. According to Nyerere, "Socialism is essentially distributive. Its concern is to see that those who sow reap a fair share of what they have sown."[119] Similarly, Azikiwe identifies socialism with the distribution or use of wealth, rather than with public ownership of production and distribution. In a speech to the annual convention of the NCNC, he said: "It is not inconsistent for a Socialist through hard work to acquire a limited amount of wealth to enable him to co-exist with his capitalist counterparts. It is not the volume of wealth that makes it obnoxious to the Socialist, but it is the use to which wealth is put that matters."[120]

Nyerere holds that a socialist society must satisfy simple human needs like the abolition of poverty and the provision of food, shelter, and education. Every state has sufficient wealth to satisfy these simple needs. African socialism must reassign wealth to this original purpose—the raising of the standard of living of the African people. Both capitalism and communism have concentrated more on acquiring power and prestige than on realizing fundamental human needs. As capitalism rests on exploitation, so communism is based on inevitable human conflict. The real division in the world today is between the rich and poor countries, not between communism and capitalism.[121]

Azikiwe makes a similar critique of capitalism. Ignoring human needs for material things, capitalism operated in prewar Nigeria only to secure profits. It failed to build hospitals, schools, and housing; instead, it concentrated on bridges, railways, electricity. African socialism must return to a humanistic, philanthropic foundation; the new economics must be based on community needs and welfare.[122]

Both Azikiwe and Nyerere urge that Africans shun capitalism and return to the communal virtues of precolonial society. In the view of Aizikiwe, traditional African society had a "communalistic" nature. Consistent with his ideas of democracy, Nyerere wants the extended family to form the basis of a socialist economy. As in the operation of a family, the individual and group must work for the good of the other:

> We want Tanganyika to become an African socialist country. . . . To this end we shall try to build on the past African tradition in which every family was responsible for all its members, and every member responsible for the family. We are simply trying to extend the family. We believe this can be done through the development of cooperative enterprises in every field of economic and social activity.[123]

According to Nyerere, African society, unlike European states, never knew antagonistic classes. While European socialism is based on feudalism and capitalism, on the division between the landed and landless and between the capitalist and proletariat, African socialists look upon all men as members of an extending family. Under this *Ujamaa,* or familyhood, the individuals work for the community, and the community cares for the individuals' needs. In contrast to precolonial Africa, however, contemporary African states can no longer confine the idea of family to a tribe or nation. Rather African socialists must extend the principles of familyhood and sharing of wealth to the whole African continent.[124]

Chief Obafemi Awolowo interprets socialism to mean "life more abundant"; he urges the government to help the poorer, less fortunate citizens:

> I have always had before me the supreme objective of a welfare state which is denoted by our motto of "Freedom for all and Life more abudant." At the same time, I do recognize that this objective can be realized only if the state is prepared to step into the breach to help the needy, especially the young ones, both to discover and develop their talents and natural bents.[125]

Awolowo attacks the influx of uncontrolled capitalist firms into the nation. In his view, economic development must be linked to the Nigerian national interest, not to the self-interest of foreign investors. Foreign investors must go into partnerships with Nigerians. Furthermore, Awolowo wants the establishment of a planned, controlled economy. A permanent economic planning commission must produce five-year development programs. The first economic priority in this plan ought to be the rapid development of agriculture. In industrial and commercial fields that private firms are not willing to enter, the government must establish public enterprises.[126]

Recently Chief Awolowo has sounded a more explicit socialist note. In 1961, he called upon the young Action Group leaders to draw up a series of papers defining democratic socialism. Despite this move toward a more pronounced socialist position, however, Awolowo still maintains a non-Marxist outlook. In his view, as in that of Nyerere and Azikiwe, welfare-state socialism must ensure that private and public sectors co-operate to realize a more equal distribution of economic resources.

IV. The Concept of Independence

When African leaders speak of independence, they reiterate many of the themes stressed in their interpretations of democracy and socialism. The values of popular sovereignty, the collective will, the national interest, community solidarity, equality, organization, flexibility, and co-operation are again affirmed in the concept of independence. Democracy and socialism have primary significance within the framework of an independent state. Only when Africans win territorial independence can they work out a democratic and socialist program. In a general sense, democracy thus refers to African control of political power, and socialism means economic benefits for the whole African population.

The term "independence" does not refer solely to gaining political power; Sékou Touré suggests that independence means a consummation of freedom in all spheres of life: "Politically, we have defined independence as a means of real and total emancipation. . . . We have concluded that it was the best way towards a rapid evolution of our society, a real improvement of the standard of living of the people, a greater social equity, and true prospects of happiness for every citizen, male or female."[127] African leaders focus on several such expressions or facets of independence as the political struggle for self-government, the affirmation of the spiritual values of Africa, the psychological quest for an African personality, the aesthetic expression of Negro African values, and the assertion in foreign policy of positive nonalignment and Pan-Africanism.

All African leaders regard political independence, not as an end in itself, but merely as a means to more meaningful goals—human dignity, self-respect, spiritual development, economic improvement, and cultural emancipation. They emphasize this interpretation in order to dampen the high expectations engendered during the period of nationalist agitation, when the attainment of self-government seemed destined to bring the millennium, and to encourage the masses to work for the reconstruction of an independent African society. For example, Prime Minister Balewa told the Nigerian House of Representatives: "Independence is not an end in itself. It is the means whereby we are determined to ensure that Nigeria plays her full part in world affairs and whereby Nigerians are enabled to enjoy a higher standard of living both materially and spiritually. In working for independence we are creating a national self-respect."[128] African leaders link the political independence of their territory with freedom movements elsewhere on the African continent. Sékou Touré feels that Guinea occupies a "pilot position" in relation to the rest of Africa. The independence of Guinea will accelerate the liberation of the African fatherland. The success of the Guinean experience will mean the triumph of African unity and independence.[129] President Nkrumah has a similar interpretation of African self-government. In a famous passage, he linked the political independence of Ghana with the all-African struggle against colonialism:

I have never regarded the struggle for Independence of the Gold Coast as an isolated incident but always as a part of a general world historical pattern. The African in every territory of this continent has been awakened and the struggle for freedom will go on. . . . Our task is not done and our own safety is not assured until the last vestiges of colonialism have been swept from Africa.[130]

The language of African nationalism expresses the drive for independence in spiritual and psychological, as well as in political, terms. African leaders favorably contrast Africa's "spiritual" values of community, altruism, and solidarity with the more "materialistic" values of Western Europe. The affirmation of the African personality highlights the need for Africans to recover their original identity. Sékou Touré speaks of the need for an intellectual "decolonization." Africans must get rid of the colonial mentality, ways of thinking, conceptions, and uncontrolled behavior patterns in order to realize a "total reconversion of attitudes and thoughts."[131] Even less militant West African leaders like President William Tubman of Liberia have moved closer to asserting a distinctively African identity. Although before 1957, the year of Ghanaian independence, the "civilized states" of Europe and America were his main sources of comparison, he has recently come to identify Liberia more directly with Africa as a whole. Referring to "old mother Africa" as the cradle of humanity and the area that first gave civilization and culture to the world, Tubman defines the new role for Liberia in an independent Africa: "Liberia must be no longer an 'asylum from the most grinding oppression.' She must be the pride of a race, the emblem of hope and aspiration, as well as the trailblazer of an emerging concept of human relationships distinctively African."[132] In South Africa, the problem of asserting the African identity becomes more acute than in the relatively color-blind atmosphere of West Africa. Albert Luthuli, although urging interracial cooperation, has still expressed his purely African identity as a protest against Afrikaner-English supremacy: "It was no more necessary for the [African] pupils to become Black Englishmen, than it was for the teachers to become White Africans. . . . I remain an African. I think as an African, I speak as an African, I act as an African. . . ."[133]

The philosophy of *négritude* illustrates the aesthetic approach to independence. As Africans must assert their distinctive, original personality, so must they express their unique Negro African values through poetry, literature, music, and painting. Léopold Senghor, the poet-President of Senegal, has achieved as much of a reputation in the cultural as in the political world. His poetry expresses the twin themes of unity and liberation, the demands also echoed by Pan-Africanists.

The Struggle for Political Independence

During the era of nationalist agitation beginning at the end of World War II, African leaders concentrated on the struggle to win political self-government. The words "freedom" and *Uhuru* express this urge toward African nationhood. By 1960, nearly all West African states had attained territorial sovereignty. In southern Africa, the drive toward political independence proceeded more haltingly. Southern Rhodesia, Angola, Mozambique, and the Republic of South Africa presented the greatest difficulties for African assumption of political power. A combination of factors—ethnic group rivalry, control by white settlers, and colonial autocracy—have hindered quick assumption of African control.

All African leaders, both "moderate" and "militant," focus on the acquisition of political power as the first step toward full independence. In French-speaking Africa, Sékou Touré and Habib Bourguiba, despite different political styles, assert the drive for independence mainly in political terms. Both leaders find national political unity in African history and in the French colonial experience. Strongly affirming the political sovereignty of Tunisia, President Bourguiba looks back to the first Tunisian dynasty at the time of Charlemagne. Recalling the struggles of his Tunisian ancestors, especially of Jugurtha, against the Romans, Bourguiba argues that the Tunisians are not merely a population. They compose a nation with a civilization and history.[134] In a similar vein, President Touré refers to African history and the precolonial struggle for independence. When Guinea sought independence, she remained faithful to African historical traditions, to the spirit of men like El Hadj Omar, Ba Demba, Behenzin, Alpha Yaya, and especially l'Almamy Samory who fought against the French intrusion.[135]

Bourguiba and Touré look to France, as well as to African history, for reinforcement of their national political identities. In their view, despite the French policy of assimilation and incorporation of the territory into the *métropole,* colonialism stimulated the national identity of African peoples. According to Bourguiba, although the colonialists created artificial frontiers, they did unify the people of each territory and taught them the value of collective struggle. French colonialism aroused formerly "civilized" peoples from their lethargy and made them more ready to assume their national responsibilities.[136] In the same spirit, Sékou Touré cites as a value of colonialism the sense of nationhood that Europeans brought to Africa. Although the colonial rulers stimulated inter-African disunity, they nevertheless created a feeling of belonging to a larger community than that of family or tribe. These larger units were more effective in challenging European power than were weak tribes.[137]

According to both Touré and Bourguiba, political independence can be secured only through the dominance of organization. African leaders need powerful organizations like political parties and trade unions to win the anticolonial struggle against Europe. According to Bourguiba, organization is of foremost importance in the campaign for self-government. His party, the Neo-Destour, must solidly organize the Tunisian masses in all aspects of life. The party embodies the Tunisian drive for liberation. It educates the people, gives them a soul, and brings them out of social and economic misery.[138] To accomplish these tasks, Bourguiba has established under the Neo-Destour a large network of organizations that include nearly the whole population. Instead of the numerous intermediate groups found in Western pluralistic societies, the party organizations comprise clubs, societies, youth and scout groups, women's leagues and professional associations of farmers, traders, manufacturers, and workers, in addition to parochial, civic, and local organizations. Although these groups affiliated with the Neo-Destour have some organizational autonomy, they do not constitute independent centers of power. Rather, under the direction of the party cell leaders, they are used to mobilize and educate the masses.[139]

Similarly, in Guinea Sékou Touré has linked the dominance of organization to the struggle for political independence. Frequently stating his belief that the Guinean population must be well organized, he early put this dictum into practice. When Touré became secretary-general of the Parti Démocratique de Guinée in 1952, he organized it into a mass movement with roots among village peasants and trade-union workers. Within five years, despite French opposition, the PDG won fifty-seven of sixty seats in the Guinean national assembly and formed the government. In 1958, Guinea was the only French African territory to vote for independence outside the French community.

Beside utilizing political parties to gain national independence, Habib Bourguiba and Sékou Touré have also employed trade unions in the struggle against colonialism. On the eve of national independence, the Tunisian president affirmed the integral unity between party and unions: "The Tunisian working class is an integral part of liberation and . . . social liberation can only be conceived and realized in and by the political liberation of the nation."[140] Today the Tunisian trade unions, stronger than in any other Arab country, are controlled by the Neo-Destour. Bourguiba believes that the workers must now develop a national, rather than a class, point of view; their movement, the Union Générale des Travailleurs Tunisiens, should therefore be closely tied to the political party that embodies the movement for national liberation.

Similarly, Sékou Touré asserts that the African trade-union movement must play a vanguard role in the struggle for liberation from France. Organizing first the Confédération Générale des Travailleurs d'Afrique, which severed its ties with the Communist-dominated World Federation of Trade Unions, and later the Union Générale des Travailleurs d'Afrique Noire, the Guinean President insists that unions must set a priority on general political objectives rather than on the narrower goals of the working class. The winning of political power will create conditions for greater economic development: "It is the political struggle that every anticolonialist trade union leads, for the affirmation of the right of free conditions for people is a political choice and implies political action."[141] The economic liberation of the working class would only prolong national liberation. Sékou Touré regards UGTAN as a revolutionary union organization, for it aims to eliminate colonialism by winning independence for all African territories. In contrast, reformist unions, those preoccupied with improving the economic status of the workers, aim only to mitigate some of the worst effects of colonialism and capitalism.[142]

Although strongly asserting the right of political independence, neither Bourguiba nor Touré rejected postindependence co-operation with France. For them, political independence, the achievement of self-government, must ensure co-operation between Africa and Europe as equal sovereign states. Since the early 1930s, Bourguiba has called for Tunisian independence protected and guided by France, an independence effected in co-operation with France but without any spirit of domination.[143] The winning of political power thus brings an independence based upon mutual respect as sovereign nations. Before General de Gaulle abruptly withdrew French technicians from Guinea in 1958, Sékou Touré held a similar view of the need for Africa to transfer the links of dependence into ties of equality and co-operation with France. Nearly a month after the 1958 referendum in which Guinea voted *non* to the Franco-Africa Community, Touré stated his wish for continued collaboration with France: "Since our independence, without bitterness, without any preconceived idea, without any ulterior motive, we have extended our hand to France. What we want, what we continue to want, is for new relations to be established between the French nation and the young Guinean nation for the greatest good of the two peoples."[144]

Although stressing the need for equal relations between Africa and Europe, Bourguiba has always been more oriented toward Europe than has Touré. The Tunisian leader argues that the advanced technology and industry of Western Europe and the United States will permit the exploitation of the resources on the African continent and will thus diminish the gap between the two areas.[145] In contrast, President Touré, especially right after Guinea voted for independence, has tended to assert more emphatically than Bourguiba the complete emancipation of Africa from Europe. Nevertheless, since 1962 Guinea has moved to re-establish closer ties with France. The end of the Algerian war and the disappointing results of economic assistance from Russia and Eastern Europe have led Touré to look more favorably toward France.

In another respect, Touré and Bourguiba differ in their interpretations of political independence. Touré has shown less disposition toward compromise and gradualness; in his view, "clever compromises" and lack of "revolutionary firmness" lead to general discontent and anarchy. Only a policy of immediate independence will restore African equality and dignity.[146] On the other hand, Bourguiba tends to stress a more gradual time perspective. His doctrine of independence articulates the themes of flexible tactics and methods, combined with unyielding objectives. Tunisia should adapt her methods to the reactions of France. If the French choose conciliation, then Tunisia must make a similar response. If France becomes obstinate, Tunisa ought to respond with pressure. Pressure and concessions must thus be alternated in order to secure the desired objective. The main goal is to liberate Tunisia and re-establish a fully sovereign state. "Good" compromises advance Tunisia toward victory; "bad" compromises hinder the struggle for national liberation.[147] As Bourguiba argues for flexibility in tactics, so he urges caution and patience with respect to time perspective. Proximity to France and the presence of the *colons* led him to seek political independence through gradual stages. Scorning "verbal demagogy which obtains no desired results," Bourguiba encouraged the Tunisians to win national independence through "fruitful and reflective action which, to prepare for the future, takes its basis of support in reality."[148] Bourguiba thus combines flexible tactics and powerful mass organization to advance the political independence of Tunisia. Although more militant than Bourguiba, Touré has shown a similar commitment to flexibility.

The Spiritual Expression of Independence

The demand for African independence has found expression in religious, as well as in political, concepts. This tendency to employ Christian concepts when speaking of African liberation reflects an earlier phase of nationalism in Africa. In West Africa after the Second World War, the stress on organization—political parties and trade unions—largely overshadowed the prewar Christian note. In East, Central, and South Africa, however, where nationalism developed under greater restrictions, the language of Christianity played a more important part in the struggle for independence. Nnamdi Azikiwe, leader of the Nigerian nationalist movement, frequently articulated political demands in terms of religious concepts. Stressing the necessity for African redemption, he identified the gospel of renascent Africa with the triumph of Nigerian independence:

> At this stage of my life, I cannot be mere flesh. I cannot be part of the corruptible phase of man's organism. I am a living spirit of an idea—the idea of a New Africa. . . . Happily for the gospel according to the New Africa, there exist today on this continent Renascent Africans . . . who have expressed to me, by their words and deeds, during the last few days of the crucial moments of the existence of my flesh on this earth, that the New Africa is born to me.[149]

This use of religous themes reflects both the strength of Christian churches in the territory and the personal background of the leader. Most nationalist leaders were educated in mission schools. Significantly, in 1953 more than 50% of the total population of the Eastern Region of Nigeria belonged to Christian churches, by far the highest percentage of any region.[150] During the 1930s, Azikiwe formulated a belief later used by postwar African nationalists. Writing in 1934 about Liberia, the only independent West African state, at that time he contrasted the spiritual and moral values of African states with the materialistic temper of Western Europe. Precolonial Africa was oriented toward religious and humanitarian values. In Liberia lay the hope of an African civilization based on spiritual needs. Consistent with the indigenous African tradition, Liberia had chosen the "spiritual pathway" toward political solidarity.[151]

In multiracial East and South Africa, African leaders have faced severe hardships in organizing political parties and trade unions. There the demand for political independence has assumed the language of the Christian missions. Kenneth Kaunda and Albert Luthuli both articulate the strategy of nonviolence on the basis of Christian ethics. This theme reflects in part the importance of African churches in serving as an alternative to political expression, as well as the education most African leaders have received at mission schools. The father of Kaunda was an ordained Nyasa priest, while Luthuli is the son of a Congregationalist mission interpreter.

In Northern Rhodesia, Kaunda links nonviolence to Christian humanitarian principles. Nonviolence will lead to greater tolerance and spiritual and moral understanding. The dictates of the Christian conscience, as well as the demands of expedience, suggest a nonviolent strategy for attaining national independence. By adopting passive resistance, rather than yielding to violence, African nationalists will achieve a spiritual rebirth.[152] In South Africa, Chief Albert Luthuli sounds a similar nonviolent note. African churches flourish especially in the urban areas, and these religious groups provide an organizational basis for political activity. Luthuli equates the necessity of sacrifice with the historic experiences of the Christian martyrs: "The Road to Freedom is via the CROSS."[153] For Luthuli, who has long served in South African churches, his work in the African National Congress exemplifies his Christian belief about the need to improve society in this world, rather than to wait for an apocalyptic new world. As a Christian, he feels the call to work toward African independence, for the Afrikaner nationalists seek "to debase the God-factor in Man [and] to set a limit beyond which the human being in his black form might not strive to serve his Creator to the best of his ability."[154] Preparing African nationalists for the trials ahead, Luthuli argues that the Christian faith will enable the oppressed to withstand any suffering. A non-violent strategy, based on Christian ethics, thus represents the most humane and expedient method to secure eventual African emancipation.

As one who led Northern Rhodesia to independence by nonviolent means, Kenneth Kaunda has been successful where Chief Luthuli has failed. In South Africa, the higher percentage of white settlers and the fanatical policies of the Afrikaner Nationalist government have blocked peaceful forms of opposition. Kaunda successfully restrained his followers from provoking widespread violence. Leadership in South Africa has passed from Luthuli to men oriented toward more apocalyptic visions and determined to use violence in overthrowing the Nationalists. Faced with a seemingly hopeless situation, Africans have reluctantly turned away from passive resistance to the open advocacy of violence.

The Psychological Expression of Independence

The philosophy of nonviolence reflects the politico-religious basis of African independence. The African personality is an expression of the desire to secure "mental emancipation" from the colonial presence. Against the feelings of inferiority, alienation, and disequilibrium produced by colonialism, African leaders stress equality, dignity, identification with Africa, and a balance between African and European values. In the ideology of African leaders appears the constant plea for a distinctive African identity. As Erik Erikson has perceptively observed, the search for identity is linked to individual strivings for self-esteem and meaningful personal achievement. Especially among young people, who are most prone to self-hatred and self-repudiation, the receptivity to ideology stems from the need to achieve a coherent "world image," an integrated point of view that provides a meaningful orientation to life.[155] In contemporary Africa, youth is the most ideological, the most receptive to radical nationalist appeals. As the West African studies of Gustav Jahoda have revealed, African adolescents with intermediate formal education feel most inferior toward whites. In contrast to the more highly educated, who can more harmoniously integrate African and European elements, the Standard VI and VII boys feel a conflict between Western and traditional values.[156] Possessed of feelings of inferiority, alienation, and psychosocial disequilibrium, they have formed the vanguards of the Nigerian and Ghanaian nationalist movements.

The early writings of Nnamdi Azikiwe, one of the first Nigerian nationalists to call for "mental emancipation," reflect the effort to become free of the imposed feeling of racial inferiority. The British educational system created the image of Western white superiority and Nigerian inadequacy. The young Nigerians were most receptive to Azikiwe's message. In 1943, he wrote, "The myth of the mental and physical inferiority of the African has been rationalised and proselytized by racialists so that the world has been hood-winked to believe that the African is incapable of exercising political power."[157] Through the dissemination of his political beliefs, Azikiwe wanted to create a favorable "positive identity" for Africans and to obliterate a "negative identity." Those Africans under the spell of "Uncle Tomism" constituted, for Azikiwe, a negative identity. In their roles as intermediaries between the colonial administration and the Nigerian populace, they acted in a cringing, ignorant, and fearful manner toward their supposed white "masters." To replace the "psychosis" of Uncle Tomism, Azikiwe appealed to Africans to assert a positive identity, to affirm their African dignity and human equality with whites.[158]

In French-speaking West Africa, Sékou Touré has been the main exponent of psychological rehabilitation. According to Touré, the arrogant, paternalistic colonial spirit led to the degradation of African man; in particular, French education depersonalized and dehumanized the African. Through the policy of assimilation, the French convinced Africans of the white man's superiority. Only by a vigorous campaign against the habits and attitudes arising from colonialism can Africans escape this complex of inferiority and recover their original personality.[159] Touré believes that all people in the world have an equal spiritual, moral, and psychological value. Only at the level of material means do inequalities reign.[160] From Touré's perspective, colonialism not only brought to Africa the myth of racial inferiority but it also produced alienation, a feeling of "rootlessness." During the colonial era, African intellectuals were uprooted from Africa and became strangers in their own countries. They lost contact with the African *milieu* and people. To free themselves from the complexes of colonialism, Africans must henceforth become thoroughly identified with African values.[161]

In the multiracial states of Kenya and South Africa, the combination of domination by white settlers and colonial rule produced even more acute African feelings of inferiority, alienation, and disequilibrium than in racially more tolerant West Africa. In South Africa, we find the greatest need to affirm the equality of the African. There the feeling of inferiority is most strikingly associated with race. Albert Luthuli has plaintively noted the Afrikaner drive to depersonalize the blacks: "We Africans are depersonalized by the whites, our humanity and dignity is reduced in their imaginations to a minimum. . . . The pass system . . . is nothing less than an instrument of studied degradation and humiliation of us as a people, a badge of slavery, a weapon used by the authorities to keep us in a position of inferiority."[162]

In Kenya, African nationalist leaders also suffered from these feelings of alienation and psychosocial disequilibrium. Jomo Kenyatta became a victim of the imbalance colonialism imposed on African culture. A trained anthropologist, he lived in London for fifteen years but was rejected by the government in Kenya as spokesman for African rights. In a penetrating portrait of the Kikuyu nationalist, the South African novelist Peter Abrahams observed how Kenyatta felt isolated and frustrated after the war both among Europeans in Kenya, who refused to associate with him, and among his fellow tribesmen, who could not give him intellectual companionship. Kenyatta was "the victim both of tribalism and of Westernism gone sick." Abrahams wrote:

To live without roots is to live in hell, and no men chooses voluntarily to live in hell. The people who could answer his needs as a western man had erected a barrier of color against him in spite of the fact that the taproots of their culture had become the taproots of his culture too. By denying him access to those things which complete the life of western man, they had forced him back into the tribalism from which he had so painfully freed himself over the years.[163]

Kenyatta himself has written of this painful alienation and psychosocial disequilibrium:

> In the past there had been too much of "civilising and uplifting poor savages". . . . The African who is being civilised looks upon this "civilisation" with great fear mingled with suspicion. Above all, he finds that socially and religiously he has been torn away from his family and tribal organisation. The new civilisation he is supposed to acquire neither prepares him for the proper functions of a European mode of life nor for African life; he is left floundering between the two social forces.[164]

Beside securing a balance between African and European civilizations, Africans must therefore restore this organic unity of African culture.

The Aesthetic Expression of Independence

The poet-President Léopold Senghor of Senegal has become the foremost African exponent of the aesthetic approach to independence. For Senghor, as for Kenyatta, colonialism resulted in alienation. But for Senghor cultural alienation transcends political, economic, and social alienataion. The philosophy of *négritude* will end this alienation from Negro-African values and re-establish integration with African culture. The coming African renaissance will be less the work of politicians than of writers, painters, sculptors, musicians, dancers, and philosophers. To the first Conference of Negro Writers and Artists held in Paris in 1956, Senghor stated his views on the primacy of culture: "We thus want to liberate ourselves politically in order to be able to justly express our négritude, that is to say, our true black values."[165] For Senghor, cultural liberation is the prerequisite of political emancipation. Unlike Sékou Touré, who feels that art must be an instrument in the political struggle against colonialism and in the mobilization of the people,[166] Senghor denies that culture is subservient to politics: "African politicians have a tendency to neglect culture, to make it an appendage of politics. This is a mistake. . . . Culture is at once the basis and the ultimate aim of politics. . . . Culture is the very texture of society."[167]

Like his theory of socialism, Senghor's philosophy of *négritude* affirms the dignity of the traditional Negro African culture and also attempts to blend African with European values to produce a "civilization of the Universal." The assertion of one's *négritude* does not mean black racism or chauvinism. The values found in African societies are universal, yet the Negroes embody the totality of these traits and virtues in their fullest form.[168] Through a cultural blending of the fruitful elements of all civilizations, Senghor aims to achieve a "dynamic symbiosis." The task is for Europe and Africa to exchange cultures, so that by a process of cross-fertilization both cultures can receive new life. In this philosophy of *négritude,* Senghor employs a dialectic. By the dialetical process, progress results from the union of opposites. The thesis affirms, the antithesis negates, and the synthesis unites what is valid in thesis and antithesis. To Senghor the thesis is French culture, the antithesis is *négritude,* and the civilization of the universal constitutes the synthesis. All great civilizations have been mixtures of disparate elements. This mixture comes from contact between civilizations. Only through the resolution of contradictory elements does progress result.[169]

In short, both Negro African and European cultures have contributions to make in the construction of the civilization of the universal. The themes of unity and liberty are the most pervasive elements of African art and ontology. Senghor contrasts this unity and liberty with the European tendency toward disunity and dominance. European reason is discursive, analytical, and antagonistic; it breaks things down into their component parts. On the other hand, Negro reason is intuitive and sympathetic; it unites things into a synthesis. The Negro African sympathizes and identifies with the other, that is, with members of his family, ancestors, other adults, and strangers. Recognizing no intermediary between subject and object, he lives with the other in a common life. The European, in contrast, dissects the other; he distinguishes the object by holding it at a distance.[170] Furthermore, unlike the European, the Negro perceives a unitary order to the world. African society forms a series of concentric circles, all based on the family as the constituent unit. The tribe and kingdom are thus composed of a series of overlapping families.[171]

Beside expressing a unity, African culture also embodies the spirit of liberty and reciprocal independence. The European shows his desire to dominate. Possessed with a will to power, he dissects the object and uses it for practical ends. If the white man dominates the other, the Negro African discovers the other. In language as well as in art, this spirit of liberty and unity expresses itself. While Indo-European languages use a logical syntax of subordination, Negro African languages resort to an intuitive syntax of co-ordination and juxtaposition.[172] To express this spirit of liberty, the African must thus have the freedom of choice between civilizations in contact. The African must not be assimilated; he must assimilate. Between French and African cultures there ought to be reciprocal, free assimilation. The African must carefully choose what he will take from Western culture and what he must retain of Negro African civilization.[173]

From the integration of these two civilizations, Senghor hopes to realize a universal humanism. The African must not reject discursive reason, the heritage of Aristotle and Descartes. Rather, by linking discursive to intuitive reason, the new African societies can achieve an integrated concept of the world. Similarly, Africans must not reject the most obvious European contributions—technical skills and methods and machines. These contributions are complementary rather than antagonistic. Although in traditional Negro African societies, art and magic took precedence over productive labor and technical activities, contemporary African states cannot repudiate the industrial world. They need industrialization for human progress. Yet in their desire for rapid industrialization, newly independent states must not sacrifice the African spiritual, moral, and artistic values—the sense of inner piety that unifies the peasantry—for the Western technical superiority that is concerned only with the exterior of man. Only by an equilibrium between the material and moral values can African culture make a worthwhile contribution to the world.[174]

The poetry of Senghor has political, as well as purely artistic, ramifications. His poems reflect the themes of unity and liberation found in the philosophy of *négritude*. His assertion of the primacy of culture over politics does not mean that Senghor adheres to the doctrine of "art for art's sake." Like Sékou Touré, Senghor believes that African art is social and functional. Negro African art and literature serve a purpose; they are composed for all with the participation of all.[175] This selection from the poem entitled "Chaka," dedicated to the "Bantu martyrs of South Africa," illustrates the theme of African liberation. The poem expresses the struggle between Chaka, the famous nineteenth-century Zulu warrior, and a white man. Chaka voices resistance to white oppression:

La voix blanche: Ta voix est rouge de haine Chaka . . .
Chaka: Je n'ai haï que l'oppression . . .
La voix blanche: De cette haine qui brûle le cœur
    La faiblesse du coeur est sainte, pas cette tornade du feu.
Chaka: Ce n'est pas haïr que d'aimer son peuple.
    Je dis qu'il n'est pas de paix armée, de paix sous l'oppression
    De fraternité sans égalité. J'ai voulou tous les hommes frères.
La voix blanche: Tu as mobilisé le Sud contre les Blancs . . .
Chaka: Ah! te voilà Voix Blanche, voix partiale, voix endormeuse.
    Tu es la voix des forts contre les faibles, la conscience des
        possédants de l'Outre-mer. . . .[176]

In another poem, an elegy dedicated to Aynina Fall, a trade union leader on the African railways, Senghor invokes the spirit of one who struggled for the unity of Black Africa:

Il a versé son sang, qui féconde la terre d'Afrique; il a racheté
    nos fautes; il a donné sa vie sans rupture pour l'UNITE DES
    PEUPLES NOIRS.
Aynina Fall est mort, Aynina Fall est vivant parmi nous.[177]

In summary, Senghor holds that *négritude,* a form of humanism, contributes to the civilization of the universal. France has contributed strains of humanistic culture; to these strains must be joined the elements of Negro African humanism. The humanism of *négritude,* which integrates spiritual values, will help to redeem the antihumanistic civilization of the West, now dominated by materialism and machines. Through the expression of *négritude,* Africans will secure an aesthetic independence from the European elements of disunity and dominance. Only when Africans produce, as well as consume, culture will they achieve unity and liberation.

Independence in Foreign Policy and Pan-Africanism

The twin demands for independence and unity appear in the foreign policies of nonalignment and Pan-Africanism followed by most African leaders. The concept of neutralism, or nonalignment, exemplifies the African aspiration for independence from non-African controls. As in the interpretation of socialism, African leaders stress a flexible, undoctrinaire policy that maximizes freedom of action. African states hope to avoid entanglements in great power disputes, and they want to maintain sufficient flexibility to evaluate each issue on its own merits. Emphasizing a pragmatic approach, the African interpretation of neutralism affirms three priorities: the national interest, the African interest, and the interests of world peace. As Modibo Keita, President of Mali, has written:

We examine international problems in the light of our interests and of the interests of Africa, and at the same time in light of our desire for peace and for the peaceful co-existence of all countries, and we decide our policy in the light of these principles alone. If our policy then coincides with that of the Eastern or Western bloc, this is entirely a matter of chance and not the result of calculation.[178]

Most African leaders believe that a neutralist foreign policy will maximize national independence. During the first years of her independence, the United States pursued a neutralist policy toward France and England, the two great powers of that time. This policy was calculated to serve the national interests of the new American nation, notably to protect the frontier from European domination and to free the country's energies for economic growth. Similarly, African leaders hold that neutralism implies maintaining national sovereignty. According to President Nkrumah, "Non-alignment means that we seek advice and help from all, but direction or dictation from none. . . . We welcome close working relations with the West and with the East, so long as our national sovereignty is fully safeguarded."[179]

Beside expressing the priority of the national interest, the concept of nonalignment also affirms the primacy of African independence. In a 1959 address to the United Nations, Sékou Touré told the General Assembly delegates:

It is not Africa which should be asked whether it belongs to one camp or another; it is rather to the two camps, to the East as to the West, that we must put the question which we consider as fundamental: Yes or no, are you for the liberation of Africa? . . . The answer to this question will determine the attitude of Africa vis-à-vis the existing systems.[180]

Leaders as different as President Nkrumah and Prime Minister Balewa also affirm that nonalignment enables the new states to support, without previous commitment to any power bloc, all matters affecting the welfare of Africa. Nkrumah contrasts positive neutralism with negative neutralism. Negative neutralism is based on fear and timidity, on withdrawal and isolation from the world's troubles. On the other hand, positive neutralism means constructive support for the furtherance of African progress and peaceful relations.[181] Similarly, Premier Balewa has written, "Our foreign policy has never been one of neutrality, but rather non-alignment. We have never, for instance, been neutral in African affairs, nor can we be neutral in matters pertaining to world peace."[182]

In addition to affirming national and African interests, the nonalignment policy asserts the priority of world peace. African leaders hope that non-involvement in great power conflicts will help keep the Cold War out of Africa and thus free resources and manpower for concentration on national unity and rapid economic growth. They work for world peace mainly through United Nations agencies. Although African leaders all verbally support the United Nations, they differ somewhat on how it can best serve peace. In the view of President Nkrumah, the United Nations must function mainly as an agency to end colonialism. Since for him colonialism is the root of war, anti-colonial and antiwar aims are inseparable.[183] With a slightly different emphasis, Prime Minister Balewa views the United Nations as a "supreme conference." As in the federal parliament of Nigeria, leaders of differing views can meet and reconcile their differences. The United Nations is an arena of conciliation, a place to discuss frankly common problems, to negotiate, to compromise, and to achieve mediation. Here at the world level, diplomats must avoid party politics and ideological differences.[184] President Senghor of Senegal also believes that the United Nations should help bring world peace by reconciling differences. The United Nations must follow the traditional political approach of Africa — the dialogue or palaver. By conversation and discussion, by confrontation of opposition points of view, a peaceful solution to world disputes will result.[185] Senghor's interpretation of foreign policy thus reflects his similar ideas about African democracy, socialism, and *négritude*.

The concept of Pan-Africanism unifies the various aspects of independence —the political, psychological, artistic, and foreign-policy aspects. The stress on national independence, the affirmation of the African personality, and the articulation of distinctive Negro African values are all components of Pan-Africanism. In the realm of foreign policy, both neutralism and Pan-Africanism signify a flexible approach, as well as concentration upon the national and African interest. The emotional appeal of Pan-Africanism to African youth and to those out of political office and the more concrete plans for African unity proposed by governmental decision-makers lead to cross-fertilization of ideas across territorial frontiers. In the many ideas about Pan-African union, we can discern three primary reasons for all-African organization. One type of Pan-Africanism seeks to secure economic and social progress through functional unions. A second group of proposals aims to establish a sense of cultural unity among African peoples so that they may express their original values. The third form of Pan-African union is concerned mainly with ideological considerations.[186] Functional associations, cultural groupings, and ideological unions do not constitute mutually exclusive categories, for all Pan-African schemes include some proposals for functional co-operation in economic, cultural, and political fields. Rather, the classifications reflect the dominant reason for organization.

Leaders favoring a more gradual approach to independence support the functional type of Pan-African union. They focus on the need to maintain existing national boundaries and to refrain from interference in the internal politics of other states. The functional idea offers attractive features to the newly independent African territories. Functionalism provides an alternative to power politics, a way of dealing with specific problems in a flexible manner, a method of meeting the demand for rapid socioeconomic change, and finally a means of sharing sovereignty without insisting that the individual nation yield completely its territorial control to a central authority. The advocates of functional Pan-Africanism express a patient attitude. For them, a Pan-African union must grow, rather than be imposed. Time is necessary to assess problems carefully, to gain understanding, and to formulate solutions appropriate to the situation.

In French-speaking West Africa, President Félix Houphouët-Boigny of the Ivory Coast has taken leadership of the movement for functional co-operation. He played a major role in creating the Union Africaine et Malgache, as well as the more geographically limited Conseil de l'Entente. By the arrangements of the Conseil, the Ivory Coast agreed to subsidize the Upper Volta, Niger, and Dahomey; this "solidarity fund," supplied by 10% of the customs revenues of the four territories, is allocated according to need. Under Houphouët's direction, the Union Africaine et Malgache has achieved the

greatest practical results of all supranational African unions. It has a permanent secretariat, defense organization, a postal and telecommunications
union, an economic co-operation organization with a common customs code,
an airline (Air Afrique), and joint United Nations representation. It has
taken steps to establish a union of development banks, a shipping line, and
a diplomatic structure.

These concrete accomplishments reflect the self-professed realism of
Houphouët. For the Ivory Coast President, the politics of "realism" dictates
modesty of plans rather than verbal utopias; co-operation with Europe instead
of complete separation; and reliance on French, rather than Communist, aid.
He has frequently drawn a contrast between African dreams and realities:

> The dream is African unity, political unity with a central unitary or federal govern-
> ment, a central or unitary parliament. That is the dream—that is the wish we all
> formulate. But that is not the reality of today. And we have been realistic enough to
> prefer reality to this dream. This reality consists of a unity of constructive aspirations,
> in the respect, in the affirmation, of the personality of each State.[187]

Political realism also imposes the primary concept of interdependence of
peoples, both African and European. From the point of view of Houphouët,
leaders like President Nkrumah express too strong a hatred for colonialism.
Condemning those who disagree as "balkanizers," such militant Pan-Africanists
seek to establish African unity around themselves or their countries.
Houphouët, in contrast, prefers to continue ties with a prosperous country
like France, which has brought positive benefits to Africa, rather than to
become dependent on an economically underdeveloped African country. To
affirm grand principles has some merit, but to elaborate methods precisely
and to put principles into practice is better. Houphouët feels that the Conseil
de l'Entente, which operates according to national equality and solidarity, and
the Union Africaine et Malgache, which has set up practical means of co-operation, have followed this path of inter-African realism.[188]

President Houphouët-Boigny enjoys many advantages in leading a Pan-
African union. The nations within the UAM share a common currency,
administrative background, and the French language. Houphouët has "fraternal
links" with Sékou Touré and Modibo Keita; the three were founding members
of the interterritorial party, the Rassemblement Démocratique Africain.
Houphouët has recently tried to establish better relations with his former
comrades. Known for his pragmatic realism and ideological temperance, he
may emerge with the greatest concrete Pan-African successes in the functional
field.

In English-speaking West Africa, Nigeria has taken the lead in encouraging
functional Pan-African co-operation. For Balewa and Azikiwe, the removal of
practical barriers must precede any political union. Like Houphouët, both
believe that the economic and social integration of Africa must come before
the yielding of territorial sovereignty to a "political leviathan."[189] Premier
Balewa favors an exchange of ideas, better communications, and co-operation
in nonpolitical matters before attempting to form a political organization.
His plans envisage a natural growth toward Pan-Africanism rather than
imposition by a dominant personality:

> I do not think myself that ideas of political union are practicable in the immediate

future. I do not rule out the possibility of eventual union but for the present it is un-
realistic to expect countries to give up sovereignty which they have so recently acquired,
and I am quite sure that it is wrong to imagine that political union could of itself bring
the countries together: on the contrary, it will follow as the natural consequence of
cooperation in other fields.[190]

In contrast to Kwame Nkrumah, who asserts the primacy of the political
realm, Balewa believes that political organisms grow and cannot be "artificially" created by political means.

In East Africa, Julius Nyerere has most strongly advocated a Pan-African
union. In 1959, he suggested that a future federation be based on the existing
East African High Commission, which managed transport and communication services for Kenya, Uganda, and Tanganyika. After gaining independence
in December, 1961, Tanganyika remained in the functional organization,
now renamed the East African Common Services Organization. Although
Tanganyika receives the fewest benefits from the East African common
market, Nyerere has strongly campaigned for a more tightly knit federation.
He realizes that a functional union with a central bank and common tariff
rates will attract greater amounts of capital to Tanganyika. The poorest
territory in the proposed federation, Tanganyika currently benefits from the
common services provided by the EACSO.[191] This campaign for a functional
East African Federation illustrates Nyerere's concept of the relationship
between African political independence and Pan-Africanism. He has written,
"Africa must understand that the role of African nationalism is different—
or should be different—from the nationalisms of the past. That the African
national state is an instrument for the unification of Africa, and not for
dividing Africa. That African Nationalism is meaningless, is dangerous, is
anachronistic, if it is not at the same time Pan-Africanism."[192]

While the functionalists advocate Pan-Africanism as a means for sharing
technical skills and material resources, such exponents of cultural unity as
Léopold Senghor desire to achieve cultural solidarity based on the traditional
African and European civilizations. In Negro African society, the person was
integrated into a network of particular horizontal and vertical solidarities.
Vertically, the family, village, tribe, kingdom, and empire constituted the
progressively higher forms of territorial integration. Age grades, brotherhoods
of secret rites, castes, and professional or trade corporations formed the
principal horizontal links.[193] Senghor believes that a Pan-African union must
reproduce these traditional African vertical and horizontal solidarities. French-
speaking states have already achieved horizontal solidarity. These ties must
be extended to include the English-speaking states in Africa. The French-
speaking African states continue to have vertical links with France. Since,
at the present time, African economies are competitive rather than complementary, Senghor realizes that it would be difficult to establish an African Common
Market. By joining the European Common Market, Senegal would gain from
the co-operation and cohesion. In contrast to President Nkrumah, Senghor
feels that continentalism is a form of autarchy. Instead of becoming continental
chauvinists, African states must extend the vertical solidarities to the rest of
Europe and to America, the "daughter" of Europe. By realization of these
horizontal and vertical solidarities, Africa will contribute positively to the
construction of the civilization of the universal.[194]

President Nkrumah of Ghana has shown no commitment to a universal civilization. In his view, Africa must break its ties of dependence on Europe. Africa is not an extension of any other continent. Ghana and, to a lesser extent, Guinea and Mali have most militantly supported an African-oriented ideological union. According to Sékou Touré, a Pan-African union must not be based on colonial zones of influence like French-speaking West Africa or British Africa. There must also be no dependence on the highly developed countries. In fact, the motivation behind African unity lies in the unequal economic relationship between Africa and Europe. Where now the developed countries tend to exploit economically and to dominate the underdeveloped African states, a strong Pan-African union would overcome the social and economic inequalities that are weakening Africa. When establishing this transterritorial union, African leaders ought to consider the ideological views of the prospective states rather than types of political structure inherited from the colonial era. Touré has said, "Our conception of union . . . depends more on the degree of political consciousness of the people of the African countries than on their present political structures."[195] President Modibo Keita of Mali has taken a similar view. According to him, the basis for a surrender of sovereignty to a Pan-African organization must be conformity of ideological views on domestic and foreign policy, that is, views that concur with those of Mali.[196]

Just as President Touré considers Guinea to be in the "pilot position" of a future United States of Africa, so does Kwame Nkrumah look upon Ghana as the driving force behind Pan-Africanism. With a kind of chiliastic urgency, the Ghanaian president has advocated the formation of an immediate Pan-African union based on the members' total commitment to full independence and political unity:

The African struggle for independence and unity must begin with political union. A loose confederation of economic co-operation is deceptively time-delaying. It is only a political union that will ensure a uniformity in our foreign policy, projecting the African personality and presenting Africa as a force to be reckoned with. . . . The fight is for the future of humanity, and it is a most important fight. . . . Our salvation and strength and our only way out of these ravages in Africa lie in political union.[197]

Compared with the functionalists, militant leaders like Nkrumah have a more urgent, immediate time perspective on Pan-Africanism. The respective stress on immediacy or gradualism reflects in part the internal divisions within a territory. Countries like Ghana, Guinea, and Mali, which have established strong political dominance of party over state, have a more short-run orientation. Territories like Nigeria, the Ivory Coast, and Senegal, characterized by more diversity and pluralism within the political structures, stress a longer-range view. From the point of view of leaders like Balewa, Houphouët, and Senghor, African politicians must not underestimate contemporary "micro-nationalisms." They must respect present territorial frontiers, even if they are "artificial."

Because of this flexibility, allowance for diversity, and concern for gradualism, proposals for functional co-operation have so far met with greater success, as the African Summit Conference held in Ethiopia during May, 1963, demonstrated. Functionalism allows more time to reconcile differences than does political federation. The focus on nation-building, on creating national identity, and on achieving rapid modernization impedes the formation of a Pan-African political union. Even democracy and socialism, ideologically universal creeds, have become linked to national separateness. In the contemporary world of nation-states, socialism is identified with national modernization, and democratic processes take place through national institutions. The association of the political with conflict and coercion further increases the reluctance of independent states to submit their newly won autonomy to a political "leviathan." For these reasons, even those supporting ideological Pan-Africanism have recently shown greater interest in the functional approach to Pan-Africanism. President Nkrumah now apparently believes that African states can form a strong, effective union in the fields of economic planning, common foreign policy, and joint military command without an unnecessary revision of present territorial boundaries. Sékou Touré has never laid down the precise form of the all-African union he wants. In recent years, he has moved closer in his point of view to the Ivory Coast and Nigerian leaders. African politicians' views on Pan-Africanism exemplify the same flexibility as their beliefs about democracy and socialism. Each leader seems willing to make some compromises and shifts in opinion to realize greater African unity.

V. Conclusion

We can summarize the general nature of African political ideologies by analyzing the structure of these beliefs. The structural components include differentiation and organization of these beliefs, centrality of certain aspects of a belief system, and time perspective.[198]

The beliefs of African leaders reveal certain structural similarities. First, most leaders differentiate between African and European forms of democracy, between the institutions and essence of democracy. In their opinion, African society embodies the democratic spirit—free discussion, equality, widespread participation, universal suffrage, popular sovereignty, and checks against the arbitrary exercise of power. The institutions found in a European democracy —a two-party or multiparty system, the parliamentary form, a neutral civil service, an independent judiciary—do not form the essence of democracy.

The concept of socialism is differentiated between its humanistic and purely economic aspects, among African socialism, European socialism, and Russian communism. African society embodies the humanistic essence of socialism— community welfare, concern for the people's needs, respect for human dignity, equality, and social justice. The economic aspects of African socialism include various forms, although there is a widespread preference for a mixed system of public and private sectors. All leaders reject the class struggle, which is relevant to Europe, and total nationalization, which characterizes the Soviet Union's economy.

The concept of independence is differentiated between political and economic emancipation, between "nominal" and "real" independence. For all African leaders, the achievement of self-government is only the first step toward eventual full independence. When African economies are free of excessive dependence on the developed countries and when African societies have restored their cultural and spiritual values, complete liberation will be attained.

Second, in terms of the centrality of various aspects of the ideologies, African leaders regard the democratic spirit as most salient and the institutions as secondary. The welfare of the collectivity takes precedence over protection of minority rights. Similarly, the concept of socialism posits economic abundance, minimal conflict, African control, social justice, and the absence of class privileges as its central features. Beliefs about independence postulate the centrality of Africa; African values, the African way of thinking, and African ontology are the most salient aspects. Sékou Touré expresses this attitude:

> Every time that we adopt a solution genuinely African in its nature and conception, we shall solve our problems easily, for those who implement it will not be bewildered or surprised at what they have to do; they will grasp without difficulty the way they should work, act, or think. In making full use of our specific qualities, we shall accelerate our historic evolution.[199]

Third, African politicians adopt a long-range time perspective on the development of a democracy with institutionalized opposition groups. For most leaders, African society has already realized the essence of democracy. The legitimation of institutions allowing for institutionalized opposition will occur some time after the close of the "national emergency" period. For instance, Tom Mboya has written:

> When a country has just won its independence . . . such a situation can only leave room for a very weak and small opposition often with less impressive leadership, at least in the initial period. Unless a split occurs in the ranks of the new nationalist government, this situation may continue for ten or even more years. This does not mean the abandonment of democracy, but it is a situation which calls for great vigilance on the part of the people in respect to their individual freedoms.[200]

In their concepts of socialism, African leaders take a similar long-range view toward the realization of economic abundance. Africa is undeveloped, not underdeveloped. Socialism, in the form of simplicity of tastes, social equality, and the absence of privileges, characterized Africa before the colonial presence. Yet the accumulation of capital and industrialization of the economy will take considerable time; therefore the need for hard work and sacrifice. The attainment of full independence will also be reached gradually. African leaders expect all territories to achieve political independence in the short run. The majority recognizes, however, that economic independence and the unification of independent African states will occur only through stages. In general, most leaders have a long-range optimism, produced by the combined effect of Christian missionary education and Marxist teachings. They optimistically feel that the achievement of national independence will soon bring the benefits of democracy and socialism to the African continent.

NOTES

1. "Africanists Hold First Congress in Ghana," *Ghana Today*, VI (January 2, 1963), 1.
2. For this interpretation of socialism, see Henry Smith, *The Economics of Socialism Reconsidered* (London, 1962), pp. 97, 117, 155, 158, 210.
3. Joseph A. Schumpeter, *Capitalism, Socialism, and Democracy* (3rd ed.; New York, 1962), pp. 269-73.
4. Kwame Nkrumah, *I Speak of Freedom: A Statement of African Ideology* (New York, 1961), p. 158.

5. Haile Selassie I, *Speeches Delivered on Various Occasions,* May, 1957, to December, 1959 (Addis Ababa, 1960), p. 19.

6. Abubakar Tafawa Balewa, "Foreword," in Chief H. O. Davies, *Nigeria: The Prospects for Democracy* (London, 1961), p. x.

7. Léopold Senghor, *African Socialism: A Report to the Constitutive Congress of the Party of African Federation,* trans. Mercer Cook (New York, 1959), p. 36.

8. For a critical analysis of the nature of democracy in a primary group setting, see Sidney Verba, *Small Groups and Political Behavior: A Study of Leadership* (Princeton, 1961), pp. 212-32.

9. Sékou Touré, *Toward Full Re-Africanisation: Policy and Principles of the Guinea Democratic Party* (Paris, 1959), p. 76.

10. Touré, *La planification économique* (Conakry, 1960), pp. 379, 382.

11. Touré, *Guinée: prélude à l'indépendance* (Paris, 1958), p. 150.

12. Touré, *The International Policy of the Democratic Party of Guinea* (Cairo, 1962), pp. 219-20.

13. Touré, *Texte des interviews accordées aux représentants de la presse* (Conakry, 1959), p. 127.

14. Touré, *La Guinée et l'émancipation africaine* (Paris, 1959), p. 217; see also *Toward Full Re-Africanisation,* pp. 27, 54-5.

15. Touré, *La Guinée et l'émancipation africaine,* p. 127.

16. *Ibid.,* pp. 233, 234-5.

17. Touré, *Expérience guinéenne et unité africaine* (Paris, 1961), pp. 393-4.

18. Touré, *La Guinée et l'émancipation africaine,* p. 232; *The International Policy,* p. 207.

19. Touré, *Toward Full Re-Africanisation,* p. 38; see also *The International Policy,* p. 208.

20. Touré, *Guinée: prélude à l'indépendance,* p. 147.

21. See Bernard Charles, "Un parti politique africain: Le Parti Démocratique de Guinée," *Revue française de science politique,* XII (Juin, 1962), 315.

22. Touré, *Toward Full Re-Africanisation,* p. 37.

23. Touré, *The International Policy,* pp. 204-5.

24. Touré, *Toward Full Re-Africanisation,* pp. 35, 89.

25. See *ibid.,* p. 90; *La planification économique,* p. 62.

26. Touré, *The Political Action of the Democratic Party of Guinea for the Emancipation of Guinean Youth* (Cairo, 1961), p. 21.

27. Bernard Charles, "Le Parti Démocratique de Guinée," *Revue française de science politique,* XII (Juin, 1962), 312-59, has a perceptive analysis of the theory and structure of the PDG.

28. Robert Michels, *Political Parties,* trans Eden and Cedar Paul (New York, 1962), p. 214.

29. For a discussion of institutional charisma, see Reinhard Bendix's description of the Roman Catholic Church, *Max Weber: An Intellectual Portrait* (Garden City, 1962), pp. 308-18.

30. Touré, *The International Policy,* p. 189.

31. Nkrumah, *I Speak of Freedom,* p. 158.

32. "One Government for All Africa," *Ghana Today,* April 26, 1961, p. 2.

33. "Sessional Address Delivered by President Nkrumah to the Ghana National Assembly, October 2, 1962," Supplement to *Ghana Today,* October 10, 1962, p. 4.

34. See Kwame Nkrumah, "On Freedom's Stage: Extracts from a Speech Delivered to the Legislative Assembly in November, 1956," *Africa Today,* IV (March-April, 1957), 6-8.

35. Nkrumah, *I Speak of Freedom,* p. 209.

36. "Text of an Address Broadcast from Accra, April 8, 1961," Supplement to *Ghana Today,* April 12, 1961, p. 2. For an analysis of recent party-political developments in Ghana, see David E. Apter, "Ghana," in J. S. Coleman and C. G. Rosberg, eds., *Political Parties and National Integrations in Tropical Africa* (Berkeley and Los Angeles, 1964), and *Ghana in Transition* (New York, 1963).

37. Nkrumah, *Speech Delivered on the Occasion of the Tenth Anniversary Celebrations of the Party,* June 12, 1959 (Accra, 1959), p. 19.

38. "The Birth and Growth of the CPP," *The Party,* No. 2, March, 1961, p. 11.

39. See Jacques Boyon, "Une idéologie africaine: le nkrumaïsme," *Revue française de science politique,* XIII (Mars, 1963), 79.

40. Kofi Baako, "Nkrumaism—Its Theory and Practice," in Paul E. Sigmund, Jr., ed., *The Ideologies of the Developing Nations* (New York, 1963), p. 196.

41. Nkrumah, "Sessional Address Delivered by President Nkrumah to the Ghana National Assembly, October 2, 1962," Supplement to *Ghana Today,* October 10, 1962, p. 3.

42. Julius Nyerere, "One-Party Government," *Spearhead,* I (November, 1961), 7.

43. Nyerere, "The African and Democracy," in James Duffy and Robert Manners, eds., *Africa Speaks* (New York, 1961), pp. 32-3.

44. Nyerere, "Will Democracy Work in Africa?" *Africa Special Report,* V (February, 1960), 3.

45. Nyerere, "One Party System," *Spearhead,* II (January, 1963), 12, 13, 21, 23.

46. *Ibid.,* p. 21.

47. Nyerere, "One-Party Government," *Spearhead,* I (November, 1961), 8.

48. Nyerere, "One-Party System," *Spearhead,* II (January, 1963), 16.

49. *Ibid.,* pp. 14, 20.

50. *Ibid.,* p. 20.

51. *Ibid.*

52. For a statement of the need to integrate real and formal authority, see Nyerere, "How Much Power for a Leader?" *The Observer* (London), June 3, 1962, p. 10.

53. Nyerere, "One Party System," p. 23.

54. Colin Leys, "Tanganyika: The Politics of Independence," *International Journal,* XVII (Summer, 1962), 251-68; John B. George, "How Stable Is Tanganyika?" *Africa Report,* VIII (March, 1963), 3-9; Margaret L. Bates, "Tanganyika," in Gwendolen M. Carter, ed., *African One-Party States* (Ithaca, 1962), pp. 444-59.

55. For Senghor's views on democracy, see *Nation et voie africaine du socialisme* (Paris, 1961, pp. 115-7; "Ce que l'homme noir apporte," *L'homme de couleur* (Paris, 1939), pp. 301-2; "L'Esprit de la civilisation ou les lois de la culture négro-africaine," *Présence Africaine,* Juin-Novembre, 1956, p. 62; *African Socialism,* p. 34.

56. Obafemi Awolowo, *Awo: The Autobiography of Chief Obafemi Awolowo* (London, 1960), p. 271.

57. *Ibid.,* p. 304.

58. Awolofo, *Path to Nigerian Freedom* (London, 1947), pp. 55, 54.

59. With the creation of a Mid-West region, the Action Group, which formerly governed the Western region, suffered a severe loss of political power. Due to limited resources, the proposed Mid-West region will remain heavily dependent on the central government. See *West Africa,* April 21, 1962, pp. 421-2.

60. Awolowo, *Path to Nigerian Freedom,* pp. 66, 65.

61. Nigeria House of Representatives *Debates,* I (April, 1960), 376.

62. Balewa, "Foreword," in Chief H. O. Davies, *Nigeria: The Prospects for Democracy,* pp. x-xi.

63. Nnamdi Azikiwe, *The Evolution of Federal Government in Nigeria* (Orlu, 1955), p. 23.

64. See *Report of the CSA Meeting of Specialists on the Basic Psychological Structures of African and Madagascan Populations,* Tananarive, August 27-September 3, 1959. Synthetic Report Prepared under the Supervision of Dr. S. Biesheuvel, p. 37.

65. Albert Luthuli, *Let My People Go* (New York, 1962), pp. 209-10.

66. Luthuli, "A Program for a New South Africa," *Saturday Night,* LXXVII (January 20, 1962), 12.

67. *Ibid.*

68. *Ibid.,* p. 11.

69. Luthuli, *Let My People Go,* p. 87.

70. Luthuli, "A Program for a New South Africa," 18.

71. Tom Mboya, *Kenya Faces the Future, Africa Today,* Pamphlet No. 3 (New York, 1959), p. 32.

72. Mboya, *The Kenya Question: An African Answer,* Fabian Tract No. 302 (London, 1956), p. 37.

73. Kenneth Kaunda and Colin Morris, *Black Government?* (Lusaka, 1960), pp. 98, 111.

74. "One Government for All Africa," *Ghana Today,* April 26, 1961, p. 1.

75. Max Weber, *The Protestant Ethic and the Spirit of Capitalism,* trans. Talcott Parsons (New York, 1958), p. 62.

76. Nyerere, "An African View: Communitarian Socialism," *Liberation,* VII (Summer, 1962), 14.

77. For an insightful interpretation of Marxism, see Herbert Marcuse, *Soviet Marxism* (New York, Vintage Books, 1961), esp. pp. 105-20.

78. Touré, *La planification économique,* p. 68.

79. Touré, *Texte des interviews,* p. 107.

80. Touré, *La planification économique,* p. 81.

81. Touré, *Expérience guinéenne et unité africaine,* p. 438.

82. Touré, *La planification économique,* p. 309.

83. *Ibid.,* p. 290.

84. *Ibid.,* pp. 84-8.

85. Touré, *La Guinée et l'émancipation africaine,* p. 52.

86. Touré, *The Political Action . . . for the Emancipation of Guinean Youth,* pp. 12-15.

87. Touré, *La planification économique*, p. 428.
88. Touré, *Texte des interviews*, pp. 7, 17; *La Guinée et l'émancipation africaine*, pp. 17, 71, 122.
89. Touré, *La Guinée et l'émancipation africaine*, p. 68.
90. Touré, *Texte des interviews*, pp. 149-51.
91. Touré, *La planification économique*, p. 104; *La Guinée et l'émancipation africaine*, p. 211.
92. Touré, *La planification économique*, pp. 292, 293-6.
93. The sources of these four quotations are "Text of an Address Broadcast from Accra, April 8, 1961," Supplement to *Ghana Today*, April 12, 1961, p. 1; "Trade Unions Must Contribute to Africa's Political Unity," *Ghana Today*, April 11, 1962, p. 2; *Speech Delivered on the Occasion of the Tenth Anniversary Celebrations of the Party*, June 12, 1959, p. 21; *I Speak of Freedom*, p. 165.
94. Nkrumah, *Towards Colonial Freedom: Africa in the Struggle Against World Imperialism* (Accra, 1957), p. 31.
95. Nkrumah, *Guide to Party Action* (Accra, 1962), p. 4; "African Freedom and Unity," Supplement to *Ghana Today*, June 20, 1962, p. 7.
96. For this interpretation of socialism, see *The Party*, No. 2, March, 1961, p. 16; *Guide to Party Action*, p. 6.
97. See *For Work and Happiness*, Program of the Convention People's Party (Accra, 1962).
98. Senghor, *African Socialism*, p. 29.
99. Mamadou Dia, *Contribution à l'étude du mouvement coopératif en Afrique noire* (Paris, 1958), pp. 11, 13, 17; *Réflexions sur l'économie de l'Afrique noire* (new ed.; Paris, 1960), p. 27; "Économie et culture devant les élites africaines," *Présence africaine*, Juin-Septembre, 1957, pp. 66-7.
100. Senghor, *Nation et voie africaine du socialisme*, pp. 123-4.
101. Senghor, *African Socialism*, p. 32.
102. Senghor, "L'Avenir de la France dans l'outre-mer," *Politique Étrangère*, XIX (Août-Octobre, 1954), 421; *Nation et voie africaine du socialisme*, pp. 94, 106.
103. Senghor, *Nation et voie africaine du socialisme*, pp. 116, 124.
104. Senghor, "African-Style Socialism," *West Africa*, XLV (November 11, 1961), 1245; *Nation et voie africaine du socialisme*, p. 106.
105. Dia, *Réflexions sur l'économie*, p. 70; "Économie et culture devant les élites africaines," *Présence africaine*, Juin-Septembre, 1957, p. 64.
106. Dia, *L'Économie africaine: études et problèmes nouveaux* (Paris, 1957), pp. 35-7.
107. Dia, *Réflexions sur l'économie*, pp. 60-7, 81-4.
108. *Ibid.*, pp. 17, 27.
109. Senghor, *African Socialism*, p. 41.
110. Dia, "Proposition pour Afrique," *Présence africaine*, Avril-Mai, 1957, p. 46.
111. Dia, *The African Nations and World Solidarity*, trans. Mercer Cook (New York, 1961), p. 51.
112. Senghor, "A Community of Free and Equal Peoples with the Mother Country," *Western World*, October, 1958, p. 39; "Éléments constructifs d'une civilisation d'inspiration négro-africaine," *Présence africaine*, Février-Mai, 1959, p. 278.
113. Dia, *Réflexions sur l'économie*, pp. 135-6, 168.
114. Dia, *The African Nations and World Solidarity*, p. 91.
115. Dia, *Réflexions sur l'économie*, pp. 36-41.
116. Dia, *L'Économie africaine*, p. 72.
117. *Ibid.*, pp. 78-82.
118. Senghor, "The African Path to Socialism," *Venture*, XIII (November, 1961), 7; *African Socialism*, p. 18.
119. Nyerere, "Communitarian Socialism," *Liberation*, VII (Summer, 1962), 13.
120. Nnamdi Azikiwe, "Opportunity Knocks at Our Door," Speech Delivered October 28, 1957, to the Annual Convention of the NCNC, quoted in Richard Sklar, *Nigerian Political Parties* (Princeton, 1961), p. 230.
121. Nyerere, "Scramble for Africa," *Spearhead*, I (February, 1962), 14-15.
122. Azikiwe, *Economic Reconstruction of Nigeria* (Lagos, 1944), pp. 8, 42, 50.
123. Nyerere, "It's Up to Us," *Africa Today*, VIII (December, 1961), 5.
124. Nyerere, "Communitarian Socialism," *Liberation*, VII (Summer, 1962), 15.
125. Awolowo, *Awo*, p. 267.
126. Nigeria, House of Representatives *Debates*, I (April, 1960), 31-2; and II (April, 1960), 208, 210.
127. Touré, *Toward Full Re-Africanisation*, pp. 69-70.
128. Nigeria, House of Representatives *Debates*, III (August, 1959), 288.

129. Touré, *Expérience guinéenne et unité africaine*, p. 347; *La Guinée et l'émancipation africaine*, p. 60.
130. Nkrumah, *Ghana: The Autobiography of Kwame Nkrumah* (New York, 1957), p. 288.
131. Touré, *La Guinée et l'émancipation africaine*, p. 170.
132. E. Reginald Townsend, ed., *President Tubman of Liberia Speaks* (London, 1959), pp. 61, 277, 296-7.
133. Luthuli, *Let My People Go*, p. 31.
134. Habib Bourguiba, *La Tunisie et la France* (Paris, 1954), pp. 202-3, 342; *Electoral Campaign Speeches* October 26 - November 5, 1959 (Tunis, 1959), p. 23.
135. Touré, *Expérience guinéenne et unité africaine*, p. 221.
136. Bourguiba, *The Advancement of Africa* (Tunis, n.d.), p. 116; "The Outlook for Africa," *International Affairs*, XXXVII (October, 1960), 430.
137. Touré, "The Republic of Guinea," *International Affairs*, XXXVI (April, 1960), 169.
138. Bourguiba, *La Tunisie et la France*, pp. 91, 106, 156.
139. See Clement Henry Moore, "The Neo-Destour Party of Tunisia," *World Politics*, XIV (April, 1962), 461-82.
140. Bourguiba, "Le Syndicalisme tunisien de M'hamed Ali à Ferhat Hached," *Temps Modernes*, IX (November, 1953), 905.
141. Touré, *Congrès Générale de l'U.G.T.A.N. rapport d'orientation et de doctrine* (Paris, 1959), p. 34.
142. *Ibid.*
143. See Bourguiba, *La Tunisie et la France*, p. 46; "Le problème franco-tunisien est un problème de souveraineté," *Temps modernes*, VII (Mars, 1952), 1970.
144. Touré, *Guinée: prélude à l'indépendance*, pp. 166-7.
145. Bourguiba, *The Advancement of Africa*, p. 42.
146. Touré, *The International Policy*, pp. 219-20.
147. Bourguiba, *Vers la libération économique* (Tunis, 1957), p. 31; *Address Delivered on March 2, 1959, at the Sixth Neo-Destour Party Congress, Sousse* (Tunis, 1959), pp. 17, 23-9, 43.
148. Bourguiba, *La Tunisie et la France*, p. 139.
149. Azikiwe, *Zik: A Selection from the Speeches of Nnamdi Azikiwe* (London, 1961), p. 57.
150. James S. Coleman, *Nigeria: Background to Nationalism* (Berkeley and Los Angeles, 1958), p. 95.
151. Azikiwe, *Liberia in World Politics* (London, 1934), pp. 266, 331, 396.
152. Kaunda and Morris, *Black Government?* pp. 99-100; Kaunda, *Zambia Shall Be Free* (London, 1962), p. 154.
153. Luthuli, *Let My People Go*, p. 238.
154. Luthuli, "Africa and Freedom: Text of the Nobel Lecture Delivered at Oslo University," *Présence africaine*, Fourth Quarterly, 1962, p. 9.
155. See Erik H. Erikson, "Identity and the Life Cycle," *Psychological Issues*, I (1959), 89-90; *Young Man Luther* (New York, 1958).
156. Gustav Jahoda, *White Man: A Study of the Attitudes of Africans to Europeans before Independence* (London, 1961), pp. 108-17.
157. Azikiwe, *Political Blueprint of Nigeria* (Lagos, 1943), p. 58.
158. *Ibid.*, pp. 8, 65. See also Azikiwe, *Before Us Lies the Open Grave* (N. P., 1947), p. 3.
159. Touré, *La Guinée et l'émancipation africaine*, pp. 164, 170; *Toward Full Re-Africanisation*, pp. 9, 11, 48.
160. Touré, *Expérience guinéenne et unité africaine*, p. 101.
161. Touré, *La Guinée et l'émancipation africaine*, p. 170; "Africa's Future and the World," *Foreign Affairs*, XLI (October, 1962), 147.
162. Luthuli, *Let My People Go*, pp. 155, 244.
163. Peter Abrahams, "The Blacks," in Langston Hughes, ed., *An African Treasury* (New York, 1960), p. 52.
164. Jomo Kenyatta, *Facing Mt. Kenya* (New York, 1962), p. 120.
165. Léopold Sédar Senghor, *Présence africaine*, Juin-Novembre, 1956, p. 215.
166. Touré, *La Guinée et l'émancipation africaine*, pp. 163-72.
167. Senghor, *African Socialism*, p. 32.
168. Senghor, "African-Negro Aesthetics," *Diogenes*, No. 16 (Winter, 1956), p. 37.
169. Senghor, "Some Thoughts on Africa: A Continent in Development," *International Affairs*, XXXVIII (April, 1962), 189, 191; *Présence africaine*, Juin-Novembre, 1956, p. 216.
170. Senghor, *Nation et voie africaine du socialisme*, pp. 100-1; "L'Esprit de la civilisation ou les lois de la culture négro-africaine," *Présence africaine*, Juin-Novembre, 1956, pp. 52-3.
171. Senghor, "African-Negro Aesthetics," p. 26.

172. Senghor, "Éléments constructifs d'une civilisation d'inspiration négro-africaine," *Présence africaine*, Février-Mai, 1959, p. 255; "L'Esprit de la civilisation ou les lois de la culture négro-africaine," *Présence africaine*, Juin-Novembre, 1956, p. 62.

173. Senghor, "Vues sur l'Afrique noire, ou assimiler, non être assimilés," in Robert Lemaignen, Léopold Sédar Senghor, Prince Sisowath Youtevong, *La communauté impériale française* (Paris, 1945), p. 65; *Présence africaine*, Juin-Novembre, 1956, p. 216.

174. Senghor, "Subir ou choisir?" *Présence africaine*, No. 8-9, issue entitled *Le monde noir*, pp. 438-42; "Éléments constructifs d'une civilisation d'inspiration négro-africaine," *Présence africaine*, Février-Mai, 1959, p. 277; "Discours de Léopold Sédar Senghor, Inauguration de l'Université de Dakar, le 9 decembre, 1959," *Réception du Général de Gaulle*, p. 24; "On Negrohood: Psychology of the African Negro," *Diogenes*, No. 37 (Spring, 1962), p. 14.

175. Senghor, "L'Esprit de la civilisation ou les lois de la culture négro-africaine," *Présence africaine*, Juin-Novembre, 1956, pp. 56-7.

176. Senghor, *Éthiopiques* (Paris, 1956), pp. 40-1.

177. Senghor, *Nocturnes* (Paris, 1961), p. 81.

178. Modibo Keita, "The Foreign Policy of Mali," *International Affairs*, XXXVII (October, 1961), 438.

179. "Achievements in 1961," Supplement to *Ghana Today*, January 3, 1962, p. 4.

180. Touré, "Africa's Destiny," *Africa Speaks*, pp. 45-6.

181. "Appeal for World Peace," Supplement to *Ghana Today*, September 13, 1961, p. 3; *I Speak of Freedom*, p. 199.

182. Abubakar Tafawa Balewa, "Nigeria Looks Ahead," *Foreign Affairs*, XLI (October, 1962), 139.

183. "Africa Speaks to the United Nations: Kwame Nkrumah," *International Organization*, XVI (Spring, 1962), 316.

184. "The 99th Member Speaks at UN," *Federal Nigeria*, III (September-October, 1960), 13.

185. "Africa Speaks to the United Nations: Léopold Sédar Senghor," *International Organization*, XVI (Spring, 1962), 324.

186. For a more complete account of the nature and intellectual sources of Pan-Africanism, see Charles F. Andrain, "The Pan-African Movement: The Search for Organisation and Community," *Phylon*, XXIII (Spring, 1962), 5-17.

187. Félix Houphouët-Boigny, "Les chances de l'Afrique," *Revue politique et parlementaire*, Juillet, 1961, p. 5.

188. For a brief statement of Houphouët's beliefs, see *ibid.*, pp. 4-6; *Rapport du Président Houphouët-Boigny au Congrès Extraordinaire du Rassemblement Démocratique Africain* (Abidjan, 1959), pp. 7, 10, 14, 19.

189. Azikiwe, "Nigeria in World Politics," *Présence africaine*, No. 32-3, 1960, pp. 27-8; Abubakar Tafawa Balewa, "Nigeria Looks Ahead," *Foreign Affairs*, XLI (October, 1962), 137.

190. "The 99th Member Speaks at UN," p. 13.

191. For an analysis of the historical development and prospects of a federation linking Kenya, Uganda, and Tanganyika, see Carl G. Rosberg, Jr., and Aaron Segal, "An East African Federation," *International Conciliation*, No. 543 (May, 1963).

192. Nyerere, "Scramble for Africa," p. 16.

193. Senghor, "Éléments constructifs d'une civilisation négro-africaine," pp. 263, 266.

194. Senghor, *Nation et voie africaine du socialisme*, pp. 119-20; "Some Thoughts on Africa," *International Affairs*, XXXVIII (April, 1962), 189-92.

195. Touré, *Texte des interviews*, pp. 115, 47, 54, 112-3; "Africa's Future and the World," *Foreign Affairs*, XLI (October, 1962), 147.

196. Modibo Keita, "The Foreign Policy of Mali," *International Affairs*, XXXVII (October, 1961), 435-6.

197. Nkrumah, *I Speak of Freedom*, pp. 253, 220-1.

198. For a more detailed description of these structural components, see M. Brewster Smith, Jerome S. Bruner, and Robert W. White, *Opinions and Personality* (New York, 1956), pp. 33-7, 242-6.

199. Touré, *The Political Action . . . for the Emancipation of Guinean Youth*, pp. 107-8.

200. Tom Mboya, "Vision of Africa," *Africa Speaks*, pp. 25-6.

The Nature of Belief Systems
in Mass Publics

BY *PHILIP E. CONVERSE*

BELIEF SYSTEMS have never surrendered easily to empirical study or quantification. Indeed, they have often served as primary exhibits for the doctrine that what is important to study cannot be measured and that what can be measured is not important to study. In an earlier period, the behaviorist decree that subjective states lie beyond the realm of proper measurement gave Mannheim a justification for turning his back on measurement, for he had an unqualified interest in discussing belief systems.[1] Even as Mannheim was writing, however, behaviorism was undergoing stiff challenges, and early studies of attitudes were attaining a degree of measurement reliability that had been deemed impossible. This fragment of history, along with many others, serves to remind us that no intellectual position is likely to become obsolete quite so rapidly as one that takes current empirical capability as the limit of the possible in a more absolute sense. Nevertheless, while rapid strides in the measurement of "subjective states" have been achieved in recent decades, few would claim that the millennium has arrived or that Mannheim could now find all of the tools that were lacking to him forty years ago.

This article makes no pretense of surpassing such limitations. At the same time, our substantive concern forces upon us an unusual concern with measurement strategies, not simply because we propose to deal with belief systems or ideologies, but also because of the specific questions that we shall raise about them. Our focus in this article is upon differences in the nature of belief systems held on the one hand by elite political actors and, on the other, by the masses that appear to be "numbered" within the spheres of influence of these belief systems. It is our thesis that there are important and predictable differences in ideational worlds as we progress downward through such "belief strata" and that these differences, while obvious at one level, are easily overlooked and not infrequently miscalculated. The fact that these ideational worlds differ in character poses problems of adequate representation and measurement.

The vertical ordering of actors and beliefs that we wish to plumb bears some loose resemblance to the vertical line that might be pursued downward through an organization or political movement from the narrow cone of top leadership, through increasing numbers of subordinate officials, and on through untitled activists to the large base formally represented in membership rolls. It is this large base that Michels noted, from observations of political gatherings, was rarely "there", and analogues to its physical absence do not arise accidentally in dealing with belief systems. On the other hand, there is no perfect or necessary "fit" between the two orderings, and this fact in itself has some interest.

That we intend to consider the total mass of people "numbered" within the spheres of influence of belief systems suggests both a democratic bias and a possible confusion between numbers and power or between numbers and the outcomes of events that power determines. We are aware that attention to numbers, more or less customary in democratic thought, is very nearly irrelevant in many political settings. Generally, the logic of numbers collides head on with the logic of power, as the traditional power pyramid, expressing an inverse relation between power and numbers, communicates so well. "Power" and "numbers" intersect at only one notable point, and that point is represented by the familiar axiom that numbers are one resource of power. The weight of this resource varies in a systematic and obvious way according to the political context. In a frankly designed and stable oligarchy, it is assumed to have no weight at all. In such a setting, the numbers of people associated with particular belief systems, if known at all, becomes important only in periods of crisis or challenge to the existing power structure. Democratic theory greatly increases the weight accorded to numbers in the daily power calculus. This increase still does not mean that numbers are of overriding importance; in the normal course of events it is the *perception* of numbers by democratic elites, so far as they differ from "actual" numbers, that is the more important factor. However this may be, claims to numbers are of some modest continuing importance in democratic systems for the legitimacy they confer upon demands; and, much more sporadically, claims to numbers become important in nondemocratic systems as threats of potential coercion.

I. Some Clarification of Terms

A term like "ideology" has been thoroughly muddied by diverse uses.[2] We shall depend instead upon the term "belief system," although there is an obvious overlap between the two. We define a *belief system* as a configuration of ideas and attitudes in which the elements are bound together by some form of constraint or functional interdependence.[3] In the static case, "constraint" may be taken to mean the success we would have in predicting, given initial knowledge that an individual holds a specified attitude, that he holds certain further ideas and attitudes. We depend implicitly upon such notions of constraint in judging, for example, that, if a person is opposed to the expansion of social security, he is probably a conservative and is probably opposed as well to any nationalization of private industries, federal aid to education, sharply progressive income taxation, and so forth. Most discussions of ideologies make relatively elaborate assumptions about such constraints. Constraint must be treated, of course, as a matter of degree, and this degree can be measured quite readily, at least as an average among individuals.[4]

In the dynamic case, "constraint" or "interdependence" refers to the probability that a change in the perceived status (truth, desirability, and so forth) of one idea-element would *psychologically* require, from the point of view of the actor, some compensating change(s) in the status of idea-elements elsewhere in the configuration. The most obvious form of such constraint (although in some ways the most trivial) is exemplified by a structure of propositions in logic, in which a change in the truth-value of one proposition necessitates changes in truth-value elsewhere within the set of related propositions. Psychologically, of course, there may be equally strong constraint among idea-elements that would not be apparent to logical analysis at all, as we shall see.

We might characterize either the idea-elements themselves or entire belief systems in terms of many other dimensions. Only two will interest us here. First, the idea-elements within a belief system vary in a property we shall call *centrality,* according to the role that they play in the belief system as a whole. That is, when new information changes the status of one idea-element in a belief system, by postulate some other change must occur as well. There are usually, however, several possible changes in status elsewhere in the system, any one of which would compensate for the initial change. Let us imagine, for example, that a person strongly favors a particular policy; is very favorably inclined toward a given political party; and recognizes with gratification that the party's stand and his own are congruent. (If he were unaware of the party's stand on the issue, these elements could not in any direct sense be constrained within the same belief system.) Let us further imagine that the party then changes its position to the opposing side of the issue. Once the information about the change reaching the actor has become so unequivocal that he can no longer deny that the change has occurred, he has several further choices. Two of the more important ones involve either a change in attitude toward the party or a change in position on the issue. In such an instance, the element more likely to change is defined as less central to the belief system than the element that, so to speak, has its stability ensured by the change in the first element.[5]

In informal discussions of belief systems, frequent assumptions are made about the relative centrality of various idea-elements. For example, idea-elements that are logically "ends" are supposed to be more central to the system than are "means." It is important to remain aware, however, that idea-elements can change their relative centrality in an individual's belief-system over time. Perhaps the most hackneyed illustration of this point is that of the miser, to whom money has become an end rather than a means.

Whole belief systems may also be compared in a rough way with respect to the *range* of objects that are referents for the ideas and attitudes in the system. Some belief systems, while they may be internally quite complex and may involve large numbers of cognitive elements, are rather narrow in range: Belief systems concerning "proper" baptism rituals or the effects of changes in weather on health may serve as cases in point. Such other belief systems as, for example, one that links control of the means of production with the social functions of religion and a doctrine of aesthetics all in one more or less neat package have extreme ranges.

By and large, our attention will be focussed upon belief systems that have relatively wide ranges, and that allow some centrality to political objects, for they can be presumed to have some relevance to political behavior. This focus brings us close to what are broadly called *ideologies*, and we shall use the term for aesthetic relief where it seems most appropriate. The term originated in a narrower context, however, and is still often reserved for subsets of belief systems or parts of such systems that the user suspects are insincere; that he wishes to claim have certain functions for social groupings; or that have some special social source or some notable breadth of social diffusion.[6] Since we are concerned here about only one of these limitations—the question of social diffusion—and since we wish to deal with it by hypothesis rather than by definition, a narrow construction of the term is never intended.

II. Sources of Constraint on Idea-Elements

It seems clear that, however logically coherent a belief system may seem to the holder, the sources of constraint are much less logical in the classical sense than they are psychological—and less psychological than social. This point is of sufficient importance to dwell upon.

Logical Sources of Constraint

Within very narrow portions of belief systems, certain constraints may be purely logical. For example, government revenues, government expenditures, and budget balance are three idea-elements that suggest some purely logical constraints. One cannot believe that government expenditures should be increased, that government revenues should be decreased, and that a more favorable balance of the budget should be achieved all at the same time. Of course, the presence of such objectively logical constraints does not ensure that subjective constraints will be felt by the actor. They will be felt only if these idea-elements are brought together in the same belief system, and there is no guarantee that they need be. Indeed, it is true that, among adult American citizens, those who favor the expansion of government welfare services tend to be those who are more insistent upon reducing taxes "even if it means putting off some important things that need to be done."[7]

Where such purely logical constraint is concerned, McGuire has reported a fascinating experiment in which propositions from a few syllogisms of the Barbara type were scattered thinly across a long questionnaire applied to a student population. The fact that logical contingencies bound certain questions together was never brought to the attention of the students by the investigator. Yet one week later the questionnaire was applied again, and changes of response to the syllogistic propositions reduced significantly the measurable level of logical inconsistency. The conclusion was that merely "activating" these objectively related ideas in some rough temporal contiguity was sufficient to sensitize the holders to inconsistency and therefore to occasion readjustment of their beliefs.[8]

On a broader canvas, such findings suggest that simple "thinking about" a domain of idea-elements serves both to weld a broader range of such elements into a functioning belief system and to eliminate strictly logical inconsistencies defined from an objective point of view. Since there can be no doubt that educated elites in general, and political elites in particular, "think about" elements involved in political belief systems with a frequency far greater than that characteristic of mass publics, we could conservatively expect that strict logical inconsistencies (objectively definable) would be far more prevalent in a broad public.

Furthermore, if a legislator is noted for his insistence upon budget-balancing and tax-cutting, we can predict with a fair degree of success that he will also tend to oppose expansion of government welfare activities. If, however, a voter becomes numbered within his sphere of influence by virtue of having cast a vote for him directly out of enthusiasm for his tax-cutting policies, we cannot predict that the voter is opposed as well to expansion of government welfare services. Indeed, if an empirical prediction is possible, it may run in an opposing direction, although the level of constraint is so feeble that any comment is trivial. Yet we know that many historical observations rest directly upon the assumption that constraint among idea-elements visible at an elite level is mirrored by the same lines of constraint in the belief systems of their less visible "supporters." It is our argument that this assumption not only can be, but is very likely to be, fallacious.

Psychological Sources of Constraint

Whatever may be learned through the use of strict logic as a type of constraint, it seems obvious that few belief systems of any range at all depend for their constraint upon logic in this classical sense. Perhaps, with a great deal of labor, parts of a relatively tight belief system like that fashioned by Karl Marx could be made to resemble a structure of logical propositions. It goes without saying, however, that many sophisticated people have been swept away by the "iron logic" of Marxism without any such recasting. There is a broad gulf between strict logic and the quasi-logic of cogent argument. And where the elements in the belief system of a population represent looser cultural accumulations, the question of logical consistency is even less appropriate. If one visits a Shaker community, for example, one finds a group of people with a clear-cut and distinctive belief system that requires among other things plain dress, centrality of religious concerns, celibacy for all members, communal assumptions about work and property, antagonism to political participation in the broader state, and a general aura of retirement from the secular world. The visitor whose sense of constraint has been drawn from belief configurations of such other retiring sects as the Amish is entirely surprised to discover that the Shakers have no abhorrence of technological progress but indeed greatly prize it. In their heyday, a remarkable amount of group energy appears to have been reserved for "research and development" of labor-saving devices, and among the inventions they produced was a prototype of the washing machine. Similar surprise has been registered at idea-elements brought together by such movements as Perónism and Italian Fascism by observers schooled to expect other combinations. Indeed, were one to survey a limited set of ideas on which many belief systems have registered opposite postures, it would be interesting to see how many permutations of positions have been held at one time or another by someone somewhere.

Such diversity is testimony to an absence of any strict logical constraints among such idea-elements, if any be needed. What is important is that the elites familiar with the total shapes of these belief systems have *experienced* them as logically constrained clusters of ideas, within which one part necessarily follows from another. Often such constraint is quasi-logically argued on the basis of an appeal to some superordinate value or posture toward man and society, involving premises about the nature of social justice, social change, "natural law," and the like. Thus a few crowning postures—like premises about survival of the fittest in the spirit of social Darwinism—serve as a sort of glue to bind together many more specific attitudes and beliefs, and these postures are of prime centrality in the belief system as a whole.

Social Sources of Constraint

The social sources of constraint are twofold and are familiar from an extensive literature in the past century. In the first place, were we to survey the combinations of idea-elements that have occurred historically (in the fashion suggested above), we should undoubtedly find that certain postures tend to co-occur and that this co-occurrence has obvious roots in the configuration of interests and information that characterize particular niches in the social structure. For example, if we were informed that dissension was rising within the Roman Catholic Church over innovations designed to bring the priest more intimately into the *milieu* of the modern worker, we could predict with a high degree of success that such a movement would have the bulk of its support among the *bas-clergé* and would encounter indifference or hostility at the higher status levels of the hierarchy.

Of course, such predictions are in no sense free from error, and surprises are numerous. The middle-class temperance movement in America, for example, which now seems "logically" allied with the small-town Republican right, had important alliances some eighty years ago with the urban social left, on grounds equally well argued from temperance doctrines.[9] Nonetheless, there are some highly reliable correlations of this sort, and these correlations can be linked with social structure in the most direct way. Developmentally, they have status similar to the classic example of the spurious correlation—two terms that are correlated because of a common link to some third and prior variable. In the case of the belief system, arguments are developed to lend some more positive rationale to the fact of constraint: The idea-elements go together not simply because both are in the interest of the person holding a particular status but for more abstract and quasi-logical reasons developed from a coherent world view as well. It is this type of constraint that is closest to the classic meaning of the term "ideology."

The second source of social constraint lies in two simple facts about the creation and diffusion of belief systems. First, the shaping of belief systems of any range into apparently logical wholes that are credible to large numbers of people is an act of creative synthesis characteristic of only a miniscule proportion of any population. Second, to the extent that multiple idea-elements of a belief system are socially diffused from such creative sources, they tend to be diffused in "packages," which consumers come to see as "natural" wholes, for they are presented in such terms ("If you believe this, then you will also believe that, for it follows in such-and-such ways"). Not that the more avid consumer never supplies personal innovations on the fringes—he is very likely to suppress an idea-element here, to elaborate one there, or even to demur at an occasional point. But any set of relatively intelligent consumers who are initially sympathetic to the crowning posture turns out to show more consensus on specific implications of the posture as a result of social diffusion of "what goes with what" than it would if each member were required to work out the implications individually without socially provided cues.

Such constraint through diffusion is important, for it implies a dependence upon the transmission of information. If information is not successfully transmitted, there will be little constraint save that arising from the first social source. Where transmission of information is at stake, it becomes important to distinguish between two classes of information. Simply put, these two levels are what goes with what and why. Such levels of information logically stand in a scalar relationship to one another, in the sense that one can hardly arrive at an understanding of why two ideas go together without being aware that they are supposed to go together. On the other hand, it is easy to know that two ideas go together without knowing why. For example, we can expect that a very large majority of the American public would somehow have absorbed the notion that "Communists are atheists." What is important is that this perceived correlation would for most people represent nothing more than a fact of existence, with the same status as the fact that oranges are orange and most apples are red. If we were to go and explore with these people their grasp of the "why" of the relationship, we would be surprised if more than a quarter of the population even attempted responses (setting aside such inevitable replies as "those Communists are for everything wicked"), and, among the responses received, we could be sure that the majority would be incoherent or irrelevant.

The first level of information, then, is simple and straightforward. The second involves much more complex and abstract information, very close to what Downs has called the "contextual knowledge" relevant to a body of information.[10] A well informed person who has received sufficient information about a system of beliefs to understand the "whys" involved in several of the constraints between idea-elements is in a better position to make good guesses about the nature of other constraints; he can deduce with fair success, for example, how a true believer will respond to certain situations. Our first interest in distinguishing between these types of information, however, flows from our interest in the relative success of information transmission. The general premise is that the first type of information will be diffused much more readily than the second because it is less complex.

It is well established that differences in information held in a cross-section population are simply staggering, running from vast treasuries of well organized information among elites interested in the particular subject to fragments that could virtually be measured as a few "bits" in the technical sense. These differences are a static tribute to the extreme imperfections in the transmission of information "downward" through the system: Very little information "trickles down" very far. Of course, the ordering of individuals on this vertical information scale is largely due to differences in education, but it is strongly modified as well by different specialized interests and tastes that individuals have acquired over time (one for politics, another for religious activity, another for fishing, and so forth).

Consequences of Declining Information for Belief Systems

It is our primary thesis that, as one moves from elite sources of belief systems downwards on such an information scale, several important things occur. First, the contextual grasp of "standard" political belief systems fades out very rapidly, almost before one has passed beyond the 10% of the American population that in the 1950s had completed standard college training.[11] Increasingly, simpler forms of information about "what goes with what" (or even information about the simple identity of objects) turn up missing. The net result, as one moves downward, is that constraint declines across the universe of idea-elements, and that the range of relevant belief systems becomes narrower and narrower. Instead of a few wide-ranging belief systems that organize large amounts of specific information, one would expect to find a proliferation of clusters of ideas among which little constraint is felt, even, quite often, in instances of sheer logical constraint.[12]

At the same time, moving from top to bottom of this information dimension, the character of the objects that are central in a belief system undergoes systematic change. These objects shift from the remote, generic, and abstract to the increasingly simple, concrete, or "close to home." Where potential political objects are concerned, this progression tends to be from abstract, "ideological" principles to the more obviously recognizable social groupings or charismatic leaders and finally to such objects of immediate experience as family, job, and immediate associates.

Most of these changes have been hinted at in one form or another in a variety of sources. For example, "limited horizons," "foreshortened time perspectives," and "concrete thinking" have been singled out as notable characteristics of the ideational world of the poorly educated. Such observations have impressed even those investigators who are dealing with subject matter rather close to the individual's immediate world: his family budgeting, what he thinks of people more wealthy than he, his attitudes toward leisure time, work regulations, and the like. But most of the stuff of politics—particularly that played on a national or international stage—is, in the nature of things, remote and abstract. Where politics is concerned, therefore, such ideational changes begin to occur rapidly below the extremely thin stratum of the electorate that ever has occasion to make public pronouncements on political affairs. In other words, the changes in belief systems of which we speak are not a pathology limited to a thin and disoriented bottom layer of the *lumpenproletariat*; they are immediately relevant in understanding the bulk of mass political behavior.

It is this latter fact which seems to be consistently misunderstood by the sophisticated analysts who comment in one vein or another on the meaning of mass politics. There are some rather obvious "optical illusions" that are bound to operate here. A member of that tiny elite that comments publicly about political currents (probably some fraction of 1% of a population) spends most of his time in informal communication about politics with others in the same select group. He rarely encounters a conversation in which his assumptions of shared contextual grasp of political ideas are challenged. Intellectually, he has learned that the level of information in the mass public is low, but he may dismiss this knowledge as true of only 10 to 20% of the voters, who affect the course of mass political events in insignificant ways if at all.[13] It is largely from his informal communications that he learns how "public opinion" is changing and what the change signifies, and he generalizes facilely from these observations to the bulk of the broader public.[14]

III. Active Use of Ideological Dimensions of Judgment

Economy and constraint are companion concepts, for the more highly constrained a system of multiple elements, the more economically it may be described and understood. From the point of view of the actor, the idea organization that leads to constraint permits him to locate and make sense of a wider range of information from a particular domain than he would find possible without such organization. One judgmental dimension or "yardstick" that has been highly serviceable for simplifying and organizing events in most Western politics for the past century has been the liberal-conservative continuum, on which parties, political leaders, legislation, court decisions, and a number of other primary objects of politics could be more—or less—adequately located.[15]

The efficiency of such a yardstick in the evaluation of events is quite obvious. Under certain appropriate circumstances, the single word "conservative" used to describe a piece of proposed legislation can convey a tremendous amount of more specific information about the bill—who probably proposed it and toward what ends, who is likely to resist it, its chances of passage, its long-term social consequences, and, most important, how the actor himself should expect to evaluate it if he were to expend further energy to look into its details. The circumstances under which such tremendous amounts of information are conveyed by the single word are, however, twofold. First, the actor must bring a good deal of meaning to the term, which is to say that he must understand the constraints surrounding it. The more impoverished his understanding of the term, the less information it conveys. In the limiting case—if he does not know at all what the term means—it conveys no information at all. Second, the system of beliefs and actors referred to must in fact be relatively constrained: To the degree that constraint is lacking, uncertainty is less reduced by the label, and less information is conveyed.

The psychological economies provided by such yardsticks for actors are paralleled by economies for analysts and theoreticians who wish to describe events in the system parsimoniously. Indeed, the search for adequate overarching dimensions on which large arrays of events may be simply understood is a critical part of synthetic description. Such syntheses are more or less satisfactory, once again, according to the degree of constraint operative among terms in the system being described.

The economies inherent in the liberal-conservative continuum were exploited in traditional fashion in the early 1950s to describe political changes in the United States as a swing toward conservatism or a "revolt of the moderates." At one level, this description was unquestionably apt. That is, a man whose belief system was relatively conservative (Dwight D. Eisenhower) had supplanted in the White House a man whose belief system was relatively liberal (Harry Truman). Furthermore, for a brief period at least, the composition of Congress was more heavily Republican as well, and this shift meant on balance a greater proportion of relatively conservative legislators. Since the administration and Congress were the elites responsible for the development and execution of policies, the flavor of governmental action did indeed take a turn in a conservative direction. These observations are proper description.

The causes underlying these changes in leadership, however, obviously lay with the mass public, which had changed its voting patterns sufficiently to bring the Republican elites into power. And this change in mass voting was frequently interpreted as a shift in public mood from liberal to conservative, a mass desire for a period of respite and consolidation after the rapid liberal innovations of the 1930s and 1940s. Such an account presumes, once again, that constraints visible at an elite level are mirrored in the mass public and that a person choosing to vote Republican after a decade or two of Democratic voting saw himself *in some sense or other* as giving up a more liberal choice in favor of a more conservative one.

On the basis of some familiarity with attitudinal materials drawn from cross-section samples of the electorate,[16] this assumption seems thoroughly implausible. It suggests in the first instance a neatness of organization in perceived political worlds, which, while accurate enough for elites, is a poor fit for the perceptions of the common public. Second, the yardstick that such an account takes for granted—the liberal-conservative continuum—is a rather elegant high-order abstraction, and such abstractions are not typical conceptual tools for the "man in the street." Fortunately, our interview protocols collected from this period permitted us to examine this hypothesis more closely, for they include not only "structured" attitude materials (which merely require the respondent to choose between prefabricated alternatives) but also lengthy "open-ended" materials, which provided us with the respondent's current evaluations of the political scene in his own words. They therefore provide some indication of the evaluative dimensions that tend to be spontaneously applied to politics by such a national sample. We knew that respondents who were highly educated or strongly involved in politics would fall naturally into the verbal shorthand of "too conservative," "more radical," and the like in these evaluations. Our initial analytic question had to do with the prevalence of such usage.

It soon became apparent, however, that such respondents were in a very small minority, as their unusual education or involvement would suggest. At this point, we broadened the inquiry to an assessment of the evaluative dimensions of policy significance (relating to political issues, rather than to the way a candidate dresses, smiles, or behaves in his private life) that seemed to be employed *in lieu of* such efficient yardsticks as the liberal-conservative continuum. The interviews themselves suggested several strata of classification, which were hierarchically ordered as "levels of conceptualization" on the basis of *a priori* judgments about the breadth of contextual grasp of the political system that each seemed to represent.

In the first or top level were placed those respondents who did indeed rely in some active way on a relatively abstract and far-reaching conceptual dimension as a yardstick against which political objects and their shifting policy significance over time were evaluated. We did not require that this dimension be the liberal-conservative continuum itself, but it was almost the only dimension of the sort that occurred empirically. In a second stratum were placed those respondents who mentioned such a dimension in a peripheral way but did not appear to place much evaluative dependence upon it or who used such concepts in a fashion that raised doubt about the breadth of their understanding of the meaning of the term. The first stratum was loosely labeled "ideologue" and the second "near-ideologue."

In the third level were placed respondents who failed to rely upon any such over-arching dimensions yet evaluated parties and candidates in terms of their expected favorable or unfavorable treatment of different social groupings in the population. The Democratic Party might be disliked because "it's trying to help the Negroes too much," or the Republican Party might be endorsed because farm prices would be better with the Republicans in office. The more sophisticated of these group-interest responses reflected an awareness of conflict in interest between "big business" or "rich people," on the one hand, and "labor" or the "working man," on the other, and parties and candidates were located accordingly.

It is often asked why these latter respondents are not considered full "ideologues," for their perceptions run to the more tangible core of what has traditionally been viewed as ideological conflict. It is quite true that such a syndrome is closer to the upper levels of conceptualization than are any of the other types to be described. As we originally foresaw, however, there turn out to be rather marked differences, not only in social origin and flavor of judgmental processes but in overt political reactions as well, between people of this type and those in the upper levels. These people have a clear image of politics as an arena of group interests and, provided that they have been properly advised on where their own group interests lie, they are relatively likely to follow such advice. Unless an issue directly concerns their grouping in an obviously rewarding or punishing way, however, they lack the contextual grasp of the system to recognize how they should respond to it without being told by elites who hold their confidence. Furthermore, their interest in politics is not sufficiently strong that they pay much attention to such communications. If a communication gets through and they absorb it, they are most willing to behave "ideologically" in ways that will further the interests of their group. If they fail to receive such communication, which is most unusual, knowledge of their group memberships may be of little help in predicting their responses. This syndrome we came to call "ideology by proxy."

The difference between such narrow group interest and the broader perceptions of the ideologue may be clarified by an extreme case. One respondent whom we encountered classified himself as a strong Socialist. He was a Socialist because he knew that Socialists stood four-square for the working man against the rich, and he was a working man. When asked, however, whether or not the federal government in Washington "should leave things like electric power and housing for private businessmen to handle," he felt strongly that private enterprise should have its way, and responses to other structured issue questions were simply uncorrelated with standard socialist doctrine. It seems quite clear that, if our question had pointed out explicitly to this man that "good Socialists" would demand government intervention over private enterprise or that such a posture had traditionally been viewed as benefiting the working man, his answer would have been different. But since he had something less than a college education and was not generally interested enough in politics to struggle through such niceties, he simply lacked the contextual grasp of the political system or of his chosen "ideology" to know what the appropriate response might be. This case illustrates well what we mean by constraint between idea-elements and how such constraint depends upon a store of relevant information. For this man, "Socialists," "the working man," "non-Socialists" and "the rich" with their appropriate valences formed a tightly constrained belief system. But, for lack of information, the belief system more or less began and ended there. It strikes us as valid to distinguish such a belief system from that of the doctrinaire socialist. We, as sophisticated observers, could only class this man as a full "ideologue" by assuming that he shares with us the complex undergirding of information that his concrete group perceptions call up in our own minds. In this instance, a very little probing makes clear that this assumption of shared information is once again false.

The fourth level was, to some degree, a residual category, intended to include those respondents who invoked some policy considerations in their evaluations yet employed none of the references meriting location in any of the first three levels. Two main modes of policy evaluation were characteristic of this level. The first we came to think of as a "nature of the times" response, since parties or candidates were praised or blamed primarily because of their temporal association in the past with broad societal states of war or peace, prosperity or depression. There was no hint in these responses that any groupings in the society suffered differentially from disaster or profited excessively in more pleasant times: These fortunes or misfortunes were those that one party or the other had decided (in some cases, apparently, on whim) to visit upon the nation as a whole. The second type included those respondents whose only approach to an issue reference involved some single narrow policy for which they felt personal gratitude or indignation toward a party or candidate (like social security or a conservation program). In these responses, there was no indication that the speakers saw programs as representative of the broader policy postures of the parties.

The fifth level included those respondents whose evaluations of the political scene had no shred of policy significance whatever. Some of these responses were from people who felt loyal to one party or the other but confessed that they had no idea what the party stood for. Others devoted their attention to personal qualities of the candidates, indicating disinterest in parties more generally. Still others confessed that they paid too little attention to either the parties or the current candidates to be able to say anything about them.[17]

The ranking of the levels performed on *a priori* grounds was corroborated by further analyses, which demonstrated that independent measures of political information, education, and political involvement all showed sharp and monotonic declines as one passsed downward through the levels in the order suggested. Furthermore, these correlations were strong enough so that each maintained some residual life when the other two items were controlled, despite the strong underlying relationship between education, information, and involvement.

The distribution of the American electorate within these levels of conceptualization is summarized in Table I. The array is instructive as a port-

TABLE I — Distribution of a Total Cross-Section Sample of the American Electorate and of 1956 Voters, by Levels of Conceptualization

	Proportion of total sample	Proportion of voters
I. Ideologues	$2\frac{1}{2}\%$	$3\frac{1}{2}\%$
II. Near-ideologues	9	12
III. Group interest	42	45
IV. Nature of the times	24	22
V. No issue content	$22\frac{1}{2}$	$17\frac{1}{2}$
	100%	100%

rait of a mass electorate, to be laid against the common elite assumption that all or a significant majority of the public conceptualizes the main lines of politics after the manner of the most highly educated. Where the specific hypothesis of the "revolt of the moderates" in the early 1950s is concerned, the distribution does not seem on the face of it to lend much support to the key assumption. This disconfirmation may be examined further, however.

Since the resurgence of the Republicans in the Eisenhower period depended primarily upon crossing of party lines by people who normally considered themselves Democrats, we were able to isolate these people to see from what levels of conceptualization they had been recruited. We found that such key defections had occurred among Democrats in the two bottom levels at a rate very significantly greater than the comparable rate in the group-interest or more ideological levels. In other words, the stirrings in the mass electorate that had led to a change in administration and in "ruling ideology" were primarily the handiwork of the very people for whom assumptions of any liberal-conservative dimensions of judgment were most far-fetched.

Furthermore, within those strata where the characteristics of conceptualization even permitted the hypothesis to be evaluated in its own terms, it was directly disproved. For example, the more sophisticated of the group-interest Democrats were quite aware that Eisenhower would be a more pro-business president than Stevenson. Those of this group who did defect to Eisenhower did not, however, do so because they were tired of a labor-oriented administration and wanted a business-oriented one for a change. Quite to the contrary, in the degree that they defected they did so *in spite of* rather than *because of* such quasi-ideological perceptions. That is, their attitudes toward the respective interests of these groups remained essentially constant, and they expressed misgivings about an Eisenhower vote on precisely these grounds. But any such worries were, under the circumstances, outweighed by admiration for Eisenhower's war record, his honesty, his good family life, and (in 1952) his potential for resolving the nagging problem of the Korean War. Among respondents at higher levels (ideologues and near-ideologues), there was comparable attraction to Eisenhower at a personal level, but these people seemed more careful to hew to ideological considerations, and rates of Democratic defection in these levels were lower still. In short, then, the supposition of changing ideological moods in the mass public as a means of understanding the exchange of partisan elites in 1952 seems to have had little relevance to what was actually going on at the mass level. And once again, the sources of the optical illusion are self-evident. While it may be taken for granted among well educated and politically involved people that a shift from a Democratic preference to a Republican one probably represents a change in option from liberal to conservative, the assumption cannot be extended very far into the electorate as a whole.

IV. Recognition of Ideological Dimensions of Judgment

Dimensions like the liberal-conservative continuum, as we have observed, are extremely efficient frames for the organization of many political observations. Furthermore, they are used a great deal in the more ambitious treatments of politics in the mass media, so that a person with a limited understanding of their meaning must find such discussions more obscure than enlightening. Aside from active cognitive use, therefore, the simple status of public comprehension of these terms is a matter of some interest.

It is a commonplace in psychology that recognition, recall, and habitual use of cognized objects or concepts are rather different. We are capable of *recognizing* many more objects (or concepts) if they are directly presented to us than we could readily *recall* on the basis of more indirect cues; and we are capable of recalling on the basis of such hints many more objects (or concepts) than might be *active* or *salient* for us in a given context without special prompting. In coding the levels of conceptualization from free-answer material, our interest had been entirely focused upon concepts with the last status (activation or salience). It had been our assumption that such activation would be apparent in the responses of any person with a belief system in which these organizing dimensions had high centrality. Nevertheless, we could be sure at the same time that if we presented the terms "liberal" and "conservative" directly to our respondents, a much larger number would recognize them and be able to attribute to them some kind of meaning. We are interested both in the proportions of a normal sample who would show some recognition and also in the meaning that might be supplied for the terms.

In a 1960 reinterview of the original sample whose 1956 responses had been assigned to our levels of conceptualization, we therefore asked in the context of the differences in "what the parties stand for," "Would you say that either one of the parties is more *conservative* or more *liberal* than the other?" (It was the first time we had ever introduced these terms in our interviewing of this sample.) If the answer was affirmative, we asked which party seemed the more conservative and then, "What do you have in mind when you say that the Republicans (Democrats) are more conservative than the Democrats (Republicans)?" When the respondent said that he did not see differences of this kind between the two parties, we were anxious to distinguish between those who were actually cynical about meaningful party differences and those who took this route to avoid admitting that they did not know what the terms signified. We therefore went on to ask this group, "Do you think that people generally consider the Democrats or the Republicans more conservative, or wouldn't you want to guess about that?" At this point, we were willing to assume that if a person had no idea of the rather standard assumptions, he probably had no idea of what the terms meant; and indeed, those who did try to guess which party other people thought more conservative made a very poor showing when we went on to ask them (paralleling our "meaning" question for the first group), "What do people have in mind when they say that the Republicans (Democrats) are more conservative than the Democrats (Republicans)?" In responding to the "meaning" questions, both groups were urged to answer as fully and clearly as possible, and their comments were transcribed.

The responses were classified in a code inspired by the original work on levels of conceptualization, although it was considerably more detailed. Within this code, top priority was given to explanations that called upon broad philosophical differences. These explanations included mentions of such things as *posture toward change* (acceptance of or resistance to new ideas, speed or caution in responding to new problems, protection of or challenge to the *status quo*, aggressive posture towards problems *vs.* a *laissez-faire* approach, orientation toward the future or lack of it, and so forth); *posture toward the welfare state, socialism, free enterprise, or capitalism* (including mention of differential sensitivity to social problems, approaches to social-welfare programs, governmental interference with private enterprise, and so forth); *posture toward the expanding power of federal government* (issues of centralization, states' rights, local autonomy, and paternalism); and *relationship of the government to the individual* (questions of individual dignity, initiative, needs, rights, and so forth). While any mention of comparably broad philosophical differences associated with the liberal-conservative distinction was categorized in this top level, these four were the most frequent types of reference, as they had been for the full "ideologues" in the earlier open-ended materials.

Then, in turn, references to differences in attitude toward various interest groupings in the population; toward spending or saving and fiscal policy more generally, as well as to economic prosperity; toward various highly specific issues like unemployment compensation, highway-building, and tariffs; and toward postures in the sphere of foreign policy were arrayed in a descending order of priority, much as they had been for the classification into levels of conceptualization. Since respondents had been given the opportunity to mention as many conservative-liberal distinctions as they wished, coding priority was given to the more "elevated" responses, and all the data that we shall subsequently cite rests on the "best answer" given by each respondent.[18]

The simple distributional results were as follows. Roughly three respondents in eight (37%) could supply no meaning for the liberal-conservative distinction, including 8% who attempted to say which party was the more conservative but who gave up on the part of the sequence dealing with meaning. (The weakest 29% will, in later tables, form our bottom stratum "V," while the 8% compose stratum "IV.") Between those who could supply no meaning for the terms and those who clearly did, there was naturally an intermediate group that answered all the questions but showed varying degrees of uncertainty or confusion. The situation required that one of two polar labels (conservative or liberal) be properly associated with one of two polar clusters of connotations and with one of two parties. Once the respondent had decided to explain what "more conservative" or "more liberal" signified, there were four possible patterns by which the other two dichotomies might be associated with the first. Of course, all four were represented in at least some interviews. For example, a respondent might indicate that the Democrats were the more conservative because they stood up for the working man against big business. In such a case, there seemed to be a simple error consisting in reversal of the ideological labels. Or a respondent might say that the Republicans were more liberal because they were pushing new and progressive social legislation. Here the match between label and meaning seems proper, but the party perception is, by normal standards, erroneous.

The distribution of these error types within the portion of the sample that attempted to give "meaning" answers (slightly more than 60%) is shown in Table II. The 83% entered for the "proper" patterns is artifically increased to

TABLE II — Association of Ideological Label with Party and Meaning

Ideological label	Meaning	Party	Proportion of those giving some answer
Conservative	Conservative	Republican	83%
Liberal	Liberal	Democrat	
Conservative	Liberal	Republican	
Liberal	Conservative	Democrat	5
Conservative	Conservative	Democrat[a]	
Liberal	Liberal	Republican	6
Conservative	Liberal	Democrat	
Liberal	Conservative	Republican	6
			100%

a. While this pattern may appear entirely legitimate for the southern respondent reacting to the southern wing of the Democratic Party rather than to the national party, it showed almost no tendency to occur with greater frequency in the South than elsewhere (and errors as well as lacunae occurred more frequently in general in the less well educated South). Data from a very different context indicate that southerners who discriminate between the southern wing and the national Democratic Party take the national party as the assumed object in our interviews, if the precise object is not specified.

an unknown degree by the inclusion of all respondents whose connotations for liberalism-conservatism were sufficiently impoverished so that little judgment could be made about whether or not they were making proper associations (for example, those respondents whose best explanations of the distinction involved orientations toward defense spending). The error types thus represent only those that could be unequivocally considered "errors." While Table II does not in itself constitute proof that the error types resulted from pure guesswork, the configuration does resemble the probable results if 20-25% of the respondents had been making random guesses about how the two labels, the two polar meanings, and the two parties should be sorted out. People making these confused responses might or might not *feel* confused in making their assessments. Even if they knew that they were confused, it is unlikely that they would be less confused in encountering such terms in reading or listening to political communications, which is the important point where transmission of information is concerned. If, on the other hand, they were wrong without realizing it, then they would be capable of hearing that Senator Goldwater, for example, was an extreme conservative and believing that it meant that he was for increased federal spending (or whatever other more specific meaning they might bring to the term). In either case, it seems reasonable to distinguish between the people who belong in this confused group at the border of understanding and those who demonstrate greater clarity about the terms. And after the confused group is set aside (stratum III in Tables III-VI), we are left with a proportion of the sample that is slightly more than 50%. This figure can be taken as a maximum estimate of reasonable recognition.

We say "maximum" because, once within this "sophisticated" half of the electorate, it is reasonable to consider the quality of the meanings put forth to explain the liberal-conservative distinction. These meanings varied greatly in adequacy, from those "best answers" that did indeed qualify for coding under the "broad philosophy" heading (the most accurate responses, as defined above) to those that explained the distinction in narrow or nearly irrelevant terms (like Prohibition or foreign-policy measures). In all, 17% of the total sample gave "best answers" that we considered to qualify as "broad philosophy."[19] This group was defined as stratum I, and the remainder, who gave narrower definitions, became stratum II.

Perhaps the most striking aspect of the liberal-conservative definitions supplied was the extreme frequency of those hinging on a simple "spend-save" dimension *vis-à-vis* government finances. Very close to a majority of all "best" responses (and two-thirds to three-quarters of all such responses in stratum II) indicated in essence that the Democratic Party was liberal because it spent public money freely and that the Republican Party was more conservative because it stood for economy in government or pinched pennies. In our earlier coding of the levels of conceptualization, we had already noted that this simple dimension seemed often to be what was at stake when "ideological" terms were used. Frequently there was reason to believe that the term "conservative" drew its primary meaning from the cognate "conservation." In one rather clear example, a respondent indicated that he considered the Republicans to be more conservative in the sense that they were ". . . more saving with money and our *natural resources*. Less apt to slap on a tax for some non-essential. More conservative in promises that can't be kept." (Italics ours.)

Of course, the question of the proportion of national wealth that is to be spent privately or channeled through government for public spending has been one of the key disputes between conservatives and liberal "ideologies" for several decades. From this point of view, the great multitude of "spend-save" references can be considered essentially as accurate matching of terms. On the other hand, it goes without saying that the conservative-liberal dialogue does not exhaust itself on this narrow question alone, and our view of these responses as an understanding of the differences depends in no small measure on whether the individual sees this point as a self-contained distinction or understands the link between it and a number of other broad questions. On rare occasions, one encounters a respondent for whom the "spend-save" dimension is intimately bound up with other problem areas. For example, one respondent feels that the Republicans are more conservative because ". . . they are too interested in getting the budget balanced—they should spend more to get more jobs for our people." More frequently when further links are suggested, they are connected with policy but go no further:

[Republicans more conservative because] "Well, they don't spend as much money." [What do you have in mind?] "Well, a lot of them holler when they try to establish a higher interest rate but that's to get back a little when they do loan out and make it so people are not so free with it."

Generally, however, the belief system involved when "liberal-conservative" is equated with "spend-save" seems to be an entirely narrow one. There follow a number of examples of comments, which taken with the preceding citations, form a random drawing from the large group of "spend-save" comments:

[Democrats more conservative because] "they will do more for the people at home before they go out to help foreign countries. They are truthful and not liars."

[Republicans more liberal judging] "by the money they have spent in this last administration. They spent more than ever before in a peace time. And got less for it as far as I can see."

[Republicans more conservative because] "Well, they vote against the wild spending spree the Democrats get on."

[Republicans more conservative because] "they pay as you go."

[Democrats more conservative because] "I don't believe the Democrats will spend as much money as the Republicans."

[Republicans more conservative because] "it seems as if the Republicans try to hold down the spending of government money." [Do you remember how?] "Yes," [by having] "no wars."

From this representation of the "spend-save" references, the reader may see quite clearly why we consider them to be rather "narrow" readings of the liberal-conservative distinction as applied to the current partisan scene. In short, our portrait of the population, where recognition of a key ideological dimension is concerned, suggests that about 17% of the public (stratum I) have an understanding of the distinction that captures much of its breadth. About 37% (strata IV and V) are entirely vague as to its meaning. For the 46% between, there are two strata, one of which demonstrates considerable uncertainty and guesswork in assigning meaning to the terms (stratum III) and the other of which has the terms rather well under control but appears to have a fairly limited set of connotations for them (stratum II). The great majority of the latter groups equate liberalism-conservatism rather directly with a "spend-save" dimension. In such cases, when the sensed connotations are limited, it is not surprising that there is little active use of the continuum as an organizing dimension. Why should one bother to say that a party is conservative if one can convey the same information by saying that it is against spending?

Since the 1960 materials on liberal-conservative meanings were drawn from the same sample as the coding of the active use of such frames of reference in 1956, it is possible to consider how well the two codings match. For a variety of reasons, we would not expect a perfect fit, even aside from coding error. The earlier coding had not been limited to the liberal-conservative dimension, and, although empirical instances were rare, a person could qualify as an "ideologue" if he assessed politics with the aid of some other highly abstract organizing dimension. Similarly, among those who did employ the liberal-conservative distinction, there were no requirements that the terms be defined. It was necessary therefore to depend upon appearances, and the classification was intentionally lenient. Furthermore, since a larger portion of the population would show recognition than showed active use, we could expect substantial numbers of people in the lower levels of conceptualization to show reasonable recognition of the terms. At any rate, we assumed that the two measures would show a high correlation, as they in fact did (Table III).

Of course, very strong differences in education underlie the data shown in Table III. The 2% of the sample that occupy the upper left-hand cell have a mean education close to seven years greater than that of the 11% that occupy the lower right-hand cell. Sixty-two per cent of this lower cell have had less formal education than the least educated person in the upper corner. The differences in education show a fairly regular progression across the intervening surface of the table (see Table IV). Although women have a higher mean education than men, there is some sex bias to the table; for women

TABLE III — Levels of Conceptualization (1956) by Recognition and Understanding of Terms "Conservatism" and "Liberalism" (1960)

| | | LEVELS OF CONCEPTUALIZATION | | | | |
	Stratum	Ideologue	Near ideologue	Group interest	Nature of the times	No issue content
Recognition	I	51%	29%	13%	16%	10%
and	II	43	46	42	40	22
understanding[a]	III	2	10	14	7	7
	IV	2	5	6	7	12
	V	2	10	25	30	49
		100%	100%	100%	100%	100%
Number of cases		(45)	(122)	(580)	(288)	(290)

a. The definitions of the strata are: I. recognition and proper matching of label, meaning, and party and a broad understanding of the terms "conservative" and "liberal"; II. recognition and proper matching but a narrow definition of terms (like "spend-save"); III. recognition but some error in matching; IV. recognition and an attempt at matching but inability to give any meaning for terms; V. no apparent recognition of terms (does not know if parties differ in liberal-conservative terms and does not know if anybody else sees them as differing).

are disproportionately represented in the lower right-hand quadrant of the table. Furthermore, although age is negatively correlated with education, there is also rather clear evidence that the sort of political sophistication represented by the measures can accumulate with age. Undoubtedly even sporadic observation of politics over long enough periods of time serves to nurture some broader view of basic liberal-conservative differences, although

TABLE IV — Levels of Conceptualization (1956) and Term Recognition (1960) by Mean Years of Formal Education

| | | LEVELS OF CONCEPTUALIZATION | | | | |
	Stratum	Ideologue	Near ideologue	Group interest	Nature of the times	No issue content
	I	14.9[a]	14.2	12.3	11.1	11.9
Recognition	II	13.9	11.9	10.7	10.7	11.5
and	III	*	11.1	10.6	9.8	9.6
understanding[b]	IV	*	*	10.4	9.9	10.3
	V	*	10.0	9.5	8.5	8.2

    * Inadequate number of cases.

    a. The cell entry is mean number of years of formal education. Partial college was arbitrarily assumed to represent an average of 14 years, and work toward an advanced degree an average of 18 years.

    b. See Table III for definitions of the five strata.

of course the same sophistication is achieved much more rapidly and in a more striking way by those who progress greater distances through the educational system.

    It is not surprising that political sophistication goes hand in hand with political activism at the "grass roots" (Table V). The relationship is certainly

TABLE V — Amount of 1956-1960 Political Activity by Level of Conceptualization (1956) and Term Recognition (1960)

| | | LEVEL OF CONCEPTUALIZATION | | | | |
	Stratum	Ideologue	Near ideologue	Group interest	Nature of the times	No issue content
	I	3.8[a]	2.6	2.5	2.6	2.2
Recognition	II	3.4	3.0	1.7	1.8	1.3
and	III	*	2.5	2.2	1.5	1.1
understanding[b]	IV	*	*	1.9	1.5	.8
	V	*	1.7	1.0	.8	.4

    * Inadequate number of cases.

    a. The cell entry represents a mean of the number of acts of political participation exclusive of voting reported for the two presidential campaigns of 1956 and 1960. For 1956, a point was awarded to each respondent for party membership, campaign contributions, attendance at political rallies, other party work, attempts to convince others through informal communication, and displaying campaign buttons or stickers. In 1960, essentially the same scoring applied, except that on two items more differentiated information was available. A point was awarded for attending one or two political rallies, two points for three to six rallies, and three points for seven or more. Similarly, a second point was awarded for people who reported having attempted in 1960 to convince others in more than one class (friends, family, or coworkers). A total score of 15 was possible, although empirically the highest score was 14. Only about 1% of the sample had scores greater than 9.

    b. See Table III for definitions of the five strata.

not perfect: About 20% of those in the most sophisticated cell engaged in none of the forms of participation beyond voting that were surveyed (see note a, Table V) in either the 1956 or 1960 election campaigns, and there is more "stray" participation than has sometimes been suspected among those who express little interest in politics or comprehension of party differences yet who may, for example, happen on a political rally. Furthermore, even the active hard core is not necessarily sophisticated in this sense: Two of the thirteen most active people fall in the lower right half of the table, and their activism is probably to be understood more in terms of mundane social gratifications than through any concern over the policy competition of politics.

Nonetheless, persistent and varied participation is most heavily concentrated among the most sophisticated people. This fact is important, for much of what is perceived as "public reaction" to political events depends upon public visibility, and visibility depends largely upon forms of political participation beyond the vote itself. Anyone familiar with practical politics has encountered the concern of the local politician that ideas communicated in political campaigns be kept simple and concrete. He knows his audience and is constantly fighting the battle against the overestimation of sophistication to which the purveyor of political ideas inevitably falls prey. Yet, even the grass-roots audience that forms a reference point for the local politician is, we suspect, a highly self-selected one and quite sophisticated relative to the electorate as a whole.

Since we have 1960 information on the number of political rallies attended by each of our respondents, we may simulate the "sophistication composition" of the typical political gathering. "Typical" is loosely used here, for real gatherings are various in character: A dinner for the party faithful at $15 a plate obviously attracts a different audience from the one that comes to the parade and street rally. Nonetheless, the contrast between the electorate and an hypothetical average rally is instructive (Table VI). People located in the three upper left-hand corner cells of the matrix (6% of the electorate) form more than 15% of the composition of such rallies, and probably, in terms of further rally participation (vocal and otherwise), seem to form a still higher proportion. Yet on election day their vote (even with a

TABLE VI — The Sophistication Composition of a "Typical" Political Rally, Compared to the Composition of the Total Electorate[a]

		A RALLY						THE ELECTORATE			
	High				Low		High				Low
High	5%	5%	11%	11%	2%		2%	3%	6%	3%	2%
	6	8	11	11	4		1	4	18	9	5
	0	5	9	0	*		*	1	6	1	2
	*	0	1	*	*		*	*	3	2	3
Low	*	2	7	1	0		*	1	11	7	11

* Less than half of 1%.

a. Both five-by-five matrices are those employed in Tables III, IV, and V. Aside from rounding error, the proportions entered in each matrix total 100%. The table should be read by observing differences between proportions in the same regions of the two tables. For example, the three least sophisticated cells in the lower right-hand corner constitute 21% of the electorate and 1% of a typical rally audience.

100% turnout) is numerically outweighed by those votes mustered by people in the single cell at the opposite corner of the table who do not attend at all.

One of the most intriguing findings on the surface of the matrix is that strength of party loyalty falls to one of its weakest points in the upper left-hand corner cell of the matrix. In other words, among the most highly sophisticated, those who consider themselves "independents" outnumber those who consider themselves "strong" partisans, despite the fact that the most vigorous political activity, much of it partisan, is carried on by people falling in this cell. If one moves diagonally toward the center of the matrix, this balance is immediately redressed and redressed very sharply, with strong partisans far outnumbering independents. In general, there is a slight tendency (the most sophisticated cell excepted) for strength of party loyalty to decline as one moves diagonally across the table, and the most "independent" cell is that in the lower right-hand corner.[20]

This irregularity has two implications. First, we take it to be one small and special case of our earlier hypothesis that group-objects (here, the party as group) are likely to have less centrality in the belief system of the most sophisticated and that the centrality of groups as referents increases "lower down" in the sophistication ordering. We shall see more handsome evidence of the same phenomenon later. Second, we see in this reversal at least a partial explanation for the persistence of the old assumption that the "independent voter" is relatively informed and involved. The early cross-section studies by Lazarsfeld and his colleagues turned up evidence to reverse this equation, suggesting that the "independent voter" tends instead to be relatively uninformed and uninvolved. Other studies have added massively to this evidence. Indeed, in many situations, the evidence seems so strong that it is hard to imagine how any opposing perceptions could have developed. The perception is somewhat easier to understand, however, if one can assume that the discernment of the informed observer takes in only 5, 10, or 15% of the most sophisticated people in the public as constituting "the public." This "visible" or "operative" public is largely made up of people from the upper left-hand corner of our preceding tables. The illusion that such people are the full public is one that the democratic sample survey, for better or for worse, has destroyed.

V. Constraints among Idea-Elements

In our estimation, the use of such basic dimensions of judgment as the liberal-conservative continuum betokens a contextual grasp of politics that permits a wide range of more specific idea-elements to be organized into more tightly constrained wholes. We feel, furthermore, that there are many crucial consequences of such organization: With it, for example, new political events have more meaning, retention of political information from the past is far more adequate, and political behavior increasingly approximates that of sophisticated "rational" models, which assume relatively full information.

It is often argued, however, that abstract dimensions like the liberal-conservative continuum are superficial if not meaningless indicators: All that they show is that poorly educated people are inarticulate and have difficulty expressing verbally the more abstract lines along which their specific political beliefs are organized. To expect these people to be able to express what they know and feel, the critic goes on, is comparable to the fallacy of assuming that people can say in an accurate way why they behave as they do. When it comes down to specific attitudes and behaviors, the organization is there nonetheless, and it is this organization that matters, not the capacity for discourse in sophisticated language.

If it were true that such organization does exist for most people, apart from their capacities to be articulate about it, we would agree out of hand that the question of articulation is quite trivial. As a cold empirical matter, however, this claim does not seem to be valid. Indeed, it is for this reason that we have cast the argument in terms of constraint, for constraint and organization are very nearly the same thing. Therefore when we hypothesize that constraint among political idea-elements begins to lose its range very rapidly once we move from the most sophisticated few toward the "grass roots," we

TABLE VII — Constraint between Specific Issue Beliefs for an Elite Sample and a Cross-Section Sample, 1958 [a]

	DOMESTIC				FOREIGN			
Congressional candidates	*Employment*	*Education*	*Housing*	*F.E.P.C.*	*Economic*	*Military* [b]	*Isolationism*	*Party preference*
Employment	—	.62	.59	.35	.26	.06	.17	.68
Aid to education		—	.61	.53	.50	.06	.35	.55
Federal housing			—	.47	.41	−.03	.30	.68
F.E.P.C.				—	.47	.11	.23	.34
Economic aid					—	.19	.59	.25
Military aid						—	.32	−.18
Isolationism							—	.05
Party preference								—
Cross-Section Sample								
Employment	—	.45	.08	.34	−.04	.10	−.22	.20
Aid to education		—	.12	.29	.06	.14	−.17	.16
Federal housing			—	.08	−.06	.02	.07	.18
F.E.P.C.				—	.24	.13	.02	−.04
Economic aid					—	.16	.33	−.07
Soldiers abroad [b]						—	.21	.12
Isolationism							—	−.03
Party preference								—

a. Entries are tau-gamma coefficients, a statistic proposed by Leo A. Goodman and William H. Kruskal in "Measures of Association for Cross Classifications," *Journal of the American Statistical Association*, 49 (Dec., 1954), No. 268, 749. The coefficient was chosen because of its sensitivity to constraint of the scalar as well as the correlational type.

b. For this category, the cross-section sample was asked a question about keeping American soldiers abroad, rather than about military aid in general.

are contending that the organization of more specific attitudes into wide-ranging belief systems is absent as well.

Table VII gives us an opportunity to see the differences in levels of constraint among beliefs on a range of specific issues in an elite population and in a mass population. The elite population happens to be candidates for the United States Congress in the off-year elections of 1958, and the cross-section sample represents the national electorate in the same year. The assortment of issues represented is simply a purposive sampling of some of the more salient political controversies at the time of the study, covering both domestic and foreign policy. The questions posed to the two samples were quite comparable, apart from adjustments necessary in view of the backgrounds of the two populations involved.[21]

For our purposes, however, the specific elite sampled and the specific beliefs tested are rather beside the point. We would expect the same general contrast to appear if the elite had been a set of newspaper editors, political writers, or any other group that takes an interest in politics. Similarly, we would expect the same results from any other broad sampling of political issues or, for that matter, any sampling of beliefs from other domains: A set of questions on matters of religious controversy should show the same pattern between an elite population like the clergy and the church members who form their mass "public." What is generically important in comparing the two types of population is the difference in levels of constraint among belief-elements.

Where constraint is concerned, the absolute value of the coefficients in Table VII (rather than their algebraic value) is the significant datum. The first thing the table conveys is the fact that, for both populations, there is some falling off of constraint *between* the domains of domestic and foreign policy, relative to the high level of constraint *within* each domain. This result is to be expected: Such lowered values signify boundaries between belief systems that are relatively independent. If we take averages of appropriate sets of coefficients entered in Table VII however, we see that the strongest constraint *within* a domain for the mass public is less than that *between* domestic and foreign domains for the elite sample. Furthermore, for the public, in sharp contrast to the elite, party preference seems by and large to be set off in a belief system of its own, relatively unconnected to issue positions (Table VIII).[22]

TABLE VIII — Summary of Differences in Level of Constraint within and between Domains, Public and Elite (based on Table VII)

	Average Coefficients			
	Within domestic issues	Between domestic and foreign	Within foreign issues	Between issues and party
Elite	.53	.25	.37	.39
Mass	.23	.11	.23	.11

It should be remembered throughout, of course, that the *mass* sample of Tables VII and VIII does not exclude college-educated people, ideologues, or the politically sophisticated. These people, with their higher levels of constraint, are represented in appropriate numbers, and certainly contribute to such vestige of organization as the mass matrix evinces. But they are grossly outnumbered, as they are in the active electorate. The general point is that the matrix of correlations for the elite sample is of the sort that would be appropriate for factor analysis, the statistical technique designed to reduce a number of correlated variables to a more limited set of organizing dimensions. The matrix representing the mass public, however, despite its realistic complement of ideologues, is exactly the type that textbooks advise against using for factor analysis on the simple grounds that through inspection it is clear that there is virtually nothing in the way of organization to be discovered. Of course, it is the type of broad organizing dimension to be suggested by factor analysis of specific items that is usually presumed when observers discuss "ideological postures" of one sort or another.

Although the beliefs registered in Table VII are related to topics of controversy or political cleavage, McClosky has described comparable differences in levels of constraint among beliefs for an elite sample (delegates to national party conventions) and a cross-section sample when the items deal with propositions about democracy and freedom—topics on which fundamental consensus among Americans is presumed.[23] Similarly, Prothro and Grigg, among others, have shown that, while there is widespread support for statements of culturally familiar principles of freedom, democracy, and tolerance in a cross-section sample, this support becomes rapidly obscured when questions turn to specific cases that elites would see as the most direct applications of these principles.[24] In our estimation, such findings are less a demonstration of cynical lip service than of the fact that, while both of two inconsistent opinions are honestly held, the individual lacks the contextual grasp to understand that the specific case and the general principle belong in the same belief system: In the absence of such understanding, he maintains psychologically independent beliefs about both. This is another important instance of the decline in constraint among beliefs with declining information.

While an assessment of relative constraint between the matrices rests only on comparisons of absolute values, the comparative algebraic values have some interest as well. This interest arises from the sophisticated observer's almost automatic assumption that whatever beliefs "go together" in the visible political world (as judged from the attitudes of elites and the more articulate spectators) must naturally go together in the same way among mass public. Table VII makes clear that this assumption is a very dangerous one, aside from the question of degree of constraint. For example, the politician who favors federal aid to education could be predicted to be more, rather than less, favorable to an internationalist posture in foreign affairs, for these two positions in the 1950s were generally associated with "liberalism" in American politics. As we see from Table VII, we would be accurate in this judgment considerably more often than chance alone would permit. On the other hand, were we to apply the same assumption of constraint to the American public in the same era, not only would we have been wrong, but we would actually have come closer to reality by assuming no connection at all.

All the correlations in the elite sample except those that do not depart significantly from zero exhibit signs that anybody following politics in the newspapers during this period could have predicted without hesitation. That is, one need only have known that Democrats tended to favor expansion of government welfare activities and tended to be internationalists in foreign affairs, to have anticipated all the signs except one. This exception, the -.18 that links advocacy of military aid abroad with the Republican Party, would hold no surprises either, for the one kind of international involvement that Republicans came to accept in this period limited foreign aid to the military variety, a view that stood in opposition to "soft" liberal interests in international economic welfare. If these algebraic signs in the elite matrix are taken as the culturally defined "proper" signs—the sophisticated observer's assumption of what beliefs go with what other beliefs—then the algebraic differences between comparable entries in the two matrices provide an estimate of how inaccurate we would be in generalizing our elite-based assumptions about "natural" belief combinations to the mass public as a whole. A scanning of the two matrices with these differences in mind enhances our sense of high discrepancy between the two populations.

To recapitulate, then, we have argued that the unfamiliarity of broader and more abstract ideological frames of reference among the less sophisticated is more than a problem in mere articulation. Parallel to ignorance and confusion over these ideological dimensions among the less informed is a general decline in constraint among specific belief elements that such dimensions help to organize. It cannot therefore be claimed that the mass public shares ideological patterns of belief with relevant elites at a specific level any more than it shares the abstract conceptual frames of reference.

Constraints and Overt Behavior

There is still another counter-hypothesis that deserves examination. This view would grant that the political belief systems of the less well educated may be more fragmented and chaotic. It would maintain at the same time, however, that this fact is inconsequential in the determination of behavior. The presence, absence, or incoherence of these "intervening" psychological states is thus epiphenomenal: Social structure commits behavior to certain channels quite independent of specific cognitions and perceptions of the actors themselves.[25] In other versions, researchable intervening mechanisms are suggested. The "opinion leader" model is one of them. If it is true that the mass of less knowledgeable people rely upon informal communication from a few more informed people for cues about desirable or appropriate behavior, then the lines of behavior choices followed in politics might indeed show strong sociostructural patterns, even though many uninformed actors have little of the opinion leaders' coherent and organized understanding of why one behavior is more appropriate than another. What these points of view have in common is the insistence that strong constraints can be expected to operate between sociostructural terms and conscious behavior choices quite apart from the presence or absence of appropriate intervening psychological "definitions of the situation."

Figure 1 is addressed to such arguments. The graphs indicate the varying degrees of association between objective class position and partisan preference in the 1956 presidential election, as a function of differences in the nature of political belief systems captured by our "levels of conceptualiza-tion." If objective locations in the social structure served to produce be-havioral consequences regardless of the presence or absence of relevant

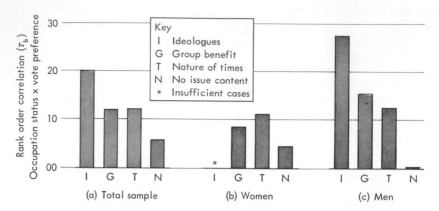

Figure 1. The Correlation of Occupation and Vote Preference within Levels of Conceptualization.

intervening organizations of conscious beliefs, then we would not expect any particular slope to the progression of bars within each graph. As Figure 1(a) shows for a sample of the adult electorate as a whole, however, the differences in intervening belief organization produce very marked and orderly differences in the degree to which partisanship reflects sociostructural posi-tion. Of course, from one point of view, this observation seems only common sense, yet the doctrinaire position that the intervening psychological terms are unimportant or epiphenomenal continues to be argued with more vehe-mence than empirical evidence.

Since it can be seen that a perfectly functioning opinion-leader model would also produce something approaching a rectangular distribution of bars in Figure 1, the slope depicted in Figure 1(a) can also be taken as a com-mentary on the practical imperfections with which opinion leader processes operate in this domain. That is, the "ideologues" and "near-ideologues" re-presented by the first bar of each graph are opinion leaders *par excellence*. While they tend to be disproportionately well educated, they nevertheless include representatives from all broad social *milieux*. Empirically they differ sharply from the less sophisticated in their attention to new political events and in the size of their store of information about past events. They get news firsthand and, presumably, form opinions directly from it. By their own report, they are much more likely than the less sophisticated to attempt to persuade others to their own political opinions in informal communica-tions. Finally, much social data leads us to assume that the bulk of these informal communications is addressed to others within their own social *milieu*. Since social-class questions are important for these opinion leaders and since their own partisan preferences are rather clearly geared to their own class, we would suppose that "opinion leading" should serve to diffuse this connection between status and behavior through less knowledgeable mem-

bers of their *milieu*, whether or not the more complicated rationales were diffused. In other words, most of what goes on in the heads of the less informed
of our respondents would indeed be irrelevant for study if the respondents
could at least be counted upon to follow the lead of more informed people
of their own *milieu* in their ultimate partisanship. And to the extent that
they can be counted on to behave in this way, we should expect Figure 1 to
show a rectangular distribution of bars. The departure from such a pattern
is very substantial.

Now there is one type of relationship in which there is overwhelming
evidence for vigorous opinion-leading where politics is concerned in our
society. It is the relationship within the family: The wife is very likely
to follow her husband's opinions, however imperfectly she may have
absorbed their justifications at a more complex level. We can do a fair job
of splitting this relationship into its leader-follower components simply by
subdividing our total sample by sex. As Figure 1(b) suggests, our expectation
that the presence or absence of intervening belief systems is of reduced importance among sets of people who are predominantly opinion followers is
well borne out by the relatively flat and disordered progression of bars among
women. Correspondingly, of course, the same slope among men becomes
steeper still in Figure 1(c).[26]

The fact that wives tend to double their husbands' votes is, from a broader
"system" point of view, a relatively trivial one. If we are willing to consider
the family as the basic voting unit, then Figure 1(c) suggests that diffusion of
the sociostructurally "proper" behavior without diffusion of understanding
of that behavior through simple opinion-leading processes is a very feeble
mechanism indeed across the society as a whole, at least where political decisions of this sort are concerned.[27] The organization of partisanship among
those who give no evidence of intervening issue content shows no trace
whatever of those residual effects that should be left by any systematic
opinion-following (and that are visible among comparable women). Thus,
while we are in no way questioning the existence of some opinion-leading,
it seems doubtful that it represents the dominant, effective phenomenon
sometimes supposed, a phenomenon that succeeds in lending shape to mass
politics despite the absence of more detailed individual comprehension of
the political context.[28]

Much more broadly, we have become convinced that this class of finding—
the declining degree of constraint between a term representing social structure and one representing an important political choice as one moves from
the more to the less politically sophisticated in the society—is a powerful
and general one. It is powerful (for readers not accustomed to the statistics
employed) in the simple sense that the variation in constraint as a function
of sophistication or involvement is extremely large: There are no other
discriminating variables that begin to separate populations so cleanly and
sharply as these measures. It is a general finding in at least two senses.
First, it replicates itself handsomely across time: In every instance within
the span of time for which appropriate data are available, the finding is present where class and partisanship are concerned. Secondly, it has some
incipient claim to generality where sociostructural terms other than "social
class" are concerned: The same sharp finding emerges, for example, when

the relationship between religion and partisanship (Protestant *vs.* Catholic) is examined.

And, of course, if class or religious membership is considered to constitute one set of idea-elements and the predispositions that lead to particular partisan preferences and final choice to form another, then the whole phenomenon takes its place as another large class of special cases of the decline of constraints and the narrowing of belief systems to which this paper is devoted.

VI. Social Groupings as Central Objects in Belief Systems

While for any unbiased sampling of controversial belief items we would predict that the relevant elite would show a higher level of internal constraint among elements than those shown by their publics, we would predict at the same time that it would be possible to bias a choice of issues in such a way that the level of constraint in the public could surpass that among the elites. This possibility exists because of the role that visible social groupings come to play as objects of high centrality in the belief systems of the less well informed.[29]

Such a reversal of the constraint prediction could be attained by choosing items that made it clear that a particular grouping, within the population and visible to most respondents, would be helped or hurt by the alternative in question. Consider, by way of illustration, the following set of items:

Negroes should be kept out of professional athletics.
The government should see to it that Negroes get fair treatment in jobs and housing.
The government should cut down on its payments (subsidies) on peanuts and cotton, which are raised mainly by Negroes in the South.
The government should give federal aid only to schools that permit Negroes to attend.
Even though it may hurt the position of the Negro in the South, state governments should be able to decide who can vote and who cannot.
If this country has to send money abroad, the government should send it to places like Africa that need it, and not to countries like Britain and France.

The strategy here is obvious. The questions are selected so that the same group is involved in each. In every case but one, this involvement is explicit. Some American adults would not know that Africa's population is largely Negro, for these people, the level of constraint between this item and the others would be relatively low. But the majority would know this fact, and the total set of items would show a substantial level of constraint, probably higher than the general level shown by the "mass" items in Table VII. Furthermore, the items are chosen to cut across some of those more abstract dimensions of dispute (states' rights, the strategy of economic development abroad, the role of the federal government in public education, and so forth) customary for elites, which means that constraint would be somewhat lowered for them.

The difference between the mass and elite responses would spring from differences in the nature of the objects taken to be central in the beliefs represented. For the bulk of the mass public, the object with highest centrality is the visible, familiar population grouping (Negroes), rather than questions of abstract relations among parts of government and the like. Since these latter questions take on meaning only with a good deal of political information and understanding, the attitude items given would tend to boil down for many respondents to the same single question: "Are you sympathetic to Negroes as a group, are you indifferent to them, or do you dislike them?" The responses would be affected accordingly.

While we have no direct empirical evidence supporting this illustration, there are a few fragmentary findings that point in this direction. For example, following the same format as the issue items included in Table VII, we asked our cross-section sample an attitude question concerning the desirability of action on the part of the federal government in the desegregation of public schools. Since we had also asked the question concerning fair treatment for Negroes in jobs and housing, these two items form a natural pair, both of which involve Negroes. The correlation between the two (in terms comparable to Table VII) is .57, a figure very substantially greater than the highest of the twenty-eight intercorrelations in the "mass" half of Table VII. It seems more than coincidence that the only pair of items involving the fortunes of a visible population grouping should at the same time be a very deviant pair in its high level of mutual constraint.

A parallel question was asked of the elite sample of Table VII, although the comparability was not so great as for those items presented in the table. This question was, "If Congress were to vote to give federal aid to public schools, do you think this should be given to schools which are segregated?" While the question was worded in such a manner as to avoid responses based on attitudes toward federal aid to education, a number of elite respondents insisted on answering in the negative, not because they were necessarily against desegregation, but rather because they were against any kind of federal aid to education. (The additional element of federal aid to schools was not present at all in the item for the cross-section sample.) Setting aside those respondents who gave indications that they were deviating from the intention of the question (7% of the elite sample), the correlation between the desegregation item and the F.E.P.C. item was nevertheless only .31, or very much to the *low* side of the elite intercorrelations on domestic issues, instead of being uniquely to the *high* side as it was for the mass sample.

We may summarize this situation in the following manner. Out of twenty-eight "trials" represented by the intercorrelations in Table VII, in only three cases did the mass sample show an intercorrelation between issues that was of the same sign and of greater absolute magnitude than its counterpart for the elite sample. Two of these "reversals" were completely trivial (.02 and .04), and the third was not large (.08). With respect to the only pair of items that explicitly involved the fortunes of a well-known social grouping, however, there not only was a reversal, but the reversal was large: The constraint for the mass sample, by a simple difference of coefficients, is .26 greater. This isolated test certainly provides some striking initial support for our expectations.

Up to this point, we have discussed two broad classes of findings. The first, as exemplified by Table VII and our more recent elaborations on it, suggests that groups as attitude objects (groups *qua* groups) have higher centrality in the belief systems of the mass than of the elite. The second is exemplified by the many findings that the alignment of an individual's social-group membership (like class or religious membership) and his political behavior is sharpest among the most politically involved and sophisticated third of a mass sample and fades out progressively as involvement and sophistication decline.

In case these propositions do not seem to square perfectly with one another, Figure 2 provides a schematic view of the situation that may clarify the matter for the reader. Of course, the details of the figure (like the precise characters of the functions) are sheer fancy. But the gross contours seem empirically justified. The elite of Table VII would naturally be represented by a line along the top of Figure 2, which would be thin to the vanishing point. The "relative elite" of the mass sample, which defines "the public" as perceived by most impressionistic observers, might sweep in the top 2%, 5%, or 10% of the graph, as one chose. In the upper reaches of the group centrality graph, we have already seen glimmers of the inverse relationship between group centrality and sophistication in such diverse items as the falling-off of party loyalty at the very "top" of the mass sample or the lowered constraint for the Negro items in the elite sample.

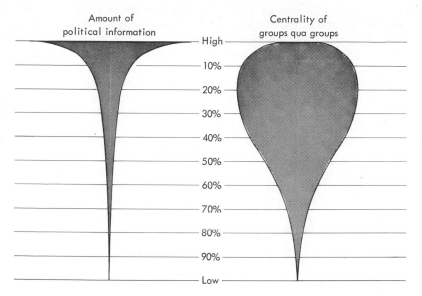

Figure 2. Political Information and the Centrality of Groups as Objects in Belief Systems.

On the other hand, why is it that when we work downward from the more sophisticated third of the population, the centrality of groups begins once again to diminish? We are already committed to the proposition that differences in information are crucial, but let us consider this point more fully. The findings that lead us to posit this decline come from a class of situations in which the actor *himself* must perceive some meaningful link between membership in a particular group and preference for a particular party or policy alternative. These situations are most typically those in which the link is not made explicit by the very nature of the situation (as we made it explicit in our battery of Negro questions above). In these cases, the individual must be endowed with some cognitions of the group as an entity and with some interstitial "linking" information indicating why a given party or policy is relevant to the group. Neither of these forms of information can be taken for granted, and our key proposition is that, as the general bulk of political information declines, the probability increases that some key pieces of information relevant to this group-politics equation will not show up.

The first item—the individual's cognition that a group exists—is a very simple one and may not even seem plausible to question. For certain groups at certain times and places, however, the possibility that such a cognition is absent must be recognized. All groups, including those that become important politically, vary in their visibility. Groups delimited by physical characteristics "in the skin" (racial groups) are highly visible, if specimens are present for inspection or if the individual has been informed in some rather vivid way of their existence. Similarly, groups that have buildings, meetings, and officers (church, congregation, and clergy for example) are more visible than groups, like social classes, that do not, although the salience of any "official" group *qua* group may vary widely according to the individual's contact with its formal manifestations.

Some groups—even among those to which an individual can be said to "belong"—are much less visible. Two important examples are the social class and the nation. Where social class is concerned, virtually all members of a population are likely to have absorbed the fact that some people have more means or status than others, and most presumably experience some satisfaction or envy on this score from time to time. Such perceptions may, however, remain at the same level as reactions to the simple fact of life that some people are born handsome and others homely; or, as Marx knew, they may proceed to cognitions of some more "real" and bounded groups. The difference is important.

Much the same kind of observation may be made of the nation as group object. On the basis of our analysis, it might be deduced that nationalist ideologies stand a much better chance of penetrating a mass population than would, for example, the single-tax ideology of the physiocrats and Henry George, for nationalist ideologies hinge upon a simple group object in a way that single-tax notions do not. This kind of deduction is perfectly warranted, particularly if one has in mind those Western nations with systems of primary education devoted to carving the shape of a nation in young minds as a "real" entity. But Znaniecki has observed, for example, that the vast majority of peasants in nineteenth-century Tsarist Russia was "utterly unconscious that they were supposed to belong to a Russian society united by a common culture." Again he reports that a 1934-1935 study in the Pripet marshes showed that nearly half of those inhabitants who were ethnically White Ruthenian had no idea that such a nationality existed and regarded themselves as belonging at most to local communities.[30] The nation as a bounded, integral group object is difficult to experience in any direct way, and its psychological existence for the individual depends upon the social transmission of certain kinds of information. What is deceptive here, as elsewhere, is that decades or even centuries after the *literati* have come to take a nation concept for granted, there may be substantial proportions of the member population who have never heard of such a thing.[31]

While cognitions of certain groups are not always present, the much more typical case is one in which the interstitial or contextual information giving the group a clear political relevance is lacking. For example, a substantial proportion of voters in the United States is unable to predict that any particular party preference will emerge in the votes of different class groupings, and this inability is particularly noticeable among the least involved citizens, whose partisan behavior is itself essentially random with respect to social class.[32]

One important *caveat* must be offered on the generalization represented in Figure 2. From a number of points we have made, it should be clear that the figure is intended to represent an actuarial proposition and nothing more. That is, it has merit for most situations, given the typical state of distribution of political information in societies as we find them "in nature." In certain situations, however, the cues presented to citizens concerning links between group and party or policy are so gross that they penetrate rapidly even to the less informed. In such cases, the form representing group centrality in Figure 2 would taper off much less rapidly with declining over-all information in the lower strata of the population.

For example, the linking information that made religion particularly relevant in the 1960 election was extremely simple, of the "what goes with what" variety. It was expressible in five words: "The Democratic candidate is Catholic." Studies have shown that, once Kennedy was nominated, this additional item of information was diffused through almost the entire population with a speed that is rare and that, we suspect, would be impossible for more complex contextual information. The linking information that made social class unusually relevant after World War II was, however, precisely this vague, contextual type.[33] It can be readily demonstrated with our data that the impact of the religious link in 1960 registered to some degree in the behavior of even the least sophisticated Protestants and Catholics, while the incremental impact of social-class cues in the earlier period had not registered at these lower levels.

The precise form of the centrality function in Figure 2 depends heavily therefore upon the character of the linking information at issue in the special case. Furthermore, if we wished to "tamper," it would not be difficult to supply a poorly informed person with a very tiny increment of linking information, too small to change his over-all amount of political information visibly yet large enough to increase considerably the centrality of a specific group in a specific situation. However this may be, Figure 2 is valid in an actuarial sense, for in "natural" populations the probability that any given individual possesses such linking information declines as over-all information becomes less.

VII. The Stability of Belief Elements over Time

All of our data up to this point have used correlations calculated on aggregates as evidence of greater or lesser constraint among elements in belief systems. While we believe these correlations to be informative indicators, they do depend for their form upon cumulations among individuals and therefore can never be seen as commenting incisively upon the belief structures of individuals.

It might then be argued that we are mistaken in saying that constraint among comparable "distant" belief elements declines generally as we move from the more to the less politically sophisticated. Instead, the configuration of political beliefs held by individuals simply becomes increasingly idiosyncratic as we move to less sophisticated people. While an equally broad range of belief elements might function as an interdependent whole for an unsophisticated person, we would find little aggregative patterning of belief combinations in populations of unsophisticated people, for they would be out of the stream of cultural information about "what goes with what" and would therefore put belief elements together in a great variety of ways.

For the types of belief that interest us here, this conclusion in itself would be significant. We believe however, that we have evidence that permits us to reject it rather categorically, in favor of our original formulation. A fair test of this counterhypothesis would seem to lie in the measurement of the same belief elements for the same individuals over time. For if we are indeed involved here in idiosyncratic patterns of belief, each meaningful to the individual in his own way, then we could expect that individual responses to the same set of items at different points in time should show some fundamental stability. They do not.

A longitudinal study of the American electorate over a four-year period has permitted us to ask the same questions of the same people a number of times, usually separated by close to two-year intervals. Analysis of the stability of responses to the "basic" policy questions of the type presented in Table VII yields remarkable results. Faced with the typical item of this kind, only about thirteen people out of twenty manage to locate themselves even on the same *side* of the controversy in successive interrogations, when ten out of twenty could have done so by chance alone.

While we have no comparable longitudinal data for an elite sample, the degree of fit between answers to our issue items and congressional roll-calls is strong enough to suggest that time correlations for individual congressmen in roll-call choice on comparable bills would provide a fair estimate of the stability of an elite population in beliefs of this sort. It is probably no exaggeration to deduce that, in sharp contrast to a mass sample, eighteen out of twenty congressmen would be likely to take the same positions on the same attitude items after a two-year interval. In short, then, we feel very confident that elite-mass differences in levels of constraint among beliefs are mirrored in elite-mass differences in the temporal stability of belief elements for individuals.

We observed much earlier that the centrality of a specific belief in a larger belief system and the relative stability of that belief over time should be highly related. From our other propositions about the role of groups as central objects in the belief systems of the mass public, we can therefore arrive at two further predictions. The first is simply that pure affect toward visible population groupings should be highly stable over time, even in a mass public, much more so in fact than beliefs on policy matters that more or less explicitly bear on the fortunes of these groupings. Second, policy items that do bear more rather than less explicitly upon their fortunes should show less stability than affect towards the group *qua* group but more than those items for which contextual information is required.

Figure 3 gives strong confirmation of these hypotheses.[34] First, the only question applied longitudinally that touches on pure affect toward a visible population grouping is the one about party loyalties or identifications. As the figure indicates, the stability of these group feelings for individuals over time (measured by the correlation between individual positions in two successive readings) registers in a completely different range from that

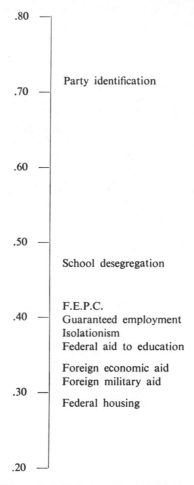

Figure 3. Temporal stability of Different Belief Elements for Individuals, 1958-60[a].

a. The measure of stability is a rank-order correlation (tau-beta) between individuals' positions in 1958 and in 1960 on the same items.

characterizing even the most stable of the issue items employed.[35] This contrast is particularly ironic, for in theory of course the party usually has little rationale for its existence save as an instrument to further particular policy preferences of the sort that show less stability in Figure 3. The policy is the end, and the party is the means, and ends are conceived to be more stable and central in belief systems than means. The reversal for the mass public is of course a rather dramatic special case of one of our primary generalizations: The party and the affect toward it are more central within the political belief systems of the mass public than are the policy ends that the parties are designed to pursue.

Figure 3 also shows that, within the set of issues, the items that stand out as most stable are those that have obvious bearing on the welfare of a population grouping—the Negroes—although the item concerning federal job guarantees is very nearly as stable. In general, we may say that stability declines as the referents of the attitude items become increasingly remote, from jobs, which are significant objects to all, and Negroes, who are attitude objects for most, to items involving ways and means of handling foreign policy.

Although most of the less stable items involve foreign policy, the greatest instability is shown for a domestic issue concerning the relative role of government and private enterprise in areas like those of housing and utilities. Interestingly enough, this issue would probably be chosen by sophisticated judges as the most classically "ideological" item in the set, and indeed Table VII shows that the counterpart for this question in the elite sample is central to the primary organizing dimension visible in the matrix. Since the item refers to visible population groupings—"government" and "private business" —we might ask why it is not geared into more stable affect toward these groups. We do believe that measures of affect toward something like "private business" (or better, perhaps, "big business") as an object would show reasonable stability for a mass public, although probably less than those for more clearly bounded and visible groups like Negroes and Catholics. The question, however, is not worded in a way that makes clear which party— government or private business—will profit from which arrangement. Lacking such cues, the citizen innocent of "ideology" is likely to make rather capricious constructions, since the issue is probably one that he has never thought about before and will never think about again except when being interviewed.

In short, all these longitudinal data offer eloquent proof that signs of low constraint among belief elements in the mass public are not products of well knit but highly idiosyncratic belief systems, for these beliefs are extremely labile for individuals over time. Great instability in itself is *prima facie* evidence that the belief has extremely low centrality for the believer. Furthermore, it is apparent that any instability characterizing one belief sets an upper limit on the degree of orderly constraint that could be expected to emerge in static measurement between this unstable belief and another, even a perfectly stable one. While an aggregate might thus show high stability despite low constraint, the fact of low stability virtually ensures that constraint must also be low. This kind of relationship between stability and constraint means that an understanding of what underlies high instability is at the same time an understanding of what underlies low constraint.

The fact that we have asked these questions at more than two points in time provides a good deal of leverage in analyzing the processes of change that generate aggregate instability and helps us to illuminate the character of this instability.[36] For example, in Figure 4 we discover, in comparing our indicators of the degree of instability associated with any particular belief as they register between t_2 and t_3 with the same figures for t_1 and t_2, that estimates are essentially the same. This result is an important one, for it assures us that within a medium time range (four years), differences among issues in degree of response stability are highly reliable.

Far more fascinating, however, is another property that emerges. Quite generally, we can predict t_3 issue positions of individuals fully as well from a knowledge of their t_1 positions alone as we can from a knowledge of their t_2 positions alone. In other words, the turnover correlations between different time points for these issues tend to fit the scheme shown in Figure 4.

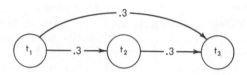

Figure 4. Pattern of Turnover Correlations between Different Time Points.

It can be shown that there is no single meaningful process of change shared by all respondents that would generate this configuration of data.[37] In fact, even if we assume that there is a relatively limited number of change processes present in the population, we find that only two such models could generate these observations. The first of these models posits that some of the respondents managed in a deliberate way to locate themselves from one measurement to another on the opposite side of an issue from the one they had selected at the preceding measurement. It would have to be assumed that a person who chose a leftish alternative on a certain issue in the first measure would be motivated to remember to seek out the rightish alternative two years later, the leftish again two years after that, and so on. Naturally, an assumption that this behavior characterizes one member of the population is sufficiently nonsensical for us to reject it out of hand.

Once this possibility is set aside, however, there is only one other model involving a mixture of two types of process of change that fits the observed data. This model is somewhat surprising but not totally implausible. It posits a very sharp dichotomy within the population according to processes of change that are polar opposites. There is first a "hard core" of opinion on a given issue, which is well crystallized and perfectly stable over time. For the remainder of the population, response sequences over time are statistically random. The model does not specify what proportions of the population fall into these two categories: This matter is empirically independent, and it is clear that the size of the turnover correlations between any two points in time is a simple function of these relative proportions.[38]

In view of our earlier remarks, this "black and white" model is credible in its assumption that a mass public contains significant proportions of people who, for lack of information about a particular dimension of controversy, offer meaningless opinions that vary randomly in direction during repeated trials over time. We may be uncomfortable, however, at using a model that suggests such a rigid and polar division of the population, leaving no room for the "gray" area of meaningful change of opinion or "conversion." In this respect, while the randomness posited by the model is a discouraging property substantively, it is an empowering property mathematically, for aggregate randomness has certain predictable consequences For example, if the model were to fit the data, we would know that some people who are responding to the items as though flipping a coin could, by chance alone, supply the same responses at three trials in a row and would therefore have response paths indistinguishable from those of perfectly stable respondents but for entirely different reasons. While we could not enter the stable group and "tag" such random people, we would at least have an excellent estimate of the number of them that lingers after three trials to pollute the set of genuinely stable respondents. Most important, however, is the fact that the very character of the model makes it possible to test quite rigorously the goodness of fit of the data to the model.

For our initial test, we singled out the issue that seemed on *a priori* grounds most likely to fit the model. It was the most "ideological" item in the battery yet the one that had shown the highest degree of temporal instability: the question about the respective roles of private enterprise and government in areas like housing and electrical power. It is important to understand in detail the grounds on which this item was chosen. The model requires that some people have unswerving beliefs on the subject and that other people have no beliefs at all. It also requires that there be no middle ground, no set of people whose beliefs on the subject are in the process of evolution. For these requirements, the "government *vs.* private enterprise issue," more than any of the others, seemed "sheltered" from meaningful change. This isolation was true in two senses. First, it involved a very basic area of political controversy, and people understanding the stakes involved in a more ideological way would not be readily dissuaded from their respective positions. Secondly, while events like the crisis at Little Rock and exposés of waste in foreign aid were occurring in this period to touch off meaningful evolutions of opinion, little was occurring that might intuitively be expected to shake true beliefs on one side or the other. At the same time, of course, the relationships to be judged in the item were sufficiently remote and abstract from the experience of most people to make many meaningless responses likely.

The fit between the data collected at three time points on this issue and our black and white model was virtually perfect.[39] This result lends remarkable assurance that our understanding of the "change" processes affecting the issue responses was accurate: The only change that occurred was random change. We naturally went on to apply this test of fit to the other issues, for which the black and white model had seemed less credible. And indeed, these other items showed a somewhat poorer fit with the model. None strays a great distance, but it is unlikely that any would survive significant tests of goodness of fit.[40] What, then, can we say about the character of beliefs touched by these other items?

Strictly speaking, as soon as we encounter data that depart in any significant measure from the black and white model, we lose all mathematical anchors, in the sense that, unless we insert a variety of restrictive assumptions, the number of models (even simple ones) that could *logically* account for the data becomes very large indeed. Despite this loss of power, the existence of one issue that does fit the black and white model perfectly provides at least an intuitive argument that those that depart from it in modest degrees do not require a totally different class of model. In other words, we come to suppose that these other items depart from the model only because of the presence of a "third force" of people, who are undergoing meaningful conversion from one genuine opinion at t_1 to an opposing but equally genuine opinion at t_2. This "third force" is small, and the dominant phenomenon remains the two segments of the population, within one of which opinions are random and within the other of which opinions have perfect stability. Nevertheless, the presence of any third force suffices to disrupt the fit between the data and the black and white model, and the degree of departure is a function of the size of the third force.

It should be reiterated that this view cannot be subjected to any unequivocal mathematical test but rather depends for its reasonableness upon the excellence of the fit shown by one issue and the approaches to fit shown by the others. It seems likely that responses to other issues of a similar type are generated in similar fashion. And while it is true that competing attitude models could be applied to describe most of these data, their assumptions simply lose all plausible ring when confronted with the results from the private-enterprise issue.[41]

Or, in another vein, the discouragingly large turnover of opinion on these issues in the total mass public might be taken as evidence that the questions were poorly written and thus extremely unreliable—that the main lesson is that they should be rewritten. Yet the issues posed are those posed by political controversy, and citizens' difficulties in responding to them in meaningful fashion seem to proffer important insights into their understanding of the same political debates in real life. More crucial still, what does it mean to say that an instrument is perfectly reliable *vis-à-vis* one class of people and totally unreliable *vis-à-vis* another, which is the proper description of the black and white model? The property of reliability is certainly not inherent *solely* in the instrument of measurement, contrary to what is commonly supposed.

As another check on the question of reliability, we decided to examine the temporal stability of belief elements of this sort among very limited sets of people whose broader interviews gave us independent reasons to believe they had particular interest in narrower belief areas (like the Negro question). We took advantage once again of interviews with a good deal of open-ended material, sifting through this voluntary commentary to find people who had shown "self-starting" concern about particular controversies. Then we went back to the relevant structured issue questions to examine the stability of these belief elements for these people over time. The turnover correlations for these limited subpopulations did increase substantially, beginning to approach the levels of stability shown for party identification (see Figure 3). Once again, the evidence seemed clear that extreme instability is associated with absence of information, or at least of interest, and that item reliability is adequate for people with pre-existing concern about any given matter.[42]

The substantive conclusion imposed by these technical maneuvers is simply that large portions of an electorate do not have meaningful beliefs, even on issues that have formed the basis for intense political controversy among elites for substantial periods of time. If this conclusion seems self-evident, it is worth reflecting on the constancy with which it is ignored and on the fact that virtually none of the common modes of dealing empirically with public beliefs attempts to take it into account. Instead, it is assumed that a location must be found for all members of a population on all dimensions of controversy that are measured. Our data argue that, where any single dimension is concerned, very substantial portions of the public simply do not belong on the dimension at all. They should be set aside as not forming any part of that particular *issue public*. And since it is only among "members" of any given issue public that the political effects of a controversy are felt (where such "effects" include activated public opinion expressed in the writing of letters to the editor, the changing of votes, and the like), we come a step closer to reality when we recognize the fragmentation of the mass public into a plethora of narrower issue publics.

VIII. Issue Publics

Our longitudinal data on eight specific political issues permit us to sketch crudely the boundaries of a sampling of eight issue publics.[43] While details of specific publics are not appropriate here, the general picture that emerges provides some final confirming glimpses into the character of political belief systems in a mass public.

First, of course, these publics vary in size, although none embraces any clear majority of the electorate. As would be expected, relative size is almost perfectly correlated with the ranking of issue stability (Figure 3), and the smallest issue public (that associated with the "ideological" private-enterprise issue) includes less than 20% of the electorate.

Since all members of the same population fall either within or outside eight different issue publics, a second analytic question involves the structure that would be revealed were we to map several issue publics at once. What proportions of the electorate would fall at the intersection of two, three, or even more issue publics? One logically possible outcome of such mapping would be a set of concentric rings, suggesting that these issue concerns are cumulative in Guttman's sense. That is, the picture might show that, if a person fell within the bounds of one fairly narrow issue public embracing only 20% of the population, then he would be nearly certain to fall within some other related issue public encompassing 40% of the population.

The reality does not approach such neatness, however. Memberships and overlapping memberships in issue publics are quite dispersed phenomena, although distribution is not entirely random. It can be shown, for example, that the number of respondents who warrant inclusion in all eight of the issue publics exceeds chance expectation by a factor greater than five. Exactly the same is true for the number of people who fall in none of the eight issue publics. Furthermore, the proportions of people who lie at the intersections of two or more issue publics tend to show increments above the chance level that, while much smaller, are nevertheless relatively large where the joint content of the issues would lead one to expect greater overlap. At any rate, the departure from a Guttman cumulative structure is extreme, and the simple conclusion seems to be that different controversies excite different people to the point of real opinion formation. One man takes an interest in policies bearing on the Negro and is relatively indifferent to or ignorant about controversies in other areas. His neighbor may have few crystallized opinions on the race issue, but he may find the subject of foreign aid very important. Such sharp divisions of interest are part of what the term "issue public" is intended to convey.

Since one of our early comparisons in this paper had to do with the general levels of constraint among an elite and a mass public on a sampling of belief elements, it is interesting to ask what degree of constraint can be found among the belief elements of those who fall at the intersection of any pair of issue publics. In such a case, we have some assurance that both sets of beliefs are important to the actor, and it is not therefore surprising that these correlations tend to be much stronger. A matrix of intercorrelations parallel to those of Table VII for people at these respective intersections looks more like the elite matrix than like the mass matrix. Of course, this "intersection" matrix is a spurious one, representing no particular population: Very few people contribute to all of the intercorrelations, a substantial number contribute to none, and the set contributing to each cell is quite variable in composition. Nevertheless, the fact remains that removal from analysis of individuals who, through indifference or ignorance, lie outside the issue publics in question serves to close much of the gap in constraint levels between mass and elite publics.

IX. Summary

Our discussion of issue publics has brought us full circle, for there is an obvious relationship among the divisions of the common citizenry into relatively narrow and fragmented issue publics, the feeble levels of constraint registered among specific belief elements of any range, and the absence of recognition or understanding of overarching ideological frames of reference that served as our point of departure. For the truly involved citizen, the development of political sophistication means the absorption of contextual information that makes clear to him the connections of the policy area of his initial interest with policy differences in other areas; and that these broader configurations of policy positions are describable quite economically in the basic abstractions of ideology. Most members of the mass public, however, fail to proceed so far. Certain rather concrete issues may capture their respective individual attentions and lead to some politically relevant opinion formation. This engagement of attention remains narrow however: Other issue concerns that any sophisticated observer would see as "ideologically" related to the initial concern tend not to be thus associated in any breadth or number. The common citizen fails to develop more global points of view about politics. A realistic picture of political belief systems in the mass public, then, is not one that omits issues and policy demands completely nor one that presumes widespread ideological coherence; it is rather one that captures with some fidelity the fragmentation, narrowness, and diversity of these demands.

Such a description is not particularly economical, and the investigator is confronted by the fact that, in coping with a poorly constrained system, he must choose between parsimony and explanatory power. This dilemma confronts him only in the degree that he insists upon dealing with the issue or ideological base of mass politics. That is, the very diffusion of this issue base at the mass level means that many of the threads cancel themselves out and can be ignored at one level of description. With good information on basic party loyalties in a population, with knowledge of sudden disruptions of economic expectations, and with freedom to treat other short-term perturbations in mass political behavior in terms of such inelegant factors as candidate popularity, there is no reason to feel that mass political phenomena are difficult to understand or predict in relatively economical terms. But such accounts do not probe to the level that supplies for many the fundamental "why" of politics—its issue or ideological base.

If we insist on treating this base and choose economy over explanatory power, then we are likely to select one or two ideological threads to follow, with recognition that the consequences of substantial numbers of other threads must be ignored. If the limited threads are well chosen, this strategy has a number of strengths, and a "good" choice of threads is likely to involve visible and competing population groupings, for reasons sketched above.

This latter strategy is essentially that employed by Lipset in tracing the imprint of social class upon mass political behavior across time and nationality in *Political Man*. His choice of threads is good, in part because of the ubiquity of social-class differences historically and cross-nationally and in part because, among issue threads, social class is one of the more reliably prominent. Despite the great diversity of issue concerns in the American public in the 1950s, if one were required to pick the single thread of ideological relevance most visible and persistent, it undoubtedly would be related to social class.

On the other hand, there is a major sacrifice of explanatory power here. For example, when we argue that social-class concerns represent the most prominent, unitary "issue" thread in mass American politics in the past decade, the scope of our statement should not be overestimated. Given the diversity and number of such threads, it need only mean (as is probably the case) that such concerns have made some greater or lesser contribution to the significant political behaviors—for the mass, largely in voting—of 20 to 40% of the American population in this period. This contribution is enough, of course, to leave a clear imprint on mass political phenomena, although it does not constitute even substantial explanation.[44]

Furthermore, it may well be that, in pluralist societies with other highly visible group cleavages, these cleavages may often have greater penetration into mass publics than do class differences, as far as consequences for political behavior are concerned. Religious pluralism is a case in point. While class differences mark every society, not all current democracies contain fundamental religious differences. Where such differences exist and can in some measure be separated from social class differences—the Netherlands, Austria, and the United States are good examples—there is fair reason to believe that they are fully as important, if not more important, in shaping mass political behavior than are class differences. Even in current France, one can predict with greater accuracy whether a citizen will be a partisan of the "left" or of the "right" by knowing his position on the "clerical question" than by knowing his position on the more central class issues typically associated with the left-right distinction. And this accuracy is possible despite several decades during which French elites have focused primary attention on other more gripping controversies and have frequently attempted to deflate the clerical question as a "phony" issue.[45]

Whatever problems are posed for description by the diffuseness of the issue base of mass politics, the most important insights are to be gained from the fact that ideological constraints in belief systems decline with decreasing political information, which is to say that they are present among elites at the "top" of political systems, or subsystems and disappear rather rapidly as one moves "downward" into their mass clienteles. We see the importance of this fact in a number of standard phenomena of both routine and crisis politics.

Perhaps the simplest and most obvious consequences are those that depend on the fact that reduced constraint with reduced information means in turn that ideologically constrained belief systems are necessarily more common in upper than in lower social strata. This fact in turn means that upper social strata across history have much more predictably supported conservative or rightist parties and movements than lower strata have supported leftist parties and movements.

These facts have further bearing on a number of asymmetries in political strategy, which typically arise between elites of rightist and leftist parties. These elites operate under rather standard ideological assumptions, and therefore recognize their "natural" clienteles in the upper and lower strata of the society respectively. The cultural definitions that separate upper and lower in most if not all modern societies are such that the lower clientele numerically outweighs the upper. The net result of these circumstances is that the elites of leftist parties enjoy a "natural" numerical superiority, yet they are cursed with a clientele that is less dependable or solidary in its support. The rightist elite has a natural clientele that is more limited but more dependable.

Asymmetrical elite strategies therefore emerge. They are best summed up perhaps in terms of an increasingly *overt* stress on group loyalty and cohesion *per se* as one moves from right to left across party spectra in most political systems. This difference has a great number of concrete manifestations. For example, where political institutions encourage multiparty development, there is likely to be less party fragmentation on the left than on the right. Where political institutions permit interparty differences in the stringency of party discipline at the legislative level, it is common to find a rather steady progression in strength of discipline exacted as one moves from right to left. At an electoral level, rightist candidates are more likely to run as individual *notables,* dissociating themselves from party *per se* or claiming positions "above the parties" and priding themselves on the independence of their consciences from party dictation.

Entirely parallel asymmetries arise in the relations between party elites and elites of organized interest groups based "outside" the political order as it is narrowly conceived. These relations tend to be more overtly close as one moves from the right to the left. Trade unions have with some frequency created or coalesced with leftist parties, and, where such coalition has not occurred, trade unions (and particularly those with the less politically sophisticated memberships) publicize political endorsements that link them rather unequivocally with specific leftist parties. Associations of professional and business people, to the degree that they perform public political activity at all, tend toward non-partisan exhortations to "work for the party of your choice" and in other ways maintain or are kept at a "proper" distance from rightist parties so far as self-publicized connections are concerned. All these differences flow from the simple fact that, for leftist parties, the transmission of gross, simple, group-oriented cues is a functional imperative. For rightist parties, there is much to lose and nothing to gain in such publicity, for the basic clientele can be counted on for fair support without blatant cues, and the tactical needs are to avoid the alienation of potentially large-scale "haphazard" support from the lower-status clientele.

These simple social biases in the presence of ideological constraints in belief systems thus register to some degree in the calculations of practical political elites. Fully as interesting, however, are the miscalculations that arise when the low incidence of these constraints in the middle and lower reaches of mass publics is forgotten. While this forgetting is more common among academic commentators than among practical politicians, it is sometimes hard to avoid—particularly where an elite with a distinctive ideology captures a broad surge of mass support. Here it is difficult to keep in mind that the true motivations and comprehensions of the supporters may have little or nothing to do with the distinctive beliefs of the endorsed elite. Yet we believe that such hiatuses or discontinuities are common and become more certain in the degree that (1) the distinctive elements of the elite ideologies are bound up in abstractions or referents remote from the immediate experience of the clientele; (2) and that the clientele, for whatever reason, is recruited from the less informed strata of a population. We shall close by applying these propositions to historical cases.

Abolition and the Rise of the Republican Party

Historians have devoted a great deal of prose to the rise of abolitionist ferment in the North after 1820. Popular sentiment against slavery seems to have gathered momentum in the relatively unbroken line that is so typical of *successful* reform movements, from the persistent agitations of Lundy and William Lloyd Garrison through the formation of antislavery societies in the 1830s, the development of the underground railroad, the birth of the Republican Party in the name of abolition, and its final electoral triumph in a popular majority for Lincoln outside the South in 1860. A number of figures are commonly cited to express the deep penetration of the ferment into the consciousness of the general public, including the membership of 200,000 attracted by the American Anti-Slavery Society in the seven short years after 1833 and the truly remarkable sales of *Uncle Tom's Cabin* in 1852 and after.

We obviously do not challenge the mountains of evidence concerning the high pitch of this controversy. We assume from the outset that this ferment among the elites and near-elites was in point of fact most noteworthy and has been accurately described. If we take the figures at face value, for example, we can compute that the Anti-Slavery Society's membership amounted to between 3 and 4% of the adult population outside of the South at that time.[46] Against what we have considered to be the commonly "visible" part of the political public (5 to 15% of the total adult public), this figure does indeed represent a vigorous development of antislave sentiment. What interests us instead is the gap between the figure of 4% indicative of a sturdy ideological movement, and the 46% of the nonsouthern popular presidential vote won by the Republican Party two years after its conception in Wisconsin and birth in Michigan under the pure banner of abolition. The question is, Essentially what part did beliefs in abolition play in attracting the votes of the mass base that made the Republican Party a political success?

The question seems particularly worth asking, for among events or çauses that have commonly been assumed to have had some substantial resonance among the mass public in American history, few would strike us as less plausible than abolition. Panics, the promise of free land in the West, railroad charges for transportation of farm produce, and competition by immigrants for urban jobs could all be expected to have had some immediate impact on at least limited portions of the mass public. Similarly, the threat of abolition would have had some concrete and day-to-day meaning for many citizens in the South. But it is hard to imagine that the ordinary nonsoutherner in 1855 would have had reason to be concerned about the plight of his "black brother" in a land several days' journey away—certainly not reason sufficient to make any visible contribution to his political responses. Indeed, we are tempted to the heresy that there were very substantial portions of the nonsouthern population in that period who were only dimly aware that slavery or a controversy about it existed.

If this latter statement seems dubious in the light of the torrents of literature poured out on the subject in the 1850s, the reader might reflect upon the feeble impact registered in the mass public by "the communist hysteria" of the McCarthy era in the early 1950s. At an elite level, the controversy was bitter and all-pervasive for a considerable period of time. Yet, during the nationally televised hearings that climaxed the affair, Stouffer found that 30% of a cross-section public could not think of any senator or congressman investigating internal communism, and the low salience of the whole controversy for most of the public was clearly demonstrated in other ways as well.[47] In the 1952 presidential campaign, the Republican charges against the Democratic Party were summed up in the handy slogan "Corruption, Korea and Communism." Our materials drawn at the time from a mass electorate showed a strong spontaneous response to the issues of corruption and Korea (although there was little understanding of the "Great Debate" that was in full swing over how the Korean conflict should be terminated) but almost no response at all to the third item, even though it referred to a controversy that, like abolition in the 1850s, has tended to remain in elite minds as the principal struggle of its period.[48] And evidence of this lack of public recognition or resonance emerges despite the existence of a population that relative to that of 1850, was highly literate, leisured, and exposed to mass media of a speed, breadth, and penetration that simply had no counterpart in an earlier day.[49] The controversy over internal communism provides a classic example of a mortal struggle among elites that passed almost unwitnessed by an astonishing portion of the mass public. Quite clearly, there is no necessary connection between the noise, acrimony, or duration of an elite debate and the mass penetration of the controversy, however automatically the equation is made. A better guide to penetration seems to be the character of the issue itself.

A student recently decided to analyze the contents of caches of letters from the 1850s and 1860s, which had been preserved by old families in the various attics of a small Ohio community. He was interested in tracing the development of abolitionist sentiment, and Ohio had been the first state to give the new Republican Party a mass base in the election of 1854. The problem was that no references to abolition were ever found in any of the letters, despite the fact that their writers necessarily represented the "upper" stratum of the community, the stratum that, by all odds, would be most likely to have some awareness of the controversy. In letters written on the eve of the Civil War, there were increasing "ideological" references to the disruption of the Union. Once political events had passed to the dramatic point at which the South was clearly in treasonable rebellion against the Union, the mass penetration of the controversy in the North is not difficult to understand. But it is likely that this stage was reached at a mass level much later than is customarily assumed. And for the preceding period, the Ohio letters betrayed no concern for abolition.[50]

There is, furthermore, a major leap from some awareness that a controversy is in the air to opinion formation of a strength sufficient to register in an individual's own political behavior. Once again, modern data are instructive. Although civil rights and the race question have been primary controversies in the past five years and although a very large majority of the public was aware of the struggles at Little Rock and the University of Mississippi, opinion formation on the subject among a cross-section of nonsouthern whites was far from intense. While everybody responds to opinion items on the matter, the true issue publics are made up very disproportionately of Negroes and southerners. A sprinkling of nonsouthern whites shows some genuine interest in the issue, and the bulk of them is positively disposed toward the Negro. But a measure of the salience of the Negro question as a political problem stringent enough to register two-thirds of nonsouthern Negroes as intensely concerned leaves scarcely one nonsouthern white out of ten qualifying at the same level. It should be remembered that this indifference is evident at a time when the Negro has become an important problem in urban areas outside the South, a situation that did not exist in 1850 or 1860. Most northern whites with intense positive or negative concern also live in areas where Negroes live or are inordinately interested in politics. In the hinterland, opinion is superficial or indifferent.

If the population of the hinterland that gave initial mass impetus to the

Republican Party had indeed felt some deep humanitarian concern about the plight of the Negro in the South, then we would be forced to conclude that empathy in human nature has suffered an astonishing decline in the past century. In fact, however, there are enough anomalies in the voting records of the period to leave room for fair doubt about the nature of the Republican mass base in its first three years. Fringe votes for the earlier abolitionist parties (the Liberty and Free Soil Parties) were never strong in the urban centers—Boston and New York—which were generating much of the intellectual ferment about abolition, although they were concentrated in smaller towns in Massachusetts and New York outside these centers and probably reflect the lines of genuine if thinly sprinkled abolitionist feeling. When, however, the Whig Party no longer presented itself as an alternative to the Democrats and when broad-gauged mass support had to turn either to the Republicans or to the anti-Catholicism of the "Know-Nothing" American Party, the patterns were somewhat different. In 1856 the largest northeastern centers (excluding all but the potentially abolitionist North[51]), where intellectuals had pursued abolition most doggedly and where Catholic immigrants were accumulating, gave the Know-Nothings their clearest mass support and the Republicans their weakest harvest of former Whig or Free-Soil votes. The capacity to move these votes into the Republican column was greater in those surrounding areas that had shown the strongest traces of support for the earlier abolition parties, although in many of these areas the Know-Nothings cut into the vote as well. The least blemished successes of the new Republican party lay in the deeper hinterland, which had given the feeblest support to abolition in preceding elections.[52]

While any evidence pertaining to the thoughts and motivations of the mass of citizens who did not make public speeches or leave written records must be circumstantial, it is worth suggesting that there was probably an important discontinuity between the intransigent abolitionism associated with the Republican Party at an elite level in its early phases and its early mass successes. How great this discontinuity was we do not and doubtless shall not ever know, although we have some confidence that, if the truth were known, the discontinuity would be large enough to shock many students of documents and data from more elite levels.

Of course, from the point of view of historical outcomes, all that is important is that this particular conjunction of circumstances occurred when it did and was interpreted as it was by political elites in both North and South. These facts shaped history and placed the abolitionist movement in the forefront of "popular" American reforms, set apart from other reforms that have either achieved general elite acceptance without need for mass support or have faded into semioblivion because times were not propitious for the capture of a mass base. Nonetheless, our understanding of history may be improved at some points if we recognize the possibility that such discontinuities can occur.

The Mass Base of the Nazi Party

The rise of the Nazi Party in Germany between the two World Wars entrained such a tragic sequence of events that the experience has provoked diagnoses from every school of thought concerned with people, politics, or societies. Typically, the question has been, How could the German people have lent support to a movement with an ideology as brutal and authoritarian as that of the Nazis? Some years ago, Bendix argued that it was important to differentiate between the top Nazi leaders, the party members, and the masses whose sudden surge of support at the polls converted the National Socialists from simply another extremist fringe group of the sort that many societies harbor much of the time to a prominence that permitted them to become masters of Germany soon after 1932.[53]

Few would now question that the simple magnitude of economic collapse Germany suffered in the wake of World War I was the critical catalyst, both for the organizational strength the cadre of Nazi activists had attained prior to 1930 and for the sweeping successes they attained at the polls in that year. Once this point is made, however, we concur with Bendix that the explanatory paths for the mass and the elite are likely to diverge. Our interest here has to do solely with the relationship between the new-found mass of Nazi voters and the ideology of the movement they endorsed.

Who was particularly attracted to this mass base? Once again, there is fair agreement among analysts that there was a significant connection between the marked increase in voter turnout and the sudden surge in Nazi votes that marked the 1928-1932 period. Bendix noted that the staggering increase of $5\frac{1}{2}$ million votes picked up by the Nazi Party in 1930 over its 1928 totals coincided with a rapid influx into the active electorate of nearly $2\frac{1}{2}$ million adults who had failed to vote in 1928. These figures for new voters are exclusive of the estimated 1,760,000 young people who became eligible and voted for the first time, and there is reason to believe that these young people flocked to the Nazis in disproportionate numbers.[54] In addition, there is convincing evidence from Heberle and others that, among older voters, the most dramatic shifts from other parties to the Nazi Party occurred in rural areas and especially among peasants.[55] We conclude therefore that, whatever the social backgrounds or motivations of the activist cadre of the Nazis, its mass base was disproportionately recruited from among customary non-voters, the young and the peasantry.

Of course, chronic nonvoters would lie at the bottom of any scale of political sophistication or ideological comprehension. In a matrix constructed after the fashion of Table III, there is a very sharp gradient in voting fidelity from the upper left-hand corner to the lower right. As we have noted, too, there is a decline in average age from the upper right-hand corner to the lower left, despite the negative correlation between age and education: The young are also the most politically unsophisticated age grade, despite their higher average education. Finally, for American data at least, it is clear that political information and political involvement decline systematically with declining mean education from urban areas to increasingly rural areas. Even taken as a whole, farmers in modern America are more remote from and comprehend less of the normal political process than do the lower echelons of the urban occupational hierarchy.[56] Furthermore, the Heberle data for Germany suggest that, among farmers, it was the most isolated and the poorest educated who shifted in the most dramatic proportions to the Nazi ticket in the crucial years.[57] In sum, it seems safe to conclude that the mass base of the Nazi movement represented one of the more unrelievedly ill-informed clienteles that a major political party has assembled in a modern state.

Heberle, who was anxious to show that Nazi popularity in Schleswig-Holstein was not the result of an ingrained antidemocratic bias, commented on how incredible it seemed that the Nazis should be so widely acceptable to these "generally sober-minded and freedom-loving North Germans, who were not at all accustomed to a tradition of authoritarian government." He devoted a lengthy analysis to an attempt to find comparable belief elements in earlier ideational movements of Schleswig-Holstein that could explain the area's receptiveness to the new ideology. While occasional common threads could be discerned, their number was meager enough to be quite accidental, and antithetical elements predominated.[58] Heberle concluded that farmers and other rural people respond to politics less in terms of "ideologies and general political ideals" than in terms of "concrete advantages and disadvantages" of one party relative to another, and he closed with the hope that, under better circumstances, these rural people would "revert" to their more innocuous attitudes of the past.[59]

Even had the clientele of the Nazi Party been of average education and political sophistication, there would be strong reason to doubt the degree to which prior awareness of Nazi ideology among its voters could be claimed. In view of the actual peculiarities of its mass base, the question verges on the absurd. The Nazis promised changes in a system that was near collapse. Under comparable stresses, it is likely that large numbers of citizens in any society (and particularly those without any long-term affective ties to more traditional parties) would gladly support *ad hoc* promises of change without any great concern about ideological implications. And typically, they would lack the contextual information necessary to assess these implications, even if some stray details were absorbed. We believe this response would be true of any mass public and not only those that, like Germany, had experienced only a brief democratic tradition.[60]

To the farmers in particular, the Nazis promised a moratorium on, if not an abolition of, all debts.[61] Furthermore, they had the disciplined and motivated party organization capable of disseminating such propaganda through the hinterland. While they had conceived of themselves as an urban party (which by origin and personnel they were), the Nazis appeared to have made a conscious discovery in the late 1920s that a golden harvest of votes had ripened in rural areas, and they set about to exploit this fact systematically, having become quite discouraged with their lack of progress in urban areas. The Communists had preceded them among the peasantry—but in an earlier and less propitious period—and they had relaxed their efforts. Furthermore, in view of Marxist dogma on the dubious political utility of the peasant, it is unlikely that their energies had ever been concentrated in quite the same manner. In principle, however, there is no reason to believe that, had the Communists instead of the Nazis arrived freshly on the rural scene at the same point and with similar vigor and sketchy propaganda, European history would not have taken a dramatically different turn. All evidence suggests that, in this historical case, the link between specific ideology and mass response was probably of the weakest.

X. Conclusion

We have long been intrigued, in dealing with attitudinal and behavioral materials drawn from cross-section publics, at the frequency with which the following sequence of events occurs. An hypothesis is formed that seems reasonable to the analyst, having to do with one or another set of systematic differences in perceptions, attitudes, or behavior patterns. The hypothesis is tested on materials from the general population but shows at best some rather uninteresting trace findings. Then the sample is further subdivided by formal education, which isolates among other groups the 10% of the American population with college degrees or the 20% with some college education. It frequently turns out that the hypothesis is then very clearly confirmed for the most educated, with results rapidly shading off to zero within the less educated majority of the population.

We do not claim that such an analytic approach always produces findings of this sort. From time to time, of course, the hypothesis in question can be more broadly rejected for all groups, and, on rare occasions, a relationship turns out to be sharper among the less educated than among the well-educated. Nevertheless, there is a strikingly large class of cases in which confirmation occurs only, or most sharply, among the well educated. Usually it is easy to see, after the fact if not before, the degree to which the dynamics of the processes assumed by the hypothesis rest upon the kinds of broad or abstract contextual information about currents of ideas, people, or society that educated people come to take for granted as initial ingredients of thought but that the most cursory studies will demonstrate are not widely shared. As experiences of this sort accumulate, we become increasingly sensitive to these basic problems of information and begin to predict their results in advance.

This awareness means that we come to expect hypotheses about wide-ranging yet highly integrated belief systems and their behavioral consequences to show results among relative elites but to be largely disconfirmed below them. It is our impression, for example, that even some of the more elaborate "ideological" patterns associated with the authoritarian personality syndrome follow this rule. Some recent results that have accumulated in connection with the Protestant-ethic hypothesis of Weber seem to hint at something of the same pattern as well.[62]

In this paper, we have attempted to make some systematic comments on this kind of phenomenon that seem crucial to any understanding of elite and mass belief systems. We have tried to show the character of this "continental shelf" between elites and masses and to locate the sources of differences in their belief systems in some simple characteristics of information and its social transmission.

The broad contours of elite decisions over time can depend in a vital way upon currents in what is loosely called "the history of ideas." These decisions in turn have effects upon the mass of more common citizens. But, of any direct participation in this history of ideas and the behavior it shapes, the mass is remarkably innocent. We do not disclaim the existence of entities that might best be called "folk ideologies," nor do we deny for a moment that strong differentiations in a variety of narrower values may be found within subcultures of less educated people. Yet for the familiar belief systems that, in view of their historical importance, tend most to attract the sophisticated observer, it is likely that an adequate mapping of a society (or, for that matter, the world) would provide a jumbled cluster of pyramids or a mountain range, with sharp delineation and differentiation in beliefs from elite apex to elite apex but with the mass bases of the pyramids overlapping in such profusion that it would be impossible to decide where one pyramid ended and another began.

NOTES

1. Karl Mannheim, *Ideology and Utopia* (New York, 1946), especially pp. 39 ff.
2. Minar has compiled a useful if discouraging survey of this diversity. See David W. Minar, "Ideology and Political Behavior," *Midwest Journal of Political Science,* V (November, 1961), No. 4, 317-31.
3. Garner uses the term "constraint" to mean "the amount of interrelatedness of structure of a system of variables" when measured by degree of uncertainty reduction. Wendell R. Garner, *Uncertainty and Structure as Psychological Concepts* (New York, 1962), pp. 142ff. We use the term a bit more broadly as relief from such polysyllables as "interrelatedness" and "interdependence."
4. Measures of correlation and indices of the goodness of fit of a cumulative scale model to a body of data are measures of two types of constraint.
5. Definitions of belief systems frequently require that configurations of ideas be stable for individuals over long periods of time. The notion of centrality fulfills this requirement in a more flexible way. That is, once it is granted that changes in the perceived status of idea-elements are not frequent in any event and that, when change does occur, the central elements (particularly in large belief systems) are amply cushioned by more peripheral elements that can be adjusted, it follows that central elements are indeed likely to be highly stable.
6. Minar, *loc. cit.*
7. See A. Campbell, P. E. Converse, W. Miller, and D. Stokes, *The American Voter* (New York, 1960), pp. 204-9.
8. William J. McGuire, "A Syllogistic Analysis of Cognitive Relationships," in Milton J. Rosenberg, Carl I. Hovland, William J. McGuire, Robert P. Abelson, and Jack W. Brehm, *Attitude Organization and Change,* Yale Studies in Attitude and Communication, Vol. 3 (New Haven, 1960), pp. 65-111.
9. Joseph R. Gusfield, "Status Conflicts and the Changing Ideologies of the American Temperance Movement," in Pittman and Snyder, eds., *Society, Culture and Drinking Patterns* (New York, 1962).
10. Anthony Downs, *An Economic Theory of Democracy* (New York, 1957), p. 79.
11. It should be understood that our information dimension is not so perfectly correlated with formal education as this statement implies. Since educational strata have a more ready intuitive meaning, however, we shall use them occasionally as convenient ways of measuring off levels in the population. In such cases, the reader may keep in mind that there are always some people of lesser education but higher political involvement who are numbered in the stratum and some people with education befitting the stratum who are not numbered there because their interests lie elsewhere and their information about politics is less than could be expected.
12. There is a difference, of course, between this statement and a suggestion that poorly educated people have no systems of belief about politics.
13. This observation is valid despite the fact that surveys showing ignorance of crucial political facts are much more likely to run in a range from 40–80% "unaware." At the height of the 1958 Berlin crisis, 63% of the American public did not know that the city was encircled by hostile troops. A figure closer to 70% is a good estimate of the proportion of the public that does not know which party controls Congress.
14. In this regard, it was enlightening to read the stunned reactions of the political columnist Joseph Alsop when, during the 1960 presidential primaries, he left the elite circuits of the East Coast and ventured from door to door talking politics with "normal" people in West Virginia. He was frank to admit that the change in perceived political worlds was far greater than anything he had ever anticipated, despite his prior recognition that there would be some difference.
15. The phrase "less adequately" is used to show recognition of the frequent complaint

that the liberal-conservative dimension has different meanings in different politics at different times. More importantly, it takes into account the fact that in most politics new issues are constantly arising that are difficult before the fact to relate to such a yardstick. Some of these intrinsically "orthogonal" issues may remain unrelated to the dimension, and, if they become of intense importance, they can split existing parties and redefine alignments. More typically, however, elites that are known on some other grounds to be "liberal" or "conservative" ferret out some limited aspect of an issue for which they can argue some liberal-conservative relevance and begin to drift to one of the alternative positions in disproportionate numbers. Then, either because of the aspect highlighted or because of simple pressures toward party competition, their adversaries drift toward the opposing position. Thus positions come to be perceived as "liberal" or "conservative," even though such alignments would have been scarcely predictable on logical grounds. After the fact, of course, the alignments come to seem "logical," by mechanisms discussed earlier in this paper. Controversy over British entry into the European Common Market is an excellent example of such a process. Currently the conservatives are officially pro-entry, and Labour leadership has finally declared against it, but the reverse of this alignment had frequently been predicted when the issue was embryonic.

16. All American data reported in this paper, unless otherwise noted, have been collected by the Survey Research Center of The University of Michigan under grants from the Carnegie Corporation, the Rockefeller Foundation, and the Social Science Research Council.

17. This account of the "levels of conceptualization" is highly abbreviated. For a much more detailed discussion and rationale, along with numerous illustrations drawn at random from interviews in each stratum, see Campbell, et al., op. cit., Chapter 10.

18. Some modest internal support for the validity of the distinction between those who spoke in terms of broad philosophy and those who offered narrower explanations may be seen in the fact that only 5% of the former category had previously judged the Democrats to be more conservative than the Republicans. Among those giving less elevated "best answers," 14% deemed the Democrats the more conservative party. And, to give some sense of the "continental shelf" being explored here, among those who had responded that a certain party was more conservative than the other but who subsequently confessed that they did not know what the distinction implied, 35% had chosen the Democrats as the more conservative, a figure that is beginning to approach the 50–50 assignment of sheer guesswork.

19. In all candor, it should probably be mentioned that a teacher grading papers would be unlikely to give passing marks to more than 20% of the attempted definitions (or to 10% of the total sample) We made an effort, however, to be as generous as possible in our assignments.

20. This cell is laden, of course, with people who are apathetic and apolitical, although more than half of them vote in major elections. Flanigan, working with the total sample, set aside those who never vote as politically inconsequential and then set about comparing the remainder of self-styled independents with strong partisans. Some of the customary findings relating political independence with low involvement and low information then became blurred or in some cases reversed themselves altogether. Our highly sophisticated independents contribute to this phenomenon. See William H. Flanigan, "Partisanship and Campaign Participation" (Unpublished doctoral dissertation, Yale University, 1961).

21. As a general rule, questions broad enough for the mass public to understand tend to be too simple for highly sophisticated people to feel comfortable answering without elaborate qualification. The pairing of questions, with those for the mass public given first, are as follows:

Employment. "The government in Washington ought to see to it that everybody who wants to work can find a job." "Do you think the federal government ought to sponsor programs such as large public works in order to maintain full employment, or do you think that problems of economic readjustment ought to be left more to private industry or state and local government?"

Aid to Education. "If cities and towns around the country need help to build more schools, the government in Washington ought to give them the money they need." "Do you think the government should provide grants to the states for the construction and operation of public schools, or do you think the support of public education should be left entirely to the state and local government?"

Federal Housing. "The government should leave things like electric power and housing for private businessmen to handle." "Do you approve the use of federal funds for public housing, or do you generally feel that housing can be taken care of better by private effort?"

F.E.P.C. "If Negroes are not getting fair treatment in jobs and housing, the government should see to it that they do." "Do you think the federal government should establish a fair employment practices commission to prevent discrimination in employment?"

Economic Aid. "The United States should give economic help to the poorer countries of the world even if those countries can't pay for it." "First, on the foreign economic aid program, would you generally favor expanding the program, reducing it, or maintaining it about the way it is?"

Military Aid. "The United States should keep soldiers overseas where they can help countries that are against Communism." "How about the foreign military aid program? Should this be expanded, reduced, or maintained about as it is?"

Isolationism. "This country would be better off if we just stayed home and did not concern ourselves with problems in other parts of the world." "Speaking very generally, do you think that in the years ahead the United States should maintain or reduce its commitments around the world?"

22. We are aware that drawing an average of these coefficients has little intepretation from a statistical point of view. The averages are presented merely as a crude way of capturing the flavor of the larger table in summary form. More generally, it could be argued that the coefficients might be squared in any event, an operation that would do no more than heighten the intuitive sense of contrast between the two publics. In this format, for example, the elite-mass difference in the domestic-issue column of Table VIII would shift from .53 *vs.* .23 to .28 *vs.* .05. Similarly, that in the party column would become .15 *vs.* .01.

23. Herbert McClosky, "Consensus and Ideology in American Politics," *American Political Science Review*, LVIII (June, 1964), No. 2.

24. James W. Prothro and C. W. Grigg, "Fundamental Principles of Democracy: Bases of Agreement and Disagreement," *Journal of Politics*, 22 (May, 1960), No. 2, 276-94.

25. There is unquestionably a class of social behaviors for which this description is more rather than less apt, although one need not have recourse to mystical or unexplained terms to understand the processes involved. In any social system, some beliefs and behavior patterns are learned by the young in such a way that there is no awareness of the possibility of alternatives. Where beliefs are concerned, a phrase like "unspoken cultural assumptions" provides an appropriate description, and there are analogues in socially learned behaviors. Most of politics, however, involves competition between explicit alternatives, which means that conscious belief systems and conscious behavior choices have an important influence—which is *not* to say that these belief systems are not often better understood if one takes account of the sociostructural position of the actor who holds them. It *is* to say that, whether or not they are present is not a matter of indifference for the course of behavior, as we shall see.

26. The reader is cautioned, in comparing Figures 1(b) and 1(c), that women classed (for example) as "no issue content" are not necessarily the wives of husbands who are also "no issue content." Indeed, the point of the comparison is that wives tend themselves to be qualified at less elevated levels than their husbands but organize their behavior in terms of their husband's "opinion leadership."

27. It should be remembered in assessing Figure 1(c) that the complete absence of this kind of opinion-leading would not produce a graph with a single tall bar at the left and an absence of height for the three other bars. That is, opinion-leading quite aside, we should expect some kind of slope, albeit a steep one, since people represented by the second and (to a fainter degree) the third bars have cruder versions of the intervening images of politics that we are arguing have key behavioral importance. It is only the people represented by the fourth bar who give no evidence of this type of intervening organization at all.

28. The empirical base for this argument becomes even more dramatic than is shown by Figure 1 if we consider all the psychological terms that a class orientation in voting presupposes. That is, Figure 1 treats the relationship between objective status and vote. To the degree that there are ideologues whose class identifications are not what their objective statuses would lead us to expect, they lower the degree of the association. Figure 13-3 of Campbell, *et al., op. cit.,* p. 352, which is conceptually parallel to Figure 1 of this paper, shows that ideologues with reported awareness of their social classes have a towering monopoly on the association of *subjective status* and vote partisanship.

29. Much of the ensuing passage can be read as a slight restatement of Herbert Hyman's insights concerning "reference groups." If we add anything at all, it is to suggest some of the circumstances under which groups *qua* groups are more or less likely to be central in individual belief systems (more or less potent as points of reference), as opposed to other kinds of belief object.

30. Florian Znaniecki, *Modern Nationalities* (Urbana, 1952), pp. 81-2.

31. Even in the modern United States, there are scattered pockets of the population that are rather vague about national identity. We encounter respondents, for example, who when asked if they were born in the United States, answer "No, I was born in Georgia," in what is clearly ignorance rather than a throwback to secession or kittenish state pride.

32. McClosky observes more generally: "Members of the active minority" [the political

elite sample] "are far better able than the ordinary voter to name reference groups that fit both their party affiliation and their doctrinal orientation. . . . Clearly the political stratum has a much better idea than the public has of where its political sympathies lie and who its ideological friends and enemies are. The ability to recognize favorable or unfavorable reference groups is, on the whole, poorly developed in the populace at large." McClosky, *op. cit.*

33. With regard to the postwar increase in relevance of social class, see Philip E. Converse, "The Shifting Role of Class in Political Attitudes and Behavior," in E. L. Maccoby, T. W. Newcomb, and E. E. Hartley, eds., *Readings in Social Psychology* (New York, 1958), p. 388.

34. The items portrayed in Figure 3 are the same as those in Table VII and are described at that point.

35. We regret that we did not get measures of pure affect for other groupings in the population, for all population members. A copious literature on intergroup attitudes in social psychology contains, however, much presumptive evidence of extreme stability in these attitudes over time.

36. Unfortunately we lack the longitudinal data for elites that would permit the following analysis to be comparative. Let us keep in mind, however, that the relatively high constraint among belief elements already demonstrated for elites is almost certain proof of high stability of these elements over time as well. The phenomenon we are analyzing is thus a mass not an elite phenomenon.

37. More technically, such a configuration is mathematically incompatible with the assumption based on simple Markov chain theory that a single matrix of transition probabilities can account for the change process. For the benefit of the nontechnical reader, we use the phrase "change process" in the singular to denote a single specified matrix of transition probabilities.

38. This model has been discussed as a hypothetical case in Lee M. Wiggins, "Mathematical Models for the Interpretation of Attitude and Behavior Change: The Analysis of Multi-Wave Panels" (Unpublished doctoral dissertation, Columbia University, 1955).

39. The logic of the test is rather simple. If the model pertains, then any respondents who change sides of an issue between t_1 and t_2 are from the random part of the population, while those who do not change sides are a mixture in known proportions of perfectly stable people and random people who happened to have chosen the same side twice by chance. If we divide the population into these two parts on the basis of their t_1-t_2 patterns and if the model is appropriate to the situation, then the turnover correlations between t_2 and t_3 for each of the two divisions of the population are determinate. The purely random group should show a correlation of .00 between t_2 and t_3; the adulterated stable group should show a correlation that falls short of unity as a direct function of the known proportions of random people still in the group. For our critical test, the original total-population turnover correlation (1956-1958) was .24. With the population properly subdivided as suggested by the model, this over-all correlation could be expected to fork into two correlations between t_2 and t_3 of .00 and .47, *if the model was applicable.* The empirical values turned out to be .004 and .49.

40. For instance, in terms parallel to the expectations of the final sentence of Note 39, the correlations may fork into a pair that are .07 and .35, rather than .00 and .47.

41. For example, a random path of responses would be laid down over time by a set of people for whom the content of the item was very meaningful, yet put each individual in such a quandary that his pro-con response potential balanced exactly at .50-.50. In such cases, it could be assumed that slight rewording of the item, making it "harder" or "easier" in a Guttman sense, would shift the response potentials away from this .50-.50 balance and would thus begin to produce correlations between individual responses over time. This view cannot be challenged in any decisive way for issues generating responses that depart from our black and white model, since, in these cases, a distribution of the population continuously across the total range of response probabilities is entirely compatible with the data. It is even possible to describe the empirical situation surrounding the private-enterprise item in these terms. The problem is that such a description seems patently absurd, for it implies that the question was somehow constructed so that the content drew highly unequivocal responses from one class of people but left all the rest in perfect and exquisite conflict. Intermediate classes—people with probabilities of responding to the content positively at a level of .6, .7, .8 or .9—are simply not necessary to account for the data. Such a description lacks verisimilitude. Our assumption is rather that, had the private-enterprise item been rendered "harder" or "easier" in a Guttman sense, the respondents we call "random" would have *continued* to respond randomly, at least across a zone of items so broad as to bracket any plausible political alternatives. In other words, the problem is not one of specific wording that puts the respondent in particularly delicate conflict; it is rather that the whole area from which this item is drawn is so remote to the respondent that he has not been stimulated to any real opinion formation within it.

42. Results of this sort lend considerable weight to Scott's proposals for assessing cultural values through analysis of responses to open-ended questions. William A. Scott, "Empirical Assessment of Values and Ideologies," *American Sociological Review,* 24 (June, 1959), No. 3, 299-310.

43. The definition of these boundaries is necessarily crude. While we have means of improving upon it in the future, it rests for the moment upon the exclusion of those people with unstable opinions, along with those who at one point or another confessed that they had no opinions. We know that each public, so defined, contains some respondents who give stable patterns of response by chance alone and therefore do not belong in the issue-public conceptually. On the other hand, for those issues where it is necessary to posit some small "third force" undergoing conversion on the issue, these people are inadvertently overlooked. Nonetheless, these two contingents appear to be small, and the issue-public boundaries are thus roughly accurate.

44. And if we take as a goal the explanation of political *changes* touched off by movements in mass political decisions in this period, as opposed to questions of more static political structure, then the explanatory utility of the social-class thread is almost nil, for the ideological class voters were least likely to have contributed to these changes by corresponding changes in their voting patterns.

45. P. E. Converse and G. Dupeux, "Politicization of the Electorate in France and the United States," *Public Opinion Quarterly,* 26 (Spring, 1962). For complementary evidence covering an earlier period, see Duncan MacRae, "Religious and Socioeconomic Factors in the French Vote, 1945-1956," *American Journal of Sociology,* LXIV (November, 1958), No. 3.

46. This figure is for 1840, and it undoubtedly advanced further in the next decade or two, although one deduces that the expansion of membership slowed down after 1840. Our estimates do not take into account, however, the standard inflation of claimed membership (intentional or unintentional) that seems to characterize all movements of this sort.

47. S. A. Stouffer, *Communism, Conformity and Civil Liberties* (New York, 1955).

48. Campbell, *et al., op. cit.,* pp 50-51.

49. In 1954, the average circulation of daily newspapers amounted to about 20% more papers than households. In 1850, one newspaper had to stretch across five households. These estimates are calculated from Bureau of the Census figures in *Historical Statistics of the United States* (Washington, D.C., 1961).

50. Informal communication from Professor Robert L. Crane.

51. We set aside Pennsylvania, Delaware, and Maryland, all of which had been slow in moving toward complete abolition and which tended to follow southern voting patterns through the election of 1856.

52. A simple ordering of potentially abolitionist states according to apparent success in transfer of 1852 Free-Soil and Whig votes to the Republicans in 1856 is negatively correlated with an ordering of these states according to the relative amount of fringe support they had tended to contribute to the abolitionist parties of the 1840s.

53. Reinhard Bendix. "Social Stratification and Political Power," in Bendix and S. M. Lipset, eds., *Class, Status and Power* (New York, 1953), pp. 596-609.

54. Bendix, *ibid.,* pp. 604-5.

55. Rudolf Heberle, *From Democracy to Nazism* (Baton Rouge, 1945). See also Charles P. Loomis and J. Allen Beegle, "The Spread of German Nazism to Rural Areas," *American Sociological Review,* 11 (December, 1946), 724-34.

56. See Campbell *et al., op. cit.,* Chap. 15. The above remarks on the Nazi movement are a condensation of a case study originally written as part of this chapter.

57. The most extreme shifts to the Nazis, arriving at a peak of between 80 and 100% of the votes in some hamlets, occurred in the central zone of Schleswig-Holstein, the *Geest.* To the East and West lay the sea, a somewhat more cosmopolitan coast, better farmland with larger estates, and a more stratified rural population. While the farmers of the *Geest* owned their own family farms and have been designated as "lower middle class," they appear to have been subsistence farmers on land that did not interest gentry. Heberle describes them as being "in mentality and habits still more of a real peasant" than farmers in the other sectors, who regarded the *Geest* farmer "very much as the Southern hillbilly or redneck is looked upon by the planters." Heberle, *ibid.,* p. 39.

58. Heberle and others have argued that the Nazi Party had particular appeal for villagers and rural people living in simple *gemeinschaft* societies because it demanded a degree of active and disciplined participation not required by other parties and such rural folk had a need to give themselves totally to a cause. At another point, however, Heberle implies that, although Schleswig-Holstein was the "most Nazi" province at the polls in both 1930 and 1932, it contributed but a meager share of activists or members to the party. See Heberle, *ibid.,* p. 87. What the mass base of the Nazi Party in its urban and rural segments seemed to share, in addition to a desperate desire for a change that would

bring respite from economic duress, was low education or, in the case of the young, low political sophistication.

59. Heberle, *ibid.*, pp. 100, 124.

60. This is not to challenge the importance of a lengthening democratic tradition or of the bearing of its absence in the German case. But we suspect that once beyond the stabilizing influence of mass identifications with standard parties, the primary salutary effects of a longer democratic tradition are limited to elite political processes. Two hundred years of democracy and several decades of elementary civics courses in the United States have not given the model citizen much capacity to recognize antidemocratic maneuvers and movements, particularly when they occur "at home."

61. Heberle, *ibid.*, p. 112.

62. All investigators have had success in showing high "achievement motivation" among American Jews (a remarkably well educated group). Furthermore, some early findings confirmed Weber's thesis, in a modern setting, by showing higher achievement motivation among Protestants than among Catholics. Veroff, Feld, and Gurin, working with a national sample, were able, however, to replicate these findings only among higher-status Catholics and Protestants (with income the criterion) in the Northeast. This more sophisticated subpopulation is alleged to be the one within which the original confirmations were found. See J. Veroff, S. Feld, and G. Gurin, "Achievement Motivation and Religious Background," *American Sociological Review*, 27 (April, 1962), No. 2, 205. While even poorly educated adherents of differing creeds can probably be counted on for fairly accurate knowledge of concrete matters of ritual and mundane taboos, they would be much less likely to absorb the broad and abstract theological conceptions that are the crucial "intervening variables" in the Weberian hypothesis.

America's Radical Right:
Politics and Ideology*

BY *RAYMOND E. WOLFINGER, BARBARA KAYE WOLFINGER,*
KENNETH PREWITT, AND *SHEILAH ROSENHACK*

EXTREME RIGHT-WING movements have been a recurring feature of American political life. The antilibertarian pronouncements and tactics of these movements, as well as the frequently deviant character of their demands, lead many observers to consider them a threat to prevailing political values. For the most part, their influence has not been enduring at the national level. They seem to have their greatest success in local communities, chiefly in intimidating educators and librarians. But at every level of government these movements influence the course of events by distracting and limiting political discussion. The profound dissatisfactions they express seem to reflect deep stresses in American society. For this reason, social scientists have tried to understand the sources of right-wing extremism and to discern the characteristics of the people who are attracted to it.

The manifestation of this political tendency in the early 1960s is known as the radical right. It has attracted much scholarly and journalistic attention.[1] While a good deal is known about the radical right's organizations, doctrines, tactics, and leaders, there is little information, albeit much speculation, about the composition and motivations of its following. This article describes a study of the attitudes, political behavior, and demographic characteristics of 308 people who attended and supported an "Anti-Communism School" presented by the Christian Anti-Communism Crusade in Oakland, California, early in 1962.

* The authors are more than ordinarily indebted to people whose generosity and skill aided them at every stage of this research. Hugh Schwartz played an important role in planning the data collection, which was done by an unusually talented and dedicated group of students at Stanford University. At succeeding stages, we profited greatly from the advice of Bo Anderson, Adam Haber, and Morris Zelditch, Jr. Ian Dengler and Peter Lyman kindly volunteered their services for coding. Charles E. Lindblom, Dean Manheimer, Nelson W. Polsby, Martin Shapiro, Aaron Wildavsky, and Professor Zelditch made many helpful comments on earlier drafts of this article. Drs. Fred C. Schwarz and Joost Sluis graciously gave free tickets to the interviewers. Additional financial support was provided by the Stanford Committee for Research on Public Affairs, the Dean of the Stanford Graduate School, and the Stanford Computation Center. A previous version of this article was read at the 1963 Annual Meeting of the American Political Science Association in New York City.

I. The Christian Anti-Communism Crusade

The numerous groups on the radical right express a wide range of policy proposals and a variety of perceptions of the political world. All of them share a central concern with communism. To the radical right, the main communist danger does not come from the Soviet Union and Communist China or from the appeal of communism to the underdeveloped nations. Instead, rightists emphasize the threat of domestic communism. They tend to attribute unacceptable events to communist influence and to characterize their critics as communists or dupes. This preoccupation with the danger and pervasiveness of communism has come to be the defining characteristic of the radical right.

Among the dozens of groups and leaders of the radical right, only Robert Welch and his John Birch Society have attracted more attention than the Christian Anti-Communism Crusade and its president, Dr. Fred C. Schwarz.[2] The Crusade's manifest objective is to fight communism by means of radio and television broadcasts, rallies, banquets, pamphlets, and other techniques. At the peak of its popularity, it had a paid staff of thirty in its southern California headquarters and an annual income in excess of $1 million.[3] By early 1963, more than a million copies had been sold of Dr. Schwarz's book, *You Can Trust the Communists*,[4] the primary source of Crusade doctrine. "Schools" are the Crusade's best known activities. Sponsored by local *ad hoc* committees and staffed by a dozen or more experienced speakers, these affairs have been held in a number of cities, most successfully in the area extending from southern California to the Gulf Coast.

Almost every social scientist or journalist who has described the Crusade considers it a radical-right organization. Schwarz vigorously denies this contention. He insists that the Crusade is a nonpolitical educational organization dedicated to promoting the proposition that communism is a monstrous threat and to encouraging people to fight it through "a continued program of study and applied citizenship to transform acquired knowledge into local, national and international programs."[5] There are good reasons for skepticism about Schwarz's protestations. The speakers at Crusade schools usually have an intemperate style seldom associated with educational activities. Some are well known for advocacy of measures to restrict freedom of expression in the name of anticommunism.[6] Crusade speakers often suggest or allege that secret communist influence lies behind many sorts of behavior, from foreign-policy decisions to the authorship of *Lolita*.[7] Although Schwarz chooses these "faculty members," he disclaims responsibility for them, explaining that they have academic freedom and that "the viewpoint expressed by every speaker is not necessarily the official policy of the school."[8]

The inevitable corollary of the central Crusade message is an insinuation of major communist penetration of American institutions.[9] Schwarz has predicted that at the communists' present rate of progress, they will win control of the world by 1973.[10] He suggests that this progress is so advanced that Americans are reluctant to express anticommunist sentiments openly. In this alarming situation, Schwarz sees his own role as crucial. Contemplating an impending Crusade school, he said, "many are praying that this event will mark a turning-point in the heretofore disastrous battle with Communism."[11] His assessment of a completed school: "For the first time the forces of the Communist appeasers are on the defensive. People are proud to be classed as anti-Communists."[12] Schwarz commonly suggests that criticism of the Crusade is a function of communist influence.[13]

Crusade officials estimate that the organization has inspired the formation of more than 5000 local "study groups."[14] The only available information about these groups comes from two psychologists who belonged to one of them in Ann Arbor, Michigan.[15] They report that the group's programs were largely indoctrinations in such radical right-wing doctrines as the pervasiveness of communist influence in American life revealed by progressive education, fluoridated water, Supreme Court decisions, and so forth. The other group members shared these views of the world.

There is some conjecture that the main effect of the Crusade is to activate potential recruits of organizations that have more explicit extremist doctrines and more direct action programs than the Crusade itself. Robert Welch has said, "Dr. Schwarz is doing a grand job of waking up people to the Communist menace. Many of our members help to set up Dr. Schwarz's schools . . . and we frankly do our best to take the people who have been stirred up and awakened and alarmed by him to get them together into the John Birch Society as action groups to do something about it all."[16] In Michigan, Crusade study groups are working with an organization called Freedom-in-Action. This organization, based in Houston, has a rather extreme ideology.[17]

We have described the Crusade in some detail because of Schwarz's contention that it is not a right-wing organization. Actually, even some of his followers seem to disagree with him. We asked the ninety-four pro-Schwarz respondents who were personally interviewed what other organizations were active in the same cause as the Crusade. Unfortunately, fifty of these respondents either claimed that they did not know of any similar organizations or refused to answer the question. But of those who did answer, 82% named right-wing groups, chiefly the John Birch Society.

II. The Research

The San Francisco Bay Region School of Anti-Communism was held in the Oakland Auditorium from January 29 through February 2, 1962. Tuition for the week was $20. Ministers, teachers, students, policemen, firemen, and servicemen were admitted for half price. A number of free passes (called "scholarships" by Dr. Schwarz) were distributed; almost 30% of our respondents did not pay for their tickets. Classes ran from 9 a.m. to 10 p.m., with breaks for lunch and dinner. The faculty included Senator Thomas Dodd (D. Conn.), Representative Walter H. Judd (R. Minn.), and a variety of speakers from the right-wing circuit. Dr. Schwarz spoke in the mornings and evenings. Evening classes were televised.

The school was preceded by an extensive publicity campaign, featuring a number of appearances around the Bay Area by Dr. Schwarz. At one of these appearances, he suggested that San Francisco was a particularly appropriate locale for his school because Nikita Khrushchev had selected the city's Mark Hopkins Hotel as the site for his headquarters when the Soviet Union took over the United States in 1973.[18]

Previous Crusade schools evidently had not encountered much local opposition. But in the San Francisco area the school met a barrage of criticism. One newspaper was vociferously and conspicuously hostile, two were cool, and only the Knowland family's *Oakland Tribune* gave the school enthusiastic backing and a great deal of space. The Northern California-Nevada Council of Churches, the Alameda County Central Labor Council, the Attorney General of California, and several groups of prominent citizens publicly denounced the school. The secretary of the local *ad hoc* school committee resigned with an attack on the organization. At the end of the school, when it was clear that it was not so successful as had been hoped, the chairman of the *ad hoc* committee attributed this disappointment partly to the Communist Party's alleged strength in the Bay Area.[19]

The controversy surrounding the school probably had the effect of providing cues about the school's place on the political spectrum, and thus reducing the number of nonconservatives who attended. Conversely, it probably enhanced the rightist composition of the student body.

We used two methods of data collection, personal interviews and a mail questionnaire. Most of the questions in these instruments were taken from The University of Michigan Survey Research Center's national election studies, Samuel A. Stouffer's research of a decade ago for *Communism, Conformity and Civil Liberties*,[20] and Martin Trow's study of attitudes toward Senator Joseph McCarthy in Bennington, Vermont.[21] We thus had normative data with which we compared our respondents' replies. The questions in our personal interviews and mail questionnaires were similar, but the latter contained additional items on political activities and attitudes.

The interviewing and the distribution of questionnaires were carried out by the authors and by students in an advanced undergraduate seminar in political science at Stanford University. The students were briefed on interviewing techniques and conducted practice interviews prior to the data collection. The interviews for this study were conducted during the afternoon and evening of the second day of the school. The mail questionnaires, covering letters describing our project as a manifestation of Stanford students' interest in the political opinions of their elders, and stamped envelopes addressed to the Stanford Department of Political Science were distributed on the second and three subsequent days of the school's operation.

A description of our reception at the school will aid understanding of both the character of the audience and the limitations of our data. There were several factors in our favor: Although Dr. Schwarz had given us free tickets, he was unaware that we were interested in his audience rather than in his message until we had collected a good many interviews and had attracted the attention of the press.[22] A number of respondents evidently felt that, since Schwarz had given us "scholarships," he approved of our research. Stanford has a respectable, upper-class reputation in the Bay Area. The interviewers' wholesome, youthful appearance seemed to evoke a desire on the part of many respondents to "save" them from the malign influence of subversive professors.

Observation of the atmosphere at the school made it clear that it would be necessary for our interviewers to abandon the customary researcher's air of impartiality if we were to gather much data. The Stanford students clapped when the audience did and rose for the numerous standing ovations.

Nevertheless, we encountered suspicion, hostility, and abuse. It appeared that the greatest immediate causes of these responses were the interviewers' academic connections and their clipboards, which suggested to the Crusaders that petitions were being circulated.[23] Most of the unfriendly remarks were made before the interviewers could say more than a few words or were volunteered by people who had not been approached. The undergraduates bore the brunt of these accusations, but, in some instances, they were regarded merely as dupes of their professor. Some Crusaders evidently assumed that since he was a professor he was also a communist, but one claimed more specific knowledge, telling one interviewer that the latter's Stanford instructor had been the leader of a local communist front for the past seven years.

We were unable to use systematic sampling methods in this situation. Strictly speaking, we do not have a sample, and, therefore, we shall not use tests for significance of difference. Interviewers were instructed to pick potential respondents to "represent" the audience in terms of age, sex, and style of dress. They tried to avoid choosing only people who seemed most willing to be interviewed. They also tried to avoid interviewing or giving questionnaires to minors or more than one person in a family. (Questionnaires inadvertently given to minors have been excluded from the analysis.) About forty people refused to be interviewed, and about 100 refused even to accept mail questionnaires. Since these refusals often were accompanied by invective and accusations of subversive intent, it is likely that the most extreme members of the audience are underrepresented in our sample. Those who refused appeared to be no different from the respondents in age, sex, dress, or manner of speech.

One hundred and eight personal interviews were completed. About 625 mail questionnaires were distributed, of which 244, or 39%, were returned. The attitudinal and demographic findings on the mail and personal samples are virtually identical. It is possible, however, that the educational distribution in each group is skewed upward: in the mail-questionnaire group for the obvious reason that such instruments are more congenial to the educated and in the personal-interview group because the undergraduates may have tended, despite instructions, to approach people who appeared closest to themselves in socioeconomic status. There is no way of knowing how representative of the population attending the school our "sample" is. Several independent observers, including a newspaper reporter, have estimated that about 2000 people came to one or more sessions of the school. While the representativeness of our sample is unknown, our respondents therefore constitute a good proportion of the total population.[24]

Eighty-eight per cent of the respondents said that they were in favor of Schwarz and the Crusade. The following analysis is based on the attitudes and characteristics of these 308 supporters of the Crusade, of whom ninety-four were interviewed and 214 completed and returned mail questionnaires. Previous empirical studies of radical rightists and McCarthyites have been concerned with respondents who, in one form or another, expressed approval of the John Birch Society or of Senator McCarthy. Our respondents meet a stronger test—they are not passive supporters of the Crusade but active participants. They were concerned enough to attend the school, in most cases at some cost in money and time.

Four cautions must be expressed against generalizing from our data to the contemporary radical right as a whole: The Crusade's name and some aspects of its publicity tactics probably minimize its attraction to Catholics and Jews and maximize its appeal to devout Protestants; the Crusade does not take positions on many public issues and therefore has a more generic appeal than many other radical-right groups; compared to many of these organizations, the Crusade is rather moderate; while attendance at the Oakland school demonstrated more than passive endorsement of the Crusade, it was a relatively mild form of activity compared to putting cards on Polish hams, forming discussion groups, or disrupting PTA meetings.

III. Demographic Characteristics of the Respondents

This sample is strikingly different from the San Francisco Bay Area population with respect to demographic characteristics. Although 12% of the area's population is Negro and Oriental, all our respondents are white.[25] In attending the school for five days, we saw no more than a handful of nonwhites.

The Crusaders are predominantly an upper-status group. More than half are businessmen or professionals or have husbands in such occupations;[26] this proportion is twice that found in the white Bay Area population. Forty-one per cent of the Crusaders reported annual family incomes in excess of $10,000, compared to 26% of the Bay Area population. Almost 80% have attended college, and 52% have been graduated. This figure is exactly four times the percentage of college graduates in the adult white population of the area. The sample contains a somewhat disproportionate number of people over the age of fifty. These data are summarized in Table I.

Slightly more than three-quarters of the Crusaders are Protestants. Only 8% are Catholics, compared to about 24% of the white Bay Area population.[27] The Crusaders' rate of church attendance is quite similar to that of northern white Protestants who have attended college.[28] In sum, these data suggest that the Crusade's appeal is to the well educated and well-to-do.[29]

Seymour M. Lipset has analyzed California Poll data on attitudes toward the John Birch Society.[30] He reports that "A supporter of the Society is more likely . . . to be better educated, and to be in a higher economic category."[31] His findings are consistent with ours, with one exception: He found that Catholics were slightly more likely than Protestants to endorse the Birch Society. This difference may be due to the religious aspects of the Crusade's image. This point should be kept in mind as an important qualification of generalizations about the radical right on the basis of our data.

IV. The Crusaders' Political and Attitudinal Characteristics

The Crusaders are almost unanimously Republican in their voting behavior. Ninety-two per cent of those who voted in the 1960 presidential

TABLE I — Demographic Characteristics of the Sample and the White Bay Area Population

	Crusaders N = 308	White residents of the Bay Area[a]
Occupation of head of household[b]		
Professional and technical	31%	14%
Businessmen, managers, and officials	27	12
Clerical and sales personnel	14	17
Skilled, semiskilled, unskilled, and service workers	11	50
Other	6	1
No answer	11	6
	100%	100%
Annual family income before taxes		
$15,000 and over	21%	8%
$10,000 to $14,999	20	18
$7,000 to $9,999	22	28
$4,000 to $6,999	20	30
Below $4,000	9	16
No answer	8[c]	—
	100%	100%
Education[d]		
Completed college	52%	13%
Some college	26	14
Completed high school	11	29
Some high school	5	19
Grammar school or less	3	25
No answer	3	—
	100%	100%
Age[e]		
Under fifty years old	52%	64%
Fifty years old and over	45	36
No answer	3	—
	100%	100%

a. Source: U.S. Bureau of the Census, *U.S. Census of Population: 1960, General Social and Economic Characteristics. California. Final Report PC (1)-6C* (Washington: U.S.G.P.O., 1962).

b. Bay Area occupation data are for all employed males, including nonwhites.

c. Most of these respondents had high-income occupations.

d. Normative data are for people twenty-five years old and older.

e. Normative data are for all white urban residents of California twenty-years old and older.

election supported Richard M. Nixon. Sixty-six per cent of the Crusaders identified themselves as Republicans, 19% as independents, and 8% as Democrats.[32] Furthermore, they lean toward the conservative wing of the Republican Party. When asked to choose between Nixon and Senator Barry Goldwater for the 1964 Republican presidential nomination, 58% of those who chose one of the two men picked Goldwater. When our data were collected, Nixon was by far the leading candidate, in the nation as a whole, for the 1964 nomination. At about this time, the Gallup organization asked a national sample of Republicans to choose among ten leading contenders for the 1964 Republican nomination. Forty-six per cent chose Nixon, and 13% picked Goldwater.[33] It seemed possible that the Crusaders' preference for Goldwater might have been even higher, except for Nixon's long participation in California politics. Many of the old-time Californians in our sample may, in assessing the two candidates, think of Nixon chiefly in his former role as the scourge of domestic communists. Accordingly, we analyzed preferences for the two men by length of residence in the Bay Area. As Table II indicates, we found that respondents who had lived in the Bay Area since the beginning of Nixon's career split about evenly in their support of the two men, while newcomers to the area were two to one for Goldwater.[34]

TABLE II — Preference for Nixon or Goldwater as Republican Presidential Candidate in 1964—by Crusaders' Length of Residence in the Bay Area

| | Crusaders who have lived in the Bay Area[a] | |
	16 years or less	More than 16 years
Prefer Goldwater	66%	47%
Prefer Nixon	34	53
	100%	100%
N	115	111

a. "No answers" and "no preference" responses have been removed from the bases.

In addition to their Republican inclinations, the Crusaders are united in their fears of internal subversion. When asked, "How great a danger do you feel that American Communists are to this country at the present time?" nine out of ten Crusaders replied "great" or "very great," as Table III indicates. This figure is double the proportion of college-educated respondents who made such replies in Stouffer's study, which was conducted at the height of the McCarthy period.

TABLE III — Perceptions of the Internal Communist Threat by Crusaders and College-Educated Americans, 1954

Think internal Communist threat is	Crusaders	College-educated Americans[a]
A very great danger	66%	18%
A great danger	21	24
Some danger	9	43
Hardly any danger	2	10
No danger	—	2
Don't know and no answer	2	3
	100%	100%
N	308	485

a. Source: data from the national survey conducted by the National Opinion Research Center in 1954 for Stouffer's study of attitudes toward communism and civil liberties, obtained from the Inter-University Consortium for Political Research.

Seventy-one per cent of our respondents said that the danger to this country from domestic communists is greater than the danger from the Soviet Union and Communist China.

We also asked questions about communist influence in several specific sectors of American life. As Table IV shows, 91% of the Crusaders thought that communist professors had a great deal of influence in colleges and universities. About half thought that communists had a great deal of influence in the Democratic Party, and a fifth even thought they were influential in the Republican Party. More than a third of the Crusaders said that communists were living in their neighborhoods.

TABLE IV* — Crusaders' Perceptions of Substantial Communist Influence or Presence in Various Aspects of American Society

	Agree	Disagree	Don't know	Total
Communists have a lot of influence in				
"Colleges and universities"	91%	9	—	100%
"The Democratic Party"	55%	38	7	100%
"The Republican Party"	20%	72	8	100%
"Communists live in my neighborhood"	36%	36	28	100%

* In this and all subsequent tables marked with asterisks, the bases have not been reported because the tables include different questions, to which the number of "No answers" varied

What kinds of people in this country do the Crusaders think are likely to be communists? Twenty-nine per cent nominated professors and intellectuals, and 45% mentioned youths, students, and "the ignorant." Only 7% mentioned foreigners or members of minority groups, and hardly any mentioned government officials. These answers are interesting both for what they include and for what they omit. The prime villains are not defined in ethnic, economic, or governmental terms. Rather, they are those people who communicate ideas and information and those who are most vulnerable to being misled. Stouffer reported somewhat similar findings. Most of his respondents were unable to give more than the vaguest kind of generalized answer ("they do bad things") when asked what communists do. But 42% were able to give more specific replies: Eight per cent said that communists committed acts of sabotage, and 8% more thought they were spies; 28% said that they converted people to communism and spread their insidious ideas.[35]

The Crusaders' responses suggest that, to adherents of the radical right, "communists" are people who spread a kind of mental infection that causes people to adopt repellent ideas. One can also infer that the Crusaders reject the idea that communism may feed on deprivation or injustice. The Crusaders' recommendations on what the government should do to fight communism in this country reflect their view that communism is an intellectual malady. Forty-eight per cent of the Crusaders recommended education, chiefly on the evils of communism[36]; 15% were in favor of supporting present anticommunist policies and institutions; and 46% called for harsher measures, ranging from the death penalty to denial of citizenship.[37]

It is sometimes asserted, most often by left-wing commentators, that adherents of the radical right are warmongers, eager for a nuclear exchange with the Soviet Union. At least one writer has explained the radical right's strength in California in these terms: Since the state's economy is dependent on defense spending, Californians will support any movement advocating a more belligerent policy toward communist countries.[38] Our data do not support this proposition. We asked the Crusaders the same question that Stouffer used a decade ago: "Of these three ways of dealing with Russia, which do you think is best for America now?"[39] As Table V shows, less than a fifth of the Crusaders were in favor of fighting Russia. Furthermore, a good many of these respondents indicated, by marginal comments, that they interpreted "fight" to mean "vigorously oppose."[40]

TABLE V — Attitudes toward Dealing with the Soviet Union

	Crusaders	National sample, 1954[a]
Believe the United States should		
Talk over problems with Russia	28%	61%
Have nothing to do with Russia	37	17
Fight Russia	18	14
Other	2	—
Don't know	1	8
No answer	13	—
	99%[b]	100%
N	308	4933

a. Source: Stouffer, *op. cit.* p. 77.
b. Does not add up to 100% because of rounding.

The current tendency to describe attitudes on policy toward the communist nations on a belligerence-negotiation dimension obscures another aspect of American opinion, one that dominated our perspectives on foreign policy until the Second World War: isolationism. As Table V shows, the Crusaders' most striking difference from Stouffer's sample is the extent of their aversion to any involvement with the Soviet Union. We suggest that isolationism, rather than aggressiveness, is the hallmark of many radical rightists' foreign-policy sentiments.

So far we have seen that, although the Crusaders are united in their alarm about the dangers of internal subversion, they display considerable diversity of opinion on proposals for dealing with communism in both its foreign and domestic manifestations. As Table VI shows, the same pattern occurs on other foreign policy issues; the Crusaders are somewhat conservative but by no means unanimously so on any particular issue. About 40% of them support American involvement in the United Nations, and about two-thirds are in favor of foreign aid, although some of the latter group would give aid only to friendly nations. Those respondents with the most extreme perceptions of the power of American communists, the fifty-six respondents who think that communists have a great deal of influence in both major political parties, are consistently more conservative than the rest of the sample. But even these alarmists are rather heterogeneous in their attitudes on substantive issues.

TABLE VI* — Attitudes on Foreign Policy Issues

	Among Crusaders who see communist influence in both major parties	Among all other Crusaders
Proportion saying		
"The United Nations is bad for the U.S."	69%	58%
"The U.S. should give little or no foreign aid"[a]	40%	30%

a. Thirty-two per cent of the respondents who favor more aid are opposed to present methods of administering the aid program or are against giving aid to communist or neutral nations.

The Crusaders share a general feeling that the federal government is too bountiful: Eighty-six per cent agreed that "the American people would have more get up and go if the government would stop giving them things." But on a less general level, 40% to 60% of the Crusaders took liberal positions on several specific issues, as Table VII shows. For instance, almost two-thirds of them are opposed to the southern position on desegregation, and more than half are in favor of at least some federal aid to education. Once again, the alarmists about domestic communist influence are somewhat more conservative on substantive issues.

TABLE VII* — Attitudes on Domestic Issues[a]

	Among Crusaders who see communist influence in both major parties	Among all other Crusaders
Proportion saying		
"South is right on integration"	44%	35%
"Opposed to federal aid to education"	56%	40%
"Opposed to medicare"[b]	69%	59%
"Unions do more harm than good"	60%	56%
"Big corporations control too much business"	35%	27%

a. With the exception of the last two items in Table VII, the questions in Tables VI and VII were asked on the mail questionnaire only.

b. Answers to this question did not vary appreciably with age.

The Crusaders' level of political tolerance is somewhat uncertain. Our comparative measure is three questions from Trow's Bennington study modified to agree-disagree form: "In peacetime the Socialist party should *not* be allowed to publish newspapers in this country"; "Newspapers should be allowed to criticize our form of government"; "Members of the Communist Party in this country should be allowed to speak on radio and television."[41] Trow's respondents were men, and, since the Crusaders are no exception to the generalization that women are less tolerant than men,[42] we compared only the male Crusaders to Trow's Bennington respondents. We controlled for education, since tolerance usually increases with years of schooling. As Table VIII shows, those Crusaders who have attended college are slightly less tolerant than the corresponding group of

Bennington residents. The Crusaders' slightly higher tolerance at the lowest educational level is probably due to the fact that 60% of the Crusaders in that group had been graduated from high school compared to 38% of the corresponding Bennington respondents.

TABLE VIII* — Political Tolerance of Male Crusaders and the Bennington Sample—by Education

	Percentage agreeing	
	Among male Crusaders	Among Bennington respondents[a]
"Socialists should be allowed to publish newspapers"		
High school graduates or less	69%	60%
Some college	79%	90%
College graduates	89%	93%
"Newspapers should be allowed to criticize our form of government"		
High school graduates or less	79%	81%
Some college	88%	91%
College graduates	92%	97%
"Communists should be allowed to speak on radio and television"		
High school graduates or less	24%	20%
Some college	24%	31%
College graduates	33%	47%

a. Recomputed by the authors from data in Trow, "Right Wing Radicalism," p. 261.

We are not satisfied that the Crusaders are even as tolerant as Table VIII indicates. For one thing, they tend to be particularly intolerant of communists' civil rights, and, as we have seen, they tend to believe that a great many people are communists. Second, the respondents who score as tolerant on the Bennington questions are only slightly less likely to support harsh measures against American communists than are the intolerant Crusaders. It is safest to conclude that our sample's level of tolerance compared to the general population is an unknown quantity. For purposes of intrasample comparison, we will use a four-point intolerance index constructed from the three Bennington items, giving one point for each intolerant response.

Numerous studies have shown that, in the general population, attitudes on political issues ordinarily are strongly related to demographic characteristics like income, education, sex, and age.[43] These relationships are remarkably weak in our sample. For example, well educated Crusaders are not notably more tolerant than those who did not attend college, while the Bennington respondents' responses vary greatly by education (see Table VIII). While conservatism on domestic welfare issues normally increases with income, this trend is visible only among the Crusaders with annual incomes above $15,000, as Table IX indicates.[44] Similarly, conservatism increases with age only among respondents over sixty years old. The demographic variable that produces the largest difference is sex. Women generally are somewhat more conservative than men, particularly on issues concerning communism[45]; even here, however, the relationships are not strong among the Crusaders.

TABLE IX — Domestic Conservatism—by Income[a]

Score on domestic conservatism index	Below $7.000	$7000 to $10,000	$10,000 to $15,000	$15,000 and over
Low 0	39%	34%	38%	23%
1	32	30	27	26
High 2	29	36	35	51
	100%	100%	100%	100%
N	44	47	52	47

a. "No answers" have been removed from the bases.

No matter what cross tabulations we made or what independent variables we controlled, we were unable to find meaningful distinctions related to demographic variables. This failure may be a consequence of the sample's limited range in both demographic factors (most respondents are upper-status) and political predispositions (the Crusaders are conservative). There may not be sufficient range within each set of variables for them to interact significantly.

The relative unimportance of demographic variables in intrasample variation may have a specific meaning in this context, however. It is possible that, once an individual has pledged his political allegiance, once he has become an active member of a political organization, ideological considerations become salient for him. Commitment to other reference groups may yield to the pressures of political commitment. If this proposition is true, we should expect that, among people active in the Democratic Party for example, attitudes would not vary so much by demographic factors as they would among a group of inactive Democrats. This proposition has not been tested with voting behavior data.

Crusaders who engage in more than one form of campaign work are more likely to take conservative positions on issues than are those who are less active. For example, 47% of the former group was opposed to both federal aid to education and federally financed medical care for the aged, compared to 24% of the latter group. This disparity is in line with findings that the political attitudes of people deeply involved in politics tend to be more consistent and congruent with their party identification.[46]

The voting behavior studies have shown that relationships between party identification and attitudes on political issues are often very weak; Republicans often are as likely to endorse a particular liberal position as Democrats.[47] Trow found that, with education controlled, McCarthy supporters were no more intolerant than the Senator's opponents, while Lipset reports weak relationships between attitudes toward McCarthy and conservative positions on a number of foreign-policy issues.[48] Despite this evidence, there seems to be a tendency to assume that supporters of the radical right have a consistent set of attitudes far outside the normal political spectrum. Instead, it appears that extremism is not unidimensional; deviant opinions in one area may coexist with quite conventional views on other issues.[49]

Many leaders of the radical right have attracted a good deal of derision for their policy proposals, which range from military adventurism abroad to complete *laissez-faire* in domestic matters. The Crusaders share the alarmist attitude toward subversion characteristic of the radical right. Their attitudes on various political issues incline to the conservative pole, but they are by no means united on any of these issues. Thus attempting to deduce their attitudes from radical-right ideology would be no more valid than would deducing the opinions of a group of Republicans from the Republican platform.[50]

Failure to distinguish between the pronouncements of political leaders and the opinions of their supporters involves some grave risks in attempting to explain the appeal of the radical right. In the first place, it is not very wise to reach conclusions about the right's sources of support on the basis of an examination of its ideology. Second, the appeal of the radical right is not limited to those individuals who will accept extreme doctrines in their entirety. Any particular bizarre doctrinal point is not sufficient to destroy a right-wing group's attractiveness to all prospective members. Robert Welch's famous remark about President Eisenhower's communist allegiance has not put an end to the growth of the John Birch Society. Although such embarrassments undoubtedly do not make recruiting easier, they do not seem to have destroyed the Birch Society's appeal. The potential supporters of the radical right are therefore more numerous than might be assumed from an examination of its ideology.

V. The Sources of the Radical Right

In the past dozen years, a good deal of intellectual effort has been expended in attempts to explain who is attracted to movements like the radical right and for what reasons. Much of this effort has been offhand speculation, but some has been based on sophisticated social-science theory and has produced provocative hypotheses. Some of these propositions are derived from theoretical orientations growing out of attempts to explain Nazism and other extremist movements. Senator McCarthy's impact on American political life resulted in another stream of investigations. Most recently, attempts have been made to explain the radical right. There is thus a body of propositions that we can use to examine our data.

Most of these propositions are concerned with ethnicity or socioeconomic status. The San Francisco Bay Area is a suitable testing ground for these propositions, since it is characterized by demographic heterogeneity. It has a variety of ethnic groups in various stages of assimilation, as well as many white Protestants in the process of bettering their positions in life. The area has been settled long enough to have established wealthy families, and its continuing economic growth produces plenty of *nouveaux riches*. In fact, the Bay Area contains sizable numbers of almost every group considered receptive to the radical right, with the exception of Texas oil millionaires. We shall begin by examining several propositions that are not congruent with our data and then proceed to more fruitful hypotheses.

Alienation

One of the most popular—and untested—themes in modern social science is "alienation." Uprooted from his customary setting by industrialization and urbanization, cut loose from the assured life of a stable class structure and traditional mores, deprived of meaningful associations and satisfactions by the formless bustle of modern life, alienated man is regarded as the most malleable and volatile of creatures. In his quiet state, he is apathetic, withdrawing from politics as from all forms of civic activity. But such quietude only increases his desperation, which must be expressed in some form of political extremism: "Mass theory leads to the expectation that the unattached and alienated of all classes are more attracted to extremist symbols and leaders than are their class-rooted counterparts."[51]

There are difficulties in designing research on alienation, which perhaps explain why these ideas have remained unverified. It is uncertain what objective indicators can be used to measure alienation. For example, using group membership as an index of class alienation, as we do, poses a question: Can we conclude that an individual without formal group memberships is any less "class-rooted" than one who belongs to half a dozen organizations? Are such superficial experiences as membership in a Rotary Club proof that an individual is not alienated? Furthermore, the literature on alienation is by no means clear about the nature of the "extremist movements" that supposedly appeal to alienated men.

Our findings relevant to alienation should be examined with these qualifications in mind. First, the Crusaders do not seem to be social isolates. As Table X shows, they have a somewhat higher level of membership in all kinds of organizations—church committees, civic groups, veterans organizations, and so forth—than do the business, professional, and white-collar respondents in the 1952 Survey Research Center study.

TABLE X — Group Memberships of Crusaders Compared to Business, Professional, and Clerical Heads of Household in National Sample, 1952

Number of group memberships	Crusaders	National sample, 1952[a]
None	11%	26%
One	29	28
Two	27	16
Three or more	34	30
	101%[b]	100%
N	294	164

a. Source: SRC 1952 election study.
b. Does not total 100% because of rounding.

It is quite conceivable that one can be socially integrated yet feel politically alienated. We used the index of sense of political efficacy developed by the SRC to measure our respondents' feelings of political effectiveness.[52] It does not appear that the Crusaders are possessed by feelings of powerlessness. As Table XI shows, they have a slightly higher sense of political efficacy than do white northerners who have attended college.

Some writers have taken the view that the radical right offers a means

TABLE XI — Crusaders' Sense of Political Efficacy Compared to College-Educated White Northerners

Sense of political efficacy	Crusaders[a]	White northern college educated[b]
High 4	40%	29%
3	32	39
2	18	23
1	6	5
Low 0	4	4
	100%	100%
N	269	262

a. Respondents who did not answer all four questions in the political efficacy index were excluded from this table.

b. Source: SRC 1960 election study.

of political expression for people detached from or frustrated by the American two-party system. Our data suggest that the opposite is the case. Fully 98% of the eligible Crusaders reported that they voted in the 1960 presidential election, while 54% of all respondents said that they had sent letters, postcards, or telegrams to government officials during the previous year. As Table XII shows, the Crusaders' rate of participation in political campaigns is extraordinarily high. Almost two-thirds of them make financial contributions to political parties or candidates. The same proportion attends meetings or rallies, and more than a third does other kinds of campaign work. Seventy-nine per cent of the Crusaders engaged in at least one type of campaign activity. It should be noted that these items do not refer indiscriminately to any kind of political activity but to activity in the two-party context—more specifically, to work for the Republican Party. As we have seen, the most politically active Crusaders were more conservative than the inactive ones.

TABLE XII* — Crusaders' Political Campaign Activity Compared to that of College-Educated White Northerners

Percentage saying they	Among Crusaders[a]	Among white northern college educated[b]
"Give money or buy tickets to help the campaign for one of the parties or candidates"	62%	23%
"Go to political meetings, rallies, dinners or things like that"	62%	13%
"Do any other work for one of the parties or candidates"	37%	8%
"Belong to any political club or organization"	27%	9%

a. These questions were asked on our mail questionnaire only.

b. Source: SRC 1960 election study. The questions were the same in both studies, except that the first three questions were phrased in the past tense in the SRC study.

Status Anxiety

The best known efforts to identify the sources of Senator McCarthy's support are the essays by noted social scientists collected in *The New American Right*.[53] This book, supplemented by articles on the radical right, has recently been reissued.[54] Several contributors to these books base their explanations of McCarthyism or the radical right on what they call "status politics," that is, a situation in which people project their anxieties about social status onto political objects. Since "status anxiety" is a very broad concept and can be applied to so much of the population, it has little explanatory value.[55] We shall discuss several specific applications of this notion that attribute susceptibility to the radical right to particular groups in the population.

The first and simplest fomulation is that upward mobile people are inclined to support the radical right. Presumably such people, newly arrived in the middle class, feel some sort of status insecurity, which they express by superpatriotism and exaggerated hostility to "communists." This proposition is not confirmed by our data. We compared the fathers' occupations of the businessmen and professional Crusaders to those of the white northern businessmen and professionals interviewed in the 1956 SRC election study. As Table XIII indicates, Crusaders have at least as much status stability as the comparison group. Furthermore, within our sample, the status-stable businessmen and professionals were more likely than the upward mobile ones to choose conservative positions on every attitude measure. The status-stable were also much more active politically.

TABLE XIII — Occupational Mobility of Businessmen and Professionals

	Businessmen and Professionals only	
	Among Crusaders[a]	*Among white northerners*[b]
Father's Occupation		
Businessmen and professionals	41%	37%
Clerical and sales	8	6
Blue collar	12	38
Farmer	16	16
No answer	23	3
	100%	100%
N	179	290

a. In the case of married female respondents, the father-in-laws' and spouses' occupations are used.

b. Source: SRC 1956 election study.

A second proposition asserts that downward mobile individuals are attracted to the radical right because it provides both an explanation for their misfortunes and a scapegoat for their consequent hostility. This proposition does not seem to explain the Crusade's appeal, for few of our respondents had experienced downward mobility.

A third explanation is also based on social mobility—but in the context of ethnic hostility. In this view, upward-mobile second- and third-generation Americans affirm their patriotism and new middle-class status by supporting the radical right. As Hofstadter puts it, "Many Americans still have problems about their Americanism and are still trying, psychologically speak-

ing, to naturalize themselves."[56] Also, to the extent that right-wing sentiments involve attacks on old-family liberals, revenge may play a part in
attracting ethnic-group members to the radical right; what better way to
take advantage of one's new position than by turning on the old Yankees who
patronized one's ancestors? This proposition was based on survey findings
that Catholics were more likely than Protestants to support McCarthy, as
well as on McCarthy's attacks on the Harvard-Acheson-striped-pants set.

Another proposition mingling mobility and ethnic hostility suggests that the
ethnics' success drives old Americans toward the right:

> These people, although very often quite well-to-do, feel that they have been pushed out
> of their rightful place in American life, even out of their neighborhoods. Most of them
> . . . have felt themselves edged aside by the immigrants, the trade unions, and the urban
> machines in the past thirty years. When the immigrants were weak, these native elements
> used to indulge themselves in ethnic and religious snobberies at their expense. Now the
> immigrant groups have developed ample means . . . of self-defense. . . . Some of the
> old family Americans have turned to find new objects for their resentment among
> liberals. . . .[57]

Whatever the utility of these assorted ethnic hostility theses as explanations
for the appeal of McCarthyism, they seem to have very little relevance to
today's radical right. For one thing, it is clear that the attack of the right is
on intellectuals, not on old Americans. More important, it is in New England
and the Middle Atlantic states, where old-settler hostility to immigrants was
most pronounced, where ethnic hatred was— and is—bitterest, and where the
political and geographic displacement of Yankees by ethnics is more
thorough, that the radical right has been least successful.[58] In contrast, its
promoters find their warmest reception in areas where hostility between
immigrants and old settlers has been minimal, in the wide-open societies of
the Rocky Mountains, the Southwest, and southern California.[59] Finally,
although the underrepresentation of Catholics in our sample may be a function of the title of the Crusade, we find no overrepresentation of recent
immigrants. On the contrary, when we compared our non-Catholic respondents to the white, non-Catholic respondents in a representative sample of
San Francisco adults,[60] we found that the former group had a much smaller
proportion of foreign-born respondents and a somewhat smaller percentage
of second-generation Americans, as Table XIV shows.

TABLE XIV — Comparison of Nativity and Parentage of Non-Catholic Crusaders and White
Non-Catholic, Adult San Franciscans

	Crusaders	San Franciscans[a]
Foreign born	8%	23%
Native born of foreign parents	20	26
Native born of native parents	67	51
No answer	4	—
	99%[b]	100%
N	283	576

a. Source: California Department of Public Health cross-section study of San Francisco
adults.

b. Does not total 100% because of rounding.

Another status hypothesis is that right-wing movements draw support from individuals with "status discrepancies," that is, from people whose education, income, and social standing are not congruent—from college-educated truck drivers and illiterate businessmen. As Lipset puts it, "such status incongruities were presumed to have created sharp resentments about general social developments, which predisposed individuals to welcome McCarthy's attack on the elite and on the New Deal."[61] As this statement suggests, one of the difficulties in trying to verify the hypothesis is that it refers as much to a state of mind as to an objectively definable condition. Perhaps for this reason, attempts to relate objective status discrepancies to support for McCarthy were not successful.[62]

We had the same experience with the Crusaders. We compared the occupations of three educational groups with those of white northerners in the 1960 SRC study, as shown in Table XV. If the status-discrepancy hypothesis had any validity for our respondents, we would expect to find that more of the well educated Crusaders had menial jobs or more of the poorly educated ones were in high-status occupations. There are scarcely any differences between the two samples at the two higher educational levels, except for a slight tendency for more Crusaders, at each level, to be businessmen. With respondents who have attended high school but not college, this difference becomes quite marked; 37% of the Crusaders in this group are businessmen, compared to 12% of the SRC group. There are, however, only forty-three Crusaders in this group; the difference from the SRC group accounts for only eleven respondents. This difference appears to be the result of chance and the generally higher occupational level of the Crusaders.

TABLE XV — Occupation by Education—Crusaders and White Northerners

	College graduates		Some college		Attended high school[a]	
	Crusaders	Northerners[c]	Crusaders	Northerners[c]	Crusaders	Northerners[c]
Occupation[b]						
Professional	54%	59%	25%	34%	7%	6%
Businessmen	31	19	30	17	37	12
Clerical and sales	11	14	22	23	26	20
Blue collar	3	9	22	25	30	62
	99%[d]	101%[d]	99%[d]	99%[d]	100%	100%
N	140	108	63	149	43	545

a. Since only 3% of the Crusaders did not attend high school, no lower educational category has been used.

b. Farmers, students, and "no answers" have been excluded from bases.

c. Source: SRC 1960 study.

d. Do not total 100% because of rounding.

American society is characterized by a relatively high degree of occupational mobility, quite high levels of education, and a rather weak system of status ascription by inheritance. One would expect that such a fluid social system would continue to produce a good deal of "status anxiety" in various forms. For this reason, explanations linking these phenomena to McCarthyism and the radical right may be considered pessimistic. It should therefore be a source of some comfort that, whatever the causes of the radical right, they do not seem to include strains resulting from the characteristic openness of the American social system.

Provincialism

According to another proposition, the radical right feeds on provincial resentment of the increasing social, economic, and cultural dominance of large cities. The radical right, like Prohibition and the Scopes trial, is interpreted as another rear-guard action against modernity. As Daniel Bell puts it, "what it seeks to defend is its fading dominance, exercised once through the institutions of small-town America, over the control of social change."[63] If this explanation were valid, we would expect to find a greater proportion of people with farm and small-town backgrounds in our sample than in the general population. Comparing Crusaders to white San Franciscans and to the white northerners in the 1960 SRC study, we do not find that a disproportionate number of Crusaders comes from farm families, as Table XVI shows. Nor do we find that a highly disproportionate number was raised in small towns.[64]

TABLE XVI — Proportion of Respondents Whose Fathers were Farmers—by Occupation

	Per cent with farmer fathers[a]		
	Crusaders	*White northerners*[b]	*White San Franciscans*[c]
Occupation of head of household			
Businessmen and professionals	16%	11%	14%
Clerical and sales	12%	15%	13%
Blue collar	32%	31%	25%

a. "No answers" have been excluded from the bases.
b. Source: SRC 1960 study.
c. Source: Public Health San Francisco study.

So far we have discussed hypotheses that, whatever their utility in explaining other manifestations of right-wing sentiment, are not helpful when applied to the Crusaders. Now we shall look at some propositions that do seem to have value in explaining our respondents.

Fundamentalism

A number of writers have noted that the radical right seems to be attractive to fundamentalist Protestants.[65] Various explanations have been offered for this attraction. The most convincing ones point to affinities between fundamentalist dogma and radical-right interpretations of history. Belief in the literalness and purity of Biblical teachings makes fundamentalists resistant to social and cultural change; they are affronted by moral relativism, increasingly lenient sexual mores, the decline of parental authority, and other aspects of the secular modern world. The fundamentalist sees "the world as strictly divided into the saved and the damned, the forces of good and the forces of evil."[66] The main danger to the faithful is from the corrosion of faith by insidious doctrines—a danger from within. This argument is given added credence by the revivalist style and trappings of many "anticommunist" leaders.[67]

Slightly more than three-quarters of the Crusaders are Protestants. Twenty-six per cent of the Protestant Crusaders are Baptists or members of minor fundamentalist denominations, compared to 13% of the white, college-educated Protestants in the San Francisco sample. These fundamentalists, who comprise 20% of the total sample, are not significantly different from the other respondents on either demographic or attitudinal measures. But a more sensitive measure of the intermingling of politics and religion isolates a group that seems to confirm the explanations of affinities between the radical right and fundamentalists.[68] We asked our respondents how they happened to come to the Crusade. Those who came because of church influence (forty-three respondents) are different from the rest of the sample in a number of ways, as Table XVII demonstrates. They are not nearly so well off or well educated. They are slightly more likely to have rural backgrounds and considerably more likely to be devout, religiously active members of fundamentalist denominations.

TABLE XVII* — Comparison of the Demographic Characteristics of the "Church Group" (Those Who Came because of Church Influence) and All Other Crusaders

	Among "church group"	Among all other Crusaders
Proportion who		
Are fundamentalists	66%	15%
Attend church regularly	90%	45%
Belong to church committees	89%	37%
Were raised on farms	30%	19%
Are clerical or manual workers	54%	24%
Have annual incomes under $10,000	78%	51%
Belong to unions	21%	15%
Did not complete college	62%	44%

The members of the "church group" are considerably more liberal on domestic issues than is the remainder of the sample. Only 8% of them favor the southern position on segregation, compared to 42% of the other respondents. Almost twice as many of the church group are in favor of medical care for the aged and federal aid to education. This relative liberalism is not merely a reflection of their lower status. Among nonchurch-group Crusaders, low-income respondents are as conservative on domestic issues as high-income respondents

These data suggest that members of the church group were not attracted to the Crusade by economic self-interest.[69] We suggest that their religious beliefs lead them to look on communism as an earthly manifestation of the devil.

TABLE XVIII* — Comparison of Attitudes of the "Church Group" and All Other Crusaders

	Among "church group"	Among all other Crusaders
Proportion who		
"Prefer Nixon to Goldwater"	60%	39%
"Are low on index of domestic conservatism"	56%	30%
"Do *not* regard unions as harmful"	62%	41%
"Are opposed to the South's position on integration"	92%	58%
"Are opposed to teaching Darwin's theories in schools"	52%	30%
"Believe atheists are persons likely to be Communists"	31%	11%
"Are high on index of perception of internal Communist danger"a	64%	50%
"Engage in no more than one form of political activity"	57%	41%

a. Perception of the internal communist danger is measured by a five-point index, with one point each for thinking that American communists are a very great danger, that communist professors have a great deal of influence, that communists are very influential in the Democratic Party, and that they are very influential in the Republican Party.

As one of these Crusaders put it, "I'm a Bible student and am convinced that the Communist movement is satanic in its origins, principles, and ultimate aims." While only a third of the church group named atheists as likely to be communists, this proportion was three times that in the rest of the sample.

Although members of the church group are more liberal than the other Crusaders, they are even more extreme in their perceptions of the extent of communist infiltration in American life, which suggests that for them "communism" is a handy label for all the works of the devil, from sexual immodesty to permissive child-rearing practices. It appears that people who came to the Crusade through their churches were attracted for essentially religious reasons, an interpretation supported by their lower level of political activity.

It is possible that the Crusade's religious aura was an essential part of its appeal to such people, who might not find all radical-right organizations equally attractive. They might more likely be drawn to a group like Billy James Hargis's Christian Crusade than to a secular organization like the Birch Society.

Old-fashioned Individualists

Just as fundamentalists are hostile to the secularism and moral looseness of contemporary society, some other people are supposedly resentful of another modern trend: the development of immense bureaucratic organizations that have crowded individual enterprise to the wall. Such old-fashioned types have "a wistful nostalgia for a golden age of small farmers and businessmen and also . . . strong resentment and hatred toward a world which makes no sense in terms of older ideas and which is conducted in apparent violation of old truths and values of economic and political life."[70] It has been suggested that such people have been drawn to support of McCarthy and the radical right because they have a "political orientation which has no institutionalized place on the political scene."[71] Small businessmen are thought to be the chief examples of this type.

There are thirty-eight self-employed businessmen in our sample. They do not differ from other respondents in any meaningful pattern, except that half of them report making more than $15,000 a year, which raises some question about all of them being small businessmen.

Testing this antibureaucratic hypothesis with respect to McCarthyism, Martin Trow isolated a group of his Bennington respondents whom he called "nineteenth-century liberals." This group consisted of those respondents who were hostile both to labor unions and big business, the major examples of impersonal mass institutions. Trow found that these "liberals" were much more likely to approve of McCarthy than people who were favorable both to unions and big business or favorable to one and hostile to the other. He interpreted their support of McCarthy as an expression of hope that the Senator would turn back the tide of gigantic bureaucracy.

We used the same questions about unions and big business to isolate a similar group of "nineteenth-century liberals" among the Crusaders. These "liberals" composed 14% of Trow's sample and 17% of ours. (Only two of our "liberals" are also in the church group.) These respondents are a fairly distinct group. As Table XIX shows, they are characterized by political intolerance, a low sense of political efficacy, conservatism on foreign policy, low political participation, and belief that there is no difference between the Democratic and Republican Parties.

TABLE XIX* — Comparison of the Attitudes of "Nineteenth-Century Liberals" and All Other Crusaders

	Among "nineteenth-century liberals"	Among all other Crusaders
Proportion who are		
"High on index of intolerance"[a]	53%	24%
"Low on index of sense of political efficacy" (score of 0, 1, or 2)	48%	24%
"High on index of foreign policy conservatism"	74%	51%
"Engage in no more than one form of political activity"	59%	40%
"Believe that there is no difference between the major political parties"	43%	18%

a. Intolerance is measured by a four-point index, with one point for a "disagree" response to each of the three items in Table VIII; "high" is a score of two or three.

The most remarkable feature of these findings is the "liberals'" lack of involvement in two-party politics; unlike the other Crusaders, they seem to be estranged from conventional means of political expression. Many of them apparently feel that neither political party is a vehicle through which they can protest the eclipse of individualism. If "communism" represents secularism to the fundamentalists, it may well symbolize bureaucratic organization to the "liberals."

The church group and the nineteenth-century liberals together account for about one-third of the sample. It does not appear that the presence at the Crusade of the remainder of the sample can be explained by any of the sociological propositions that we have discussed. In pursuing this problem further, it may be useful to consider who was *not* susceptible to the appeal of the Crusade.

Most obviously, the Crusade was not attractive to Jews, Orientals, Negroes, or Catholics.

Second, it did not seem to have much appeal to lower-status people, except for fundamentalists. On this point, the radical right may differ from McCarthyism, which had considerable appeal for people with less education and more menial jobs.[72] This difference between the two movements may be due to several factors. One possibility is that, at present, the radical right lacks a single commanding leader who dominates the movement and symbolizes it to the public. McCarthy, of course, was more than a symbol; he was the embodiment of his movement. For people with little education, unaccustomed to thinking in abstract terms, a single highly visible leader offers a much easier point of reference. Another possibility is that the ideology of the radical right does not offer much that is attractive to lower-status people.

Studies of public opinion and voting behavior have shown that communist subversion was not a salient issue to many people in the early 1950s, despite the volume of political oratory on the subject.[73] There are some indications that McCarthy's popularity with lower-status people was due to his denunciations of the old American upper class, an attack that would appeal both to Yankee-hating ethnic-group members in the Northeast and to Middle Western anglophobes. Trow's research suggests that many of McCarthy's Bennington supporters saw him as a kind of spiritual Robin Hood, taking the rich and well-born down a peg in behalf of the common man.[74] There is none of this antipatrician tone in the radical right, which enshrines in one of its slogans the proposition that the United States is not a democracy.

Third, on the basis both of our data and our contacts with the Crusaders, we do not believe that they are social or psychological cripples. Most of them hold responsible positions in business or the professions, and the vast majority is active in a variety of community organizations. Unfortunately, we do not have data on personality variables. Possibly the Crusaders would score higher than members of the general population on a measure of authoritarianism. Indeed, some research on McCarthy supporters suggests that this would be the case.[75] The Crusaders' beliefs about the extent of internal subversion may be regarded as paranoid, but, despite the deviant quality of some of their political attitudes, they are functioning members of society.

Fourth, and most important, the Crusade was not for Democrats. The most striking single distinguishing characteristic of our sample is the scarcity of Democrats. This scarcity is not a reflection of our respondents' high socioeconomic status, since party identification is quite imperfectly related to SES. Furthermore, the working-class Crusaders are no less Republican than the rest of the sample; 90% of them voted for Nixon in 1960. It does not appear that the absence of Democrats is merely a reflection of concern about the dangers of domestic communism, since Stouffer reports that about as many Democrats as Republicans thought that this danger was "relatively great,"[76] and it therefore does not appear that Republicans have a monopoly on worries about subversion. Evidently this fear is not a sufficient stimulus to participation in a radical-right movement. By the same token, many Democrats have conservative attitudes on welfare issues, foreign policy, and civil liberties, particularly in California, where there are many southern Democrats. Yet even members of the "church group," who were considerably more liberal than the rest of the sample and came to the Crusade for essentially religious reasons, were as Republican as the other Crusaders.

The strong relationship between party identification and support of the radical right should not be surprising, for party is the most powerful independent variable in many other areas of political behavior.[77] For most people, party identification is the most important point of reference in evaluating political phenomena. While the attention paid to domestic communism in political oratory has varied a good deal, it has still been one of the major themes of political discourse—particularly in California—and it is a Republican theme.[78] These cognitive clues were reinforced by the statements of party leaders. By early 1962, a number of prominent Democrats had attacked the radical right, and the Democratic Attorney General of California had denounced Dr. Schwarz and the Crusade specifically. Few leading Republicans had criticized the radical right at that time. The local controversy about the Oakland school occupied a good deal of newspaper space. Politically conscious Democrats in the Bay Area, aware that their party had been belabored on the communist issue for years, could hardly have failed to conclude that a Democratic Crusader would be something of an anomaly.[79]

VI. The Social and Political Context of the Radical Right

If Republicanism and the prevalence of rightist attitudes were the only factors determining the size and importance of radical-right groups, we should expect to find such organizations throughout the country. Yet there are marked variations in the level of radical-right activity. It is most intense in certain regions like southern California and the Southwest and seems to be almost nonexistent elsewhere, especially in the Northeast. The uneven level of radical-right activity seems to be a function of the interaction of two factors: the presence of compatible attitudes and a favorable balance between institutional constraints and rewards for right-wing political agitation. We shall argue that variations in this second factor may account for variations in the strength of the radical right.

The right seems to be most successful in those states that are undergoing both major economic growth and marked changes in economic bases, life styles, and cultural geography. It may be that the politically relevant aspects of these conditions involve not so much individual gains and losses in objective social status as what might be called "lateral social change." That is, the cause may be the strains produced by the interpersonal and institutional instability that comes with rapid economic growth. There are arguments attributing the radical right's popularity in California both to rootless newcomers and discomfited old-timers. We have no normative data with which to compare our findings on the length of time the Crusaders have lived in the Bay Area and in California, and we cannot therefore contribute to this discussion.

All the states where the radical right is most active have in common a political characteristic that is conspicuously lacking in the Northeast, where the right is feeblest. Where the radical right flourishes, political party organizations are weak and lack continuity. Control of a major party is an important inducement to right-wing activity in a number of states. But where party organizations are strong, where established leaders have formidable resources for protecting their positions from challengers, and where the rewards for political action run more toward tangible benefits than ideological satisfaction, the difficulty of taking over the party discourages potential right-wing activists. The presence of a strong party organization also impedes other radical-right activity like the intimidation of school teachers and librarians.

In California and in much of the West and Southwest, "organization" is a misnomer for the collection of personalities, factions, and ideological inclinations that comprise the Democratic and Republican Parties. Party leadership is generally fragmented, in large measure because there are few resources available to co-ordinate and discipline party activists.[80] The leaders' vulnerability to concerted attack is a temptation to rebels from the right.

The second major political contextual restraint on the radical right is the presence of a Republican in the White House.[81] At the party-organization level, rightist attempts to take control of a state party during the Eisenhower years would have been restrained by awareness of the disadvantages of opposing the President. A president's ability to influence directly the outcome of a power struggle within a state party is limited but by no means negligible. Indirectly, however, his rightist critics face a considerable problem if he is Republican, for they cannot so easily attack his policies. The allegations of communist influence that play so large a part in right-wing propaganda are less convincing to the public when a Republican is president. Hope, party loyalty, and organizational alliances all restrain right-wing leaders at such times. As the case of Senator McCarthy showed, ambitious men who ignore these constraints encounter a basic truth: A concerted attack on a Republican president from the right will inevitably lead to a confrontation in which Republican politicians are forced to choose between their president and his critics. This fact is a Republican president's ultimate weapon against the radical right.

All these conditions are reversed when the White House changes party hands. There is no incumbent president to restrain right-wing dissidents in the state parties. One or more of the politicians contending for the next presidential nomination are likely to encourage radical-right activity as a means of building their own strength. Professional politicians, largely indifferent to ideological considerations, may encourage radical-right accusations as a weapon against the Democrats. During a Democratic administration, alarmism about communism is more plausible to many people.

Recent fluctuations in radical-right activity have conformed to this pattern. The current resurgence occurred after the 1960 presidential election. Although the John Birch Society was founded in 1958, it was not until 1961 that it grew enough to attract public attention. The Christian Anti-Communism Crusade was an obscure organization for the first seven years of its existence, but, in the first year of the Kennedy administration, its income increased 350%.[82]

VII. Conclusion

We have attempted to answer two interrelated questions in this paper: What kinds of people participate in the Crusade? Why are they attracted to this movement? With the exception of Lipset's and Polsby's work, previous consideration of such questions produced sociological explanations dealing with status anxiety, cultural resentment, ethnic hostility, and the like. By and large, these propositions do not seem consistent with our data. In particular, their utility is vitiated by the most salient fact about the Crusaders: Whatever else they may be, they are not Democrats.

The most economical answer we can give to the first question is that the Crusade draws its support from Republicans, chiefly those of higher socioeconomic status. The Crusaders' support for Goldwater suggests that they are Republicans dissatisfied with their party's stance in national elections. The best inference we can draw from this dissatisfaction is that it is due to acceptance of the welfare state by Republican presidential candidates. As the great reigning evil of our time, communism seems to be, for many people, a shorthand symbol for unacceptable political trends. The Crusaders' fears about the influence of communism were restrained during the Eisenhower administration by the improbability that Eisenhower was soft on communism. With Republicans out of power, "anticommunism" is a way to express resentment with maximum emotional impact and a minimum of divisiveness within the Republican Party.

The political strategy of the radical right is limited by its lack of mass appeal. It is likely, then, to be most effective in those aspects of politics where numbers are not crucial: not in general elections, but in pressure politics, party conventions, and the like. Our respondents' tremendous rates of political participation suggest that they are well placed to pursue their goals in the internal politics of the California Republican Party, pressing for control of the party's various organs, nomination of conservative candidates, and a commanding voice in determining party policy. They appear to have had some success in these endeavors.[83] Their ability to achieve both intraparty success and electoral victories has not yet been demonstrated, however, and it may well be that the interests of the radical right are not compatible with those of the Republican Party.

NOTES

1. The radical right has been covered at great length in most newspapers and national magazines. Several popular books have been written about it, including Roger Burlingame, *The Sixth Column* (Philadelphia, 1962); Mark Sherwin, *The Extremists* (New York, 1963); and Donald Janson and Bernard Eismann, *The Far Right* (New York, 1963). The only scholarly book on this subject to date is Daniel Bell, ed., *The Radical Right* (Garden City, 1963). One issue of *The Journal of Social Issues* was devoted largely to the radical right: Vol. 19, (April, 1963). The semimonthly *Reports* of Group Research, Inc. (Washington, D.C.) contain a great deal of topical information on the radical right.

2. Probably the most complete description of Dr. Schwarz and the Crusade can be found in the Anti-Defamation League's publication, *Facts*, November-December, 1962,

entitled "The Case of Fred C. Schwarz." The Crusade has been described in some detail in virtually every national magazine. Books on the radical right usually devote a chapter to it.

3. In 1961, the Crusade's gross receipts exceeded $1.2 million; they fell to just over $1 million in 1962. These figures do not include money paid indirectly to the Crusade, such as contributions for televising Crusade programs.

4. Dr. Fred Schwarz, *You Can Trust the Communists* (Englewood Cliffs, 1960). The book was issued in a paperbound edition in 1962.

5. *Christian Anti-Communism Crusade News Letter* (henceforth cited as *News Letter*), April, 1962, p. 2.

6. One Crusade speaker, a Republican member of the California State Assembly, has introduced a bill to forbid teaching in California schools any theory "opposed to recognized religious sectarian doctrines" (*San Francisco Chronicle*, May 22, 1963, p. 1). Schwarz has said that "Americans should be willing to renounce a certain measure of personal freedom in the battle against Communism" (quoted in *Facts*, p. 253).

7. See, for example, *Oakland Tribune*, February 1, 1962, pp. A-1, E-11; *Facts*, p. 254; and *San Francisco Examiner*, February 2, 1962, p. 10.

8. *News Letter*, April, 1962, p. 3.

9. In a letter to the Crusade mailing list, Schwarz remarked, "Few people would dispute the contention that a deeper understanding of Communism is desperately needed by those who formulate the national policies and programs on which the survival of freedom depends (letter dated July 19, 1963). Speaking in St. Louis, he said, "We can cry out about how awful the Communist influence is in radio, TV, the press, in government. We can just regret it all. Or we can light a candle. . . . We can personally bring our own program of light, education . . ." (quoted in *Facts*, p. 254). Schwarz also attributes a good deal of procommunist influence to American colleges and universities; see, for example, *You Can Trust the Communists*, pp. 17, 28, 33, 35, 60.

10. See, for example, U.S. House of Representatives, Committee on Un-American Activities, *International Communism* (Staff Consultation with Frederick Charles Schwarz), 85th Congress, 1st session, May 29, 1957, p. 14. Hundreds of thousands of copies of this testimony have been distributed by a manufacturing firm in Wisconsin.

11. *News Letter*, August, 1962, p. 7.

12. *Ibid.*, December, 1960, p. 2.

13. See, for example, *ibid.*, November-December, 1961; *ibid.*, May, 1962, p. 6; *San Francisco Examiner*, February 2, 1962, p. 10.

14. Two Crusade publications, "Establishing a Local Study Group," and "Meeting Manual for the Local Study Group," suggest a variety of radical-right material and offer help from headquarters to local groups.

15. Mark Chesler and Richard Schmuck, "Participant Observation in a Super-Patriot Discussion Group," *Journal of Social Issues*, 19 (April, 1963), 18-30.

16. Quoted in *Life*, February 9, 1962, p. 117. Schwarz has doggedly refused to evaluate the Birch Society, explaining, "I don't know very much about the John Birch Society" (quoted in Janson and Eismann, *op. cit.*, p. 63). The *New York Times* has quoted him as saying, "You know sometimes I get the notion Welch follows me around the country, signing up the people after I've worked them up" (reported in *Facts*, p. 249).

17. See Janson and Eismann, *op. cit.*, p. 139; and Willie Morris, "Houston's Super-patriots," *Harper's*, October, 1961, p. 56.

18. *San Francisco Chronicle*, January 9, 1962, pp. 1, 16.

19. *New York Sunday Times*, February 4, 1962, p. 51.

20. Samuel A. Stouffer, *Communism, Conformity and Civil Liberties* (Garden City, 1955).

21. Martin Trow, "Small Businessmen, Political Tolerance, and Support for McCarthy," *American Journal of Sociology*, 64 (November, 1958), 270-81. For a complete report on this research, see Trow, "Right Wing Radicalism and Political Intolerance: A Study of Support for McCarthy in a New England Town," (Unpublished doctoral dissertation, Columbia University, 1957).

22. At the end of our first evening of data collection, after he and the Northern California director of the Crusade had carefully studied the mail questionnaire, Schwarz agreed not to condemn the study to his audience, although he warned, "With one sentence, I could kill your whole project." He declined, however, to announce publicly that we had no polemic intent and that we were not associated with critical student pickets who had been vehemently denounced by members of the faculty. These negotiations were witnessed by several reporters and were described in the *San Francisco News-Call Bulletin*, January 31, 1962, p. 4. This account appeared after the personal interviews were completed and before most of the mail questionnaires were distributed. Since there were no appreciable differences between responses to the two types of instrument, we concluded that this incident had no important influence on our data.

23. In addition, there was a good deal of generalized xenophobia. The *Oakland Tribune* remarked on the Crusaders' determined and unusual reluctance to give names to reporters (January 30, 1962, p. G-11). During the evening, a lady stood on the front steps of the auditorium holding a sign bearing a crimson handprint, an American flag, and the words "Remember Hungary." She was constantly harassed by passing Crusaders, who often called her a communist and advised her to "go back" to Russia. Her critics were unmoved by her plaintive reply: "But I'm on your side."

24. Of the estimated 2000 people at the Crusade, perhaps 200 were minors and, at a conservative estimate, at least 500 came with spouses. Of a total possible population of about 1300, more than a quarter were interviewed or completed a questionnaire.

25. For this reason, we present normative data for the white population whenever possible. Unless otherwise indicated, "Bay Area" refers to the San Francisco-Oakland Standard Metropolitan Statistical Area as defined by the Census Bureau. All but nine of our respondents come from this region.

26. All discussion of the Crusaders' occupations is based on the occupation of the head of the respondent's household.

27. The best available source of information on the religious characteristics of the Bay Area population is: National Council of the Churches of Christ in the U.S.A., *Churches and Church Membership in the United States,* Series C, no. 59, 1957. According to this source, there were 595,153 Catholics in the Bay Area; this figure is 24% of the white population in 1960. The problem of defining church "membership" makes it an inadequate source of normative data on Protestant church affiliations.

28. Source: the national sample survey of the 1960 presidential election conducted by the University of Michigan Survey Research Center. All SRC election data used in this article were obtained from the Inter-University Consortium for Political Research. We are grateful to Ralph Bisco, Michael Kahan, Warren E. Miller, and Linda Wilcox of the Consortium staff for their advice and assistance. The SRC data used in the preliminary version of this article that was given at the 1963 meeting of the American Political Science Association were computed by the authors from IBM cards supplied by the Consortium. The originals of these cards subsequently were "cleaned" by the Consortium. The SRC data in this article are from the clean cards, which accounts for a few minor differences in the SRC data presented in the two versions.

29. The scarcity of lower-status persons in our sample cannot be adequately explained by the well known finding that such people have relatively low rates of political participation. While their rate of participation is lower, such persons still account for a good proportion of the audience at other kinds of public political meetings. For instance, of the white northerners who attended one or more political meetings during the 1960 election campaign, 62% had not attended college, and 65% had annual family incomes of less than $7,500 (source: the 1960 SRC election study).

30. Seymour M. Lipset, "Three Decades of the Radical Right: Coughlinites, McCarthyites, and Birchers—1962," in Bell, *op. cit.,* pp. 353-7.

31. *Ibid.,* p. 354.

32. Of the twenty-five Democrats in the sample, four are Jews, five are Catholics, and five were born in the South. There are eight Jewish respondents in all.

33. Source: *San Francisco Chronicle,* March 5, 1962, p. 34.

34. Another possible explanation of this finding is that newcomers to California are more likely to be conservative, for there is some indication that newcomers are more favorably disposed to the Birch Society than are old residents (see Lipset, *op. cit.,* p. 363). The old-time Nixon supporters, however, are more conservative on issues than the newcomers for Nixon. The old residents for Goldwater are by far the most reactionary of the four groups.

35. Stouffer, *op. cit.,* p. 158.

36. This figure may reflect Schwarz's emphasis on anticommunist "education."

37. These percentages total more than 100% because some respondents made more than one suggestion. A few Crusaders recommended withdrawal from the United Nations or cessation of all relations with communist countries.

38. Fred J. Cook, "The Ultras," *The Nation,* June 30, 1962, p. 571.

39. Stouffer, *op. cit.,* p. 77.

40. Dr. Schwarz and some of his students complained that the three alternatives given in the question provide an inadequate set of choices. We agree.

41. Trow, "Right Wing Radicalism," p. 261. Trow's respondents were chosen by modified quota-sampling methods.

42. See, for example, Stouffer, *op. cit.,* pp. 131-55.

43. A great deal of research on this point is summarized in V. O. Key, Jr., *Public Opinion and American Democracy* (New York, 1961).

44. Domestic conservatism is measured by a three-point index, with one point each for replies against medicare and aid to education. Conservative responses on the other three

items in Table VII were so weakly associated with one another and with these two questions that we did not include them in the index. The foreign-policy index has four points, with one point each for opposition to foreign aid and to the United Nations and choice of the "fight Russia" or "have nothing to do with Russia" responses in Table V.

45. Cf. Lipset, "The Sources of the Radical Right—1955," in Bell, op. cit., pp. 303-4.

46. See Key, op. cit., pp. 439-40; and Angus Campbell, P. Converse, W. Miller, and D. Stokes, The American Voter (New York, 1960), p. 208.

47. See, for example, Campbell, Converse, Miller, and Stokes, op. cit., Chap. 9.

48. Trow, "Small Businessmen," pp. 272-3; and Lipset, "Three Decades," pp. 338-40. Since support for McCarthy was related negatively both to Democratic allegiance and education, relationships between McCarthyism and conservative issue positions might have been found if party identification had been controlled.

49. We do not mean to suggest that opposition to medicare, for example, is an extreme or bizarre opinion. Our point is that support of medicare is evidence that an individual does not hold extreme rightist views on at least that issue. Regrettably, we did not ask questions about some of the more celebrated radical-right positions, such as abolition of the income tax.

50. Trow makes this point with respect to McCarthyism; see "Small Businessmen," pp. 280-1.

51. William Kornhauser, The Politics of Mass Society (New York, 1959), p. 180.

52. This well known measure of sense of political efficacy is based on these questions: "I don't think public officials care much what people like me think"; "Sometimes politics and government seem so complicated that a person like me can't really understand what's going on"; "Voting is the only way that people like me can have any say about how the government runs things"; "People like me don't have any say about what the government does." Efficacy is measured on a five-point index, with one point for each negative answer. For a detailed discussion of this measure, see Angus Campbell, Gerald Gurin, and Warren E. Miller, The Voter Decides (Evanston, 1954), pp. 187-94.

53. Daniel Bell, ed., The New American Right (New York, 1955).

54. Bell, The Radical Right.

55. The inclusiveness of "status anxiety," the diversity of the various groups that were thought to support McCarthy because of this anxiety, and the scarcity of evidence to support these speculations have led several writers to comment critically on The New American Right. See especially Trow, "Small Businessmen," pp. 270-1; and Nelson W. Polsby, "Toward an Explanation of McCarthyism," in Polsby, Robert A. Dentler, and Paul A. Smith, eds., Politics and Social Life (Boston, 1963), pp. 809-24. Polsby has an amusing table listing the many categories of people who are considered McCarthyites by one or more of the contributors to The New American Right (p. 813).

56. Richard Hofstadter, "Pseudo-Conservatism Revisited: A Postscript—1962," in Bell, The Radical Right, p. 84.

57. Hofstadter, "The Pseudo-Conservative Revolt—1955," in Bell, The Radical Right, p. 72.

58. Lipset, "Three Decades," pp. 350-2. A Crusade school held in New York in 1962 was a popular and financial fiasco; the estimated deficit was $75,000 (Facts, pp. 261-2). Of a listing of rightist groups published in 1962, 19% of the organizations were located in California, chiefly in the Los Angeles area (source: Chesler and Schmuck, "On Super-Patriotism: A Definition and Analysis," Journal of Social Issues, 19 (April, 1963), p. 38.

59. There are a great many second- and third-generation Irish and Italians in the Bay Area and appreciable numbers of them elsewhere in the West. Scandinavians and Germans are also plentiful in the area. But none of these ethnic groups encountered anything like the hostility that was so salient a feature of immigrant life in the Northeast. The ethnic groups that have suffered the most from discrimination in the West, Orientals and Mexicans, display no interest at all in the radical right.

60. Data on San Francisco are from a sample survey of adults in that city, conducted for the California Department of Public Health under the direction of Drs. Ira Cisin and Genevieve Knupfer. We are grateful to them for these data, and to Edward R. Tufte for help in tabulating the data.

61. Lipset, "Three Decades," p. 333.

62. Ibid. Lipset cites California Poll data that show a tendency for individuals with status discrepancies to be disproportionately favorable to the Birch Society (ibid., p. 363). He reports that the number of cases is far too small to warrant much confidence, however. He also cites an unpublished paper by Robert Sokol showing that persons who felt that their pay was not commensurate with their education were more likely to support McCarthy (ibid., pp. 333-4, 374). Another study uncovered relationships between status discrepancies and conservative attitudes; see Gerhard C. Lenski, "Status Crystallization: A Nonvertical Dimension of Social Status," American Sociological Review, 19 (August, 1954), 405-12.

63. Bell, "The Dispossessed—1962," in Bell, *The Radical Right,* p. 12.

64. We asked our respondents, "Were you brought up mostly on a farm, in a small town, or in a large city?" The only roughly comparable normative data available came from the Public Health San Francisco study, which asked, "Where did you live before the age of 15—on a farm, in the country but not on a farm, or in a town or city?" If respondents answered "town" or "city," the population size was asked, and the replies were coded by size. The 25,000-to-100,000 category presents some difficulties for us, since it probably includes both "small towns" and "large cities"; 10% of the San Francisco sample are in this category. A second difficulty is that in a sample of a large city one would expect that a higher proportion of the respondents had been raised in large cities than in a metropolitan-area sample where only some of the respondents come from the core city. In the light of these considerations, we can hardly claim to have comparable data, but the following table indicates that the Crusaders probably are not markedly unrepresentative of the Bay Area with respect to rural or small-town backgrounds.

Size of Place Where Raised

	Crusaders	San Franciscans
On a farm (and in the country)		
Businessmen and professionals	20%	19%
All others	25%	23%
Small town (up to 100,000 population)		
Businessmen and professionals	37%	24%
All others	34%	25%
Large city (over 100,000 population)		
Businessmen and professionals	43%	57%
All others	41%	52%

65. The most extended discussion of this relationship, although without the benefit of data, is by David Danzig, "The Radical Right and the Rise of the Fundamentalist Minority," *Commentary,* April, 1962, pp. 291-8. See also Lipset, *Political Man* (Garden City, N.Y., 1961), p. 108; Bell, *The Radical Right, passim*; and Victor C. Ferkiss, "Political and Intellectual Origins of American Radicalism, Right and Left," *The Annals of the American Academy of Political and Social Science,* 344 (November, 1962), 6.

66. Danzig, p. 292.

67. There are several right-wing movements, chiefly in the Southwest, with a strong revivalist flavor. Schwarz and other officials of the Crusade have backgrounds in various types of religious activity; see *Facts,* pp. 250-2. Schwarz's speaking style often reflects this background.

68. It should be noted that persons with fundamentalist points of view are found, in varying numbers, in all Protestant denominations. Within some denominations whose theological positions are liberal, there are individual churches that adhere to more fundamentalist positions.

69. Some writers interpret fundamentalist support of the radical right as a consequence of a recent rise from economic deprivation to prosperity; see Bell, *The Dispossessed* pp. 20-1.

70. Trow, "Small Businessmen," p. 275.

71. *Ibid.,* p. 276.

72. Lipset, "Three Decades," pp. 331-3.

73. Campbell, Gurin, and Miller, *op. cit.,* p. 52; Campbell, Converse, Miller, and Stokes, *op. cit.,* p. 51; and Stouffer, *op. cit.*

74. For evidence on this point see Trow, "Small Businessmen." Various articles in Bell, *The Radical Right,* discuss likely sources of lower-class support for McCarthy; see, in particular, Hofstadter's articles and Peter Viereck, "The Revolt Against the Elite—1955."

75. High authoritarianism scores are increasingly related to support of McCarthyism as educational level increases; see Lipset, "Three Decades," pp. 342-4. An extraordinary study of students at Ohio State University indicated that members of a right-wing organization had considerably higher F-scale scores than either uncommitted or left-wing students. The number of cases is quite small, however. See Edwin N. Barker, "Authoritarianism of the Political Right, Center, and Left," *Journal of Social Issues,* 19 (April, 1963), 63-74.

76. Thirty-four per cent of the Republicans and 30% of the Democrats saw the internal Communist threat as "relatively great" (Stouffer, p. 211). Stouffer reports that a number of other surveys have produced the same finding (p. 217).

77. Polsby was the first to draw attention to the importance of party identification as an explanation of support for McCarthy.

78. Remarks about relationships between Republicanism and support for the radical right are not applicable to those one-party states of the South and Southwest where party identification loses most of its function as a cognitive clue.

79. In polls taken within a few months after the first widespread public disclosure of the existence of the John Birch Society, Democrats compose 33% of the pro-Birch respondents in a national sample (by Gallup) and 28% in California (Lipset, pp. 352, 356). It is not reported how many of the twenty-five pro-Birch Democrats in the Gallup national sample are from the South. As time has passed and the controversy about the radical right has continued, it is quite possible that previously pro-Birch Democrats have learned the "proper" relationship between their party and the Birch Society.

80. Two recent case studies of Democratic nominations in California and Connecticut, respectively, illustrate the striking differences in party cohesion in the two states. See John H. Bunzel and Eugene C. Lee, "The California Democratic Delegation of 1960," in Edwin A. Bock and Alan K. Campbell, eds., *Case Studies in American Government* (Englewood Cliffs, 1962), pp. 133-74; and Joseph P. Lyford, *Candidate* (New York, 1959). Bunzel and Lee describe the difficulties experienced by California Democrats in preventing complete fragmentation of their party over the 1960 presidential nomination. The Governor and other leaders were unable to control the delegation. In contrast, Connecticut Democratic leaders succeeded in 1958 in forcing their convention to nominate for Congress an unknown army officer who had not lived in the state for more than twenty years.

81. Several writers in Bell, *The Radical Right,* have made this point; see Bell, p. 1; and Lipset, pp. 296-7.

82. The Crusade's reported income was $364,535 in 1960 and $1,273,492 in 1961 (*News Letter,* August, 1962, p. 6).

83. Ultraconservative forces gained control of the national Young Republicans at the organization's 1963 convention in San Francisco. For a discussion of their activities in the Republican Party see T. George Harris, "The Rampant Right Invades the GOP," *Look* (July 16, 1963), pp. 19-25.

The Age of Ideology:
Persistent and Changing*

BY *REINHARD BENDIX*

I. Ideology as an Historical Phenomenon

Introduction

ABOUT THREE CENTURIES AGO, Francis Bacon observed that words become idols and obstruct our understanding. Words in common usage designate what is "most obvious to the vulgar." Men of learning therefore, alter the common meanings of words in order to achieve accuracy through definition. Nevertheless, they often end up in dispute about words among themselves, since definitions also consist of words and these "words beget others." Bacon concluded that "it is necessary to recur to individual instances."[1] In the social sciences, his observations and advice are still valuable and nowhere more so than with regard to the phenomenon of ideology, which is examined in the essays collected in this volume.

Modern scientists—like the earlier men of learning—tend to be impatient with words in their common usages which, as Bacon put it, "stand in the way and resist change." Like Humpty Dumpty in *Through the Looking Glass,* they want the words to mean what they say the words mean. If clarity is obtained thereby, it is well worth the artificiality that results. An artificial terminology, however, has its own risks, even aside from the problem of getting other scientists to agree to it. In order to clarify definitional problems, it is often advisable to refer to "individual instances," and such references are obscured when the terms used have been formulated deductively. In addition, it must be kept in mind that the ambiguous or multiple meanings of words, as they are ordinarily used, are an important part of the evidence. Social scientists should consider this evidence with clear heads, but should not clarify it out of existence. The scientist's legitimate quest for clarity can subtly distort such evidence by supposing that, once the confusions of a term are cleared up, the problems to which it refers have disappeared also.

"Ideology" is a case in point. The word is in such bad repute that writers

---

*This essay is based in part on my earlier publication, *Social Science and the Distrust of Reason* (*University of California Publications in Sociology and Social Institutions,* Vol. I [Berkeley, 1951]), which has been out of print for a number of years.

on the subject are either apologetic about using it or prefer to substitute another term like "belief-system," as do several authors in this volume. At the same time, there are writers who continue to use it as if its meaning were well understood. Among them are those who speak of an "end of ideology," by which they mean the decline of political ideas in Western countries. This decline is attributed to the rise of totalitarianism, which diminishes controversy in the antitotalitarian camp; the rise of the welfare state, which institutionalizes the drive toward equality; and the resulting consensus on a "pluralistic" society in which power is sufficiently decentralized to leave room for individual freedom.[2] These factors probably account for the sharp reduction of ideological disputes over some aspects of domestic policy, but there is also evidence of a sharp increase of ideological disputes in other respects. We may be witnessing a change in the arena of ideological conflict, rather than an "end of ideology," even in the Western context. For if intense ideological conflict has declined domestically in some respects, it has probably increased in others, in race relations, for example. While the secret diplomacy of the nineteenth century sought to obviate ideological differences, the "diplomacy" of the Cold War has accentuated them. Again, the waning imperialist doctrines of the nineteenth century are now being replaced by the anticolonial and anti-Western doctrines of the mid-twentieth century. These considerations suggest that the phenomenon of "ideology" has an historical and structural dimension.

A Nonideological World View

If one can speak—even in a restricted sense—of an "end of ideology," then the phenomenon of ideology must also have had a beginning, unless the term is used merely as a synonym for ideas. Is there a common element in all the diverse uses of ideology, by reference to which one can distinguish one cultural epoch from another? Can one speak meaningfully of a "pre-ideological" epoch?[3] The answer is, I believe, that the term is not properly applicable in Western civilization prior to the seventeenth or eighteenth centuries, somewhat in the way that terms like "economy" or "society" or "intellectuals" do not fit the "premodern" period either. All these terms are applicable to the ways in which men think about their society. The shift is one of cultural pattern and intellectual perspective rather than of social or political structure, although the relations between these levels are important also. In practice, it is sometimes difficult to distinguish the earlier world view from that more characteristic of the subsequent, "ideological" epoch—especially during the long transitional period that began in the Renaissance when the earlier conviction became attenuated. But this difficulty does not invalidate the distinction between a culture based on belief in the Supreme Deity and another in which—in the absence of this belief—man and society, along with nature, are viewed as embodying discoverable laws, which are considered the "ultimate reality." As Carl Becker has put it:

In the thirteenth century the key words would no doubt be God, sin, grace, salvation, heaven and the like; in the nineteenth century, matter, fact, matter-of-fact, evolution, progress. . . . In the eighteenth century the words without which no enlightened person could reach a restful conclusion were nature, natural law, first cause, reason, sentiment, humanity, perfectability (these last three being necessary only for the more tender-minded, perhaps).[4]

This substitution of nature for God is especially important for an understanding of ideology as a distinctive intellectual perspective.

The ramifications of the earlier world view are observable in many different realms. In literature, for example, "reality" had been represented in a heroic and a satiric-comic mode since antiquity, a contrast that disappeared only in the realistic or naturalistic representations of nineteenth-century literature. The object of the older literature was poetic representation of reality as it should be, in terms of ideal contrasts between virtues and vices, between heroes and fools or knaves. Similarly, the facts of economic life were treated in the context of estate-management, in which instructions concerning agriculture, for example, occurred side by side with advice on the rearing of children, marital relations, the proper management of servants, and so forth. The moral approach to human relations was not at all distinguished from the economic and technical considerations of the household. Again, premodern historiography—if the word is not indeed a misnomer—consisted in what we consider a moralistic chronicling of events, an entirely unselfconscious assessment of history in terms of a moral standard accepted as given and unchanging. The basis for this moral standard was belief in a divinely ordered universe, and the common element in these premodern perspectives was therefore the effort to discover "the moral law," which had existed from the beginning of time as the central fact of a world created by God.[5] One may speak broadly of a premodern or pre-ideological epoch as long as this perspective remained intact, as long as even the most passionate controversialists did not question the existence of the moral law and the divine ordering of the universe.

In this view, history consists in the unfolding of the divine law and of man's capacity to understand it and follow its precepts. To be sure, men cannot fully understand the providential design. But through their thoughts and actions, men reveal a pattern or order of which they feel themselves to be vehicles or vessels, even though they understand it only dimly. Man's capacity to reason is not questioned, even though his development of that capacity remains forever partial, precisely as the ends of human actions are not in doubt although in an ultimate sense they remain unknown. It is when human reason and the ends of action are questioned that "ideology" comes into its own.

Sources of Error, the Ends of Action, the Uses of Theories, and Truths

In ordinary usage, "ideology" refers to:

1. The body of doctrine, myth, and symbols of a social movement, institution, class, or large group. 2. Such a body of doctrine, etc. with reference to some political and cultural plan, as that of fascism, along with the devices for putting it into operation. 3. *Philos.* a. the science of ideas. b. a system which derives ideas exclusively from sensation. 4. Theorizing of a visionary or unpractical nature.[6]

To relate these definitions to the present discussion, it is only necessary to distinguish their several elements. In the sociopolitical and philosophical realms, the definitions refer ideas back to a nonideational basis, whether it be a social movement, an institution, a class, or a physiological and psychological substratum called "sensation." In this view, ideas are derived from some extra-ideational source, however the source or the process of derivation may be conceived. I shall use the term *reductionism* to characterize this approach. Second, the definitions specify that doctrine, myth, symbol, or theory is oriented to the future, in the sense that it embodies a political or cultural plan of action. In this sense, ideology is a type of goal-orientation, a special aspect of the teleology that is characteristic of all human action. I shall speak of *goal-orientation* or *the ends of action* when I refer to this attribute. The last definition refers to theorizing as visionary or impractical, thus raising a question about *the uses of theories.* The accent is polemical, setting up an invidious contrast between a visionary and a realistic approach, the latter term referring presumably to theories and truths (or statements of fact) that are practical or concrete. Here "ideology" is used in its pejorative sense, about which we shall say more presently.

The distinction between the "ends of action" and the "uses of theories and truths" requires comment. The action primarily considered here is the pursuit of knowledge, so that in the present context the "ends of knowledge" are distinguished from the "uses of knowledge." The distinction is necessary even though the relationship between the ends and uses of knowledge is sometimes close. But for the men of knowledge, the pursuit of truth is often a large and ill defined good, which is never fully realized by the uses of truths even in the ideal case, since all knowledge is proximate. Furthermore the "uses of theories and truths" are often in the hands of men of affairs, and even where theories and truths are abused from the point of view of the scientist as a citizen, such abuse does not invalidate the value of knowledge in his eyes, since, under favorable conditions and in the hands of wise men, the same knowledge can be put to constructive use as well. It is advisable, therefore, to refer to the *ends* and *uses* of knowledge as separate, though related, aspects of the action-involvement of ideas.

These three aspects together—the reductionist tendency in the analysis of ideas; plans of action for man and society, including the pursuit of knowledge for the sake of human progress, and the invidious contrast between realism and illusion—are the constituent elements of ideology as I shall use the term.

Historically, the Age of Ideology came into its own when critical questions were raised concerning man's ability to reason and the degree to which he is capable of defining and realizing the ends of his actions. Reductionism in the analysis of ideas and concern with the ends of knowledge are important elements in Francis Bacon's programmatic statements. Critical questions about the use of theories, especially in society, arose much later toward the end of the eighteenth and the beginning of the nineteenth century.

Bacon's declaration of independence from the scholastic learning of an earlier age has the stirring power of all acts of emancipation. Nevertheless, it contains uncertainties about man's reason and the ends of his pursuit of knowledge. In its attempt to lay the foundations of modern knowledge, Bacon's manifesto seeks to guard scientific inquiry against the errors that typically obstruct human understanding. In his "theory of idols," analysis of the sources of error becomes an important part of the quest for knowledge. We must guard against the influence of interests and wishful thinking that is found in all men (idols of the tribe); against the individual's character and experience, which prompt him to dwell on some ideas with peculiar satisfaction (idols of the cave); against the "ill and unfit choice of words" (idols of the market-place); and against the received systems of philosophy (idols of the theater). In thus classifying recurrent sources of error, Bacon intends only to safeguard the pursuit of truth, not to open the floodgates for an ever more probing analysis of the nonideational foundations of knowledge.

Furthermore, he approaches these critical questions in a spirit of optimism.

> Human knowledge and human power meet in one; for where the cause is not known, the effect cannot be produced. Nature to be commanded must be obeyed; and that which in contemplation is as the cause is in operation as the rule.

Accordingly, Bacon refers to the *kingdom of man,* which can be won but for the

> unfair circumscription of human power, and . . . a deliberate and factitious despair; which not only disturbs the auguries of hope, but also cuts the sinews and spur of industry, and throws away the chances of experience itself, and all for the sake of having their art thought perfect, and for the miserable vainglory of making it believed that whatever has not yet been discovered and comprehended can never be discovered or comprehended hereafter.[7]

Still basing his thought on the traditional world view, Bacon believes in man's capacity to discover the divine order; even such confidence is compatible with an abiding faith. But when he considers the ends of human action and admonishes men to seek knowledge "for the benefit and use of life," Bacon is totally at variance with the traditional view, even though he reminds men to seek knowledge for charity rather than for such inferior ends as profit, fame, or power.[8] Still, Bacon wishes only to emancipate the men of his age from thralldom to a world view according to which all wisdom is already contained in the divine word and only remains to be discovered by men in their proximate fashion. He intends "the investigation of truth in nature" as a new and better means of discovering the divine wisdom.

At the same time, Bacon is well aware that the pursuit of knowledge must be safeguarded against those who are apprehensive that it will undermine the authority of religion and the state. Bacon claims that investigations of nature are "the surest medicine against superstition, and the most approved nourishment of faith," rather than a danger to religion as some people fear. And he argues against those who fear for the power of the state, declaring that investigations of nature can only enhance that power, while "matters of state" are not a proper subject for science—"these things resting on authority, consent, fame, and opinion, not on demonstration."[9] The very act of emancipation thus raises questions about human reason and the ends of human knowledge. Rather than to rely on faith in man's God-given capacity to discover the truth, it becomes necessary to protect this human capacity by rationally devised safeguards against error. And instead of faith in a providential design, which is revealed through human action whether men know it or not, it becomes necessary to make the ends of the pursuit of knowledge (and, more generally, of all actions) a conscious object that must be protected against base motives, misinterpretations, and unintended consequences.

No scientific inquiry can dispense with the two concerns Bacon formulated in his "Novum Organum." The possible sources of error must be understood and guarded against; this concern is a part of the scientific enterprise. In addition, by the act of engaging in research or inquiry, scientists commit themselves to a line of action that cannot be clearly separated from its social context. The "ends of knowledge" that they pursue are a matter of belief not of proof. We saw that Bacon raises the hopes of men for the new science but also tries to anticipate and offset the apprehensions of those who fear it. For scientific work depends upon men of affairs and the general public, and Bacon discerns some consequences of this dependence.

> It does not rest with the same persons to cultivate sciences and to reward them. The growth of them comes from great wits; the prizes and rewards of them are in the hands of the people, or of great persons, who are but in very few cases even moderately learned. Moreover, this kind of progress is not only unrewarded with prizes and substantial bene-fits; it has not even the advantage of popular applause. For it is a greater matter than the generality of men can take in, and is apt to be overwhelmed and extinguished by the gales of popular opinions.[10]

To be successful, the scientific enterprise requires special safeguards that arise from this dependence. Yet, neither the errors to which inquiry is subject nor its dependence upon public support has proved an ultimate bar to a properly conducted inquiry. On the contrary, critical awareness of the scientist's fallibility has helped to promote scientific knowledge, and the public's conditional support has not impeded its gradual advance.

At the threshold of the modern world, the task was to emancipate men from unthinking acceptance of received opinion, stimulate the critical scrutiny of ideas, and encourage the investigation of nature in the hope of benefiting mankind. Bacon initiated an era in which reason replaced faith among the mental and psychological conditions of inquiry, while the ends of that in-quiry were defined in terms of "human utility and power," rather than the greater glory of God. In the natural sciences, the Baconian program proved extraordinarily successful; as methods of research were developed and its findings proved reliable, the utility of these findings became an article of faith that was questioned less with each advance in scientific knowledge. The magnetic appeal of this new faith quickly dispelled the remaining commit-ments of scientists to the earlier world view, as well as Bacon's rather defensive declaration that "matters of state" are outside the province of scientific inquiry.[11] The new intellectual perspective came to be applied to man and society, and there also reason replaced faith in the mental and psychological conditions of inquiry and the ends of human knowledge. Yet, unlike the consequences in the natural sciences, the result was a paradox. While the search for the sources of error proceeded apace as an indispensable means for the advancement of social knowledge, the ends of inquiry re-mained uncertain, resting as they do on the borrowed belief, rather than the proven fact, that social knowledge serves "human utility and power." Accord-ingly, "ideology" came to be used in a pejorative sense, when the scientific approach was applied to man and society. Here knowledge can also be ad-vanced only if the sources of error are known and guarded against. But all too often such knowledge of error has been used as a weapon in the struggle of ideas, as a means of discrediting an opponent, rather than as a method-ological safeguard. Here also the advance of knowledge depends on public support. But the frequent absence of manifest utility makes that support more precarious and provides ready arguments for those who would discredit an opponent's views as "visionary and unpractical."

These questions came to the fore as confidence in the progress of human knowledge was extended to all types of inquiry, including those "matters of state" that Bacon had cautiously excluded from his program. I need not here review these extensions in psychology, education, political theory, and philosophy except to note that in philosophy the optimistic search for truth eventually found expression in a science of ideas entitled "ideology."[12] In his *Eléments d'idéologie* (1801, 1803, 1805) Destutt de Tracy gave a systematic exposition of this science intended for use in the schools. He stated in his preface that "ideology is a part of zoology," since human intelligence is a phenomenon of animal life and must be analyzed accordingly.[13] Tracy felt, as did his ideologue colleagues, that such a reductionist analysis of ideas— "studies on the formation of our ideas" as he called it—had arrived at the truth and no longer left room for doubt or perplexity.[14] Yet this perspective was directly associated with the republicanism and atheism of the ideologues. During Napoleon's ascendance to supreme power, a conflict quickly developed between the Emperor and these philosophers, whose association he had cultivated only a short time before. The pejorative meaning of "ideology" originated in this controversy, specifically in Napoleon's repeated denunciations of the men who had coined this term to identify a philosophical school.[15] With this emphasis on the questionable practicality of ideas or theories—Napoleon had used phrases like "obscure metaphysic" and "idealistic trash" to characterize the work of *les idéologues*—we have the third constituent element of "ideology," one that poses in a general and rather mixed-up way the question of the truth, the utility, and the political repercussions of ideas concerning man and society.[16]

The implications of this pejorative meaning of "ideology" are illuminated in the work of Edmund Burke, although he wrote before Tracy had coined the term and Napoleon had used it in polemic fashion. Burke opposes the reductionist analysis of ideas with his affirmation of sentiment and prejudice as indispensable bases of the community.

> . . . In this enlightened age I am bold enough to confess that we are generally men of untaught feeling; that instead of casting away all our old prejudices, we cherish them to a very considerable extent, and, to take more shame to ourselves, we cherish them because they are prejudices. . . . We are afraid to put men to live and trade each on his own private stock of reason; because we suspect that this stock in each man is small, and that the individuals would do better to avail themselves of the general bank and capital of nations and of ages. Many of our men of speculation, instead of exploding general prejudices, employ their sagacity to discover the latent wisdom which prevails in them. . . . Because prejudice, with its reason, has a motive to give action to that reason, and an affection which will give it permanence. Prejudice is of ready application in the emergency; it previously engages the mind in a steady course of wisdom and virtue, and does not leave the man hesitating in the moment of decision, sceptical, puzzled and unresolved Prejudice renders a man's virtue his habit; and not a series of unconnected acts. Through just prejudice, his duty becomes a part of his nature.[17]

Although this famous passage states the case for conservatism and is thus an obvious example of ideology, it is cited here because it serves to illuminate the pejorative meaning of "ideology."

Burke sets out to shock his readers by using "prejudice" as a word of praise. In the eighteenth century, that word referred to the prevailing opinions of church and state, which the philosophers of the French Enlightenment sought to discredit and unmask by theoretical reduction of all ideas to the basic "sensations" out of which they have been formed.[18] Accordingly, when Burke praises "prejudice," he seeks to put a stop to that inquiry into the "sources of error" that the Enlightenment was extending from the natural sciences to philosophy, political theory, and education. At the same time, he provides an impressive analysis of the hiatus between theory and action. Theory means detachment, while practical things are accomplished by commitment; theory deals with principles, while action involves compromises and modifications in detail; theory enlarges the horizon and endangers action by revealing its contingencies, while action is limited in its aims; theory makes provisional statements, while actions are irreversible; theory involves no presumption in favor of precedent, while action is limited by past behavior; and where theory rejects errors, prejudices, or superstitions, the statesman puts them to use.[19]

Burke thus denounces all inquiries into the conditioning of knowledge as presumptuous and unnatural, a fatal disruption of the "untaught feelings" and inherited sentiments that alone provide a sound basis of morality. Similarly, he denounces all abstract theories in politics because they will jeopardize the "art of the possible." Such theories project wholly visionary plans and state impractical principles, which undermine the resolution to act in the face of uncertain contingencies. As a conservative who seeks to preserve or to restore the older world view, Burke thus gave a pejorative meaning to the critical inquiries into the "formation of our ideas" that the French philosophers were developing, as well as to abstract political theories that attempted to define the ends of social action for the nation as a whole. He felt that the lot of men could be improved only gradually and then only if sentiments and the ends of action remain undisturbed by rational inquiry—though in making this argument he advanced a theory of his own based on a concept of reason as an outgrowth of experience and tradition. In Burke's view, the position of the philosophers of the Enlightenment has wholly pernicious repercussions, and a position that gives rise to such consequences must be false. In this type of argument, the truth of an idea is so confused with its social and political effects that the tests of truth and evaluations of the effects become interchangeable. Burke's position is, therefore, an early example of the ideologizing tendencies against which he fought so vigorously but that he helped to initiate nevertheless. By the time he wrote, the old world view had lost its hold over the minds of men; it had become difficult to look upon man's reason and the ends of his action as an ultimately unknowable part of the providential design. Even Burke, who sought to uphold this view, was forced to do so with arguments that were at variance with its basic assumptions.[20]

II. Ideological Dimensions of Social Theory

Introduction

We have seen that Bacon's programmatic declarations of three centuries ago distinguish between the ends of knowledge, the means of advancing it, and the ways in which both the pursuit of knowledge and its results may be used or misused. Bacon seeks to persuade men that the ends of knowledge are worthy ends, ends that justify the hopes of men and need not arouse their fears. Then, taking the value of knowledge as given and considering man's capacity to acquire knowledge a divine gift that is not in question, he advances his "theory of idols" to safeguard men against the errors into which they typically fall. For Bacon, inquiry into error is an unequivocal means to advance the knowledge of nature. In addition, Bacon warns against the misuse of science. He declares, for example, that science and theology must be separated strictly—for the greater enhancement of both. Here the emphasis is neither on the value of advancing science nor on the means of doing so, but on the ways in which its friends and enemies can use or misuse the investigation of nature and its results.

These distinctions—though logically valid—are more difficult to make in social theory. In this field, men have not accepted the value of knowledge to nearly the same extent as in the natural sciences, and the utility of knowledge about man and society has not been demonstrated so effectively. It can be said that men should explore such knowledge and its possible benefits to the limit, since they never know enough to determine that limit. For a long time there was resistance to the advance of knowledge in the natural sciences as well, and—in the absence of constructive alternatives—the solution of problems before us must be sought by all available avenues of detached inquiry. But these considerations, valid as they may be, do not enable us to ignore the ideological dimensions of social theory.

In studies of man and society, it is difficult to keep inquiry distinct from our conception of the purpose of inquiry and from considerations of utility. Scholars who inquire into the sources of error in order to enhance social knowledge must do so in the face of considerable uncertainty about the purpose and the utilization of such knowledge. They are not in the position of natural scientists who could point to increasing evidence of human utility as traditional faith declined. Accordingly, in the social sciences, every new insight into human fallibility raises questions about the role of reason in human affairs and tends to increase, rather than diminish, uncertainty about the ends and uses of knowledge. Here also inquiry into the sources of error is indispensable, but—in the absence of strong evidence about "benefit and uses of life"—this inquiry tends to be linked with efforts to allay uncertainty, to state the case for the value of knowledge, and to ensure that it will serve human progress.

In the twentieth century, a term like "reason" no longer possesses a widely accepted meaning. The present discussion will distinguish between *prudence* and *reason*. The first term refers to the "reason of Everyman," which Hobbes defines as "learning begot by experience which equal time bestows equally on all men." Related to this concept is "cumulative experience" in the sense in which Burke saw that institutions embody the prudence exercised by successive generations of men of affairs. Hobbes and Burke refer to "prudence" as the word is used here. Such prudence is distinguished from reason acquired by specialized experience, which Coke defined with reference to the common law as "an artificial reason acquired by much study." The paradox traced in the next section can be summed up in the statement that our general estimate of prudence has declined, while our estimate of reason acquired by "much study" has increased greatly.

Distrust of Prudence and Belief in Science

The history of social thought since the enlightenment is characterized by exaggerated confidence and doubt. The drive for social knowledge in this "age of ideology" reflects the confidence inspired by progress in the natural sciences. If it is possible to increase our knowledge of nature, then it must be possible to increase our knowledge of man and society. Such knowledge has value, it is asserted, not only for its own sake but as a means of enhancing intellectual clarity and of enlarging man's control of human affairs.[21] Properly employed, knowledge of society can improve men's material condition and enhance the joy and fullness of their lives. In this way, many social scientists might subscribe to Bacon's stirring declarations about the "kingdom of man," were it not for their reticence in propounding a borrowed belief for which supporting evidence in their own fields is not overwhelming or unequivocal.[22] More common perhaps is the approach that emphasizes scientific method, contrasts that method with mere opinion, and urges that the ends and uses of knowledge be considered constructively once our knowledge is sufficiently advanced and secure.[23] On the other hand, social thought since the Enlightenment has developed an image of man as a creature of his drives, habits, and social roles, in whose behavior prudence and choice play no decisive part. If all men are mere creatures of drives and circumstances, then social scientists are not exempt. The investigation of social life would itself be a product of social and psychological conditioning. As such, the quest for knowledge of society would have to be considered as one type of social action among many. Knowledge conceived solely as a product of social life can hold no promise for the improvement of the human condition, and, with this view of knowledge, scholars would have no motive to continue their efforts to increase it.

The paradox is an ancient one, and it is more than a mere logical puzzle.[24] If we assume that all men are products of their passions, then we shall not search for prudence and shall consider what looks like prudence to be a mere by-product of passion. Our hopes will be diminished. The question becomes: What passions do we obey in making these inquiries? Unlike their fellows in other disciplines, social scientists are subject to the restriction that their general assertions about man and society affect society directly and apply significantly to themselves as well. All social inquiry leads to a heightened self-consciousness that easily turns into skepticism, or a kind of anti-intellectualism that results in intuition or technical empiricism. But self-consciousness is also an indispensable intellectual tool. Properly handled, it may enable us to protect social research against the unexamined intrusion of intellectual fashions and thus in some measure to resist influences to which social scientists are subject as members of their societies. To this end, it is useful to explore in some depth the ideological dimensions of social theory, the implications arising from our inquiries into the sources of error, from our conception of the ends of knowledge and from our uses of theories.

Since the time of Bacon, inquiry into the sources of error has greatly advanced our knowledge of men and in the process has greatly lowered our estimate of the effect of prudence on human affairs. Our hopes for the benefits to be derived from knowledge have diminished. To appreciate this development, it is necessary to recall the eighteenth-century belief in progress through science, particularly through analysis of prejudice and the formation of our ideas.

In the view of philosophers like Condillac, Cabanis, Tracy, Helvétius, and Holbach, the good society is the product of man's quest for knowledge. The powers of the altar and the throne stand in the way of this achievement. Representatives of these powers believe they must blind the people and exploit their prejudices in order to keep them subject. To this end, religious fanatics and political rulers interfere with freedom of thought. They must be opposed in the interests of humanity by a deliberate unmasking of prevailing prejudices and by scientific inquiry into the principles of morality, which are believed to be innate in man. To the philosophers of the Enlightenment, the discoverable order of society consists of these principles, which will be revealed once knowledge of ideas and natural law has advanced. This knowledge is a great power in the battle for enlightenment, a power that is feared by those who stand for the prejudices that obscure the moral order. In this view, prejudices are no longer obstructions of the mind, as they were for Bacon, but weapons with which the leaders of established institutions defend the status quo. Vices and crimes, says Helvétius, are errors of judgment closely akin to prejudices. There must be freedom of thought to combat them; such freedom encourages discussions and disputes, which bear fruit in the advance of truth. And it is God's will that truth results from inquiry.[25]

The truths to be discovered are laws of the human mind like those that Tracy and Cabanis sought to discover through their inquiries into the "formation of our ideas." The ideologues were very confident that they knew how to discover such laws. They left the use of these discoveries rather vague, content in the belief that, once the needed educational reforms had been instituted, their philosophical ideas would be used in the schools. Their work was a starting point in the transition from philosophy to the modern sciences of man and society. Both their studies of the "formation of our ideas," as well as their belief in progress through such knowledge, became widely influential through the writings of Henri de Saint-Simon (1760-1825). Following the ideologues, Saint-Simon also makes physiology the basic scientific discipline because it—in contrast to the conjectural sciences— involves theories based on observations that can be verified.[26] With this idea, Saint-Simon actually adds little substance to earlier speculations. But— like Bacon before him—he raises men's hopes in the promise of the new science. He proposes to make morals and politics into a "positive science of Man" on the basis of the knowledge provided by physiology.

> Politics will become a positive science. When those who cultivate this important branch of human knowledge will have learned physiology during the course of their education, they will no longer consider the problems which they have to solve as anything but questions of hygiene.[27]

The implications of this idea are far-reaching, although its generic interest is negligible. Bacon had proposed a reductionist analysis (his theory of "idols") as a safeguard against error; now physiology rather than logic had become the appropriate discipline for analysis of the human mind. Men are considered animals, their physical attributes provide the clues for a properly scientific understanding of all human qualities. Saint-Simon commends this approach on the ground that, in the future, it will make human affairs as easily manageable as personal cleanliness. Rarely perhaps has so low an estimate of man been linked with so high an estimate of science and of what scientists can accomplish by analyzing all human qualities as by-products of physiological processes.

Today—about a century and a half after Saint-Simon's death—our knowledge of man has increased greatly, but our hopes for the use of that knowledge have diminished. While Saint-Simon remains noteworthy only for his attitude toward the science of man, Freud has greatly influenced our understanding of human nature and in particular our awareness of the non-ideational bases of human thought. Freud's work is relevant here as the most far-reaching development of the reductionist tradition. Where the Enlightenment philosophers sought the laws of the human mind in "sensations," Marx in the organization of production, and Nietzsche in the struggle for power, Freud sought them in man's biological make-up. All human behavior leads to pleasure or pain. Man's subjective efforts to increase the first and diminish the second are primarily reflections of a character that is formed through prior experience of drive-satisfactions (or frustrations) in the growing child's relations with his parents. Character is thus the product of what has happened to each individual's organic drives of sex and aggression; satisfaction or frustration of these drives is the primary medium through which the individual forms his patterned responses, sees himself, and relates himself to his significant others. All cultural activities and values are secondary compared with these primary sources of gratification and frustration.

Freud is an heir to the eighteenth-century tradition. Based on a theory of personality-formation, his therapy aims at the improvement of the individual. Patients may find ways out of their emotional difficulties when they have opportunities to reassess their life-experiences and especially the repressed experiences of their early childhoods. But common prudence is of minor importance in avoiding such difficulties and of no importance in finding solutions for them, since prudence is at a discount when a person is emotionally involved. Although Freud believes that men are capable of reassessing their personal histories and—to a degree—reorganizing their lives on that basis, it is catharctic experience above all that leads to this therapeutic use of cognitive and moral faculties. And that catharsis depends in turn upon the therapeutic transaction in which the patient becomes dependent upon his analyst, while the latter—with a detachment achieved through training and control analysis —seeks to help the patient master himself.

Freud does not explain why an elite of psychoanalysts seeks and is capable of attaining such self-mastery and why, in addition, it attempts to help other people attain more effective ways of life. Instead of offering a psychoanalytic interpretation of the quest for psychoanalytic knowledge, he rests his case upon belief in progress through science. In his arguments against the defenders of traditional religion, Freud puts the case of scientific inquiry in the following terms:

1. It is difficult indeed to avoid illusions, and perhaps the hopes men have

for science are illusions also. But men suffer no penalties for not sharing belief in science—in contrast to religion—and all scientific statements, though uncertain, are capable of correction.

2. Defenders of religion and science may agree that the human intellect is weak in comparison with human instincts. But the voice of the intellect, though soft, does not rest until it has gained a hearing. One may be optimistic about the future of mankind, for by its gradual development and despite endless rebuffs the intellect prevails. If, as a defender of religion,

you confine yourself to the belief in a higher spiritual being, whose qualities are indefinable and whose intentions cannot be discerned, then you are proof against the interference of science, but then you will also relinquish the interest of men.

In the name of this Baconian ideal, Freud states his belief that "in the long run nothing can withstand reason and experience."[28]

3. The illusions of religions are basically infantile; once they are discredited, there is nothing left for their believers but to despair of culture and of the future of mankind. The champions of science are free of this bondage. True, secular education probably cannot alter man's psychological nature. But if we acknowledge this fact with resignation, we do not thereby lose interest in life.

We believe that it is possible for scientific work to discover something about the reality of the world through which we can increase our power and according to which we can regulate our life. . . . Science has shown us by numerous and significant successes that it is no illusion.[29]

Those who are skeptical should remember that science is still young; in judging its results we tend to use a foreshortened time perspective. The frequency with which previously established scientific statements are replaced by closer approximations to the truth is a strong argument for the scientific procedure. "Science," Freud concludes, "is no illusion. But it would be an illusion to suppose that we could get anywhere else what it cannot give us."[30] Compared with the strident confidence of a man like Saint-Simon, Freud's advocacy of science is skeptical and subdued. For him, the solution of any human problem is highly complex, and no advance of science is likely to reduce the management of affairs to a question of hygiene.[31]

Saint-Simon's and Freud's inquiries into the "foundation of our ideas" are linked with their concepts of the ends of knowledge. Neither writer is directly concerned with analyzing in depth the implications of the steps taken to guard knowledge against error, both for our concept of the purpose of social knowledge and for the use that is to be made of its results. These ideological implications of social theory are a central theme in the writings of Karl Marx, Alexis de Tocqueville, Emile Durkheim, and Max Weber. Each of these theorists analyzes the social conditioning of knowledge, but each also believes in progress through knowledge and thus faces the task of protecting that belief against the corrosive effects of his own insights.

The Quest for Objectivity and the Uses of Ideas

Karl Marx (1818-1883)

The philosophers of the Enlightenment firmly believed that a just social order can be established through human reason, as long as discussion is free and once education is reorganized on the basis of the "science of ideas." To these men, prejudice has its source in vested interests, while the correct understanding of society results simply from unprejudiced inquiry. This easy optimism was abandoned by Marx.

He conceives of man's intellectual history as a reflection of class struggles. Ideas about society are weapons wielded by contending social classes to attack their enemies and defend their friends. Classes are formed on the basis of the organization of production, which engenders common interests and ideas among individuals who, as capitalists, shopkeepers, craftsmen, wage-earners, and others, make their livings in similar life-situations. Each individual is under the compulsion to make his living under circumstances not of his own choosing; as individuals under these compulsions share common life-experiences arising from the organization of production, they form social classes and develop class consciousness. It is from this source, that awareness of social relations and ideas about society arise, and, because of their fundamental importance, these class-compulsions affect all other aspects of consciousness as well. Accordingly, for Marx, all aspects of cultural life reflect the class struggle. Men of ideas differ among themselves only in the degrees to which they are subject to the compulsions of the class struggle and the manners in which they transform these compulsions intellectually.

In Marx's view, knowledge of man and society depends upon and changes with the class structure, and this dependence must be analyzed anew in each case. Inquiry into the "foundations of our ideas" (reductionism) is no longer a means to knowledge; it has become a type of knowledge in its own right. For Marx distinguishes social structures like feudalism, capitalism, and socialism, not only in terms of their respective class structures, but also in terms of the religious beliefs and the knowledge of social reality that "corresponds" to these structures. In the feudal period, men are easily swayed by the fantastic images of mythology and religion. Because technology is backward, material satisfactions are impossible to obtain for the masses of the people; thus men unwittingly exchange spiritual for material satisfactions. In feudal society, social relations are marked by a pervasive personal dependence, of which the members of that society are fully aware, because it is not "disguised under the shape of social relations between products of labor."[32]

This disguise of social relations arises because capitalist society is

based upon the production of commodities, in which the producers in general enter into social relations with one another by treating their products as commodities and values, whereby they reduce their individual private labor to the standard of homogeneous human labor—for such a society, Christianity with its *cultus* of abstract man, more especially in its bourgeois developments, Protestantism, Deism, etc., is the most fitting form of religion.[33]

Religion prevents men from actively changing the world in which they live, but, under feudalism, technology is backward and the promise of change small, while under capitalism, the real satisfaction of material needs is possible. On the basis of modern technology, capitalism has created an unprecedented productive potential, but its exploitative system of production has also created a misery that is unprecedented because—for the first time in history—it has become unnecessary. Under capitalism, religion prevents men from seeing that their misery can now be abolished; it is an opiate of the people in that sense. In addition, everything is reduced to the status of a commodity that is judged in terms of its price on the market, not in terms of its intrinsic value. As a result, the relations between one man and another are obscured, for their transaction appears to them in terms of its price. For example, the "personal" dependence of the worker on his employer appears to both in terms of the wage agreed upon in the employment contract. All human values become quantified and homogeneous, while social relations are mediated by the mechanism of the market. Christianity, however, helps to prevent men from recognizing the dehumanization or alienation that results from this subjection to the compulsions of the market and the organization of production.

Under socialism, these conditions are radically altered. Marx's critique of capitalism becomes clearer by means of this contrast. He never speaks in detail about the socialist society of the future, but he claims that religion will disappear, along with the reasons for its previous importance—namely, the alienation of men from control over the means of production and from their fellow men.

> Let us now picture to ourselves . . . a community of free individuals, carrying on their work with the means of production in common, in which the labor-power of all the individuals is consciously applied as the combined labor-power of the community. All the characteristics of Robinson [Crusoe's] labor are here repeated, but with this difference, that they are social, instead of individual. Everything produced by him was exclusively the result of his own personal labor, and therefore simply an object of use for himself. The total product of our community is a social product. One portion serves as fresh means of production and remains social. But another portion is consumed by the members as means of subsistence. A distribution of this portion among them is consequently necessary.

While the mode of this distribution will vary with the productive organization and the historical development of the producers,

> The social relations of the individual producers, with regard both to their labor and to its products, are in this case perfectly simple and intelligible, and that with regard not only to production but also to distribution. . . . [34]

Since alienation arises from social relations mediated by trading on a market, alienation will be abolished once men re-establish direct, unmediated relationships with their work and their fellows through control over the processes of production and distribution. Under modern conditions, such control must be collective. Once such collective control is established, the conditions that favor religious ideas and appeals will have disappeared.

> The religious reflex of the real world can, in any case, only then finally vanish, when the practical relations of everyday life offer to man none but perfectly intelligible and reasonable relations with regard to his fellow men and to nature.
> The life-process of society, which is based on the process of material production, does not strip off its mystical veil until it is treated as production by freely associated men, and is consciously regulated by them in accordance with a settled plan.[35]

But once it is so treated, the need for illusions has disappeared, because the relations among men and between men and nature have become "perfectly simple and intelligible."

Freedom from illusion about the relations of men in society is seen as a by-product of the classless society of the future. For Marx, knowledge of man and society remains ideological, an example of what he calls "false consciousness," as long as it is conditioned by the class struggle. No man is exempt from this conditioning while that struggle continues. In this context, Marx posits a nexus between existing social relations and the ordinary man's ability to comprehend them. His repeated references to the simplicity and intelligibility of social relations suggest that these relations are more intelligible in some social structures than in others. "Intelligibility" refers to the understanding of ordinary men, a kind of prudence uncontaminated by ideology that will become possible once class struggles have ceased and men have come into their own in terms of the full use of their rational and creative faculties. But Marx also contrasts his own scientific analysis with the ideological interpretations of classical economists, utopian socialists, and others.[36] He likes to compare his approach with that characteristic of the physical and biological sciences.[37] In this way, scientific knowledge of society—implicitly distinguished from the ordinary man's understanding of social relations—appears possible under capitalism. Ideological distortion is not therefore an inevitable by-product of a society rent by class conflict. Despite his distrust of prudence and reason, Marx clings to the eighteenth-century belief that scientific knowledge of society is attainable and will play an important historical role.

> . . . In times when the class struggle nears the decisive hour, the process of dissolution going on within the ruling class—in fact, within the whole range of an old society— assumes such a violent, glaring character that a small section of the ruling class cuts itself adrift and joins the revolutionary class, the class that holds the future in its hands. Just as, therefore, at an earlier period, a section of the nobility went over to the bourgeoisie, so now a portion of the bourgeoisie goes over to the proletariat, and in particular, a portion of the *bourgeois ideologists, who have raised themselves to the level of comprehending theoretically the historical movements as a whole.*[38]

In this view, the workers will provide the political momentum for the great historical change to come; they will cause a revolutionary upheaval against the material and psychological inhumanities to which they have been subjected, but they do not possess the intellectual tools to direct that upheaval. This direction will be provided by bourgeois ideologists who respond to the dissolution of their own class, the miseries of the proletariat, and the historical opportunities that arise from the intensified class struggle and the underutilization of man's productive potential.

Accordingly, Marx clings to both horns of the ideological dilemma. He insists on the reductionist analysis of ideas as emanations of the class struggle. From this perspective, illusion and ideology will finally vanish from our understanding of society only when the life process of society is regulated by freely associated men in accordance with a settled plan.[39] If truth about society will be attained only in the society of the future, then social knowledge has no constructive role here and now. But Marx does not accept this implication, which would cut the ground from under his own claim to be a scientist and a political leader. His whole work is a life-long insistence upon man's capacity to forge the intellectual instruments for the reorganization of society. Accordingly, he shifts back and forth between reductionism and the affirmation of his belief in the constructive role of ideas. The position of the working class under capitalism provides the lever for the re-organization of society (reductionist analysis), but the labor movement cannot be successful unless it is guided by the results of scientific inquiry (belief in reason). In responding to the ever more glaring contradictions of capitalist society (reductionist analysis), bourgeois ideologists "raise themselves" to an understanding of the historical movement (belief in reason).

This intellectual posture reflects the agonized twisting and turning of a man who believes, or wants to believe, in the historically constructive role of human intelligence but whose inquiries undermine that belief. By treating all knowledge as a distorting reflex of the real world, Marx casts doubt upon the ends and uses of knowledge and of all human activities. Since, under capitalism, men pervert rather than enhance the "benefit of life," all positive and undistorted use of intelligence in the present is precarious. Subsequent history and the vulgarizations of his followers have obscured the fundamental tragedy of Marx as a man of knowledge. He wants to know—accurately and dispassionately—but he also wants to make sure that the knowledge gained will play a constructive role in human affairs. Yet his theory casts doubt upon the belief in reason to which his life's work is dedicated. Perhaps these contradictions explain the passion of Marx, the wild polemics against his opponents, the promethean hope, and the undercurrent of despair. Consideration of a near contemporary, Alexis de Tocqueville, will reveal the work of a man who grappled with similar problems but did not conceal from himself the tragedy of the man of knowledge who seeks to assess and to up-grade the role of prudence in human affairs.

Alexis de Tocqueville (1805-1859)

Tocqueville is a seeker after truth, he believes in reason, and he wants to enhance the "benefit and use of life"—quite as much as Marx. But while Marx is an heir of the Enlightenment, Tocqueville is an heir of its critics. Where Marx carries forward the eighteenth-century belief in science and develops particularly the "science of ideas," Tocqueville makes no reference to the scientific approach and, if anything, opposes—as Burke had done—the reductionist analysis of ideas. Where Marx follows the model of the natural sciences and insists upon the hardheaded objectivity of his materialistic approach (despite the manifest passion of his writings), Tocqueville patterns himself after writers like Montesquieu and avows his passionate concern with moral problems.

Yet Tocqueville knows full well that the pursuit of knowledge must be guarded against bias and error and that the passions of partisanship aroused in the wake of the French Revolution jeopardize objectivity. It is characteristic of the man that his discussions of method and his claims to objectivity appear not in his published writings but in his correspondence with friends. Tocqueville does not claim to be a scientist and therefore does not publicize his procedures and erudition so that his objectivity may be checked by others, as in the natural sciences. Yet dispassionate inquiry is indispensable to sound judgment, and Tocqueville states the reasons why he believes himself to be dispassionate.

They ascribe to me alternately aristocratic and democratic prejudices. If I had been born in another period, or in another country, I might have had either the one or the other. But my birth, as it happened, made it easy for me to guard against both. I came into the world at the end of a long revolution, which after destroying ancient institutions, had created none that could last. When I entered life, aristocracy was dead and democracy as yet unborn. My instinct, therefore, could not lead me blindly either to the one or to the other. I lived in a country which for forty years had tried everything and settled nothing. I was on my guard, therefore, against political illusions. Myself belonging to the ancient aristocracy of my country, I had no natural hatred or jealousy of the aristocracy; nor could I have any natural affection for it, since that aristocracy had ceased to exist, and one can be strongly attached only to the living. I was near enough to know it thoroughly, and far enough to judge dispassionately. I may say as much for the democratic element. It had done me, as an individual, neither good nor harm. I had no personal motive, apart from my public convictions, to love or to hate it. Balanced between the past and the future, with no natural instinctive attraction towards either, I could without an effort look quietly on each side of the question.[40]

Accidents of birth and historical circumstance are here advanced as the basis of his objectivity. In reductionist analysis, the social conditioning of knowledge is ordinarily perceived as a source of error and bias, but Tocqueville attributes to that conditioning his own freedom from bias.[41] He readily acknowledges that other circumstances might have led him to adopt the aristocratic or democratic prejudices now falsely attributed to him. That it did not happen is the result of attributes entirely unique to his person and his situation. True to his aristocratic heritage Tocqueville thus guards against bias in a manner that is totally incompatible with the equalitarian tenets of science. For in science safeguards against error and bias are accepted only if they are open to public inspection and therefore in principle accessible to everyone who adopts the required procedures.

But if Tocqueville is aristocratic in his claim to objectivity, he also makes good his contention that he is dispassionate. In his view, the development of human societies toward greater equality of conditions is an established fact, decreed by providence. Unlike his fellow aristocrats, he does not deny what he considers to be inevitable or quarrel with it or resist it to the last. Instead, he seeks to understand the conditions of equality, in all their implications, as in his great work *Democracy in America*. He concludes, it is true, that under these conditions a government "cannot be maintained without certain conditions of intelligence, of private morality, and of religious belief," but he believes that these conditions can be attained, since "after all it may be God's will to spread a moderate amount of happiness over all men, instead of heaping a large sum upon a few by allowing only a small minority to approach perfection."[42] Tocqueville thus accepts the goals of democracy but attempts to "diminish the ardor of the Republican party" by showing that democracy is not an easily realized dream and—while conferring benefits on the people—is not likely to develop the "noblest powers of the human mind." At the same time, he attempts to "abate the claims of the aristocrats" by showing that democracy is not synonymous with destruction and anarchy but compatible with order, liberty, and religion. Democracy of this kind, rather than an unspeakable tyranny, can be achieved if the aristocratic opponents will not resist what they lack the power to prevent. By making the "impulse in one quarter and resistance in the other . . . less violent" Tocqueville seeks to ensure a peaceable development of society.[43]

This balance in the political sphere is matched by Tocqueville's capacity for self-scrutiny, which helps him to preserve the objectivity of his pursuit of knowledge. Aristocratic background and a realistic assessment of men lead to a somber view indeed. "I love mankind in general, but I constantly meet with individuals whose baseness revolts me."[44] Or, "If to console you for having been born, you must meet with men whose most secret motives are always actuated by fine and elevated feelings, you need not wait, you may go and drown yourself immediately."[45] Tocqueville also reminds his friends and himself, however, that in fact such high motives are predominant in a few men and that they occur even in a large majority of men from time to time. Consequently, one "need not make such faces at the human race."[46] Nor is it only a matter of general attitude. Rather one should be alert to the unwitting effect that our estimate of men has upon human affairs and upon ourselves.

Some persons try to be of use to men while they despise them, and others because they love them. In the services rendered by the first there is always something incomplete, rough, and contemptuous that inspires neither confidence nor gratitude. I should like to belong to the second class, but often I cannot. . . . I struggle daily against a universal contempt for my fellow-creatures. I sometimes succeed, at my own expense, by a minute uncompromising investigation into the motives of my own conduct.[47]

Tocqueville states that, when he tries to judge himself as if he were an indifferent spectator or opponent, he is more inclined to "drop a little in my own esteem" than to place too low an estimate on other men. And elsewhere he declares that "man with his vices, his weaknesses, and his virtues, strange combination though he be of good and evil, of grandeur and of baseness, is still, on the whole, the object most worthy of study, interest, pity, attachment, and admiration in the world, and since we have no angels, we cannot attach ourselves, or devote ourselves to anything greater or nobler than our fellow-creatures."[48]

Aristocrat though he was, Tocqueville put himself on a par with the masses of men, who were the objects of his most passionate concern. Considering the march toward greater equality inevitable, he devoted his life to the furtherance of men's understanding of the democratic societies that were emerging, so that they might be safeguarded against the dangers of despotism. Since he did not base his claim to be heard either on his background or on his standing as a scholar but solely on the strength of his concern, his personal detachment, and the persuasiveness of his reasoning, Tocqueville found a very direct relationship between his ideas and political action, even though he disclaimed not so much the ambitions, as the qualifications of great statesmanship.

No! I certainly do not laugh at political convictions; I do not consider them as indifferent in themselves, and as mere instruments in the hands of men. I laugh bitterly at the monstrous abuse that is every day made of them, as I laugh when I see virtue and religion turned to dishonest uses, without losing any of my respect for virtue and religion. I struggle with all my might against the false wisdom, the fatal indifference, which in our day saps the energy of so many great minds. I try not to have two worlds: a moral one, where I still delight in all that is good and noble, and the other political, where I may lie with my face to the ground, enjoying the full benefit of the dirt which covers it.[49]

Here, then, is detachment in the pursuit of knowledge, a passionate concern for the "good of mankind" and a direct effort to use knowledge to this end.

For Tocqueville, politics is the natural arena in which that knowledge must be applied in order to affect the course of human affairs.[50]

Tocqueville's assessment of this task is strikingly different from that of Marx. Committed to the proletarian cause as the lever for the reorganization of society, Marx nevertheless distinguishes sharply between the untutored proletariat and the bourgeois ideologists who analyze the capitalist economy and understand history. Despite his populist stance and his insistence that ultimately proletarian class consciousness and the scientific understanding of capitalism develop in response to the class struggle, Marx makes clear that, for the time being, what workers *are* is far more important than what they *think*.

It is not relevant what this or that worker or even what the whole proletariat *conceive* to be their aim, for the time being. It matters only *what* the proletariat *is* and that it will be forced to act historically in accordance with this *being*. The aim and the historical action of the proletariat are clearly and irrevocably outlined by its life situation as well as by the entire organization of present-day bourgeois society.[51]

Tocqueville, on the other hand, makes no distinction between men of knowledge and the masses of the people—despite his aristocratic background. He is convinced, furthermore, that, to influence the course of events, it will not do to "cure all our ills" by institutional means, for institutions exert "only a secondary influence over the destinies of men." For him, the "excellence of political societies" depends upon the "sentiments, principles, and opinions, the moral and intellectual qualities given by nature and education to the men of whom they consist."[52]

Accordingly, Tocqueville believes that—if men develop the moral and intellectual qualities necessary to the task—they will be able to avert the dangers of despotism implicit in democracy. His own inquiry into the natural tendencies of a democratic society seeks to point out these dangers so that by timely discovery and confrontation "we may look our enemies in the face and know against what we have to fight."[53] Tocqueville sees these "natural tendencies" in precarious balance with the forces opposing them. In concluding his *Democracy in America*, he writes:

The nations of our time cannot prevent the conditions of men from becoming more equal, but it depends upon themselves whether the principle of equality is to lead them to servitude or freedom, to knowledge or barbarism, to prosperity or wretchedness.[54]

Tocqueville does not believe that it is possible to predict the outcome of this struggle. In the face of uncertainty he wishes society to behave "like a strong man who exposes himself to the danger before him as a necessary part of his undertaking and is alarmed only when he cannot see clearly what it is."[55] On another occasion, Tocqueville makes clear the significance of this position. The eighteenth century had "an exaggerated and somewhat childish trust in the control which men and peoples were supposed to have of their own destinies." That idea may have led to many follies, but it also produced great things. Since the revolution, however, so many generous ideas and great hopes have miscarried that men have been led to the opposite extreme.

After having felt ourselves capable of transforming ourselves, we now feel incapable of reforming ourselves; after having had excessive pride, we have now fallen into excessive self-pity; we thought we could do everything, and now we think we can do nothing; we like to think that struggle and effort are henceforth useless and that our blood, muscles, and nerves will always be stronger than our will power and courage. This is really the great sickness of our age. . . [56]

It is this sickness against which Tocqueville takes his stand, an heir of the Enlightenment in the tradition of Montesquieu.

Nevertheless, Tocqueville's life was marked by profound pessimism. At the age of thirty-one, he wrote to a friend of his desire to persuade men that respect for law and religion must be combined with freedom and that to grant freedom is the best way of preserving morality and religon. "You will tell me that this is impossible; I am inclined to the same opinion; but it is the truth, and I will speak it at all risks. . . ."[57] At the age of forty-three, at the time of the 1848 Revolution, he wrote to the same friend that, if he had had children, he would warn them to be prepared for everything, for no one can count on the future.

In France especially, men should rely on nothing that can be taken away; [they should] try to acquire those things which one can never lose till one ceases to exist: fortitude, energy, knowledge, and prudence. . . .[58]

And toward the end of his life, at the age of fifty-one, he wrote to Madame Swetchine:

No tranquillity and no material comfort can in my mind make up for the loss [of liberty]. And yet I see that most of the men of my time—of the most honest among them, for I care little about the others—think only of accommodating themselves to the new system and, what most of all disturbs and alarms me, turn a taste for slavery into a virtue. I could not think and feel as they do, if I tried: it is even more repugnant to my nature than to my will. . . . You can hardly imagine how painful, and often bitter, it is to me to live in this moral isolation; to feel myself shut out of the intellectual commonwealth of my age and country.[59]

We see that Tocqueville passionately believed in freedom and rejected the reductionist analysis as false wisdom tending toward "the unfair circumscription of human power." Yet throughout his life he was haunted by the impenetrability of the future and by the melancholy realization that the truths he had discovered were *not* being used for the "good of mankind." As a result, despite his relations, neighbors, and friends, his mind had "not a family or a country."[60] The contrast with Marx is startling, if we consider that this life-long exile who had family but few friends and, one suspects, few neighbors, derived courage and confidence in his mission from the very determinism that Tocqueville rejected, from the conviction that he had "comprehended theoretically the historical movement as a whole." It is hard to resist the conclusion that the wish for power through knowledge was father to Marx's determinist and reductionist theories, while Tocqueville's quest for truth without the promise of power was linked with his willingness to face the tragedy of moral isolation.

Emile Durkheim (1858-1917)

The experience of moral isolation is as central a problem for Durkheim as for Tocqueville. Writing some of his major works during the years of the Dreyfus Affair (1895-1906), Durkheim witnessed a threat to moral standards fully as great as did Tocqueville when he observed the destruction of old institutions by the French Revolution and the failure of French society to

achieve institutional stability thereafter. The work of both men is deeply
affected by these experiences; like the critics of the Enlightenment, both are
preoccupied with questions of morality. Yet the two differ profoundly.
For Tocqueville, moral isolation was an intense, personal experience, as well
as an object of study. As a champion of liberty, he was conscious of the
degree to which liberty is jeopardized by the moral weaknesses associated
with the drive for equality; he believed that his contemporaries had abandoned the ideals of the eighteenth century, and he felt the loneliness of his
position. Durkheim was also affected by the moral decline he witnessed
about him, but moral isolation appears to have been a less personal experience for him than for Tocqueville. Belief in science furnished the moral
basis of Durkheim's approach. He is the champion of sociology as a science,
and he endeavors to introduce his chosen discipline into the scientific community. Durkheim states this purpose clearly:

> Our principal objective is to extend scientific rationalism to human behavior. It can be
> shown that behavior of the past, when analyzed, can be reduced to relationships of cause
> and effect. These relationships can then be transformed, by an equally logical operation,
> into rules of action for the future. . . . It therefore seems to us that in these times of
> renascent mysticism an undertaking such as ours should be regarded quite without appre-
> hension and even with sympathy by all those who, while disagreeing with us on certain
> points, yet share our faith in the future of reason.[61]

We shall see that, in Durkheim's view, it is science and not—as with Tocqueville—liberty, morality, and religion that will reconstruct the moral order.

To establish sociology as a science is Durkheim's central concern. In his
very first publication, his Latin thesis on *Montesquieu's Contribution to the
Rise of Social Science*, Durkheim emphasizes the distinction between science
and art.[62] Life goes on, decisions about what to do must be made quickly,
and the reasons for our actions are hastily assembled. "We improvise a
science as we go along," but such collected arguments, by which men of
action support their opinions, "do not reflect phenomena . . . but merely
states of mind."

> Even in abstract questions, no doubt, our ideas spring from the heart, for the heart
> is the source of our entire life. But if our feelings are not to run away with us, they must
> be governed by reason. Reason must be set above the accidents and contingencies of life.[63]

Accordingly, science must be advanced in complete independence and "in
utter disregard of utility." The more clear-cut the distinction between science
and art, which Durkheim defines as decisions on what to do, the more
useful science will be for art.

This distinction does not, however, prompt Durkheim to inquire into the
sources of error as a safeguard of objectivity. Instead, he proceeds to define "the conditions necessary for the establishment of social science." Each
science must have its own specific object. The only objects that admit of
scientific study are those that constitute a type, that share "features common
to all individuals of the same type," that are finite in number and ascertain-
able. But description of types must be supplemented by interpretation,
which presupposes stable relations between cause and effect, for without
them everything is fortuitous and does not admit of interpretation.[64] No social
science is possible if societies are not subject to laws. No one dares

question the possibility of natural science; the principal assumptions underlying these sciences have been tested and never found false; hence they are "also valid, in all likelihood, for human societies, which are part of nature."[65] Like Marx before him, Durkheim takes the established natural sciences for his model, but he is quite specific in his use of this model.

So long as everything in human societies seemed so utterly fortuitous, no one could have thought of classifying them. There can be no types of things unless there are causes which, though operating in different places and at different times, always and everywhere produce the same effects. And where is the object of social science if the lawgiver can organize and direct social life as he pleases? The subject matter of science can consist only of things that have a stable nature of their own and are able to resist the human will.[66]

Even then it is not enough to have a subject matter that can be investigated scientifically. Rather, a method of investigation is needed that does not exist ready-made but must be developed as social science grapples with the great complexities that confront it.

In his *Rules of Sociological Method,* Durkheim elaborates this point by stating the basic theoretical assumptions of his work.

1. Social phenomena are a reality *sui generis,* and they cannot be explained by reference to less complex or nonsocial phenomena—exactly as psychological phenomena can be understood only as such rather than by a reduction to physiological processes, for example.

2. Sociology is the study of social groups, albeit groups composed of individuals. The group, however, is a new, synthetic reality, arising from the *association* of individuals.

3. At its own level, society must be observed with regard to the consciousness that it forms of itself as a collectivity, much as the individual is observed through his consciousness. The collective thought embodied in language is an obvious example of such collective consciousness.

4. Language, like moral rules, religious beliefs and practices, myth, folklore, proverbs, popular sayings, and other aspects of culture, is *external* to the individual and exercises a *moral constraint* upon him. That is, these collective "representations" exist when the individual comes into the world. He acquires them unwittingly. The fact that he is constrained to acquire them becomes apparent only when he violates cultural norms and his violation is censured.[67]

In later comments on his work, Durkheim seeks to correct the impression that his is an entirely collectivist approach that totally subordinates the individual. He insists that society exists only in and through individuals, that the collective derivation of their thought and feeling is as natural to them as the air they breathe.[68] Accordingly, "society" is imminent in the individual at the same time that it transcends him by virtue of its greater duration and power of constraint. Even in his efforts to qualify his emphasis on the collectivity, Durkheim only re-emphasizes how far he has carried the analytical reduction of individual consciousness.

Symptomatic in this respect are two explicit discussions of individualism. Durkheim considers the cult of the individual a great threat to social solidarity, especially in the context of economic liberalism and competition. But he also appears to reconcile himself to the pervasiveness of individualism in the modern world by showing that individualism itself is a product of society.[69]

Durkheim considers the same problem again in his last writings, in which he takes cognizance of the frequent antagonism of social relations. Our bodily appetites are self-centered and are therefore the foundation of individuality, while our minds are typically preoccupied with ideas that are socially derived and therefore universal. Accordingly, *individuality* results from the biochemical nature of every person; it is a composite by-product of those purely physical attributes that make every man unique. *Personality,* on the other hand, has its source in the feelings and ideas that are shared by the members of a collectivity. This conception is consistent with Durkheim's theory that the idea of the soul and its independence from the finite existence of the body (immortality) is founded in the fact that society continues while individuals are born and die.[70] In this way, Durkheim rejects the earlier reductionism of the ideologues, who analyze all intellectual and moral activity in terms of a substratum of bodily activity (sensations), while advancing a sociological reductionism of his own that cites man's biological attributes as the only source of individuality. Paradoxically, the individual is here located in what all men have in common, while his psychological and intellectual faculties become the locus of a common humanity, despite the fact that, as Voltaire says, variety is spread over the face of the earth through cultural differences.

This concluding paradox of Durkheim's life's work brings us back to the ideological dimensions of social theory. How does Durkheim's sociological theory affect his conception of the ends of knowledge and the uses of his ideas? He analyzes how European society is characterized increasingly by an absence of valid social norms (anomie), a moral decline attributable to the increasing division of labor. If modern society is to become "healthy" once again, legal regulations are required that will not be punitive but will rather encourage co-operation; and social solidarity must be fostered by voluntary associations of occupational groups.[71] But to achieve these effects, men must now rely on knowledge, since traditional beliefs have lost their efficacy. Durkheim points out that:

Man seeks to learn and man kills himself because of the loss of cohesion in his religious society; he does not kill himself because of his learning. It is certainly not the learning he acquires that disorganizes religion; but the desire for knowledge wakens because religion becomes disorganized. Knowledge is not sought as a means to destroy accepted opinions but because their destruction has commenced.[72]

Here and throughout Durkheim's work the basic cause of a declining morality is seen as a *loss of social cohesion* of which the decline of religion, the tendency to commit suicide, and the quest for knowledge are different symptoms or consequences. But if this view is valid, then why does Durkheim expect or hope that knowledge or science, which is among these consequences, is capable nevertheless of constructing a new and more vigorous morality? His answer is:

Far from knowledge being the source of the evil, it is its remedy, the only remedy we have. Once established beliefs have been carried away by the current of affairs, they cannot be artificially reestablished; only reflection can guide us in life, after this. Once the social instinct is blunted, intelligence is the only guide left us and we have to reconstruct a conscience by its means. Dangerous as is the undertaking there can be no hesitation, for we have no choice. . . . [Science] has not the dissolvent effect ascribed to it, but is the only weapon for our battle against the dissolution which gives birth to science itself.[73]

Durkheim adds that one must not make a "self-sufficient end" out of science or education. They are only means or guides to aid us in our efforts to reconstruct a "social conscience."

But what can we hope from intelligence and science for the construction of a new morality when science tells us that moral standards remain intact only as long as sacred beliefs are shared by the members of a collectivity? Although Durkheim believes or hopes that science can achieve this end, even he shows skepticism to a degree when he refers to intelligence and science as the *only guide or weapon left to us*. Throughout his work, Durkheim demonstrates that moral norms are viable only to the extent that the social cohesion of groups remains unimpaired but that this cohesion must decline as a result of the division of labor. At the end, what remains is Durkheim's subjective faith in reason, undermined intellectually by the theory and evidence that he developed in order to sustain it.

Max Weber (1864-1920)

Of the four theorists considered here, Max Weber is certainly the one who most directly concerns himself with the problem of objectivity. He does not view scientific neutrality as a by-product of the historical process as does Marx, of circumstance and personal quality as does Tocqueville, or of the effort to establish sociology after the model of the natural sciences as does Durkheim. For Weber, objectivity results from the deliberate efforts of the scholar. While Tocqueville claims objectivity as a concomitant of personal experience, Weber seeks to achieve it through methodological clarification and self-restraint. But like Tocqueville, Weber emphasizes the importance of ideas and sentiments for an understanding of social life—in contrast to Marx and Durkheim, who continue the tradition of the ideologues. It is true that Weber, as well as Tocqueville, appreciates the insights of this tradition, which seeks to understand ideas by an analytical reduction to the organization of production or the degree of cohesion attained in human association. Nevertheless, both consider ideas an irreducible factor in social life, and it is above all in his analysis of ideas that Weber's claim to scientific objectivity must be assessed.

The intellectual vantage point of these theorists is clearest perhaps in their treatment of religion. For Marx, the "religious reflex" provides a spurious gratification of human desires, a spiritual justification of the inhumanities of man's social condition. Now that technology has advanced sufficiently to fulfill these desires, religion has become unnecessary and will disappear. Tocqueville considers religious faith among the highest manifestations of the human spirit and is aghast at the abuses and perversions to which it is subjected. To preserve liberty, even though the relations among men become more equal, it is necessary to strengthen religion and morality. Toward the end of his life, Tocqueville became personally more religious as he recognized the growth of secularism among his contemporaries. For Durkheim, religion is an object of study, as enduring a phenomenon as Tocqueville believed it to be, but not a personal concern. Science cannot accept the literal truth of religious beliefs, but it recognizes and analyzes the symbolic truth they express. For Durkheim, religion arises from the reality of group life: "It is society which the faithful worship; the superiority of the gods over men is that of the group over its members."[74] Weber's approach to religion contains all these elements. Like Marx, he recognizes the material interests involved in religious beliefs and institutions, especially the economic interests of religious functionaries. Yet, like Tocqueville, he also considers religious ideas as an aspect of human creativity. Personally areligious, Weber takes as scientific an interest in religion as does Durkheim. But unlike Durkheim, who focuses on primitive religion in order to understand its "essence," Weber concentrates on the age of religious creativity (Confucius, Buddha, Old Testament prophets) in order to understand the characteristics of Western civilization. This attempt to analyze the highest manifestations of human spirituality gives special point to Weber's concern with the problem of scientific objectivity.

All inquiry is initiated by the subjective orientation of the investigator. In the natural sciences, this orientation depends on the results previously obtained, the unresolved problems suggested by these results, and the ingenuity of the researcher. In the social sciences, cumulation is evident primarily in the collection of data. In the interpretation of these data, it is less evident and more difficult to sustain, even when it exists. The reason is that the questions raised for investigation depend more upon considerations of cultural relevance (*Wertbezogenheit*) than upon previous findings. The different approaches to the study of religion already mentioned exemplify the mutability of such considerations. But this genuine difficulty is not a bar to objectivity. If the same questions are raised about the same data, then equally competent men will arrive at the same conclusions—provided that, in their handling of the investigation, value-judgments (*Werturteile*) do not intrude. It is at this point that Weber sees the major obstacle to objectivity.

His most explicit statements in this respect are directed at those teachers who misuse their professorial positions in order to propagate political opinions under the guise of science. Weber's attack was occasioned by nationalist professors in Imperial Germany who were unable or unwilling to distinguish between their civic and their academic responsibilities. His argument in this case is simply a criticism of professional malpractice. In many settings, it is relatively easy to answer this criticism by explicit attention to the matter. The speaker or writer himself declares what his values are and warns his listeners or readers that they must not mistake certain statements for judgments authenticated by scientific findings. Rather, value-judgments must be assessed by each person in the light of his own evaluations. Along these lines, Weber's injunctions against value-judgments appear to be trivial because they are easy to follow.

Yet Weber himself does not consider them trivial. He insists passionately on the separation of value-judgments from scientific inquiry, for he is as deeply concerned with the one as with the other. Failure to observe this separation appears to him an abuse of science *and* a monstrous desecration of what men hold most dear—in contrast to Tocqueville who sees in that same separation a "false wisdom" and a "fatal indifference." At this point, the hiatus between the two men's thought could not be greater—despite affinity in other respects.

Weber is directly concerned with the formulation of concepts for research; Tocqueville is not. For Weber, the exclusion of value-judgments is the precondition of scientific inquiry about man and society. Concepts must be so formulated that they enable us to identify types of social phenomenon unequivocally and without intrusion from "the will and the affections" (Bacon). Such classification and identification are elementary scientific procedure. The zoologist hardly requires a reminder that his special liking for fox terriers has no bearing on the matter he studies. A social theorist like Weber, however, may wish to identify the magnetic appeal that commanding personalities have had for masses of people throughout history. Where the fact of this appeal is unquestioned, the concept "charisma" applies, whether the reference is to a holy man like St. Francis of Assisi or a "great bird of prey" like Alexander the Great.[75] Weber insists that the enormous ethical gulf between two such figures must be considered in its own moral terms, clearly separated from the finding that they have at least one trait in common. I shall comment later on the use and abuse of this position.

The value-neutral formulation of concepts is as crucial for Weber as is the theoretical foundation of sociology for Durkheim. Both men are committed to the advancement of knowledge, but the difference between them is marked. For Durkheim, social science becomes possible to the degree that "realities can be reduced to a type" consisting of "the features common to all individuals of the same type." A social science that characterizes a typical social phenomenon, "cannot fail to describe the normal form of social life . . . ; whatever pertains to the type is normal, and whatever is normal is healthy.[76] Durkheim subscribes to a philosophical realism that identifies the concept of type with the typicality of the phenomenon as it exists. Consequently, he considers it indispensable for social science

to discover *in the data themselves* some definite indication enabling us to distinguish between sickness and health. If such a sign is lacking, we are driven to take refuge in deduction and move away from the concrete facts.[77]

This position Weber rejects *in toto*. Terms like "health" or "sickness" are for him synonyms for "good" and "evil" when applied to society, criteria of moral worth by which men arrive at ethical judgments.[78] Accordingly, there is no normal or typical form of social life, as there is for Durkheim. Social phenomena exist for Weber in a continuity that allows no natural demarcation.[79] Instead of positing natural types with a more or less stable arrangement of their elements, as Durkheim would have it, Weber posits ideal types—benchmark concepts constructed out of a one-sided simplification and exaggeration of the evidence as it is found in society.

This basic difference in orientation has several consequences. For Durkheim, the purpose of ascertaining natural types is to understand the feature common to all individuals of a given type. By recognizing the similar social constraints to which all these individuals are subject, we can explain their actions in terms of cause and effect. This knowledge enables us to understand what is normal and healthy in social life and to act accordingly. For Weber, on the other hand, the purpose of constructing ideal types is to interpret the meaning that men in social life associate with their actions, to understand what sense it makes to them to act as they do.[80] The simplifications and exaggerations involved in this procedure are designed to give order to the multiplicity of phenomena. By referring to these artificial benchmarks, the analyst can assess the real actions documented or observed.[81] An example is the ideal type of the charismatic leader and the routinization of his charismatic appeal, perhaps through institutionalization. In Weber's view, the analyst can assess the degree to which a given action approaches the ideal type of a personal or institutionalized charisma without himself evaluating these approximations. The purpose of this procedure is not to achieve causal explanation, however. Weber makes quite clear that for him sociology is an auxiliary discipline, one that uses the comparative and classificatory procedure to distinguish between what is general and what is unique. In this way, sociology establishes what is recurrent in different societies, while history explains the unique event.[82]

It follows that Weber's conception of purpose is more cautious than that of Durkheim. The idea that men pursue knowledge for its own sake or for intellectual clarity cannot be found in Durkheim, who puts major emphasis upon enlarging man's control of human affairs. Weber subscribes to all three objectives, but he is especially circumspect with regard to the practical uses of social science—in keeping with his emphasis on the hiatus between theory and action, between the detachment of the scientist and the commitment essential to the man of action. Having once taken the position that truth is not a by-product of history, that analytical categories and criteria of "social health" do not reside in the data themselves, Weber is consistent. The scientist can ascertain the facts, point out the assets and liabilities of alternative actions, clarify value-positions in terms of their internal consistency and possible consequences, but he can do no more. His role is that of counselor, assistant, and expert, and he must first be consulted. For Weber, there is no direct link between knowledge and power in human affairs.[83]

Compared with the hopes of the Enlightenment this position is one of great resignation. In contrast to Marx and Durkheim, Weber does not have a strong faith in the power of knowledge in society. He shares Tocqueville's pessimism in this regard, though not his melancholy. In Weber's case, the hiatus between fact and value, between the scholar and the man of action is not a token of indifference, as Tocqueville sees it. It is evidence rather of Weber's simultaneous commitment to scholarship and action. In his life-long effort to achieve a creative relationship between these spheres. Weber put a premium on preserving the integrity of both and thus exposed himself, as only Tocqueville had done before him, to tension and utter frustration. To assert and search for the meaningfulness of the individual's life in a world without God, to recognize the compulsions of human existence yet assert man's capacity to act, to advance social science yet probe into the irrational foundations and consequences of knowledge—this acceptance of tension left its mark on Weber's personal life. Like Tocqueville before him, he paid a price for tolerating the ambiguities of reason in human affairs that Marx and Durkheim were less willing to accept.

III. Legacies and Emerging Problems

Scientific inquiry presupposes a belief in science. Most people adhere to this belief in the expectation that "knowledge is power." In the social sciences, however, confidence in this maxim has been undermined. Efforts to advance knowledge have led unwittingly to changes in conceptions of human nature. The advance of knowledge presupposes the control of bias. To control bias, we must understand its sources. In this respect, our understanding has advanced, while our distrust of reason and prudence has deepened—from Bacon's theory of idols to Nietzsche's and Freud's views of the organic conditioning of knowledge. The sciences of men have grown together with a skeptical view of human nature, and the latter raises questions about the utility of social knowledge.

Often these questions have been evaded, so that belief in progress through science and distrust of common prudence have gone hand in hand. The view that the mass of humanity is subject to social laws has been linked—implicitly perhaps—with the assumption that an elite of social scientists can understand these laws and enhance knowledge, human utility, and power. If not consciously, then through the work they do, social scientists belie the assertion that all men are subject to social laws. Although this exception reflects the inevitable elitism of the man of knowledge, it also reveals that "infusion of the will and the affections" against which Francis Bacon warned three centuries ago. In the face of this paradox—that everything is expected of science and nothing of man—we must take stock of our assumptions. The combination of trust in science and distrust of prudence is one of Bacon's "idols of the theatre," one of the latest "stage plays" that "wonderfully obstruct the understanding." Emancipation from received opinion in this regard and repeated examination of the mental set with which we approach the study of society are indispensable methodological tools.

Such re-examination has been attempted in this discussion by reflection on the historical and theoretical dimensions of ideology. As we contrast the nonideological world view with the questioning of human knowledge and power that marks the "Age of Ideology," we cannot conclude that the "end of ideology" is in sight.[84] Rather, the development of modern science has been accompanied from the beginning by efforts to control bias and by questions about the ends and uses of knowledge. These efforts and questions expose the action-involvement of all ideas. This involvement is greater in those fields in which every general statement applies to the man of knowledge as well as to the subject matter he investigates.

The paradox of the liar, as the ancient philosopher Zeno formulated it, is an integral part of theories about society. All social theorists are bound to begin with postulates on how they propose to investigate society dispassionately. For, in the "Age of Ideology," their efforts must be to seek truth through the quest for objectivity, not to praise God through discovery of His wisdom. Among the writers we have examined (and others as well), this effort leads to two typical variants, at least. The reductionist approach seeks to control or exclude error by reference to an impersonal source or safeguard. Truth as a by-product of the class-struggle and of characteristic features of the natural sciences are the examples we have examined. The approach through self-knowledge seeks to ensure objectivity by cautions that the investigator applies to himself. Truth as a by-product of personal experience and opportunity and of methodological inquiry and self-discipline were our examples. Such approaches do not resolve the ambiguities of knowledge in human affairs; rather they accentuate these ambiguities through dogmatism or mitigate them at the price of personal resignation. The belief in reason has been on trial ever since—in the eighteenth century—social philosophers began to employ the natural sciences as their model. Their hope was to discover universal principles of morality, as well as social laws or regularities in the behavior of men and societies. This hope presupposed remnants of an earlier nonideological world view, according to which man possesses a God-given capacity to discover uniformities underneath the diversity of appearances (whether in nature or society). The resulting knowledge would enhance man's moral stature. Eventually this view of the moral end and use of knowledge was superseded by secular goals, by the belief that knowledge would enhance man's "technical mastery of life" (Weber) and by the expectation that such mastery is inherently worthwhile. These latter assumptions are on trial today, and we are learning that social theories are not alone in having failed to resolve the ambiguities inherent in the secularization of knowledge. The ambiguities of the nonideological world view had to be resolved by faith—while, in the absence of faith, we must live with the ambiguities of the human condition.

In his essay, "Science as a Vocation," Max Weber wrote some forty years ago that scientists are professionally dedicated to the advancement of knowledge but do not ask what ends this knowledge will serve, because increased "technical mastery" is to them a self-evident good. When we observe the pain of those struck down by an incurable disease, we can certainly share this belief as we yearn for the day when these remaining scourges will have been eradicated. All of us are tender toward the sick, because the means to help them are or may be within reach; if we lacked that confidence, we could not permit ourselves to be so tender. There is a world-wide unanimity in favor of death control, and this unanimity is the spirit that has initiated and sustained the growth of medical knowledge. Yet, in the two centuries that have elapsed since the beginning of modern medicine, the *effect* of advancing knowledge has been equivocal. From ancient times until the end of the seventeenth century, the world population did not exceed 500 million people; by the 1920s, it had increased to more than two billion. A report from the United Nations predicts that, by the year 2000, it will exceed six billion. This twelvefold increase in world population over a period of 350 years could not have occurred without medical knowledge. On humanitarian and political grounds, it is impossible to withhold such knowledge from countries whose productive capacity has not and does not now keep step with their reproductive capacity. Such countries face the Sisyphean task of narrowing a gap while it increases. It is expected that the population of India will grow from 430 to 480 million during the next five-year plan; by the year 2000, the largest city in that country may contain, if that is the word, sixty-six million people. A century after the *Communist Manifesto,* a specter *is* haunting the world: the age-old prospects of famine, epidemic, and political tyranny or chaos.

Most of us recoil at the suggestion that this prospect is also a product of knowledge. Most of us hope that the tremendous advances in the productivity that other branches of knowledge have made available will enable men to banish this specter from the face of the earth. We know we must make the attempt, and, in any case, we want to advance our technical mastery for "the benefit and use of life" as Francis Bacon put it three centuries ago. Bacon made that declaration when the population of Europe was only beginning to increase after centuries of stagnation or cyclical variation. We too support this declaration or act in accordance with its spirit, but our belief in knowledge is secure no longer. In a world in which medicine by its effects on population can foster starvation, albeit indirectly, and in which increasing "technical mastery" may lead to the annihilation of life, the "inherent value" of knowledge is equivocal. Yet who will abandon the benefits of science because men are unable to control the powers science has unleashed? No advocate of ending the nuclear arms race, no man who warns against the effects of nuclear testing has been heard to suggest that, along with these destructive uses of knowledge, we discard its constructive uses also. Yet our social capacity for such constructive uses may not exceed our social capacity for destruction. Although it is unusual to call the benefits of science into question, we are all aware today that the "technical mastery of life" can lead to consequences beyond human control. So far, few men have grappled with the corollary that the advancement of knowledge may one day destroy man's "technical mastery of life." Accordingly, the ends and uses of knowledge (and that means the ideological dimensions of intellectual effort) call for critical examination—more urgently than ever.

NOTES

1. Francis Bacon, "Novum Organum," in E. A. Burtt, ed., *The English Philosophers from Bacon to Mill* (New York, 1939), pp. 40-1.
2. See Daniel Bell, *The End of Ideology* (New York, 1960), pp. 369 ff., *passim. Cf.* Seymour M. Lipset, *Political Man* (Garden City, 1960), pp. 403ff. The references in these and related writings are to the "end of ideology" in the West; it is acknowledged that there may have occurred a "rise of ideology" in Asia and Africa.
3. In principle there is also the possibility of a postideological epoch, but this eventuality lies in the future as long as we are witnessing the "end of some ideologies" rather than the "end of ideology." The more accurate phrase has less punch, however.
4. Carl Becker, *The Heavenly City of the Eighteenth Century Philosophers* (New Haven, 1932), p. 47.
5. For a brilliant portrayal of this earlier world view with special reference to social and economic thought, see Otto Brunner, *Adeliges Landleben und Europäischer Geist* (Salzburg, 1949), Chap. 2. In the field of literary history, parallel materials are found in Erich Auerbach, *Mimesis, The Representation of Reality in Western Literature* (Garden City, 1957), *passim.* For a contrast between these premodern perspectives and the "Age of Ideology" I am indebted to Brunner, "Das Zeitalter der Ideologien," *Neue Wege der Sozialgeschichte* (Göttingen, 1956), pp. 194-219.
6. *American College Dictionary* (New York, 1947), p. 599.
7. Bacon, *op. cit.*, pp. 28, 62. The subtitle of the essay is "Aphorisms Concerning the Interpretation of Nature and the Kingdom of Man."
8. For an acute analysis of the modernity of Bacon's approach in relation to classical conceptions of knowledge and action, see Hans Jonas, "The Practical Uses of Theory," *Social Research*, XXVI (Summer, 1959), 127-50.
9. The quoted phrases are found in Bacon, *op. cit.*, p. 64.
10. Bacon, *op. cit.*, p. 65.
11. The fundamental commitment of scientists to a hedonistic and secular world view is examined in detail in the study by Lewis Feuer, *The Scientific Intellectual* (New York, 1963).
12. The most comprehensive treatment of this development is contained in Ernst Cassirer, *The Philosophy of the Enlightenment* (Boston, 1955). Directly pertinent to the present discussion are Charles Van Duzer, *Contribution of the Ideologues to French Revolutionary Thought* (Baltimore, 1935); and Hans Barth, *Wahrheit und Ideologie* (Zürich, 1945), pp. 54-70.

13. See J. W. Stein, *The Mind and the Sword* (New York, 1961), p. 88 and *passim*. The term "ideology" was coined by Tracy in order to distinguish his "scientific" approach from conventional philosophy or metaphysics. See *ibid.*, p. 186, n. 33.

14. *Ibid.*, pp. 94, 107. Similarly, Cabanis—in his *Rapports du physique et du moral* (1802)—sought to analyze morality by research in physiology, a method that would make progress in education and the social sciences as rapid as it had been in the natural sciences. See p. 82.

15. See Barth, *op. cit.*, pp. 15-35; and Stein, *op. cit.*, pp. 141-71 for accounts of this episode.

16. A given proposition might be true but impractical and politically beneficial (from some point of view); it might be true, practical, but politically dangerous (from some point of view); and so forth. Since truth, practicality, and political effect have been involved in the pejorative meaning of ideology ever since Napoleon, confusions abound, especially since utility or political effects have often been employed as tests of truth in order to strengthen or weaken the appeal of theories under the guise of the prestige of science. These confusions, however, are an important part of nineteenth-century intellectual history.

17. Edmund Burke, *Reflections on the Revolution in France* (Chicago, 1955), pp. 126-7.

18. In the passage preceding the one quoted, Burke polemicizes against Rousseau, Voltaire, and Helvétius: "We know that *we* have made no discoveries, and we think that no discoveries are to be made, in morality; nor many in the great principles of government, nor in the ideas of liberty, which were understood long before we were born, altogether as well as they will be after the grave has heaped its mould upon our presumption. . . . In England we have not yet been completely embowelled of our natural entrails; we still feel within us, and we cherish and cultivate, those inbred sentiments which are the faithful guardians, the active monitors of our duty, the true supporters of all liberal and manly morals. . . . We preserve the whole of our feelings still native and entire, unsophisticated by pedantry and infidelity. . . . We fear God; we look up with awe to kings; . . . Why? Because such ideas are brought before our minds, it is *natural* to be so affected; because all other feelings are false and spurious, and tend to corrupt our minds. . . ." *Ibid.*, pp. 125-6.

19. *Cf.* Leo Strauss, *Natural Right and History* (Chicago, 1953), pp. 307-11, for an extended statement of these contrasts derived from Burke's writings.

20. *Cf.* the detailed discussion of this point in *ibid.*, pp. 294-323.

21. This formulation was made by Max Weber in his essay "Science as a Vocation." See H. H. Gerth and C. Wright Mills, eds., *From Max Weber: Essays in Sociology* (New York, 1946), pp. 150-1. It is a convenient summary of the assumptions underlying much social thought in the nineteenth century; its significance for Weber's approach is considered later.

22. Such reticence is not universal. *Cf.* George Lundberg, *Can Science Save Us?* (New York, 1961), *passim*.

23. *Cf.*, for example, the telling arguments against premature consideration of these questions of purpose in Robert K. Merton, "Social Conflict over Styles of Sociological Work," *Transactions of the Fourth World Congress of Sociology*, III (Louvain, 1961), pp. 21-44.

24. The paradox was first formulated by the Greek philosopher Zeno in the statement: "A Cretan says all Cretans are liars." Since the person making the statement is himself a member of the group of whom a lack of veracity is asserted, an infinite chain of mutually contradictory assertions follows. For our purposes the analogous statement would be: "Social scientists say that every man's knowledge of society is the product of that society," although this application lacks the simplicity of the classic model.

25. Quoted in Barth, *op. cit.*, p. 67.

26. Frank E. Manuel, *The New World of Henri Saint-Simon* (Cambridge, 1956), p. 134.

27. Quoted in *ibid.*, p. 135.

28. Sigmund Freud, *The Future of an Illusion* (Garden City, n.d.), p. 98. The numbered statements in the text are based on pp. 95-102.

29. *Ibid.*, p. 99.

30. *Ibid.*, p. 102.

31. Although the contrast between Saint-Simon and Freud suggests a diminution of hope concerning the benefits to be derived from knowledge, proof of this trend in the climate of opinion is a more complex affair and is not attempted here. Even in the eighteenth century there were great skeptics of the promise of science as applied to human affairs—men like Edmund Burke and Montesquieu—and this skepticism had numerous spokesmen throughout the nineteenth century along with the more dominant expressions of belief in progress. Hans Barth's *Wahrheit und Ideologie* contains a detailed philosophical analysis of changing conceptions of man and truth that supports the interpretation offered here. *Cf.* the writings of Karl Loewith.

32. Karl Marx, *Capital* (New York, 1936), p. 89.

33. *Ibid.*, p. 91.
34. *Ibid.*, pp. 90-1.
35. *Ibid.*, pp. 91-2.
36. See, for example, Karl Marx, *A Contribution to the Critique of Political Economy* (Chicago, 1904), p. 12.
37. See, for example, Marx, *Capital*, pp. 12-3, preface to the first edition.
38. Karl Marx and Friedrich Engels, *Manifesto of the Communist Party* (New York, 1939), p. 19. My italics.
39. This wording is adapted from Marx, *Capital*, p. 92.
40. From Tocqueville's letter to Henry Reeve, dated March 22, 1837, in Tocqueville, *Memoir, Letters and Remains*, II (Boston, 1862), 39-40.
41. There is a similar argument in Marx, but it is very general and unclear, while Tocqueville is specific and lucid.
42. *Ibid.*, I, 376. From a letter to M. Stoffels, February 21, 1835.
43. Quoted phrases are taken from the letter to Stoffels, *ibid.*
44. From a letter to M. de Kergorlay, November 13, 1833, *ibid.*, I, 299.
45. From a letter to M. Stoffels, January 3, 1843, *ibid.*, I, 392.
46. *Ibid.*
47. *Ibid.*, I, 299-300. From the letter to Kergorlay, already cited.
48. *Ibid.*, I, 393. From the letter to Stoffels, January 3, 1843.
49. *Ibid.*, I, 374-5. From a letter to M. Stoffels, January 12, 1833.
50. See *ibid.*, II, 84-5, for a vigorous statement to this effect in a letter to M. de Corcelle, October 11, 1846.
51. See Karl Marx and Friedrich Engels, *Die Heilige Familie* (Berlin, 1953), p. 138. Italics in the original; my translation. Marx constantly re-examined the labor movements in various countries for evidence of a rising class-consciousness in his sense of the word, but his judgments in this respect were notably unstable in terms of his own theoretical assumptions.
52. Tocqueville, *op. cit.*, II, 230. From a letter to M. de Corcelle, September, 17, 1853.
53. *Ibid.*, II, 13-4. From a letter to M. de Corcelle, April 12, 1835.
54. Tocqueville, *Democracy in America*, II (New York, 1954), 352.
55. From the letter to De Corcelle, April 12, 1835.
56. Tocqueville, *The European Revolution and Correspondence with Gobineau* (Garden City, 1959), pp. 231-2. From letter to Gobineau, December 20, 1853.
57. Tocqueville, *Memoir*, I, 382. From the letter to M. Stoffels, July 24, 1836.
58. *Ibid.*, I, 400. From the letter to M. Stoffels, July 21, 1848.
59. *Ibid.*, II, 305-6. From the letter dated January 7, 1856.
60. *Ibid.*, II, 335. From the letter to Madame Swetchine, October 20, 1856.
61. Emile Durkheim, *The Rules of Sociological Method* (Chicago, 1938), p. xi, from the author's preface to the first edition.
62. Emile Durkheim, *Montesquieu and Rousseau* (Ann Arbor, 1960), pp. 3ff.
63. *Ibid.*, pp. 6-7.
64. *Ibid.*, p. 10.
65. *Ibid.*, pp. 10-1.
66. *Ibid.*, p. 12.
67. My restatement here is brief in keeping with the purpose of the present discussion.
68. *Cf.* Durkheim's simultaneous insistence upon the collective origin and the individual manifestation of ideas and sentiments in *Rules*, pp. liv, n. 5, and lvi, n. 7. It may be added that Durkheim's strongly antipsychological argument, which is part of his case for sociology as an autonomous discipline, should be read in the context of nineteenth-century psychology with its emphasis on instincts and psychophysical parallelism.
69. These points are discussed in Durkheim, *The Division of Labor in Society* (New York, 1960), pp. 283ff and *passim*. Note also a later essay, published in 1898, discussed in Edward Tiryakian, *Sociologism and Existentialism* (New York, 1962), p. 57.
70. I am indebted to Tiryakian, *op. cit.*, for his analysis of this late phase of Durkheim's thought.
71. See his discussion of law and occupational groups in *The Division of Labor*, pp. 174ff., and preface to the second edition. His efforts to clarify the concepts of normality or "social health" are contained in *Rules*, Chap. III.
72. Emile Durkheim, *Suicide* (London, 1952), p. 169.
73. *Ibid.*
74. Tiryakian, *op. cit.*, p. 35.
75. The phrase is taken from Tocqueville's letter to Mrs. Grote, in *Memoirs.*
76. Durkheim, *Montesquieu and Rousseau*, pp. 8-9.
77. *Ibid.*, p. 55. My italics.
78. To consider these criteria a quality inherent in the phenomena is tantamount to the nonideological world-view discussed earlier or to its organological legacy in a man like

Durkheim. That is, facts and values are like emanation of the divine will just as body temperature and the limits of variation compatible with health are attributes of the biological organism. *Cf.* Weber *"organologische Kulturtheorien,"* Mannheim on the history of the idea of the state as an organism, and so forth.

79. "Denn gerade *wegen* der Unmöglichkeit, in der historischen Wirklichkeit scharfe Grenzen zu ziehen, können wir nur bei Untersuchung ihrer *konsequentesten* Formen hoffen, auf ihre spezifischen Wirkungen zu stossen." Max Weber, *Gesammelte Aufsätze zur Religionssoziologie,* I (Tübingen, 1947), 87.

80. I add this phrase because the term Weber employs is *Sinn* not *Bedeutung,* sense rather than meaning, although the latter word has been used in the translations.

81. *Cf.* Leo Strauss, *op. cit.,* for a comprehensive compilation of the *evaluative* terms that can be found in Weber's *empirical* works like his essays on the sociology of religion. Strauss criticizes Weber for his constant use of value-judgments in his research, but he fails to note the basic difference between assessments based on ideal-types and value-judgments in the sense of personal evaluations.

82. *Cf.* Reinhard Bendix, "Max Weber's Interpretation of Conduct and History," *American Journal of Sociology,* LI (May, 1946), 518-26.

83. See Weber's discussion in "Science as a Vocation," in Gerth and Mills, *op. cit.*

84. This end has occurred, however, where a new orthodoxy has put a stop to the uncertainties endemic in the pursuit of knowledge—hardly the meaning that those who coined the phrase had in mind. One should note in this connection the pejorative use of "ideology" in Soviet terminology as a label by which Western thought is set off from the truth of Marxism-Leninism.

Supplementary Bibliography

COMPILED BY *KAY L. LAWSON*

BOOKS

Abraham, W. E., *The Mind of Africa*. Chicago, 1962.
Almond, Gabriel, *The Appeals of Communism*. Princeton, 1954.

Balandier, Georges, *Sociologie actuelle de l'Afrique noire*. Paris, 1955.
Barth, Hans, *Wahrheit und Ideologie*. Zürich, 1945.
Bell, Daniel, *The End of Ideology*. New York, 1960.
Birnbaum, Norman, *The Sociological Study of Ideology (1940-1960)*. Current Sociology, Oxford, 1961.
Brzezinski, Z., *Ideology and Power in Soviet Politics*. New York, 1962.
Burns, Edward McNall, *Ideas in Conflict: The Political Theories of The Contemporary World*. New York, 1960.

Cailliet, Emile, *La Tradition littéraire des idéologues*. Philadelphia, 1943.
Christie, Richard, and Marie Jahoda, *Studies in The "Authoritarian Personality."* New York, 1954.
Cohn, Norman, *The Pursuit of The Millennium*. New York, 1957.

Davis, Harold E., *Latin American Social Thought Since Independence*. Washington, D.C., 1961.
Delaisi, François, *Political Myths and Economic Realities*. New York, 1925.
Destutt de Tracy, Antoine Louis Claude, *Elémens d'idéologie*, 4 vols. Paris, 1825-1827.

Fanon, Frantz, *Les damnés de la terre*. Paris, 1961.

Geiger, Theodor Julius, *Ideologie und Wahrheit*. Stuttgart, 1953.
Grimes, A. P., and R. H. Horwitz, eds., *Modern Political Ideologies*. New York, 1959.
Gross, Feliks, ed., *European Ideologies*. New York, 1948.

Horowitz, Irving Louis, *Philosophy, Science, and The Sociology of Knowledge*. Springfield, 1961.

Kaufmann, Felix, *Methodology of The Social Sciences*. New York, 1944.
Knuth, Werner, *Ideen, Ideale, Ideologien: vom Verhängnis Ideologischen Denkens, ein Beitrag zu seiner Überwindung*. Hamburg, 1955.

Lane, Robert Edwards, *Political Ideology: Why the American Common Man Believes What He Does*. New York, 1962.
Lerner, Daniel, *The Passing of Traditional Society: Modernizing the Middle East*. New York, 1958.
Levy-Brühl, Lucien, *Primitive Mentality*. New York, 1923.
Lippe-Weissenfeld, Kurt Bernhard, *Modern Ideologies and American Democracy, A Comparison*. San Francisco, 1939.
Lipset, S. M., *The First New Nation: The United States in Historical and Comparative Perspective*. New York, 1963.

Lorenz, Emil, *Der Politische Mythus*. Leipzig, Vienna, and Zurich, 1923.

Mannheim, Karl, *Ideology and Utopia: An Introduction to The Sociology of Knowledge*. New York, 1936.
Mukerji, Krishma Prasanna, *Implications of the Ideology-Concept*. Bombay, 1955.

Naess, Arne, *Democracy, Ideology and Objectivity*. Oslo, 1956.
Northrop, F. S. C., ed., *Ideological Differences and World Order*. New Haven, 1949.

Picavet, François Joseph, *Les idéologues*. Paris, 1891.
Pribram, Karl, *Conflicting Patterns of Thought*. Washington, 1949.

Sigmund, Paul E., Jr., ed., *The Ideologies of The Developing Nations*. New York and London, 1963.
Silvert, Kalman, *The Conflict Society: Reaction and Revolution in Latin America*. New Orleans, 1961.
Sorel, Georges, *Reflections on Violence*. New York, 1950.
Stark, Werner, *The Sociology of Knowledge*. New York, 1958.
Stern, F. R., *Cultural Despair and The Politics of Discontent; A Study of The 'Germanic' Ideology*. Ann Arbor, 1954.
Sundkler, Bengt, *Bantu Prophets in South Africa*. London, 1948.
Sutton, F. X., *et al.*, *The American Business Creed*. Cambridge, Mass., 1956.

Tempels, Placied, *Bantu-Philosophie, Ontologie und Ethik*. Heidelberg, 1956.

Van Duzer, Charles Hunter, *Contribution of The Ideologues to French Revolutionary Thought*. Baltimore, 1935.

Walsby, Harold, *The Domain of Ideologies: A Study of The Origin, Development and Structure of Ideologies*. Glasgow, 1947.
Weber, Max, *The Methodology of The Social Sciences*. New York, 1949.
———, *The Protestant Ethic and The Spirit of Capitalism*. New York, 1958.
Whitehead, Alfred North, *Modes of Thought*. New York, 1938.
Worsley, Peter, *The Trumpet Shall Sound: A Study of Cargo Cults in Melanesia*. London, 1957.

ARTICLES AND CONFERENCE PAPERS

Adams, J. L., "Religion and the ideologies," *Confluence*, IV (April, 1955), 72-84.
Aiken, Henry D., "The revolt against ideology," *Commentary*, XXXVII (April, 1964), No. 4.
Andrzejewski, S., "Are ideas social forces?" *American Sociological Review*, XIV (December, 1949), 758-64.
Ansari, Z. I., "Egyptian nationalism vis-a-vis Islam," *Pakistan Horizon*, XIII (January-March, 1960), No. 1, 21-47.
Arendt, H., "Ideology and terror: a novel form of government," *Review of Politics*, XV (July, 1953), 303-27.
Aron, R., "The diffusion of ideologies," *Confluence*, II (March, 1953), No. 1, 3-12.
———, "Fin de l'âge idéologique?" in *Sociologica*, Frankfurt am Main, 1955, pp. 219-33.
———, "Le rôle des idéologies dans les changements politiques." Paper presented at the Hague Congress of the International Association of Political Science, September 8-12, 1952.

Banerjee, D. N., "Political ideologies and political behavior," *Modern Review*, XCII (Calcutta, December, 1952), No. 6, 444-50.
Bastide, R., "Mythes et utopie," *Cahiers internationaux de Sociologie*, VII (January-June, 1960), No. 28, 3-12.
Bendix, Reinhard, "Industrialization, ideologies, and social structure,"*American Sociological review* XXIV (October, 1959), No. 5, 613-23.
Bennigsen, A., "L'agitation et le durcissement idéologique en U.R.S.S.," *Études*, CCXCIV (September, 1957), No. 9, 243-51.
Bergmann, G., "Ideology," *Ethics*, LXI (April, 1951), 205-18.

Bertier, F., "L'idéologie politique des Frères musulmans," *Orient*, II (October-December, 1958), No. 8, 43-57.

———, "L'idéologie sociale de la révolution egyptienne," *Orient*, II (April-June, 1958), No. 6, 49-71.

Bottomore, T. B., "Some reflections on the sociology of knowledge," *British Journal of Sociology*, VII (March, 1956), 52-8.

———, "The ideas of the founding fathers," *European Journal of Sociology*, I (1960), No. 1.

Brumberg, A., "Soviet campaign against survivals of capitalism," *Russian Review*, XII (April, 1953), 65-78.

Brzezinski, Z., "Communist ideology and power: from unity to diversity," *Journal of Politics*, XIX (November, 1957), No. 4, 549-90.

Bunn, Ronald F., "The Ideology of the Federation of German Employers' Associations," *American Journal of Economics and Sociology*, XVIII (July, 1959), No. 4, 369-79.

Bunzel, J. H., "The general ideology of American small business," *Political Science Quarterly*, LXX (March, 1955), No. 1, 87-102.

Burks, R. V., "Conception of ideology for historians," *Journal of the History of Ideas*, X (April, 1959), 183-98.

Cassinelli, C. W., "Totalitarianism, ideology and propaganda," *Journal of Politics*, XXII (February, 1960), 68-95.

Chevallier, J. J., "Le XVIIIème siècle et la naissance des idéologies," *Res Publica*, II (1960), No. 3, 194-204.

Cohen, A. A., "Religion as a secular ideology," *Partisan Review*, XXIII (Fall, 1956), 495-505.

Deninger, W. T., "Political power and ideological analysis," *Politico*, XXVI (June, 1961), No. 2, 277-98.

Dibble, V. K., "Occupations and ideologies," *American Journal of Sociology*, LXVIII (September, 1962), 229-41.

Dion, L., "Political ideology as a tool of functional analysis in sociopolitical dynamics: an hypothesis," *Canadian Journal of Economics*, XXV (February, 1959), 47-59.

Ehrenberg, H., "Ideologische und soziologische Methode. Ein Wort zur Sozialisierung der Denkart," *Archiv für systematische Philosophie und Soziologie*, XXX (1927), No. 1, 133ff.

Etzioni, Amitai, "Neo-liberalism—The turn of the sixties," *Commentary*, XXX (December, 1960), No. 6, 473-9.

Fallers, Lloyd A., "Ideology and culture in Uganda nationalism," *American Anthropologist*, LXIII (August, 1961), No. 4, 677-86.

Feuer, L. S., "The sociology of philosophic ideas," *Pacific Sociological Review*, I (Fall, 1958), No. 2, 77-80.

Friedmann, H. C., "Politics and mind: a contrast between India and the West," *Indian Yearbook of International Affairs*, I (1952), 258-65.

Galantière, L., "Ideology and political warfare," *Confluence*, II (March, 1953), No. 1, 43-54.

Geismar, Ludwig L., "Ideology and the adjustment of immigrants," *Jewish Social Studies*, XXI (July, 1959), No. 3, 155-64.

Halpern, B., "Dynamic elements of culture," *Ethics*, LXV (July, 1955), 235-49.

Hodges, Donald Clark, "The class significance of ethical traditions," *American Journal of Economics and Sociology*, XX (April, 1961), No. 3, 241-52.

Hopper, Rex D., "Aspectos ideologicos y de jefatura de la revolucion Mexicana," *Revista Mexicana de Sociologia*, XVIII (January-April, 1956), No. 1, 19-36.

Hudson, G. F., "Communist ideology in China," *International Affairs*, XXXIII (April, 1957), No. 2, 176-84.

———, "The emperor of the last days," *Commentary*, XXIV (December, 1957), No. 6, 519-24.

Huntington, S. P., "Conservatism as an ideology," *American Political Science Review*, LI (June, 1957), 454-73.

Idenburg, P. J., "De niuewe Afrikaanse staten en de Westersdemocratischc normen," *Internationale Spectator*, XV (January 8, 1961), No. 1, 3-15.

Jansson, J. M., "The role of political ideologies in politics," *International Relations*, I (April, 1959), No. 11, 529-42.
Juarez, C., "Y a-t-il une renaissance idéologique en Espagne?" *Cahiers Internationaux*, IX (December, 1957), 49-56.

Kallen, H. M., "Social philosophy and the war of the faiths," *Social Research*, XX (Spring, 1953), No. 1, 1-18.
Keyfitz, Nathan, "Western perspectives and Asian problems," *Human Organization*, XIX (Spring, 1960), No. 1, 28-31.
Khulusi, S. A., "Divergences idéologiques dans le monde arabe. Y a-t-il conflit entre panarabisme et panislamisme?" *Monde non chrétien*, XXXIV (April-June, 1955), 172-81.
Kim, Y.-C., "On political thought in Tokugawa Japan," *Journal of Politics*, XXIII (February, 1961), No. 1, 127-45.
Kirshen, H. B., "The ideology of American labor," *Politico*, XXV (September, 1960), No. 3, 581-95.
Kluke, P., "Nationalsozialistische Europaideologie," *Vierteljahrshefte für Zeitgeschichte*, III (July, 1955), No. 3, 240-75.
Koch, H., "Sowjetideologie als Weltanschauung und Wissenschaft," *Osteuropa*, VII (January, 1957), No. 1, 10-22.

Laeuen, H., "Polens Verhältnis zur Ideologie," *Osteuropa*, XI (July-August, 1961), Nos. 7-8, 517-26.
Laqueur, W. Z., "Communism and nationalism in tropical Africa," *Foreign Affairs*, XXXIX (July, 1961), No. 4, 610-21.
Lasswell, H. D., "The political role of ideologies." Paper presented at the Hague Congress of the International Association of Political Science, September 8-12, 1952.
Lefort, C., "Dynamique idéologique et structure de classe," *Transactions of the Third World Congress of Sociology*, 3 (London, 1956), 297-301.
Lenk, Kurt, "Sociology and ideology. Remarks on the discussion of Marxism from Simmel to Mannheim," *Kölner Zeitschrift für Soziologie und Sozial-Psychologie*, XIII (1961), No. 2, 227-38.
Lerner, D., *et al.*, "Comparative analysis of political ideology: a preliminary statement," *Public Opinion Quarterly*, XV (Winter, 1951-1952), No. 4, 715-33.
Lippmann, Walter, "The making of creeds," in *A Preface to Politics* (New York, 1913).
Litt, Edgar, "Civic education, community norms, and political indoctrination," *American Sociological Review*, XXVIII (1960), No. 1.
Lively, J. F., "Power and ideology in Soviet politics," *Politico*, XXVI (1961), No. 2, 407-18.
Lockwood, T. D., "A study of French socialist ideology," *Review of Politics* (April, 1959), No. 2, 402-16.
Loewenstein, K., "Political systems, ideologies and institutions: the problem of their circulation," *Western Political Quarterly*, VI (December, 1953), No. 4, 689-706.
————, "The role of ideologies in political change," *International Social Science Bulletin*, V (1953), No. 1, 51-74.
Lukic, R. D., "Means of propagating political ideologies and the conditions for their development in various parts of the world." Paper presented at the Hague Congress of the International Association of Political Science, September 8-12, 1952.

MacRae, D. G., "Class relationships and ideology," *Sociological Review*, VI (December, 1958), 261-72.
Mack, Raymond W., "Occupational ideology and the determinate role," *Social Forces*, XXXVI (October, 1957), No. 1, 37-44.
Mahar, Pauline M., "Changing caste ideology in a northern Indian village," *Journal of Social Issues*, XIV (1958), No. 4, 51-65.
Malenbaum, W., and W. Stolper, "Political ideology and economic progress," *World Politics*, XII (April, 1960), 413-21.

Matossian, Mary, "Ideologies of delayed industrialization: some tensions and ambiguities," *Economic Development and Cultural Change*, VI (April, 1958), No. 3, 217-28.

McClosky, Herbert, "Consensus and ideology in American politics," *American Political Science Review*, LVIII (June, 1964), No. 2.

Merton, Robert K., "The sociology of knowledge," *Twentieth Century Sociology* (New York, 1946).

Minar, D. W., "Ideology and political behavior," *Midwest Journal of Political Science*, V (November, 1961), No. 4, 317-31.

Nahirny, V. C., "Some observations on ideological groups," *American Journal of Sociology*, LXVII (January, 1962), 397-405.

Northrop, F. S. C., "The ideological problems of social science," *The Logic of the Sciences and the Humanities* (New York, 1956).

Ossowski, S., "Les transformations de l'idéologie nationale contemporaine," *Bulletin Internationale des Sciences Sociales*, III (été, 1951), No. 2, 268-75.

Partridge, P. H., "Politics, philosophy, ideology," *Political Studies* (Oxford), IX (October, 1961), No. 3, 217-35.

Pettee, G. S., "Ideology in America," *Confluence*, II (June, 1953), No. 2, 69-80.

Plamenatz, J., "The communist ideology," *Political Quarterly*, XXII (January-March, 1951), No. 1, 16-26.

Polanyi, Michael, "The republic of science: its political and economic theory," *Minerva*, I (Autumn, 1961), No. 1.

Pool, I., *et al.*, "On measurement of ideological change. The Radir project at Hoover Institute, Stanford University." Paper presented at the Hague Congress of the International Association of Political Science, September 8-12, 1952.

Pye, Lucian W., "Personal identity and political ideology," *Behavioral Science*, VI (July, 1961), No. 3, 205-21.

Rama, C. M., "Ideología, regiones y clases sociales en la España contemporanea," *Revista de la Facultad de Derecho y Ciencias sociales* (Montevideo), IX (July-September, 1958), No. 3, 575-612.

Rosenberg, M., "Misanthropy and political ideology," *American Sociological Review*, XXI (December, 1956), No. 6, 690-5.

Rostow, W. W., "A note on 'the diffusion of ideologies,'" *Confluence*, II (March, 1953), No. 1, 31-42.

Sanchez Agesta, L., "Ideología y orden constitucional," *Anuario de filosofía del derecho*, XII (1954), 89-101.

Schweitzer, A., "Ideological strategy," *Western Political Quarterly* XV (March, 1962), 46-66.

Scott, W. A., "Empirical assessment of values and ideologies," *American Sociological Review*, XXIV (June, 1959), No. 3, 299-310.

———, "International ideology and interpersonal ideology," *Public Opinion Quarterly*, XXIV (Fall, 1960), 419-35.

Shils, E., "Ideology and civility: on the politics of the intellectual," *Sewanee Review*, LXVI (Summer, 1958), 450-80.

Shumelda, J., "Postwar ideological difficulties in the Soviet Union," *Ukrainian Quarterly*, XI (Summer, 1955), No. 3, 227-38.

Shuval, Judith T., "The role of ideology as a pre-disposing frame of reference for immigrants," *Human Relations*, XII (1959), No. 1, 51-63.

Spencer, Robert F., "Culture process and intellectual current: Durkheim and Ataturk," *American Anthropologist*, LX (August, 1958), No. 4, 640-59.

Sperber, M., "Idéologie et société," *Preuves*, III (April, 1953), No. 26, 19-28, and (May, 1953), No. 27, 25-37.

Spiro, Melford E., "The Sabras and Zionism: A study in personality and ideology," *Social Problems*, V (Fall, 1957), No. 2, 100-10.

Spranger, E., "Wesen und Wert politischer Ideologien," *Vierteljahrshefte für Zeitgeschichte*, II (April, 1954), No. 2, 118-36.

Srinivas, P. R., "Hindu sociology and modern ideologies," *Bulletin of the Rama Krishna Mission Institute of Culture*, VI (May, 1955), No. 5, 115-9.

Stark, W., "La interpretacíon marxista de la religión y la interpretacíon religiosa del marxismo," *Revista internacional de Sociologia*, XII (January-March, 1954), No. 45, 33-44.

———, "The psychology of social messianism," *Social Research*, XXV (Summer, 1958), No. 2, 145-57.

Steckler, George A., "Authoritarian ideology in negro college students," *Journal of Abnormal Social Psychology*, LIV (May, 1957), No. 3, 396-99.

Stein, J. W., "Beginnings of ideology," *South Atlantic Quarterly*, LV (April, 1956), 163-70.

Suziki, Hiroshi, "Conception of ideology and utopia," *Japanese Sociological Review*, VII (November, 1957), No. 1, 50-4.

Svennevig, T. P., "The ideology of the Yugoslav heretics," *Social Research*, XXVII (Spring, 1960), No. 1, 39-48.

Tandon, B. C., "Some ideological approaches towards planned economics," *Indian Journal of Economics*, XXXIX (July, 1958), No. 1, 141-9.

Toch, H. H., "Crisis situations and ideological revaluation," *Public Opinion Quarterly*, XIX (Spring, 1955), 53-67.

Torres, J. A., "Ideological component of Indian development," *Ethics*, LXXII (January, 1962), 79-105.

———, "Political ideology of guided democracy," *Review of Politics*, XXV (January, 1963), 34-63.

Ulam, A. B., "Soviet ideology and Soviet foreign policy," *World Politics*, XI (January, 1959), 153-72.

Van der Kroef, Justus M., "Indonesia's first national election: a sociological analysis," *American Journal of Economics and Sociology*, XVI (April, 1957), No. 3, 237-49, and (July, 1957), No. 4, 407-20.

Williams, B., "Democracy and Ideology," *Political Quarterly*, XXXII (October, 1961), 374-84.

Winter, G., "Conception of ideology in the theory of action," *Journal of Religion*, XXXIX (January, 1959), 43-9.

Wolff, Kurt H., "A preliminary inquiry into the sociology of knowledge from the standpoint of the study of man," in *Scritti di Sociologia e Politicà in Onore di Luigi Sturzo*, 3 (Bologna, 1953), 583-621.

———, "Preliminary study of the German ideology concerning the U.S.A.," *Papers of the Liège Congress of the International Sociological Association* (1953), Sect. II, ISA, 53, doc ISA/L/IC/Int./7.

Wright, D. M., "Democracy and economics in American ideology," *Confluence*, II (March, 1953), No. 1, 55-65.

Wright, Q., "Current research on the subject of political ideologies and their dissemination." Paper presented at the Hague Congress of the International Association of Political Science, September 8-12, 1952.

Index